# PRIMITIVE
# POLYNESIAN   ECONOMY

# PRIMITIVE
# POLYNESIAN ECONOMY

By

## RAYMOND FIRTH

Professor of Anthropology in the University of London

*Illustrated*

The Norton Library

W·W·NORTON & COMPANY·INC·

NEW YORK

Books That Live
The Norton imprint on a book means that in the publisher's
estimation it is a book not for a single season but for the years.
W. W. Norton & Company, Inc.

Library of Congress Cataloging in Publication Data
Firth, Raymond William, 1901-
  Primitive Polynesian economy.
  (The Norton Library)
  Reprint of the ed. published by Routledge and K. Paul,
London.
  Includes bibliographical references and index.
  1. Tikopians. 2. Economics, Primitive. I. Title.
DU850.F55   1975        301.5'1'09935        75-6879
ISBN 0-393-00774-X

# CONTENTS

PREFACE TO FIRST EDITION . . . . ix

PREFACE TO SECOND EDITION . . . . xi

PAGE

CHAP.

I. PROBLEMS OF ECONOMIC ANTHROPOLOGY . . I

Methods in the Study of Modern Economic Anthropology—
Present Position of Economic Anthropology—Relation to
Economic Theory—Major Problems in Tikopia Economics—
Non-monetary Conditions in Tikopia—Have the Tikopia an
Economy?—Spheres of Decision-making.

II. FOOD AND POPULATION IN TIKOPIA . . . 32

Wants and their Satisfaction—The Social Context of Food—
The Population Problem—Crude Factors of Population Pressure
—Possible Changes in Agricultural Production—Population
and Land of Chiefly Groups—Command of Food Resources by
Individuals—Cultivation of the Major Food Plants—Variations
in Food Supply, 1928-9.

III. KNOWLEDGE, TECHNIQUE, AND ECONOMIC LORE . 78

The Level of Technical Achievement—Invention as a Cultural
Process—Reason and Rule in Technical Procedure—The Distribution and Transmission of Economic Lore.

IV. THE LABOUR SITUATION . . . . . 109

Division of Labour—Occupational Specialists—Types of
Co-operation in Work—Study of a Working Party at the Repair
of a Canoe—The Role of Language in Work—Case Material
on Specific Undertakings—Labour Supply—Leadership in
Work—Ideology of Production—Attitudes to Work—Efficiency
of the Tikopia Labour Organization.

V. RITUAL IN PRODUCTIVE ACTIVITY . . . 168

The General Problem of Ritual and Economics—Some
General Propositions for Tikopia—Different Forms of Ritual
of Production—Ritual of Net-making—Effects of Ritual on
Production.

VI. ECONOMIC FUNCTIONS OF THE CHIEFS . . 187

Economic Position of a Potential Chief—The Role of the
Chief in Production—The Imposition of *Tapu*—Classification
of Taboos—The Chief as Consumer—A Chief gives a Feast—
Social Effects of Feasts—The Chief's contribution in the
Tikopia Economy.

VII. PROPERTY AND CAPITAL IN PRODUCTION . . 237

Accumulation of Some Major Types of Goods : Canoes—
Pandanus Mats—Sinnet—Bark-cloth. Concept of Ownership—
Ownership of Land—Ownership of Manufactured Goods—
Theft and the Conservation of Property—Entry of Goods into
Production—Summary.

CHAP.

PAGE

VIII. PRINCIPLES OF DISTRIBUTION AND PAYMENT . 279

Apportionment of the Product of Co-operative Work—Food as Payment for Labour—Goods as Payment for Specialized Labour—Payment to Other Factors of Production—Payment for Non-labour Services—Covert Exchange—The Concept of Reciprocity.

IX. EXCHANGE AND VALUE . . . . . 314

Exchange of Goods—Forced Exchange—Borrowing, Theft, and Compensation—Ceremonial Exchange—Marriage Exchanges —Exchange in Mortuary Ceremonies—The Economic Value of Goods—The Relative Worth of Goods in Tikopia—Spheres of Exchange—Ceremonial Destruction—Exchange in a Personalized Economy.

X. CHARACTERISTICS OF A PRIMITIVE ECONOMY . 352

APPENDIX

I. SYNOPTIC RECORD OF A TIKOPIA YEAR (1928–9) . 366

Variations in Daily Production—Chart of Economic and Social Activities, 1928–9.

II. SOME LINGUISTIC CATEGORIES IN TIKOPIA DIS-TRIBUTION AND EXCHANGE . . . . 371

III. EXCHANGE RATES IN A CULTURE CONTACT SITUATION 377

INDEX . . . . . . . . 381

# LIST OF PLATES

PLATE                                                      FACING PAGE

  I. The Manufacture of Sago Flour . . . . . . . 80

 II. Making a Filter-Funnel for Turmeric Manufacture . . . 81

III. A. Carrying a Log through a Taro Field . . . . . 112
      B. Preparing a Sago Oven . . . . . . . 112

 IV. Filtering Turmeric . . . . . . . . . 113

  V. Repairing a Sacred House . . . . . . . . 208

 VI. Food for the Workers . . . . . . . . 209

VII. A. Fishing from a Canoe . . . . . . . . 240
      B. The Ariki Kafika in his Cultivation . . . . . 240

VIII. A. Funeral Exchange—Loading up Bark-cloth . . . . 241
      B. Funeral Exchange—Bowls and Sinnet Displayed . . . 241

# DIAGRAMS

PAGE

Map. Distribution of Tikopia Population . . . . . . 40

TABLES

    I. Approximate Age Limits of Working Population . . . 42
    II. Rough Indication of Nutritive Value of Tikopia Foods . . 52
   III. Changes in Group Membership of Chiefly Houses . . . 55
   IV. Economic and Ritual Values of Major Food Plants . . . 65
    V. Classification of Taboos . . . . . . . . 202
   VI. Contributions to a Chief's Income . . . . . . 221
  VII. Ownership and Manning of Canoes . . . . . . 245
VIII. Estimated Level of Production of Some Major Types of Goods . 256
   IX. Land Utilization . . . . . . . . . 262
    X. Exchange Rates in a Culture Contact Situation . . . 377

FIGS.

 1. Fish Corrals on Raveŋa Reef . . . . . . . 62
 2. Seasonal Changes in Food Production . . . . . . 74
 3. Types of Slot in Wood-Working . . . . . . . 83
 4. Netting Technique . . . . . . . . . 96
 5. A. Decoration of Canoe Hull . . . . . . . 128
    B. Plan of Canoe Ceremony . . . . . . . 128
 6. Grades of Tikopia Society . . . . . . . . 187
 7. Plan of Thatch-making Organization . . . . . . 195
 8. Marks of Ownership on Sago Slabs . . . . . . 267
 9. Marriage Exchanges . . . . . . . . . 323
10. Groupings at a Tikopia Funeral . . . . . . . 324
11. Major Exchanges at a Funeral . . . . . . . 325
12. Chart of Economic and Social Activities (1928–9) . . . 366

# PREFACE

THIS book is in a sense a supplement to my *Primitive Economics of the New Zealand Maori*. Together they provide a comparative analysis of the institutions of two Polynesian communities differing considerably in natural environment, in population, and in political organization. For the Maori I had to use primarily documentary sources, often fragmentary ; my own brief field work trips among them filled few gaps. And since the Maori have for a century been participants in an Antipodean variant of European civilization, my generalizations had to be mainly reconstructions, though some of the traditional principles of organization have shown a sturdy vitality to the present day.[1]

Tikopia, on the other hand, is a living Polynesian culture, practically autonomous. This has allowed the analysis of contemporary behaviour, based upon my first-hand observation. The present book compared with that on the Maori therefore gives a more dynamic picture of the economic processes.

I am fully conscious that the exploration of economic theory could be carried much farther than it is here, but I hope to have indicated at least some lines along which both field study and theoretical analysis may be pursued.

I wish to acknowledge the help that I have received from Dr. W. E. H. Stanner, Dr. R. Piddington, and Mr. E. R. Leach in the preparation of this book, and I am grateful to the Committee of the Rockefeller Research Fund of the London School of Economics for making their services available to me. I am indebted also to Mr. V. G. J. Sheddick for preparing the map, and to my wife for much valuable criticism. And finally, I wish to express my obligation to the Australian National Research Council, who financed my field-expedition.

*October*, 1938.

[1] This has been demonstrated by Sir Apirana Ngata, *Native Land Development* (New Zealand Parliamentary Paper, G. 10), 1931, pp. VII–XV. Cf. F. M. Keesing, *The Changing Maori* (Memoirs of Board of Maori Ethnological Research, vol. iv), 1928.

# PREFACE TO SECOND EDITION

*PRIMITIVE Polynesian Economy* was written originally as a contribution to a general theory of economic anthropology and as a step in my description and analysis of Tikopia society. After publishing an account of the social structure, in particular the kinship structure (*We, The Tikopia*, London, 1936), I analyzed the economic structure of the society because so many social relationships were made most manifest in their economic content. Indeed the social structure, in particular the political structure, was clearly dependent on specific economic relationships arising out of the system of control of resources. With these relationships in turn were linked the religious activities and institutions of the society, which I began to describe in *The Work of the Gods in Tikopia*, London, 1940, and of which my analysis has still to be completed.

In 1952, however, I had an opportunity to re-examine Tikopia society under the aegis of the Australian National University, to which I owe many facilities. With the help of a colleague, James Spillius, who remained on the island for nearly a year after I left, an intensive re-study was made of Tikopia economic, social and religious conditions. General results of this study in comparison with the situation as seen by me in 1928/29 have already been published (Raymond Firth, *Social Change in Tikopia*, London, 1959, especially Chapters 3 and 6). The description included comparative estimates in 1929 and in 1952 of capital in canoes and other major goods, plots of land in the same main cultivating area, diagrams of fish corrals on the same stretch of beach, and a table of comparative exchange rates. (See the present volume, pp. 244–262, 377–80; also Raymond Firth and James Spillius, *A Study in Ritual Modification: The Work of the Gods in Tikopia in 1929 and 1952*, London, 1963.

One of the most striking features in the changed Tikopia economic situation was the massive entry of Tikopia men into the external labour market. This was due in part to pressures of population on subsistence, exacerbated by a severe food shortage in 1952 which rose to famine proportions. It was also due to the keen interest of Tikopia young men to have experience abroad, to get money and to purchase the exciting range of new consumer goods open to them. Problems of the famine, as well as of the unsophisticated character of the initial Tikopia approach to the situation of working for wages and the interim solutions adopted have been described by Spillius, " Natural Disaster and Political Crisis in a Polynesian Society," *Human Relations*, vol. X, 1957, pp. 3–27, 113–125; " Polynesian Experiment: Tikopia Islanders as Plantation Labour," *Progress* (The Magazine of Unilever), Vol. 46, pp. 91–96, London, 1957.

Taking into consideration such attitudes towards labour and the fact that in 1928/29 hardly any Tikopia was cognisant of the use of money, the term " primitive " was understandably applied to their economic system. Nowadays many Tikopia know how to handle money and understand very well the implications of a wage economy. But the bulk of this book has been left as originally written since it sets out in detail the structure and organization of a non-monetary economic system. By implication such a description poses some basic questions about the elementary character of economic behaviour. When no monetary medium exists by which the relative value of goods and services may be estimated, a baseline is given by reference to which the operations of a partially monetized economic system, or one which is beginning to acquire monetary regulators, can be studied. In the first chapter of the original edition I examined some of these basic questions and the kind of contribution which the study of economic anthropology (then currently termed " primitive economics ") had made to them. Developments in economic anthropology over the last twenty-five years have made it necessary for me to re-write much of this chapter. On some of the issues raised in the last chapter I would now also express myself differently were I to rewrite this section of the book. From this edition I have omitted the general bibliography since ample references to relevant literature exist in various other publications, notably in *Economic Anthropology* (New York, 1952) by the late Melville J. Herskovits. Further treatment of some major issues in economic anthropology has been given in some of my other publications: *Economics of the New Zealand Maori*, Wellington, 1959; " The Social Framework of Economic Organization " (Chapter 4 of my *Elements of Social Organization*, London, 1951); " Work and Community in a Primitive Society " (*H.R.H. the Duke of Edinburgh's Study Conference on the Human Problems of Industrial Communities within the Commonwealth and Empire,*

*Oxford*, 1956, Oxford University Press, 1957); " The Place of Malinowski in the History of Economic Anthropology " (*Man and Culture: An Evaluation of the Work of Malinowski*, ed. Raymond Firth, London, 1957). I have made a detailed socio-economic study of an Oriental fishing industry, with much quantitative data, in *Malay Fishermen*, London, 1946. (A second edition of this work is now in preparation.) In collaboration with B. S. Yamey, an economist, I have also contributed to and edited a set of essays on *Capital, Saving and Credit in Peasant Societies*, London, 1964.

For facilities in revising this edition I am greatly indebted to the Behavioral Sciences Division of the Ford Foundation, for use of part of a personal grant-in-aid, and for the help of Mrs. M. Alfandary in preparing the material for publication. I have been much helped in the revision of the first chapter by some very useful suggestions by Professor B. S. Yamey. In considering this chapter especially, as in my other recent work on economic anthropology, I also owe much to the Wenner-Gren Foundation for Anthropological Research, which sponsored a Summer Symposium on Economics and Anthropology at Burg Wartenstein, Austria, in 1960. I am glad to take this further opportunity to pay a tribute to the Foundation and to its late President, Paul Fejos, for the generous help and scientific stimulus afforded me in this undertaking and in many other ways.

*March*, 1964.                                      Raymond Firth.

# PRIMITIVE POLYNESIAN ECONOMY

## Chapter I

## PROBLEMS OF ECONOMIC ANTHROPOLOGY

L ONG before the last war it had become clear that primitive societies all over the world were being subjected to the impact of an industrial system coming primarily from the West, or at least originating in the development of Western science and technology. Nowadays, partly as a result of the social and economic repercussions of the war itself, this process has become much more complex. There must now be hardly any communities in the world, except perhaps a few in the heart of New Guinea and in the South American continent, which have not acquired at least the rudiments of a steel technology and some trading relations with an external market system in which money is the prime medium of exchange. The consequent adaptation of their economic system has created many problems for them, and their difficulties have often not been fully understood.[1] Moreover, in many parts of the world political advance, including the formation of new indigenous states, has radically changed the emphases of interest. Formerly members of the community concerned were pre-occupied by their immediate problems of adaptation to unfamiliar economic and social structures and values. Representatives of the Western industrial system on the other hand were concerned primarily with ways in which local markets for industrially produced consumers' goods could be expanded, export of a local cash crop promoted or a larger and more efficient labour force secured for their mines or plantations. In modern times these emphases still exist. But concern for development of the local resources by the local communities, in their own interest, has now become much more articulate. The attitudes involved

[1] For an early example of this see Margaret Read, " Native Standards of Living and African Culture Change," Supplement to *Africa*, xi, 1938.

seem complex. Aid given in this process by more " developed " countries is regarded as benefitting both parties. If it would be cynical to assume that industrialized countries are actuated here simply by self-interest, however enlightened, it would be naive to credit them with pure philanthropy. But whatever be the motivations, the widespread general interest in " backward," " under-developed " or " developing " countries does assume publicly that welfare is the ultimate aim of trying to increase productivity. Side by side with this change of public emphasis has come also a growing recognition of the significance of social factors for economic growth.

An interest in increasing productivity need not be the sole, or even the main, concern of economic anthropologists, whose prime task is to improve our understanding of how alien economic systems work. But such practical considerations have helped to stimulate their enquiry, since, for more than half a century, social anthropologists have concentrated upon describing and analysing the institutions of communities brought into increasing relation with the Western economic system. The radical changes which have been occurring have indeed sharpened for anthropologists a number of significant theoretical issues, including the meaning of the term " economy " itself.

## METHODS IN THE STUDY OF MODERN ECONOMIC ANTHROPOLOGY

The social scientist who sets out to study primitive communities is at a disadvantage when compared with the student of the physical sciences. He cannot arrange, or have arranged for him, a neat laboratory—he must work in a house packed with people, a cattle kraal, a fishing canoe at sea, or a muddy plantation. Whatever plans he may make for his work, the way in which it is carried out must ultimately be conditioned by the human idiosyncrasies of his subject matter. Above all, he is not free to arrange controlled experiments. He can test the reactions of his subjects to his conversational inquiries or challenges to their ideas. By his intrusion into a ceremony he can observe the rigidity or elasticity of its taboos and the conditions in which participation is allowed. He can estimate loyalties and the depth of religious and social sanctions by attempting through gifts to extract secret information. But his most effective study of mourning ritual must await the occurrence of deaths; in kinship, he can best examine groups as they actually have been established or are coming into being as a result of social and individual forces beyond his control; and his observational studies of seasonal religious festivals can only be properly carried out at the time and place appointed by tradition. The conditions of the anthropologist's work then tend to be regulated, not by ideal scientific requirements, but by the actual life of a community.

The anthropologist cannot rely mainly on other workers for the collection of his raw material. There is no great body of statistical data on which he can at once proceed to base large-scale interpretations. Moreover, he often does not begin with any personal knowledge of the life of the community he studies. He has to accumulate for himself at the outset, by observation and inquiry, even the most commonplace facts about everyday behaviour. But this is not altogether a disadvantage. He is not thereby tempted to assume a knowledge of the basic institutions of these people. Impressed by the importance of the conditioning of " human nature " by culture, trained that his job is to observe how people actually do behave, he is constantly impelled towards generalizations of an inductive kind, though they may be of small range.

Over the last fifty years social anthropology has developed a fairly sensitive technique of fieldwork. Rules have been worked out for securing as accurate information as possible. The field-worker is encouraged to have maximum contact with the people he is studying, as by living in their midst. He is expected to use the vernacular, not only to avoid the misconstructions of an interpreter, but to be able to reinforce his set questions with material picked up by listening to ordinary conversation between the people themselves. He is expected not to rely on single informants for all significant data, but to indulge in a thorough process of checking. The opinions he obtains from individuals are not to be taken as objective statements of the social reality, but as reflections of the position and interests of the people who give them. Above all, generalizations about local institutions are not expected to be framed solely upon verbal data collected from informants, but to be backed up at every turn by the field-worker's own observations of the actual behaviour of the people. Precision has been facilitated by technical methods of inquiry such as the " genealogical method " developed by W. H. R. Rivers—even though this does not yield all the results

Rivers claimed for it. Increasingly, it has also come to be recognised that the way in which the investigator frames his problem conceptually tends to determine the character of the data he collects.

These modern field methods of anthropology as an inductive, observational science, have been built up by explicit formulation from the days of the first expeditions of Haddon and Boas onwards. They also owe much to the example of a host of more or less methodologically inarticulate workers, whose contribution has consisted in descriptive monographs from which the principles which guided them have been extracted by others. The intensity of modern field research may be said to have first been demonstrated in full measure by Bronislaw Malinowski, whose linguistic facility, repeated visits to the same area and acute consciousness of the problems involved enabled him to develop explicitly the " functional method " of investigation. In this an elaborately formulated scheme of inquiry was combined with a lively appreciation of the complexities of individual acts of behaviour and their subtle and inevitable inter-relationships. To his work much modern field research owes a debt, none the less real where it has received no overt acknowledgment.

Modern field-work in social anthropology, however, still continues to have two main defects. On the psychological side the field-worker is frequently not equipped with any systematic approach to guide him in his technique of observation and interview. For instance, the exact affective circumstances in which a record was made may not be taken into account, though they may influence the final generalization. And while his recognition of the significance of non-rational processes may be overt, an anthropologist's attribution of states of thinking and feeling to individuals—as in the process of symbolization—may often lack evidence and be merely a superficial guess. On the quantitative side, insufficient attention is often paid to the *frequency* of activity, and to its *representativeness*, particularly when variations of practice exist among different groups in a society. Again, apart from the system of recording genealogies, which is now fairly uniform, there are few standard instruments for the measurement of social relationships and few standard modes of classifying the relations of persons to objects. A sociological census, a population distribution map, maps of land tenure, diagrams of position at ceremonies, seasonal calendars of activity, have been used for a long time by most field-workers, but there is still no great uniformity in the type of records so made, and even in modern conditions some important systematic evidence may be omitted.

If, for example, an analysis is being made of exchange, an elaborate qualitative investigation is usually undertaken, bringing out how intimately the economic aspect of the transactions is related to the kinship structure, ritual forms and code of manners. But rarely is any systematic study made of the volume of exchange. This deficiency in quantitative material impedes any examination of the general problem of how far differences in the volume of exchange tend to modify economic and social relationships; it also blocks any estimate of the effect of the exchange upon the resources or incomes of individuals. (As a tentative hypothesis it might seem that the greater the volume of objects available for exchange the greater the tendency for secondary economic relationships to develop.) Similar quantitative material on the relation of labour supply to output, on the accumulation of goods by different sectors and categories of the population, on the differential ownership or control of natural resources and of productive equipment is necessary for effective empirical generalizations. If such material were gathered for communities of different social structure, or with similar social structure but different techniques of production, significant comparative generalizations could be more effectively formulated.

## PRESENT POSITION OF ECONOMIC ANTHROPOLOGY

Modern work in economic anthropology falls into two main categories: that produced incidentally in the course of a general description of a society, or as a by-product of a study of another problem; and that produced by explicit studies of an economic institution, or of the whole economy of a society. A few broad studies of the economics of primitive peoples in general have also been made.[1] From these studies certain positive contributions have emerged. The social parameters of different types of primi-

[1] e.g. R. Thurnwald, *Economics in Primitive Communities*, Oxford, 1932; S. Viljoen, *The Economics of Primitive Peoples*, London, 1936; D. M. Goodfellow, *Principles of Economic Sociology*, London, 1939; M. J. Herskovits, *The Economic Life of Primitive Peoples*, New York, 1940 (republished as *Economic Anthropology*, New York), 1952. R. H. Lowie, *The History of Ethnological Theory*, New York, 1937, makes brief reference to a few earlier works. For a fuller bibliography see Firth, *Economics of the New Zealand Maori*, Wellington, 1959.

tive economic system have been well presented. Technical methods of production have been carefully studied, and data accumulated on the relation of technique to resources, the role of human innovation, and the adaptation of technical process through diffusion of ideas. Though the economic problems related to this have received little explicit discussion the material basis for different types of economic structure has been closely described. Rituals associated with production, as also the relation of simple technical and scientific knowledge to beliefs in supernatural powers and beings, to dogma and to myth have also been investigated. In the more specifically economic field the organization of labour, especially as regards division of tasks and cooperation, and the principles of leadership, have been examined; as well as the systems of ownership of goods and, in particular, the principles of land tenure in a number of societies. Studies of exchange and trade, and the organization of markets, have been made in some detail, especially for Melanesian, African and American Indian societies.

This has involved a correction of some popular fallacies. It has been shown that primitive man in even the simplest types of society is not concerned solely with the food quest, that he has not a simple individual or household economy alone, that his organization of production involves forms of specialization, and that his systems of exchange cover a wide area, being even at times what may be termed of an " international " type, overstepping political and tribal boundaries. Moreover, it is clear that he does not live by a day-to-day satisfaction of his needs but shows foresight and engages in forms of economic abstinence.

More theoretical argument has also clarified questions of classification and terminology: whether a certain type of object can appropriately be described as currency or money and what is the significance of such classification; what are the economic as well as the social implications of transactions of gift, barter and ceremonial exchange; the nature of values in a non-monetary economy and the significance of ownership in terms of the sets of rights involved.

Yet economic anthropology, if not still one of the more neglected branches of anthropology, has not yet been clearly and effectively defined. This obscurity has been of several kinds. There is still a lack of clarity about the nature and the objectives of the study. Formerly economists, by implication if not specifically, regarded economic operations in primitive communities as being either so simple as not to deserve serious attention or so irrational as not to allow of any coherent explanation. Their citation of examples from the primitive field was therefore casual, and often naive. No conception emerged of the economic activities of a primitive community as being systematic, let alone complex in their articulation. Anthropologists, too, were often unclear as to what phenomena they were concerned with. They confused technological with economic process, and gave elaborate descriptions of the physical methods of cultivation or of craft work, without indicating the organization of labour and other resources and the mode of distribution of the rewards. They did not see what, if any, *economic* operations were involved. They assumed that the organization of production and distribution in a primitive society was culturally dictated, and hence that its operations did not need any economic apparatus.[1] The economist's assumption of " rationality " was believed to be inapplicable to a primitive economy. Economics, it was thought, was a set of principles, not a mode of analysis, and referred to the institutions of an industrial or analogous complex type of society. " Primitive economics " then was held to constitute not only a different *field* of economic behaviour but also a different kind of economics which it was the role of the anthropologist alone to interpret.

## RELATION TO ECONOMIC THEORY

There has always tended to be some uncertainty on the part of anthropologists as to the use they could make of economic theory. One difficulty has been the high level of abstraction displayed in much economic theorising, often with use of mathematical models. While at times the analysis looks to be of higher power than the conclusions, this kind of approach has seemed too remote for the economic anthropologist to draw upon. But a more serious difficulty has lain in the character of the assumptions from which the economist has proceeded.

---

[1] e.g. W. L. Warner argued that the Murngin did not create a separate economic structure but were dependent on their other institutions, primarily their kinship system, to regulate indirectly their technology and control their distribution and consumption of goods and service (*A Black Civilization*, 1937, 138). But the lack of what may be classed as specifically economic *institutions* does not mean the lack of economic *process*.

The method of modern theoretical economics is essentially deductive—the development of propositions by logical inference from a few very general assumptions about human conduct. The main assumptions involved have been stated in various ways. They postulate, for example, that every individual has a schedule of wants which are of different importance to him and can therefore be arranged in some sort of order; that there is an ultimate scarcity of resources to meet these wants; and that he attaches different relative evaluations to the different kinds of resources. Moreover, the individual in all his normal conduct tries to maximise the benefits which he can get by varying his use of the resources at his command according to circumstances. These assumptions have often been treated as if they are simple, indisputable facts of experience, and certainly in many contexts they appear to be borne out in practice. It may be, however, that on any very general scale they lack proof. Certainly in the eyes of many economists their value lies not in their assumed universality but in their provision of a basis for testable propositions.

In their most general form such postulates may be recognized by an anthropologist as being plausible for the analysis of primitive societies. But a difficulty as far as the anthropologist is concerned is that a modern economist from the nature of his study must introduce a number of subsidiary assumptions. Some are of a technical, institutional order, such as the assumption of the existence of markets and money prices, of banks and of joint stock companies, obviously directed by the conditions of modern industrial society. Other assumptions commonly employed and defended by an appeal to experience are also inspired, though in a more subtle way, by the conditions with which the economist is familiar in his own society.[1] One such

---

[1] This is realised by economists, though they sometimes still express their conclusions in ways which seem odd to anthropologists. W. B. Reddaway, for instance (in " The Economics of Under-Developed Countries," *The Economic Journal*, LXXIII, 1963, 2), an authority on the development of the Indian economy, stresses the importance of the assumptions made in considering the problems of " under-developed countries " and points out that all too often these assumptions are not explicitly stated. But his remedy in thinking about such problems is " to learn to make the right *instinctive* assumptions," to " realise *instinctively* what things were likely to be quantitatively important " in such circumstances (my italics). An anthropologist or sociologist, apart from questioning the use of the term " instinctive " in such a context, would suggest that more useful assumptions might be derived from one's own or other people's field experience.

assumption is that buyers in a market are indifferent as among alternative sellers, and that each buyer buys impersonally from the cheapest seller. This last postulate was re-stated by Robbins in this form: " All that it means is that my relation to the dealers does not enter into my hierarchy of ends."[1] It is true that some part of modern economic studies deals with conditions of a different order, such as discrimination between men and women in employment. But here too the assumptions brought into the analysis are necessarily of an institutional kind, alien to a primitive economic system.

Decision as to how far the anthropologist is justified in taking over some institutional assumptions may be easily made—his ordinary observations soon tell him if he is dealing with a widespread market system. His categorization of other institutional forms may not be so simple—his recognition of the existence of money-price systems, for instance, will depend upon the criteria he adopts for the definition of money. But even here the issues are relatively straightforward. What is not so simple is for the anthropologist to decide how far he may adopt the more abstract assumptions about, say, the degree of competition in an economic relationship. The situation is complicated also by the fact that some of the most elegant economic theories, involving the construction of models, rely upon sets of postulates which are either very remote from the conditions examined in practice by an economic anthropologist or are so highly abstract that it is almost impossible to determine if they be applicable.[2]

Some of the problems involved are raised by the statement quoted above from Robbins. It has been shown by economic anthropologists that economic relations between " labourer " and " employer," or between parties to an exchange are often

[1] L. Robbins, *The Nature and Significance of Economic Science*, London, 1932, 97. The work of Robbins, to which the argument of this chapter in the first edition of this book was greatly indebted, has recently been rediscovered in its relevance to economic anthropology by Robbins Burling, " Maximisation Theories and the Study of Economic Anthropology," *American Anthropologist*, vol. 64, 1962, 802–21.

[2] An example taken at random is some recent discussion on the conditions of free trade for a small country unable to influence world prices. The argument includes assumptions about unchanging technological knowledge and a diversity of occupations for any individual in the system, which might seem applicable to a traditional Tikopia situation. But most of the other " fairly severe assumptions," such as that of constant returns and infinite substitutability of productive services rendered by different individuals, and only two classes of citizens, trade lovers and trade haters (v. P. A. Samuelson, *The Economic Journal*, vol. LXXII, 1962, 820–829), are hardly meaningful for the Tikopia economy.

conditioned very largely by the kinship ties between them, which must be definitely regarded as entering into their hierarchy of ends at the time. The economist may reply that this is simply an instance for the application of the concept of maximization of net advantages in the various alternatives open. A difficulty in applying this concept to primitive or peasant conditions is that unless we know how these net advantages are regarded by the people themselves, it is not possible to explain why labourers assemble, or why exchange takes place. And even granted that they do assemble, and that there are acts of exchange, it is not possible by deductive analysis to explain by what principles the rates of reward or exchange are governed. It is simple to argue that these people would not act as they do if they were not maximizing their net advantages, but this assumption becomes a tautology unless it is translated into more concrete terms.

This assumption again, in practice, is normally taken by the deductive economist for reasons of simplicity to be equivalent to the desire for maximization of money gains, or for increase of wealth. Such an assumption is essential at certain stages of the logical development of economic theory, and is supported by empirical observation to a considerable degree—in the sense that predictions based on it are not falsified. For the student of economic anthropology the difficulty here is to decide how far he should employ the propositions of economics which do involve such an assumption, and, even more, to build up on alternative assumptions a structure of generalizations which will meet his needs. For instance we know from experience in Western industrial societies that in ordinary commercial circles, however much a person may be actuated by the desire to increase his reputation, this normally manifests itself in an attempt to maximize his money gains in his transactions. But this is by no means always the case in primitive societies, where the increase of reputation is not infrequently to be attained by prodigality in transactions, by refusing to haggle, by giving more than the recognized worth of what is offered him in an exchange. Moreover, factors of social obligation or canons of ritual often enter into economic transactions and tend to make exchange rates lower or higher than they would be in terms of ordinary economic analysis.

Most anthropologists interested in primitive and peasant economics do not doubt that a great part of modern economic theory must apply to these conditions. They see, however, from the nature of many of the assumptions which economists employ as the analysis proceeds, that other assumptions must be substituted for them, more in accord with the conditions of these non-Western societies. In the variety of these different social conditions, an empirical examination of each society is necessary in order that the assumptions shall be well founded.

I cite an example from a peasant community in Malaya which has an elaborate system of money prices and a keen competitive attitude in most economic transactions.[1] Yet in some forms of reward for labour the prices paid to certain individuals do not correspond to the general market rate. When women harvest rice for another cultivator, the ordinary wage is at the rate of M$4 per 100 bundles harvested. Alternatively payment may be made at the rate of 2 bundles per 10 harvested, or 20 bundles per 100. This means that 20 bundles are equivalent to M$4. Since a bundle of rice, unhusked, yields 2 quarts of unhusked rice grain, equivalent to one quart of husked rice, one gallon of husked rice would be worth on this basis 80c. This is cheap by local market prices, according to which a gallon of rice costs from M$1.20 upwards. The workers " naturally " prefer to receive their payment in rice. The cultivator employer " naturally," as the Malays themselves recognize, prefers to pay in cash. On the whole it would seem that labour is not very short and that the employer would have the advantage. But when I asked one woman how she managed to get rice owners to give her rice for her harvest work and to accumulate so much grain, she explained that they were kinsfolk—in fact, her brother and her cousin. She added that such kinsfolk might well give rice at more than the conventional rate, say up to 4 bundles out of 10, keeping only 6 for themselves. Kinsfolk may engage in competitive bargaining like anyone else, but in this case the claim of kinship modified the economic return. Yet a further economic consideration was also involved. The woman in fact was keeping her aged mother, and her brother was thus making some contribution to his mother's upkeep. The cousin, however, who had no such obligation, was recognizing a broader kinship claim. This incident illustrates the way in which, in the peasant economy, transactions may often have to be interpreted by reference to

[1] See Raymond Firth, *Malay Fishermen: Their Peasant Economy*, London, 1946; and Rosemary Firth, *Housekeeping Among Malay Peasants*, London School of Economics Monographs on Social Anthropology, No. 7, London, 1943.

social factors obtained from empirical scrutiny, carried out on some scale to estimate their general relevance.

Such empirical examination must include a study not only of economic behaviour in the narrow sense, but also of the social institutions of the people as a whole. Without it, one may be unable to account for many changes, to explain their relative magnitude, or to predict their possibility. For instance, in Tikopia on any given day a man has in theory a choice between working in his orchard and going out fishing, in a canoe or on the reef. It might be held that he will decide according to his preference at the time for an ultimate yield of crops or an immediate one of fish. But in practice his choice may be rigidly determined by social and ritual considerations. The recent death of a man of rank and the taboos associated with mourning may bar him absolutely from any resort to canoe fishing out at sea, although such may otherwise be his preference and would yield him a greater material return. He may be restricted to reef-fishing only. Moreover, the period of his abstention from canoe-fishing tends to vary directly in accordance with his propinquity of kinship to the dead man. A Western economist, concerned with productivity, can similarly take into his calculations the effects on work of time taken off for funerals. But without special cultural knowledge of the Tikopia he is debarred by his own assumptions from explaining or estimating in advance the extent of discontinuity of the economic process caused by their prolonged mourning rules. The anthropologist, however, with adequate study, can estimate the relative magnitude of these and similar effects in the economy, by observing the standard mortuary behaviour of members of the society, the average death rate, the extent of the repercussion in the kinship group, etc.[1]

For formal economic theory, which is primarily the development by processes of logical inference of the implications of certain postulated conditions, such analysis of the institutional framework is unnecessary. But where an attempt is made to justify such initial postulates by reference to the actual behaviour of human beings in the society, or where the generalizations reached are meant to explain, predict or to guide the course of

[1] Note that standard mortuary behaviour in itself may be modified by economic factors, as when the mourning period for close kin was reduced at a time of famine in order to allow the mourners to go out and seek food (Firth, *Social Change in Tikopia*, 1959, 88).

events, careful analysis is needed. So the economic anthropologist may hope ultimately to add something to the content of economic science, if not by an elaboration of deductive arguments, at least by the provision of some alternative assumptions for them. So he will facilitate translation of some formal principles of analysis into a system of generalizations capable of explaining and predicting economic behaviour in societies other than our own.

The lack of a well-constructed bridge between economics and anthropology helps to explain why, in spite of the great developments in the theory and methods of the latter since the beginning of the century, the concrete achievements in economic anthropology have not been greater. It also throws the major burden of construction on the anthropologist himself.

The earlier obscurity about the objectives of economic anthropology was essentially a confusion between formal and substantial propositions. As I point out later, some elements of this confusion still exist. The *formal* analysis and techniques of economics need no help from the anthropologist. Nor can there be any *other* systematic set of *formal* propositions of an *economic* order differing of necessity from the accepted economic ones just because they relate to a different social universe. In my view an analysis of a primitive economic system or of an African or Oriental peasant system can be made without sacrifice of the basic approach of modern economics. Most assumptions about resources, wants and choices made by an economist in his formal analysis are so general that they can apply to any human society. Even the oft-challenged maximisation principle can be regarded as universally valid provided that it can be understood to include reference to such elements as status and prestige, and not only to material wealth, where the inclusion of these other elements in the maximand are necessary for improving the explanatory and predictive powers of theory. But with the substantial proposition of economics it is another matter. The economist, as applied economist making statements about the real world, has, until very recently, almost inevitably made such statements within a Western institutional framework. (This was the complaint of Radhakamal Mukerjee about the Indian peasant economy.) To give such statements a more general validity it was necessary to incorporate data from a social framework other than the setting for the capitalist relations of production.

The need for the support of sociological material to help to explain economic conduct over a wide range of human societies has become more intelligible and more pressing as " developmental " programmes have come to the fore, either internally or externally stimulated.  The modern problems of economic growth are of such difficulty and magnitude as to have led economists to take an interest in any social reasons which may seem to be responsible for success or failure in this sphere.  But there has also been a parallel reason for more systematic treatment of the social element entering into economic processes.  From the theoretical point of view the swing of economic interest towards problems of incentives and problems of decision-making has emphasized the need for more careful empirical identification of the social factors involved.  A significant contribution may be made by economic anthropology in providing economists with such data, primarily from the results of field investigation, and in embodying the interpretation in social analysis.

Economic anthropology has a double role.  If one of its main tasks is to enlarge the range of data for the construction of more substantial economic propositions, the other task is to use such data and propositions for a deeper understanding of social conditions and structures in the communities the anthropologist studies.  Strictly speaking, the former type of study might be called " anthropological economics," while the second alone is given the name of " economic anthropology."  But the relation between them is so close, the second dependent on the first, that there seems no good case for separating them.

## MAJOR PROBLEMS IN TIKOPIA ECONOMICS

What is required from economic anthropology is the analysis of material from non-industrialized, often exotic communities in such a way that it will be directly comparable with the material of modern economics, matching assumption with assumption and so allowing generalizations to be ultimately framed which will subsume the phenomena of both price and non-price communities into a body of principles about human behaviour which will be truly universal.[1]

It is far from my intention to attempt this ideal task here. This book is an essay on an intermediate level of discussion, an

[1] This plea for the study of " comparative economics," the categories of which will transcend those of the Occidental industrial system, was long ago put forward by Radhakamal Mukerjee, *Principles of Comparative Economics*, 1921.

analysis of a single primitive economy. Its general inferences are put forward as a group of suggestions only, an attempt at defining certain issues for anthropology rather than for economics— though perhaps they may stimulate the economist to offer help in the process of further definition.

The material presented is taken from my first-hand study of the community of Tikopia, which is politically a part of the British Solomon Islands Protectorate and culturally a part of Western Polynesia. The island is small and until recently almost self-sufficient, and I do not claim that the generalizations given will have more than a limited validity for economic anthropology as a whole. But the study of a small-scale, relatively isolated, island community allows the operation of the factors of economic organization to be seen in direct and clear linkage with those of other aspects of the social structure.

Moreover, the character of the Tikopia society, with its emphasis on the importance of kinship grouping in economic institutions, its developed system of rank in political and religious terms, its reliance on agriculture and fishing for food, and its elaborate religious cult of ancestors and gods on whom production is supposed to depend, presents close affinities with other Polynesian cultures, particularly those in the Western Pacific, and has much in common with some other Oceanic economic systems. On the basis of our existing knowledge of such societies, then, supplemented by only a small amount of further research, it may be possible to establish some economic propositions as typical for these societies as a whole.

The basic problem of this book may be briefly posed as follows.

A main theme of modern economics has been stated as the study of the disposal of scarce means in relation to alternative ends, or again, as the analysis of market process. We have to consider, therefore, how far means are scarce in the Tikopia community, and what means are scarcer than others; to what extent ends are really alternative, and what is the scale of preferences when choice is made between them. We must also explain what these ends and means are, and the manner in which they are socially conditioned. The question of how far it is necessary to incorporate this discussion of the nature of ends or wants into the theoretical analysis will be considered in the final chapter.

The problem of the existence of market conditions in the

economist's sense must also be faced. The idea of a market implies wants to be satisfied, a demand for goods on the one hand, and an organization of producers to provide a supply of goods on the other. But in current economic analysis market conditions are regulated by prices; demand is a set of wants at a price, and producers offer their goods at a price. The question then arises for Tikopia, where there is no price system, whether these concepts can be enlarged to give a basis for generalization. Price in the economics of civilized societies means value expressed in terms of money, value given by the processes of exchange. For this primitive community, therefore, it is relevant to inquire what processes of exchange exist, what notions of value there are, what part they play in the economic system, and whether there are any objects the functions of which approximate to those of money. If there are not, how is production organized and how are the wants of consumers met, since the rationale of an economic system is to satisfy wants by the production of consumers' goods?

The attempt to satisfy wants raises other problems. Economic analysis assumes that men attempt to meet their requirements by maximizing their satisfactions on a basis of rational or consistent choice—an assumption justified by appeal to everyday experience. How far in a primitive society is choice guided by rational considerations, and what are the satisfactions which are aimed at to the maximum extent? Again, what is the system of distribution of resources in Tikopia, and are these resources directed into production in a manner calculated to secure the most adequate satisfaction of wants? Are the relations between producers and consumers free and impartial or are there any sources of " friction " e.g., conventional social patterns?

The economist assumes that for the working of the economic system there is in being a social order, and in particular a legal system that provides for the holding of property. We must inquire, therefore, what this organization is in Tikopia, and how by it the actions of producers are affected and the choices of consumers guided. One result of this study should be to show what is specifically " primitive " about the Tikopia economy.

In the light of general discussions in economic anthropology during the last quarter of a century since this book was first written, and of my own re-examination of the Tikopia society in the interim, I briefly outline some aspects of the Tikopia economic system a little further.

The economy of Tikopia in the form in which I observed it in 1928/29 can reasonably be categorised as of " primitive " type. The term primitive is a relative one. More closely applicable to an economic than to a social system, it has no very precise defining character and is variously used. My own view is that it implies a system of simple non-mechanical technology, with little or no innovation, directed to maintenance rather than increase of capital assets, and with relatively low differentiation of economic roles of people in production, entrepreneurial and management functions. Usually it is without overt market institutions or generally acceptable media of exchange for rapid conversion of one type of resource into another.

Such general features seem to be characteristic of most " primitive " societies.[1] Apart from these there are other features of a more individual character. Though the anthropologist often speaks of " primitive economics " as if there were a unitary system common to all such communities, this concept is only of a very general kind. Primitive systems of production differ according to the nature of the resources available, and the different technical methods they use for the conversion of these resources—to mention only food collecting, hunting, fishing, pastoralism, hoe and plough agriculture. Some primitive societies have a population problem with obvious pressure on the means of subsistence; others can easily satisfy their most immediate wants. Some have a system of exchange in which a concept akin to interest plays an important part; others ignore such a factor. Some have a keen appreciation of haggling in exchange (what Marshall has termed " an evil sagacity in driving a hard bargain, even with their neighbours "); others have a code of manners which rules it out, though their series of transactions is just as wide.

An economy such as that of the Tikopia was traditionally of a type often termed " subsistence economy." This term is liable to lead to some misconception; it does not refer only to food and clothing. In such an economic system the ordinary daily interest of the people may be directed primarily to food production. But it is by no means focussed completely upon

----

[1] Though some, e.g. that of the Kapauku described by L. Pospisil (1963), do have a monetary medium and a relatively efficient price system, their market processes as a whole are fairly limited, as is also their capital formation.

acquiring only enough food to support them at a minimal or relatively low level of living. When the term is applied to an economic system, it always means one in which the production of goods, including food, and the furnishing of services are undertaken in culturally dictated ways, wherein the objects of production serve a range of ends apart from simple maintenance of physical living. In a society such as Tikopia there is always a very keen interest in food production. In times when crops have been affected by hurricane or drought, this interest in sheer subsistence does become very marked indeed. At such times notions of " scarcity " become very obvious, and anxieties about the allocation of labour resources to produce food and the distribution of food are expressed in very acute form.[1] But when such environmental stringency is not so manifest, the economy is geared towards the production of a range of items with recreational and status significance which cannot be comprised under any narrow definition of " subsistence."

But by the term subsistence economy is sometimes meant a system in which there is production by individuals or small groups such as households, entirely for their own needs, and no system of exchange of products is therefore necessary. In this sense no such economy, even of the most primitive society, exists. In every economic system studied by anthropologists some forms of exchange occur. I was once asked by the late Robert Redfield to address his seminar with reference to the question, " What can one say of a man—any man? " My theme in reply was that at some points of his social existence every man will engage in acts of exchange.[2] From this point of view then the characteristic feature of a " subsistence economy " is not its lack of exchange but the fact that such exchange remains *internal* to the particular economic system. (This proposition may be put in the form that the system of exchange is correlative with the specific social system of the community concerned.) Instead of subsistence economy a more adequate expression would be " internally subsistent economy " since this implies that the economic system derives no resources by exchange from outside.

Even this, however, though theoretically clear, is empirically

---

[1] Firth, *Social Change in Tikopia*, London, 1959, Chapters 3–4.
[2] This is a point made in effect by B. Malinowski, *Argonauts of the Western Pacific*, 1922, p. 175.

correct only in very few, if any, primitive economic systems. Everywhere a primitive community which can be identified as a unitary and exclusive social entity does have relations of an exchange order with the outside world. In the interior of New Guinea, parts of which are inhabited still by tribes almost completely untouched by Western civilisation, there appears to have been for many generations inter-tribal traffic in shell and feather ornaments and other goods of economic interest. The economy of Tikopia, non-monetary as it was in 1929, and with its people not even comprehending how money might be used, had depended to a very significant degree for about a century upon vessels from the outside world for iron tools and fish hooks, as well as some tobacco and cloth. Even earlier the people had sporadic economic relations with those of other islands, whereby commodities of external origin were obtained by barter or by reciprocal gifts. The manner in which even in 1952 a visiting vessel was besieged by Tikopia offering their goods in exchange was an index to their condition of scarcity and to the operation of what may be termed strictly economic motivations among them.

## Non-monetary Conditions in Tikopia

Much of the more theoretical analysis in modern economic anthropology has rightly been devoted to consideration of the theory of exchange. This has a long history. Exchange, according to Blackstone,[1] is a transmutation of property from one man to another, in consideration of some price or value—in goods if barter, in money if sale. This is in accord with the principles of natural law then in vogue, and with the pre-supposition that it was the acts and motives of individuals which were involved. But as Maine pointed out, ancient law was concerned not with individuals but with families, not single persons but groups.[2] Moreover, while it may be assumed that exchange would not take place unless there was coincidence of interest between the parties, there seems no logical reason for assuming that this coincidence in kind need mean equality in degree. Writing about the same period, both Henry Maine and Karl Marx emphasized from very different angles the constraint which institutions put upon the actions of individuals. Marx laid stress upon the fact

---

[1] *Commentaries on the Laws of England*, 5th ed. 1773, vol. 2, 446.
[2] *Ancient Law*, 5th ed, 1874, 126, 186, 271.

that exchange relations were relations between persons, not between things, and that for the purpose of most fruitful analysis it is relations between categories of persons which are of most significance. But the point is that in considering an economic system such as Tikopia, the categories which are important to recognise are not for the most part categories of persons differentiated by their role in production but categories of persons who, both parties being producers, are defined as exchangers by their positions in the social system.

This contravenes the view of Marx, who argued that in general " The characters appearing upon the economic stage are merely personifications of the economic relations that exist between them." The argument is a well-worn one, but it rests on assumptions which are vital for the social anthropologist to consider. Marx held in essence that for objects of " use-value " to acquire " exchange-value " it is necessary for the individual owners to confront one another " as mutually independent persons." This he asserts is not possible in primitive society. " No such relation of mutual independence exists for the members of a primitive community . . . Commodity exchange begins where community life ends."[1] The fallacy here is contained in the word " community " which for Marx seems to imply completely common ownership of property. As we shall see in the Tikopia case, this is not correct. Moreover, despite the form of his argument Marx seems to rest his case upon the assumption that the exchange of commodities takes place because men want " useful " things, i.e. things which serve their *individual* specific ends. His conception of the " useful " includes no reference to the demand for commodities for more diffused social ends. For instance, Tikopia bark-cloth is in demand not only for clothing and bedding but also as institutionalized tokens of personal sympathy and social obligation at an initiation or funeral ceremony. In the " habitual social process " of exchange in a primitive community transactions take place between individuals as well as between groups, and the exchange value situation is a compound of diffuse social—even symbolic—uses as well as specifically personal material uses.

Granted that there is a fairly consistent and widespread system of exchange internally in Tikopia society, how is this

---

[1] K. Marx, *Capital* (Everyman ed.) 60, 63.

accomplished and at what level? For centuries almost certainly Tikopia had been a "primitive" economy. In resources, Tikopia was limited almost entirely to agriculture and fishing. The island had no iron from which metal tools could be made locally, and it is even doubtful whether stone suitable for efficient tool blades occurred on the island. Traditionally adze blades and chisels were made by the Tikopia from the shell of the giant clam found in the reef. A few stone blades, probably imported, tended to be reserved for critical technical tasks and to be treated as ritual objects.[1] Nor did the Tikopia have either pottery or the loom, though both of these were made and used by peoples living not much more than a hundred miles away. Traditionally they may have had pigs[2] but none were kept in recent times. They did not have innovative technology. Their most elaborate technical processes were the construction of their sea-going canoes and the preparation of turmeric pigment.[3] Tikopia in pre-European times was not a completely closed economy. Historically some contact with the Melanesian community of Vanikoro, about 120 miles over the ocean to the north west and with the Polynesian community of Anuta, about 70 miles to the north east, was maintained and some few sources of wealth were tapped therefrom. But until recent times this external exchange was very limited in scope and very sporadic. Now that this has been facilitated by occasional visits of European vessels between Tikopia and Anuta, it is significant to see how absorbed visiting Tikopia become in the technicalities of the exchange and how their major interest is focussed upon these rather than on the social aspects of their visit.[4] This exchange has operated on the basis of a series of fairly standard exchange rates in terms of gift and counter-gift, often employing credit, extended for several years owing to the infrequency of the vessels that call. Even by 1952 no general medium of exchange of what might be called a monetary character had developed to

[1] Firth, "Ritual Adzes in Tikopia," in *Anthropology in the South Seas* (ed. J. R. Freeman and W. R. Geddes), New Plymouth, 1959, 149, 153–5 and plates. If imported, this was probably a long time ago since no details are known. They certainly were not ceremonial trade items analogous to those reported by Malinowski (1922, 481–2).
[2] Firth, *Social Change in Tikopia*, 1959, 37–8.
[3] For the manufacture of turmeric, see Firth, *Work of the Gods in Tikopia*, 1940, 332–74; "Tikopia Woodworking Ornament," *Man*, 1960, No. 27.
[4] Firth, "Anuta and Tikopia : Symbiotic Elements in Social Organization", *Journal Polynesian Society*, vol. 63, 1954, 117–120.

facilitate transactions between the two communities.

In the major field of exchange, the internal Tikopia system, there was no monetary medium either. P. Einzig has classified Tikopia bark-cloth and coconut sinnet cord as "primitive currency."[1] This categorization rests upon the fact of the frequency with which they are liable to change hands, particularly in ceremonial transactions. But as I have shown later (p. 343) neither bark-cloth nor sinnet served as a true medium of exchange by facilitating directly the conversion of one object, say a service such as house building, into another object, say food. Nor, despite the fact that bark-cloth and sinnet were given in exchange for goods and services, was the value of such objects or services ever expressed in terms of so much bark-cloth or so many hanks of sinnet. The latter were treated as a kind of gift in return for service, without strict equation. In Tikopia the bark-cloth and sinnet are never units of account nor do they have the function of standards by which to measure the total value of one's possessions. They do confer on their holders purchasing power, in that they can be used according to occasion to command some other kinds of goods and services. But the kind of good or service is fairly rigorously specified by convention, and neither bark-cloth nor sinnet gives that general control of exchange potential represented by money in a Western community. The fact that they both can serve as means for unilateral payments—as e.g. a conventional token of sympathy or appreciation at a funeral—does not mean that they are set off as a different category from other objects which can serve similar functions. Moreover, Einzig's definition[2] makes an essential qualification of money its acceptance with the intention of use for future payments. This imposes a criterion which it is impossible to satisfy in practice. No field observer in Tikopia seeing a transfer of bark-cloth or sinnet can say whether the recipient intends to keep it simply for making future payments, or whether he will put it to ordinary technical use—garment or sheet in the case of bark-cloth, fishing-line or house- or canoe-lashing in the case of sinnet. Nor, in the case of bark-cloth, can one be sure that he will not set it aside to be used later as a

---

[1] *Primitive Money*, London, 1949, 46, 47. Oddly, Einzig discusses data from Tikopia and other Western Pacific communities under the head of "Eastern Pacific."

[2] P. Einzig, *op. cit.*, 319–327.

recurrent ritual offering. Indeed, if he questions the recipient he may well find that the man himself does not know. He simply puts the article into his store, against some as yet undetermined call on his resources. In short, these two types of Tikopia article are commodities of multiple function going far beyond their technical qualities, assets of considerable liquidity, but not full media of exchange. It is unimportant whether they are called " currency " or not, but it is important to distinguish clearly the various functions which they fulfil from those which they do not fulfil. Some of these functions, for example, control over purchasing power of limited range, and standard payments for certain specific services, do approach monetary uses, though only by indirectly allowing services to be exchanged from this angle. Some items such as bark-cloth may even be regarded as embryonic media of exchange (v. 343 *infra*). But looking at the Tikopia economy as a whole I think one should characterize it as non-monetary.

The lack of a developed money medium has certain implications for a primitive economic system such as that of Tikopia. There can be exchange without money. And while a formal problem can be raised about the existence of economic values (v. 332–40 *infra*), in a strict sense this does not mean the lack of concepts of evaluation in the economy. But if money in a developed sense is lacking, certain restrictions on the system exist. Firstly, it lacks a pervasive price system. The general function of a price system is the expression of values in terms of a single factor. Since these values are the meeting point of variables which may fluctuate widely over periods of time the existence of a price mechanism allows of an adjustment between supply and demand, by giving indices to producers and consumers of the pressure of wants and the level at which they can be satisfied. Different types of object and also apparently disparate services may all be included in this scheme of adjustment. The existence of some standards of measurement and some mechanisms of control of supply and demand are necessary for the operation of any economic system. But with the lack of a price mechanism the economy of most primitive societies presents certain marked features. Multiple standards of evaluation occur, particularly when services are measured against goods. There is absence of any fine adjustment of supply to demand on a large scale even if market conditions obtain. There is also a tendency to work for things directly and not for the medium by which they are procured.

Again, granted a social evaluation of resources, it may be difficult to utilise, mobilise or convert them in a form which allows future expenses to be met. The creation of additional capital goods is not then stimulated as part of people's ordinary activities. As D. M. Goodfellow[1] has shown, there is no such thing, in any practical sense, as a demand price for liberated resources which may be turned into capital goods. The absence of market prices by which surplus consumption goods can be easily turned into free equipment is one of the distinguishing features of a primitive economy. The relative liquidity of some types of resources does replace, it is true, to a limited degree the monetary function. Food, bark-cloth, pandanus mats, coconut sinnet cord in Tikopia are not only meant for ordinary consumption; they are employed in many kinds of exchanges, including payment for productive labour. They can thus be diverted from immediate consumption and injected into the process of production. Their accumulation is thus a part of capital formation (v. 272–3 infra). The convention that such goods can properly form part of a payment schedule irrespective of the precise consumer wants of the recipient does mean that the economic process can go ahead without either waiting for coincidence of wants on the part of producer and consumer or extensive borrowing. Yet the lack of money medium probably does tend to inhibit the multiplication of credit. Food, bark-cloth, sinnet cord tend to have a fairly limited range of uses, and (food especially) suffer from the drawback of lack of durability. The tendency is for consumption of them and their employment in production to be set at socially established levels, to be produced in anticipation of fairly specific demand, and not to be multiplied for the sake of mere acquisition.

## Have the Tikopia an Economy?

But, granted that Tikopia has traditionally been a primitive economic system, a fundamental question remains. How far can it be characterized as an *economy*? An economy may be defined briefly as that sphere of human activity concerned with resources, their limitations and uses, and the organization whereby they

[1] *op. cit.*, 80–2.

are brought in a rational way into relation with human wants in a given social system. The concept of rationality here is arguable, but stands for such type of conduct as is logically consistent with a given set of assumptions about the ends to which resources may be put, irrespective of what the character of these ends may be. Some recent writers[1] have argued in essence not only, as I have done earlier (infra), that those sectors of economic theory which deal with price phenomena expressed in monetary terms cannot apply directly to economic situations where no money is used. They have gone further in holding that the conventional economic notion of " scarcity " may not apply in primitive communities, and that while primitive people may engage in prudent calculation they do not have a system rightfully to be characterized as an economy. Hence, in the " traditional economy " the laws of the economy of the market do not apply. Now it is obvious that generalizations about the economic process which assume the existence of institutional forms such as business firms, banks and developed means of communication cannot apply to situations from which these are absent. Again, economic models which assume the possibility of calculation in price terms may not be applicable. In this sense then economic theory, certainly " classical " economic theory, does not supply the body of generalizations which an anthropologist may require. But does this invalidate the use of economic analysis in a primitive, non-monetary field? I do not think so. Economists have recognized in general a set of major problems relating to the functioning of an economic system: the determination of what goods and services are to be produced and in what quantities relative to one another; the determination of the relative proportions of the various factors of production required; the determination of how the total output of goods and services thus obtained shall be distributed among the participants in the economy.[2] Work already done in

---

[1] K. Polanyi, C. M. Arensberg and H. W. Pearson, *Trade and Market in the Early Empires*, Glencoe, Ill., 1957; Cl. Meillassoux, " Essai d'interprétation du phenomène économique dans les sociétés traditionelles d'autosubsistance," *Cahiers d'Etudes Africains*, 4, 1960, 38–67; G. Dalton, " Economic Theory and Primitive Society," *American Anthropologist*, vol. 63, 1961, 1–25.

[2] These problems are usually described as those of product mix, factor proportions and distribution of product. See E. E. Le Clair, " Economic Theory and Economic Anthropology," *American Anthropologist*, vol. 64, 1962, 1179–1203. Cf. F. Benham, *Economics*, 1938, 3–19; R. G. Lipsey, *An Introduction to Positive Economics*, London, 1961, 40 *et seq.*; P. A. Samuelson, *op. cit.*, 12–13.

economic anthropology allows the validity of this economic approach to be reaffirmed.[1] Some different arrangement of the concrete data than that conventionally adopted by economists may be needed and some broader supplementary assumptions. But no radically different mode of thinking about the problems is required.

I would argue then that the Tikopia in 1929 had an economy in the strict sense of the term, and that this can be studied by the basic analytical approach of an economist, infused by anthropological theory of society. Problems of scarcity were recognized by the Tikopia both in the narrow and in the broad sense. In the narrow sense they had their day-to-day difficulties of subsistence, finding at times, as e.g. after a hurricane, the problem of " making ends meet " or rather of making means meet ends, an extremely arduous one, involving much painful calculation.[2] Scarcity in the broad sense was also a concept familiar to them. Their leading men in particular commonly envisaged the economic situation of the island community as a whole, as was often demonstrated in their discussions with anthropologists and government officials. From time to time they employed measures of conservation to ensure the use of a particular resource to the best advantage (v. *infra*, 207–12). Notions of an increasing population pressing against the means of subsistence were very clear indeed to them, and were expressed to me and to other visitors, both in 1928/29 and again in 1952. By 1952 in particular the Tikopia realised they had an economy which had suffered a population explosion, and they could see no prospect of a technological revolution to relieve the situation. The notion of scarcity then obviously had for them a very concrete meaning. But that it also could have an abstract connotation is shown by the way in which they could conceptualise the issue of relation between population and resources in terms of difference of ratio at different periods of their own society and also in terms of possible economic pressures in other societies.

The term economics is sometimes used in two ways—to indicate either the theoretical study of the economy or the

---

[1] For two very interesting recent examples on this, see Pospisil, *op. cit.*; and R. F. Salisbury, *From Stone to Steel*, 1962, on the non-monetary economy of the Siane—both in New Guinea.

[2] Firth, *Social Change in Tikopia*, 1959, 51 *et seq.*

operational system of the economy itself.[1] From the latter point of view Tikopia may be said to have " economics." They operate their economy at various levels, from individual and domestic to clan and communal. Tikopia is definitely a community which economizes, in that the leaders are continually watching resources and planning their most effective use to achieve a range of ends which, though not set in completely formal and rigid terms, are fairly clearly defined—as the requirements of daily living, ceremonials of initiation, marriage and funeral, and the long-term demands of a chief's status feast. From this point of view one may examine the Tikopia economy as a whole, though there is difficulty in any " national income " calculations, in the absence of a common medium for the evaluation of goods and services.

The Tikopia economy is not a simple set of ecological responses. Its social parameters are significant for its form and its efficiency. Tikopia is not a " primitive " society at the lower end of the scale; it has a moderately complex social system, with some social differentiation. There is a set of about a score of corporate descent groups (lineages) much larger than elementary families, and a broadly ranked set of leaders of these groups, the " elders " of the major lineages. Heading the apical type of political system is a ritually ranked hierarchy of chiefs of the four clans into which the major lineages are organized. All these leaders of groups have important management functions. As indicated later (v. *infra* 233–6), the ritual respect accorded to the chiefs in particular is one of the most powerful sanctions for the functioning of the economy on a communal scale. Lineages and clans are not " equal and opposite " either theoretically or empirically. They vary considerably in manpower and in command of land resources. Moreover, over the last generation they have shown to some extent different growth rates.[2]

How far is Tikopia an economy of private enterprise? Apart from the private holding of consumers' goods such as houses, clothing and ornaments, most of the important producers' goods, including land and canoes, were definitely private property. Though not highly individualized, these were recognized as lying

---

[1] v. e.g. M. Fortes, " The Structure of Unilineal Descent Groups," *American Anthropologist*, vol. 55, 1953, 18. " In Africa one comes up against economics where in Australia or parts of North America one meets only housekeeping."
[2] See Firth, *Social Change in Tikopia*, 1959, 233–235.

in the prime control of representatives of lineages and, at the working level, of households.

There may be said to be a " public sector " in the Tikopia economy in that members of the community at large hold common rights to fish at sea and to use the resources of the reef and fore-shore in their own districts—a restriction which in the past has been somewhat ill-defined. Moreover, except in times of great scarcity, members of the public were recognized as having certain limited rights in the utilization of uncultivated land or the pluck-ing of coconuts from an orchard, provided that the general entitlement of the owner was acknowledged. Again, the power of a chief over the people of his own clan and of his own district could put limitations on the use of resources in the public interest. Communal interest in the operation of private property could work at times against the interest of individual owners. When the chief put a taboo on the use of coconuts in the district, it operated not only on his own family and lineage lands and those of his clan, but also throughout the area for property of men of other clans. This was communal interest in the allocation of private resources. But the fact that these resources were private and that to some extent there was competition for them between different individuals and social units, offered a perpetual dilemma —to match public demands with private needs. A dilemma of this kind, quite apart from the ordinary domestic operations of securing food and meeting social requirements, means a significant area of choice and decision-making.

The exercise of choice is an issue which has not been so easily accepted for analytic purposes by economic anthropologists as it has by most economists. While presumably admitting the relevance of the concept for abstract argument, some have maintained that choice is often severely restricted by the social structure within which the individual functions. " The very foundations of the theory of choice are socially conditioned."[1] No one, least of all the social anthropologist, can deny the social conditions of individual choice, nor overlook the fact that the demands of everyday living in a given natural and social environ-ment often seem to leave very few avenues of choice open. On the other hand, the field is often by no means as restricted as may appear—the individual *chooses* to conform rather than to suffer the penalties and disabilities of non-conformity. Moreover,

---

[1] D. B. Fusfeld in Polanyi, Arensberg and Pearson, *op. cit.* 343–4.

the fact that choices are so largely socially conditioned does not mean that the alternatives open for decision are without significance. I think it would be the experience of every field anthropologist that in their economic and social life men in a primitive society are often clearly in a position where they have to make choices, where they realize the implications of alternative modes of action and where their attempts to find the best solution gives them much thought and even anxiety. Economic choices vary greatly in the degree to which they are overtly realized or verbalized, in the magnitude of the issues involved and in the length of time taken to resolve them. On a sunny morning if the tide is at the right level on the reef a man may seize his scoop net and go down to the fish weir to see what he can catch without hesitation or debate. The obvious alternatives of going inland to cultivate in his orchard or to sit at leisure chewing betel nuts or gossiping are discarded. But if a cold wind is blowing, with rain, it may be a different matter. A sense of responsibility, however, may send the father of a family out to seek food in such conditions, whereas a young bachelor will not go despite the grumbles of the household. A multitude of such choices is made daily as part of the normal round of activities. Frequently such choices are concerned not only with the use of time and skill in labour but with the decision to draw upon other resources, in particular crops. Here, especially if food is short, the choice between plucking coconuts or making do with yesterday's cold breadfruit may be a matter of anxious family discussion. When periodically the need arises to make a presentation of goods in return for some funeral service, an observer can hear the members of the family concerned engaged in prolonged whispered colloquy, during which items may be added to or taken away from the funeral gift according as one opinion or other sways the group. In most if not all of these fields of choice the existence of the social matrix is very clear. But within this social mould choices are seen and resolved, and the implications of their resolution anticipated. Any theory concerned with understanding the operation of the Tikopia economy must take account of the significance of choice and decision.

## SPHERES OF DECISION-MAKING

The spheres of economic decision may be conveniently classified into three: (a) policy decisions; (b) management decisions; and (c) operational decisions. The sphere of operational decisions is one in which every Tikopia participates, as a principal in some cases and as an assistant in others. The issues are not necessarily simple, nor non-controversial. But they are essentially concerned with making the most advantageous use of the resources available within limits which have already been closely determined in relation to an immediate, specific objective. An example is the case of a fishing canoe which has gone out at night to net flying fish. Should the canoe most profitably turn upwind or downwind at a certain point in its manoeuvres? The decision here will be taken by the senior man in the crew, probably in consultation with the rest, and will be implemented by the steersman.

Management decisions can occur at all levels and can be regarded as including operational decisions. But there is a sphere beyond the immediate operational one where questions arise on the most efficient use of resources for the achievement of alternative ends. An example here in the Tikopia economy is whether the canoe is most effectively used in going out at night for flying fish or in the early morning for deep sea fishing during the day. At certain times of the year one course is definitely preferable to another as far as yield of fish is concerned. But at other times either is feasible, though not both. Management decisions of this order tend to be concentrated in the Tikopia economy largely in the hands of family heads and even of the senior members among them, the heads of lineages. Their decisions are not issued in an authoritarian manner but arise from much household and kin group discussion in which women, both members of the lineage and ones married into it, play a very considerable part. But the voice of the senior man is usually the deciding element.

Policy decisions may be expressed as being the long-range management decisions. But they are concerned not just with the most efficient use of a given set of resources but also with the use of those resources in reference to more general problems of control, maintenance and, if possible, increase. Because of the magnitude of the issues such decisions may involve political as well as economic questions. For example, if a Tikopia seagoing canoe is old and in bad repair, a decision will have to be taken as to whether to replace it by a new craft or not. This is not a purely economic decision because the canoe traditionally is dedicated to tutelary gods and as such is under the control of the clan chief. Hence, a policy decision not to renew the canoe, and to put in the equivalent skill and labour on other forms of craft work, would strike at the roots of the family's ties with the chief. While operational and management decisions are taken primarily with reference to the individual or group immediately concerned in handling the resources, policy decisions may be taken by persons who do not handle the resources themselves but control the management and operations of others. In effect, then, the decision that the family should build a new canoe might well be taken in the last resort by the chief himself. It can be argued again that policy occurs at all levels. But it is convenient to separate out, even for an economy such as that of Tikopia, a sphere of major decisions affecting a large collectivity such as clan, district, or the whole island community. Whereas operational and management decisions focus primarily on a fairly immediate situation, policy decisions look to the future. In the Tikopia economy, as this book shows, the policy-making function traditionally lay with the chiefs, in what may be termed a conjoint centralized authority system. Assisted by the counsel of other senior men, especially their executive officers (*maru*) and ritual elders (*matapure*) the actions of the chiefs illustrated the significance of the optional element in Tikopia economic behaviour and the role of decision-making at various levels of society.[1] The analysis given in this book relates primarily to the Tikopia economic system of 1928/29. In modern times the greatly increased contact of Tikopia with the outside world, the considerable export of labour overseas and the growing realization of the significance of the existence of an external market economy has brought radical changes. Among these has been a marked tendency for hitherto junior members of the society to take a much more prominent part in economic decision-making, as regards both their own behaviour and direction of the policy of the community at large.[2]

---

[1] Material on this is also given in some of my other publications, see e.g. *We, The Tikopia*, 1939, 90–102, 136–7, 149–51, 174, 376–93, 398–407; *Work of the Gods in Tikopia*, 1940, 23–4. For a striking case see my *Elements of Social Organization*, 1951, 65–6.

[2] *Social Change in Tikopia*, 1939, especially chapter V.

## CHAPTER II

# FOOD AND POPULATION IN TIKOPIA

A N analysis of the Tikopia economic system may well begin with a simple statement about the type of concrete wants to be satisfied in the community, and the aims of the people's economic activity. The broad cultural features thus sketched will show significant differences from our own society in the relative importance attached to the various wants.

## WANTS AND THEIR SATISFACTION

Whereas we think of three meals a day as a normal standard, and often take subsidiary refreshment as well, the Tikopia aim at securing one main meal a day, with only one or two snacks. The time at which this meal is taken, the early afternoon, regulates a great deal of their work. Whereas again we regard meat as a staple food the Tikopia rely primarily upon vegetable foods, either baked or compounded with coco-nut cream in a pudding, and supplement this with fish ; animal meat is unknown and the flesh of birds is rarely eaten. The clothing each requires is defined by custom as a piece of bark-cloth, varying in type and size according to age and sex, and needing little preparation, though frequently replaced. They use no head covering or footwear. Young children are not required to wear clothing. In what would correspond to a family budget in our society, therefore, food alone is the major item. Shelter, some privacy, and a domestic hearth are provided by houses of timber and sago-thatch, easily built, supplemented by cooking-huts near-by. For sleeping and resting no bed or couch is required, but a mat of plaited strips of pandanus leaf, a blanket of bark-cloth, and a pillow, this being of carved wood for men and of a pile of bark-cloth for women. Other house furniture is equally simple. The floor must be covered with coco-nut-leaf mats, but seats are not used, and since the bedding can be easily stowed away during the daytime all the floor-space can be used to capacity (apart from certain ritual restrictions).[1]

[1] *We, the Tikopia*, 75–80, for plan and description of a house interior.

Water-bottles of coco-nut, baskets, wooden bowls, grating-stools, pestles, and the earth-oven with its stones are the major items needed in the preparation of food, and in addition other standard technical equipment is required such as adzes, knives, canoes, nets, fishing rods and lines, fish-hooks, and digging sticks. The scheme of personal adornment is much the same for both sexes : a certain amount of tattoo, beads of seashell and coco-nut shell, necklets, ear tassels, and head fillets of leaf, posies of flowers and fruit ; in addition men often wear kilts of finely plaited pandanus leaf. For dancing, the principal recreation, sounding boards and beaters are needed, and for men, wooden bats and wands. The Tikopia are not a warlike people, but for display and occasional offence spear, club, and bow and arrow are part of a man's equipment.

This list is not exhaustive, but covers the main objects sought to satisfy ordinary wants.

Many of these things are roughly made and are enriched by little ornament, But if Tikopia is no luxury culture, neither is it one such as Alfred Marshall envisaged, with a level of wants hardly above that of a brute animal.[1]

I can make no attempt to deal with the psychological implications of the concept of wants, or to measure the satisfactions which the fulfilment of them gives to the Tikopia. But it will be recognized that their wants, like those of any other human beings, are defined not only by their bodily requirements, but also by the environment in which they live and by the culture in which they have been brought up. One of the notable features of such an apparently simple economy is the distribution of goods between different uses in accordance with a complex scheme of social relationships. Food is not merely an object of satisfying appetite, or of providing hospitality ; it is a means of expressing obligations to kinsfolk and chiefs, of paying for a variety of services, and of making religious offerings. Bark-cloth and mats are not required simply for personal wear or for bedding, but are transferred in satisfaction of mortuary and other obligations while even fishing lines, paddles, wooden bowls, and other technical instruments serve similar ends.

What is the degree of variability in these wants ? There is some variation according to age, though the determining factor is rather the responsibilities that age normally brings. Children of either sex are expected to accumulate only a few items of the

---

[1] *Principles of Economics*, 8th ed., 86.

simplest kind of goods, such as fish-hooks or arm-rings ; though their father may often make ceremonial gifts in their name they are merely the nominal donors. For an adult man fishing lines and a rod, a long-handled net, a paddle, a club, ornaments, sinnet cord, and a digging stick come within his range of wants. But if he is unmarried he does not normally aim at securing a canoe of his own, or accumulating a store of wooden bowls, bark-cloth, and pandanus mats ; for these he relies upon his father or married brother. It is the attainment of the social status of a *pure*, a married man and actual or potential head of a family that primarily enlarges the range of a man's wants. At times, however, there may be individual attempts to exceed the ordinary cultural standard. And the bachelors do not always accept unquestioningly the property superiority of the married men. Thus at one time during my stay there were complaints from bachelors that I had given preferential treatment to married men in my gifts, and they put forward their own claims for knives, axes and calico.

Variation according to sex goes along the same lines of status. Before marriage a woman wants little beyond a sleeping mat, a fishing net, and a few ornaments. When she marries she begins to want a number of domestic articles, such as a board on which to scrape hibiscus fibre, coco-nut frond for fans and baskets, large dry coco-nuts for water-bottles, a sinnet cord belt and other articles, together with a quantity of bark-cloth and mats for the ceremonial exchanges of herself and her husband. If one were to speak of any general level of wants among the Tikopia it would then have to be in household rather than in individual terms.

There is less differentiation in the type of wants according to rank than might be expected from a society in which chiefs have such definite social and ritual functions and privileges. They and their families require larger quantities of food and other goods to meet their commitments and keep up their position, but there is not a great difference in the quality of these goods. To some extent chiefs and their immediate relatives require and get choicer food, build somewhat larger houses and have finer mats and ornaments. But in most of their ordinary meals they eat exactly the same provisions as other people, they wear bark-cloth of the same quality and their house furniture is of the same simplicity. The interior of a chief's house is no richer in appointments, no more sumptuous than that of a commoner, though there may be more things in it.

The wants of single individuals or households in Tikopia vary considerably from time to time, not from changes in taste or fashion, which are very stable, but from the waxing and waning demands of intermittent ceremonial—initiations, marriages, or funerals—and the seasonal demands of religious ritual. On the whole the demand for food, bark-cloth, pandanus mats, and sinnet cord, the principal items circulated on such occasions, may be regarded as relatively elastic.[1] If, for instance, a large quantity of fish is secured it is absorbed by processes of redistribution in hospitality and gifts, and repayment of obligations. The fish are never preserved for future use, but I have never seen fish remain uneaten or be thrown away. Methods of preservation absorb vegetable food. The demand for technical equipment such as digging sticks, fishing tackle, and canoes is relatively inelastic. Curiously enough, the demand for houses is less inelastic than might be expected. Partly due to their desire to have shelters where they can spend a night or longer in their various orchards, partly to their custom of converting an ancient house where many of their dead have been buried into a temple, the Tikopia have many more houses than are necessary for bare accommodation, and a man of rank may have three or four in different parts of the island.

In talking of any level of wants, or their variability, in such conditions, there is an obvious difficulty in measuring them when the economy has no price-mechanism to give a standard of reference. There is no calculation of the worth of objects against one another in terms of any single unit or common denominator, and one therefore cannot construct a demand schedule in the ordinary economic sense. Yet the absence of money and prices troubles the economist more than it does the native. The latter has little difficulty in deciding what amount of an article he wants and is prepared to secure at a given time, and what he will expend for it. Moreover, the situation is not complicated for him, as it is for us, by actual or potential changes in the value of money. To refer again to Marshall, who seems to have had a superiority-complex about primitive peoples—his idea that differences on the margin of utilities of possessions can only be met in a primitive

---

[1] In the absence of a system of prices, elasticity and inelasticity must be defined in this context in the broad sense of the varying response of demand to a situation of actual or potential increase of supply, and not to a fall in price accompanying such an increase.

society by " the tedious and difficult " process of barter is erroneous.[1] As the material of Chapter IX shows, barter may be rare, and its place can be taken by a widespread system of borrowing of goods and services on a theory of social obligations, which works smoothly and easily.

On what basis of calculation does the native conduct his transactions and satisfy his wants ? In the absence of a price how is demand to be measured ? To what external phenomena other than the price paid does his demand give rise ? In some cases the amount of labour that must be expended to secure the object desired is an index, in others the goods given in payment for the labour of others, or given in return for a thing borrowed, or, more rarely, offered in exchange for a thing, must be the guide. In yet other cases a man's effective demand can be measured in terms of nothing more than the trouble that he will go to in asking for the thing that he wants. In such circumstances an economist's concept of demand must remain somewhat amorphous, or be expressed only in a series of separate equations. It must be emphasized that it is not the fewness of the native wants that allows the system to function without a price mechanism ; it is the specific social pattern of the ways in which these wants are met, and goods and services transferred. In other words, the channels of social obligation function as a substitute for a market.

It will be clear from what has been said that one may properly speak of a *system* of Tikopia economy. Wants are not engendered and satisfied by isolated individual action, but under the control of social rules. The nature of these is examined in later Chapters.

The discussion of wants so far has been primarily in terms of material goods. In the less material sphere such as the desire for leisure, outlets for energy, sex satisfaction and the procreation of children a complex set of social norms likewise regulates satisfaction. The distribution of time between work and leisure or recreation is not the result of a simple estimate of bodily fatigue and comparative physical satisfactions ; it is controlled to a considerable extent by the decisions of men of rank to hold dance festivals, and by the dictates of the seasonal cycles of ceremonies which require a period of dancing as a contribution to the Work of the Gods. The procreation of children, again, is not an end sought by every person in the community, or regulated by purely individual choice. Strong social conventions enforce celibacy upon

[1] Op. cit., 118.

some people and cause others to limit the number of their off-spring.

An indication of the resources available to the Tikopia for satisfying their wants has already been given,[1] and will be considered later in relation to the knowledge the natives possess of them, and the technological system through which they are applied. It is sufficient to say here that the Tikopia carry on a peasant economy, essentially self-contained. The isolation of the island prevents migration of labour to outside employment, and very little except a few articles of metal accrues to them from casual trade. But while their resources are very limited they are not inadequate. In spite of the fact that the island contains no minerals, little stone, and no building or pottery clay, it has a sufficiency of timber for canoes, palm frond for houses, and other vegetable materials for clothing, cordage, and vessels. And though it has no large game, it is fertile enough to supply large quantities of vegetable food, and its seas offer a great variety of fish. Materials are thus available for the satisfaction of the basic physical needs.

Instead of attempting to examine the situation of wants and resources by an abstract analysis of the forces of supply and demand it seems preferable to consider it primarily in relation to the more concrete factors of population and food supply, as it is envisaged by the Tikopia themselves.

## THE SOCIAL CONTEXT OF FOOD

Nothing illustrates so well the contrast between primitive and civilized economic ideologies as the psychology of food. Its primary value is of course nutritional, but primitive cultures often impute to it further values of a non-nutritional order ; for example, when it is employed as a means of meeting kinship responsibilities and other social obligations, or when it is displayed or even allowed to rot because of the non-material satisfactions this gives. This must be stressed in order to refute the popular misconception that the savage is occupied primarily with filling his belly. The range of values which lead to economic activity are socially determined and are not arranged in what might be termed a " natural scale ". The " primary " want of hunger is often subordinated to other less tangible economic wants which are traditionally dictated.

Any study of primitive economics deals largely with the

[1] *We, The Tikopia*, 21–8.

production and consumption of food. This is so partly because of the directness of the nutritional aim and the absence of intermediaries such as an entrepreneur and a money payment ; partly because of the relatively small range of objects of economic interest ; and partly because of the extensive use of food for other than purely nutritive purposes. These facts are patent to an outside observer, but frequently the native people themselves confirm them by their own talk about food. To this Tikopia is no exception.

In this island there is a marked concentration of interest on food, not only for immediate consumption but also for fulfilling ceremonial obligations. The general prospects of obtaining it are frequently discussed by the natives from both points of view. To get a meal is the principal work on most days, and the meal itself is not merely an interval in work but an aim in itself. Food serves as a most important material manifestation of social relationships and through it kinship ties, political loyalty, indemnity for wrong, and the canons of hospitality are expressed. It also provides a basis for the initiation of other social relations, such as bond-friendship, or pupil and teacher in the acquisition of traditional lore. Again, the major foodstuffs rest in totemic alignment with the major social groups ; ritual appeals are made to the gods and the ancestors who are regarded as the sources of food. All such situations are expressed in a body of linguistic material, rich in metaphors and circumlocutions. *Fai te kai*, " prepare food," is a Tikopia cliché which begins the description of any act of attempting an exchange, obtaining atonement, or making a weighty request. The sanction against laziness and the sentiment of a father for his children can both be expressed by reference to food, and deliberate restriction of population is encouraged in the same terms.[1] In the consumption of food a variety of units of apportionment is recognized, each type appropriate to certain situations. There are also rules of taste demanding that baked taro or breadfruit should be supplemented by fish, or by a creamed pudding, and there are certain criteria as to the quality of the pudding itself. The existence of a variety of recipes, already described, illustrates this same point of food æsthetics.[2]

---

[1] *We, The Tikopia*, 173, 415–17, 491, and p. 44 of this chapter. A diagrammatic representation of the complex relation of food to kinship and ritual is given in Table II, op. cit., 118.

[2] Op. cit., 103–110.

The Tikopia realize the existence of a food problem in general as well as in individual terms. Not only is there a tendency for families to be regulated in size according to the quantity of their orchards and other ground, but there is a conception of a total population for which food has to be provided. Though the Tikopia have no numerical reckoning of their population they use the term *fenua*, in one connotation meaning " territory,", " land " or " island ", to refer to all the people. Expressions such as " the land is many ", " the land as a whole," apply to the population ; and a clear example of such usage is seen in a statement such as "this land is a single body of kinsfolk".[1] The senior men of the island took an interest in a census I made, partly to obtain the comparative strengths of the different districts and clans, but also to ascertain the actual count of all the people. In a similar way the expression *te kai* can refer to the total food resources. Again, there is no quantitative measurement of this, but the two concepts are related in a general way in such statements as " If the ' land ' becomes very many, where will the food be found ? "

A historical background is given to the food problem by explanations of how in ancient times struggles occurred between men of rank through pressure on food supplies ; and nowadays the problem is raised both as a short-term and a long-term question.

## The Population Problem

The island of Tikopia is tiny, measuring less than three miles in greatest diameter. The population in 1929 was 1,281 persons by my house to house census. In the absence of an exact survey of the island it is impossible to calculate the density with precision. But according to the description in the *Pacific Island Pilot* and by my own estimate the area of the island must be something less than three square miles (excluding the lake). This means an average density of over 400 persons per square mile.

This figure by itself means little ; the actual distribution of the population by residence, however, is more significant. The map (p. 40), in which each dot represents five persons, shows that sea fishing requirements and ease of communication have been the dominant elements influencing settlement. Nearly all

---

[1] For native statement, see *We, The Tikopia*, 234, 236.

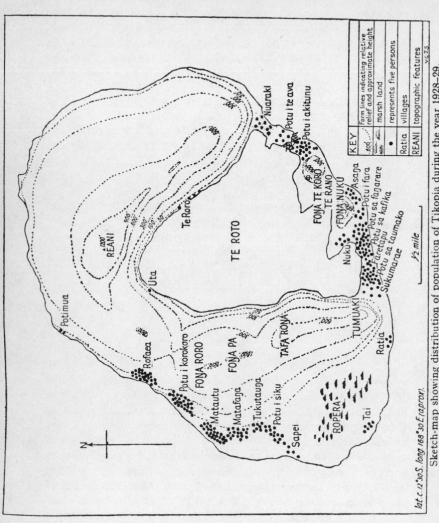

lat. c. 12°30 S. long 168°30 E (aprox).

Sketch-map showing distribution of population of Tikopia during the year 1928–29.

KEY

| | |
|---|---|
| ‒‒‒600‒‒‒ | Form lines indicating relative relief and approximate height |
| | marsh land |
| • | represents five persons |
| Ratia | villages |
| REANI | topographic features |

v.G.75

½ mile

the population is concentrated on the low lands by the coast in parts where the width of the fringing reef offers the best fishing facilities, and where to some extent the narrow reef channels allow the safest launching of canoes to sea. All the island is used for agriculture, but the northern end, which has only a narrow, breaker-lashed reef, carries no resident population. Social control also appears to have played some small part in determining settlement ; I was told that there were formerly a few houses inhabited on the higher land, but that a son of the Ariki Kafika in recent times instructed the people to come down to avoid difficulties about theft of food from cultivations there.

In terms of age groups the population was constituted as under[1] :—

|   |   | Males. | Females. | Totals. |
|---|---|---|---|---|
| i. | Children and adolescents | 338 | 249 | 587 |
| ii. | Adult to middle-aged | 249 | 250 | 499 |
| iii. | Above middle age | 100 | 95 | 195 |
|   | Total | 687 | 594 | 1,281 |

Population represents both a drain upon resources and a source of labour supply. It is interesting to try and estimate the proportion of active producers in the Tikopia community. The following Table (I) is compiled from my original census material in which I made a rough estimate of the ages of the people. No account is taken, however, of the few sick, feeble, and disabled persons. In Group I we have what can be regarded as the widest group of people engaged in production, with an age span of fifty years. In IV we have the group of maximum efficiency, with an age span of twenty-six years. But aged people participate in production as long as they are able to move about, and children begin to work with their parents from an early age, so that allowance must be made for their efforts. If we weigh the contributions of the additional persons included in Group I at one-half the value of those of persons in Group IV and add them to the latter then we get an equivalent of 666 workers of maximum efficiency, or 52 per cent of the total population.

From this we can say that the Tikopia community is supported by something like one-half of its strength computed in terms of work which would be done by able-bodied individuals.

[1] For further details of census and method of collection, see op. cit., 409–411.

TABLE I

APPROXIMATE AGE LIMITS OF WORKING POPULATION

| Limits of effective working age | No. of years | Males | Females | Total | Percentage of total population |
|---|---|---|---|---|---|
| 10–60 (inclusive) . | 51 | 446 | 392 | 838 | %<br>65 |
| 16–55 (inclusive) . | 40 | 347 | 323 | 670 | 52 |
| 16–50 (inclusive) . | 35 | 306 | 314 | 620 | 48 |
| 20–45 (inclusive) . | 26 | 244 | 251 | 495 | 38·5 |

Tikopia is a society where all food is consumed, and there is no socialized waste such as occurs for instance in the Melanesian community of the Trobriands. This would, of course, alter the situation. It would be interesting to attempt a comparison of Tikopia with other societies on these points.[1]

The next question to be considered is the trend of Tikopia population movement. Such data as are available show that there is a distinct tendency to increase. Not only did I find a considerable excess of births over deaths in 1928–9, but four years later the District Officer from Vanikoro, Mr. B. E. Crawfurd, who visited the island for a few days and took a head count, found that the population was 1,323 persons as against my figure of 1,281. These figures may not be absolutely accurate, but they must show a real trend, especially as Mr. Crawfurd's count is likely to be an under-estimate rather than an over-estimate, owing to the difficulty of ensuring that every person in the island was seen.

In former times there were several solutions to a marked population increase, or rather preventives against it. There were four direct checks : contraception of a crude kind ; infanticide ; celibacy of junior males in large families ; and in the last resort slaughter or expulsion of whole sections of the people by others. An indirect check was also provided by the practice of overseas voyaging, which from its hazards has acted as a drain on

[1] B. Malinowski, *Argonauts of the Western Pacific*, 1922, 169, 171 ; *Coral Gardens and their Magic*, 1935, i, 27, 28, 160. (No details are given, however, of any amounts of food allowed to rot, nor how far when this happens it may be regarded as the result of subsidiary food resources being available through Europeans, which has certainly tended to avert bad famines which formerly used to occur (ibid., 160).)

the young manhood. Of the 69 dead males of the chiefly houses whose group membership during the last half-dozen generations is set out in Table III, 23 were lost in *forau* (voyages). The majority of those so lost were unmarried. This proportion of one-third of male deaths due to voyaging is higher than for the rest of the population, but it is a significant factor throughout. I have termed it an indirect check since the motivation for the voyages is not to seek a solution for the population problem, but the desire for adventure. There is no doubt, however, that celibacy with its absence of immediate family obligations facilitates the freedom of action of the young men.

Contraception, celibacy, and infanticide are resorted to consciously by the Tikopia as a reflex of the population situation—*fakatau ki te kai*, " measured according to the food " as they put it. The slaughter of one major group and the expulsion of another have happened only once in Tikopia history, according to the native account ; these are the only instances of assertion of group interests on a large scale. The chiefly families have not attempted to improve their position by increase of numbers and radical sequestration of the lands of the commoner families. As the figures show they have suffered at least as much as the commoners by the operation of the checks.

In terms of sex ratios, whereas overseas voyaging has tended to diminish the proportion of males, infanticide and celibacy appear to operate more or less equally on males and females. There seems to have been no deliberate policy of checking reproduction through female infanticide alone, but merely an *ad hoc* reduction of the immediate pressure on food supplies by keeping the total number of children in each family low. In individual cases, additional female children seem to have been preserved in preference to additional males for their economic value ; one reason for this is probably that if they marry in this patrilineal society, their children are a charge upon the family lands of their husbands. But it is interesting to note that although polygyny provides an outlet in marriage for the surplus women left unwed through male celibacy, many of these women remain celibate themselves. In the genealogies the proportion of *fafine taka*, single women, is considerable. The sexual code of the Tikopia did not deprive them of sex relations, and *coitus interruptus*, with the possibility of abortion in case of pregnancy, allowed them to be free from childbirth as a compulsion to marry. How far this female celibacy was due to personal preference, and how far to lack of initiative in taking them as wives on the part of the men, it is difficult to determine. From native opinion, it seems that the former reason played a considerable part.

To show that the Tikopia are conscious of the issues involved in the adoption of these practices as population controls, I give a few brief statements made to me by various men.

A typical statement on the use of infanticide as a control against pressure on food supplies is that of Pae Sao, a commoner. He said : " A male and a female are born ; they are allowed to live ; two only ; according to the expression ' *fai tama fakaŋamua* ' (literally, ' producing foremost children,' that is, the eldest of each sex). If another child is born, it is buried in the earth and covered with stones ; it is killed. If another child is born also, it is buried in the earth. And two only are left, corresponding to the scarcity of the food."

On contraception, again, the Ariki Tafua said : " Formerly (children were) one of each only, one male and one female ; the making of branches has been done recently, by plentiful families. Formerly, if the females were two, then they were two, but there was but a single male. It was done on account of places, or orchards. The marriage is destroyed by the women. A man rises, while his wife grasps hold of our maleness (the male organ) that it may go away outside. It comes in these recent days that there is lacking what food they shall eat." It is difficult to translate neatly the old man's staccato phrases, but the points made are the former free use of *coitus interruptus* by married people to limit their families to a single son and one or two daughters, and the modern tendency to increase the numbers of children, and the chief's pessimistic failure to see where the food for them is coming from.

Before he became a Christian it was the function of the Ariki Tafua to recite formally and publicly once a year in a ceremonial proclamation known as the Fono of Rarokoka the following sentences :—

A man who sleeps with his wife
And feels (ejaculation) let him arise.
One male and one female
That is the plucking of coco-nuts and the carrying of water-
    bottles.
If a man insists on making branches (*fakauruuru*)
Where is his leaf-basis on which he will branch ?
He will make branches only to go and steal.

The term *fakauruuru* means ordinarily " sprouting into a head ", as of a bush or tree. In this connection it applies to the creation of a large family (*paito kua uruuru i tona fanauŋa*). The leaf-basis (*tafito i rakau*) is a metaphor for sources of vegetable food. The implications of the Fono are the same as the statement quoted above. In olden times contraception was a part of the moral code of the Tikopia, publicly inculcated with the weight of the chiefs and the religious values of the occasion behind it. Reference to genealogies shows that it was not carried out by all, particularly by the chiefly famiiies, but in combination with the practice of celibacy it has had a very strong effect in keeping down a pressure of population.

On the subject of celibacy I quote from Pa Motuata, a near relative of the Ariki Taumako : " In former times people were plentiful, but they went then to the ocean ; in recent times we have become very many. In former times a single male used to marry in his family ; but recently the family has married completely."

In the decade prior to 1929, owing to the nominal acceptance of Christianity over a large part of the island, and the moral influences thus brought to bear, these practices could no longer function overtly with the same force as before. They still operate to some extent, even among the " Christian " families, despite the disapproval of the Christian teacher, and threats of barring offenders from Church. Thus one case of abortion and another of infanticide came to my notice during my stay and it is probable that there were others of which I did not hear. But as against the former situation there is pressure on young people to marry, since Christianity is unwilling to give them the native freedom of sex relations outside marriage. In particular young people who have been discovered to have had an intrigue are threatened by the Mission teacher and sometimes thrust into wedlock. They tend then to produce offspring as in the former conditions they would not have done. At the same time it is true that among Christians and still more among pagans there is still a great deal of sex relationship among the unmarried.

Elderly and more responsible Tikopia are conscious of the dangers of the situation, and during my stay several of them gave expression to their concern at the growing number of children. They deplored the modern conditions, and at times asked my advice on what was to be done. They themselves saw no obvious remedy. The growing influence of Christianity seemed inevitable ; migration, suggested by European missionaries, did not appeal to them, and one of them even proposed to me that the Government at Tulagi should legalize infanticide.[1]

## CRUDE FACTORS OF POPULATION PRESSURE

The following list summarizes the crude factors tending to increase or decrease the pressure of population on resources in Tikopia at the present time, and some possible factors which may change the situation in the future.

### PRESENT FACTORS

| *Increase of pressure.* | *Decrease of pressure.* |
| --- | --- |
| New moral sanctions leading to (partial) cessation of | Purposive checks by partial :— |
| —contraception | |
| —infanticide | —contraception |
| —celibacy | —infanticide |
| —expulsion or slaughter | —celibacy |
| Sporadic (perhaps cyclical) meteorological factors such as hurricanes and drought | Drain by overseas voyaging |
| | Epidemics brought by vessels |
| Perception of increase in food supplies, leading to partial cessation of purposive checks | Enlargement of food resources by |
| | —steel tools |
| | —new food plants |
| | —" payment " of mission teachers in food and goods |
| Lack of potentialities for external trade | |

### POSSIBLE FUTURE FACTORS

| | |
| --- | --- |
| New demands which raise standard of material comfort | Expulsion or slaughter |
| | More efficient agricultural technique |
| | Exotic crops introduced for food or to allow of trade |
| Possible introduction of medical services | Migration of a section of the people |
| | Labour recruiting causing |
| | —acquisition of external purchasing power |
| | —deaths of labourers |
| | —epidemics introduced by labourers |

These mechanisms of population control may be thought to have tended in former times to operate to the advantage of the chiefly families, partly because they had command over larger areas of land, and partly because the respect for their authority gave them in the last resort the right to live as against others. As mentioned above, it does not seem that this was generally the case. The present change in social sanctions may, on the other hand, be tending to promote the increase of commoners in a greater

[1] See op. cit., 527–530.

proportion. I even heard a rumour (put about by commoners) that the chiefs were thinking of joining together and driving the commoners off to sea in order to leave the land for their own children. This I think was merely a wild fabrication, but it indicates a real anxiety based upon a feeling of population pressure.

At the present time, however, the pressure is potential rather than actual. There is no real shortage of food and no person continually goes hungry. Only after a hurricane is there a threat of famine and this might occur in any isolated island.

One may ask the question : how far is it possible for the Tikopia to cope with the situation of increasing population ? And what in fact have they already done ?

Of the cardinal environmental elements there is first the poverty of the island in raw materials or goods desired in external markets. This prevents anything in the nature of inter-island trade on a large scale so that the Tikopia are forced to rely wholly for their immediate subsistence on their own productive efforts. Such exchange with other native communities as can take place is sporadic, and minute for the economy as a whole. It consists in the rare barter of turmeric and food for a few manu-factured products such as bows and arrows or turtle-shell orna-ments from Vanikoro and other islands to the north-west. There is no importation of food. Much more important are the infrequent calls of European vessels which during the last century have enabled the Tikopia to change and amplify their technical equipment by the acquisition of steel tools. These goods have been acquired partly by barter for Tikopia mats, clubs, and other native articles, and partly also by solicitation as simple gifts. Their acquisition has meant a certain enlargement of production but as far as I could gather, no fundamental change in the economic system. The introduction of new food plants has by this agency also tended in the same direction.

These new goods have provided a permanent increase in capital and probably have increased the quantity of food available. For instance, it is easier to build a canoe than formerly and it can be made of harder wood, which demands less labour for repair and replacement, consequently giving more opportunity for spending time on obtaining fish and other food. The introduced manioc, Canarium almond, pawpaw and new varieties of banana have, with little displacement, tended to smoothe out the more violent seasonal fluctuations in food supply. Against this, however, must be offset the fact that some proportion of the population increase has probably been due to a perception of an increase in available food.

The creation of an interest in a limited range of European consumers' goods such as pipes and tobacco, calico and beads, may in the future complicate the economic position by raising the permanent standard of material comfort. For the time being this is essentially an unsatisfied (indeed unsatisfiable) demand. With no regular market for acquisition of these goods from outside, the quantity in the island is too small for there to be any substantial amount for exchange. But if contact with the external economic system were promoted, as for instance by throwing open the island for the recruiting of native labour, then the demand for such articles might become a potent factor in affecting the distribution of resources. The isolation of the island has had one important result. Recruiting of the Tikopia for labour in European plantations is prohibited by Government Ordinance,[1] the justification for which lies in the heavy death rate of these islanders in the past when brought into contact with new diseases. Recruiting then would operate as a check upon the Tikopia population. But it would be a highly selective factor and would lead to serious disturbance of the social and economic structure through changes in the sex and age ratios.

The isolation of the island means also that migration in time of any real food scarcity would be inhibited. In famine conditions escape from distress in canoes has occured but is regarded by the Tikopia as practically equivalent to suicide. Normally the dangers of the vast expanse of surrounding ocean are sufficient to check all but the unmarried men, or those who wish to throw away their lives. Moreover, the idea of any mass-migration to a permanent home elsewhere was viewed with great distaste by the Tikopia with whom I discussed it.

## POSSIBLE CHANGES IN AGRICULTURAL PRODUCTION

How far would it be possible for the Tikopia to enlarge their resources by changes in the form of their cultivation of the land ? Practically all the land is at present in active occupation. There

[1] *High Commission Gazette*, Notice 99. *Western Pacific*, 24th Sept., 1923.

are no waste areas, though there are what may be described as marginal lands which are capable of more intensive cultivation. One type of these marginal lands is that known as *kamali*, sacred for religious reasons, being ancient burial grounds. Recently, however, owing to increase of population, as the natives told me, and helped by the growing influence of Christianity, some of them have been brought into cultivation. But the area of them is small and consequently any relief to the population problem through this must be very limited.

Most of the island is divided into orchards in which stand the coco-nut and sago palms, chestnut trees, bananas, paper mulberry, and various other trees and shrubs which provide food and other raw materials. Taro, the acknowledged staple, is planted mainly in open cultivations traditionally kept for the purpose, but in addition individual and household plots of it are scattered through the orchards, together with patches of yams.

I did not collect the data for a general sketch-map of the areas under different types of cultivation. In the absence of this it is not possible for me to state accurately the amount of land used for the cultivation of taro. But a rough estimate may be formed. On the average, when taro is available, the Tikopia consume at a guess, two taro corms per person per diem, that is, about 2,500 corms per diem are needed for the whole island. Each plant has but one corm, and the seedlings are planted on the average about 2 ft. 6 in. apart. From this it may be reckoned that the amount of taro required for the whole community would be drawn from about 130 acres per annum if the crop were in constant supply. Since taro land must lie fallow for several seasons after use—perhaps two years, on an average—this means that about 390 acres of land would have to be given over to this type of cultivation, or approximately one-fifth of the available land of the whole island. But there is not a constant supply of taro, in part through the failure of individual calculation in planting but in part through reliance on other vegetable foods, particularly breadfruit, banana, and yam. Reference to Figure 2 will show periods in 1928–9 when taro was utilized to a very small extent. If the total period of low consumption of taro be put at the plausible figure of three and a half months in the year, then approximately one-seventh of the total land of the island would be required for it. On the other hand, shortages of rain, ravages by pests, and failure of some seedlings to come to maturity must result in a certain amount of wastage.[1] Hence the amount of land utilized in taro cultivation is probably between one-seventh and one-fifth of the whole area of the island.

The taro resources of the people might possibly be increased by adopting a technique of irrigation and conservation, to tide over periods of small precipitation. But this would require a radical change in their methods of cultivation, and would need specific instruction by an external agency, for which there are no facilities. If pressure of population increased greatly it would be possible with existing technique to place a certain amount of the orchard land under more intensive taro cultivation. But this would tend to limit the amount of perennial foodstuffs and of raw materials such as paper-mulberry bark and hibiscus fibre available for production. There is also the further question of the differential quality of the soil. The Tikopia differentiate types of soil, and plant taro and its allied giant *Alocasia* on that found by experience to be the best. A much more widespread resort to intensive cultivation might result in a less efficient use of the total available land.

Moreover, there is at the present time an equilibrium between the quantity of foods which are more immediately sensitive to climatic changes—particularly drought—as taro is, and foods such as coco-nut, sago, and forest fruits, which are more hardy and therefore are drawn upon when the taro crop is poor. Serious diminution in the quantity of the latter would mean that the Tikopia would be more liable to suffer from the adverse conditions which periodically recur. In such case the Tikopia can look for aid to no outside source ; after a drought or hurricane it may be the best part of a year before their plight even becomes known in other islands, and there is no guarantee of assistance from these even then.

Then there is the question of nutrition. At present coco-nut provides the Tikopia with their principal supply of vegetable oils and vegetable proteins ; to increase by a large amount their consumption of carbohydrate might quite likely have deleterious effects.

---

[1] I have no data about the weight of the product. But Faulkner and Mackie (*West African Agriculture*, 1933, 152) estimate that the average yield of " coco-yams " (taro) in Northern Nigeria is 3,000 lb. per acre. If this were the case in Tikopia then the result would be about 300 lb. of taro per person per annum which would correspond roughly with my estimate of 510 corms eaten per person per annum, as calculated above.

Table II gives a very rough indication of the comparative nutritive values of the different foods principally consumed by the Tikopia. It must be emphasized that the comparison is only of a most general kind. The representation of the different components in any one foodstuff is not meant as a quantitative expression of the ratio they bear to each other in it, nor does the Table allow any exact measure of the relative amounts of any single component through the range of foods. All that it is intended is to show in a convenient form the more important sources of the basic nutritional elements, the potentialities in this island environment for securing a qualitative balance of diet.

Comparison of this Table with Fig. 2 will give some idea of the seasonal variations in the relative quantities of material consumed. It is evident, for instance, that the intake of animal protein is most subject to fluctuation, whereas the supply of vegetable protein is maintained at a more constant level, as in time of drought when yam and manioc replace breadfruit, banana, and coco-nut. From the point of view of protein intake it is perhaps significant that there is a native convention that at a time of prolonged bad weather and consequent scarcity of fish a fermented liquid *tai*, obtained by pouring salt water into a green coco-nut and letting it stand for some days, is sometimes drunk.[1]

The Tikopia are concerned only with questions of the bulk, quality, and taste of their foods, and have no concept of the nutritional components involved.

To them two fundamental aspects of the present situation are the traditional balance observed between the various types of foodstuff, and the ownership of the land by social groups. To consider the former first—on an extreme hypothesis it might be possible to dig out the coco-nut palms and other orchard trees, and replace them by fields of taro all over the island. This might fill the bellies of a much greater number of people than are at present in occupation. But it would strike at the root of their system of food evaluation, which is of a complex conventional kind. These natives have a definite food æsthetic, a theory of taste which holds that taro alone, though satisfying, needs

---

[1] It has been suggested to me by Dr. V. M. Trikojus that the *tai* product may have some affinity with that obtained by the archaic process of " salt-raising " formerly used by housewives to procure yeast, by exposing to the air milk to which a small amount of salt has been added. The action of both yeasts and bacteria is probably involved, though no study has apparently been made of the kinds of micro-organisms actually concerned. (H. W. Conn, *Bacteria, Yeasts and Molds in the Home*, 1903, 75.)

TABLE II

ROUGH INDICATION OF NUTRITIVE VALUE OF TIKOPIA FOODS [1]

| Staple Foods | Protein | Fat | Carbo-hydrate | Mineral salts of Calcium | Potas-sium | Phos-phorus | Iron |
|---|---|---|---|---|---|---|---|
| *Taro* (Colocasia antiquorum) | | | — — — | | | | |
| *Pulaka* (Alocasia sp.) | | | — — — | | | | |
| *Mei* (Bread-fruit; *Atocarpus* sp.) | — | | — — — | — | — | — | — |
| *Futi* (Banana; *Musa* sp.) | — | — | — — | — | — | — | — |
| *Niu* (Coco-nut; *Cocos nucifera*) | — — — | — — — | — | — | — | — — | |
| *Ufi* (Yam; *Dioscorea* sp.) | — | — | — — — | — | | | |
| *Ota* (Sago; *Sagus ? vitiensis*) | | | — — — — | | | | |
| *Masoa* (Arrow-root; *Tacca* sp.) | — | — | — — — — | — | — | — | — |
| Fish | — — — | — — | | | — — | — — | |

[1] No analyses have been made of Tikopia foodstuffs, and the Table has therefore been compiled from analyses of similar foods elsewhere. In the circumstances a broad representation only can be given. A single dash represents an appreciable amount of the nutritive component, and quantitative comparison is intended only within each column. The material is insufficient to allow vitamins to be shown.

coco-nut cream to make it really appetizing. In other words, they insist on having butter with their bread. Moreover, the code of social obligation demands that gifts of food which are the basis of many social relationships should contain coco-nut cream as an emollient.[1]

Again, a serious diminution in the quantity of coco-nut would interfere with the ritual apportionment of control over the principal foodstuffs among the chiefs of the four major social groups. Despite the nominal Christianity of the Tafua chief who controls the coco-nut from the religious side this distribution is still an important factor in the rules of precedence which guide many of the relations of the chiefs. The disturbance of group interests would affect not only the balance of social privilege, but would come into direct conflict with some of the basic religious ideas of the people as a whole.

## POPULATION AND LAND OF CHIEFLY GROUPS

Some of the tendencies present in the economic situation of leading kinship groups may now be considered.

Tikopia is not a society in which wealth is equally distributed. Some men as heads of kinship groups control larger numbers of orchards and more material goods than others. But there is no division into economic classes ; merely a grading of wealth. A class division does exist, into chiefly and commoner families, but some commoners are considerably richer in land than some members of the chiefly group, even than one of the chiefs—the Ariki Faŋarere, who is lowest in rank. Where chiefly families do occupy a very prominent economic position their utilization of their resources is governed in a large degree by the claims of kinship and marriage and by ritual obligations. There can be no situation of widespread economic exploitation. (See Chapter VI.) In conventional speech wealth is reckoned largely in terms of ownership of coco-nut palms, which provide the means of enriching food for the consumption of the owner and his family and for the provision of the constant stream of gifts that goes out from his household. Moreover, when raw material is accumulated for a feast he is able to provide large quantities of the coco-nuts which are an indispensable element. Differences in wealth become a subject of comment and envy at times when supplies as a whole are short. When coco-nuts were scanty and one chief was proposing

[1] Op. cit., 103–110.

to celebrate his old age by a feast a main theme of talk in the family of another poorer chief was : " Where are our coco-nuts coming from to make the reciprocal presentation ? " But for reasons already mentioned there can be no absolute monopoly in coco-nuts.

Certain changes in the position of persons and groups seem probable in the next generation or so, from the trend of present conditions. The planting of coco-nut palms by the Ariki Tafua in two gardens formerly open to general cultivation will tend in a decade or so to elevate his resources, particularly at the expense of the people of his clan.[1] And granted the fixed allotment of lands between kinship groups, the differential increase in the size of these groups has tended to give some a distinct advantage in supply as against others, an advantage which may last for a generation or more. It is difficult to document this last point adequately, since I did not have the time needed to collect complete statistics of land ownership. But reference to genealogies of the different chiefly " houses " will show how the comparative position of members of these groups has altered in the last few generations (see Table III).

Comparison with the genealogies given in *We, The Tikopia* shows the position in each chiefly group of the ancestor whose descendants are enumerated here. The choice of six generations for analysis is not arbitrary since from this point onwards the descendants of the ancestors mentioned constitute the chiefly houses as recognized by the present Tikopia.

The separation of dead from living members in generations (3) and (4) is in order to show the existing position of each group as a whole and also to allow of comparison between one generation and the next.

The distinction between married and unmarried persons, indicated by M. and C. respectively, allows the economic position of each group to be judged more accurately. In the earlier generations most of the unmarried people are, or were, celibate from

---

[1] *We, The Tikopia*, 383.

[2] The term *generation* used in the Table represents age-group rather than kinship grade, as far as living persons are concerned. Groups 3a to 6 may be described as :—

| | |
|---|---|
| Old people | 40 upwards |
| Mature up to middle age | 20—40 |
| Children, adolescents | 1—20 |
| Infants | 0— 1 |

M. represents married ; C. celibate in each column.

## TABLE III.
### CHANGES IN GROUP MEMBERSHIP OF CHIEFLY HOUSES.

| Key | KAFIKA (Descendants of Tariariki) Males | | Females | | TAFUA (Descendants of Tarakofe) Males | | Females | | TAUMAKO (Descendants of Matakai, Pu Veterei) Males | | Females | | FAŊARERE (Descendants of Sufaŋa) Males | | Females | |
|---|---|---|---|---|---|---|---|---|---|---|---|---|---|---|---|---|
| | M. | C. | M. | C. | M. | C. | M. | C. | M. | C. | M. | C. | M. | C. | M. | C. |
| Generation [1]: | | | | | | | | | | | | | | | | |
| (1) Dead | 1 | – | – | – | 1 | 1 | – | – | 2 | – | 5 | – | 3 | – | – | – |
| (2) Dead | 3 | 8 | 3 | 2 | 6 | 2 | 0 | 2 | 2 | 2 | 2 | 4 | 3 | 2 | 1 | – |
| (3) a Dead | 4 | 1 | 1 | 0 | 6 | 3 | 4 | 0 | 1 | 1 | 0 | 6 | 5 | 1 | 3 | 4 |
| b Living | 3 | 0 | 3 | 1 | 1 | 0 | 2 | 0 | 3 | 0 | 0 | 1 | 1 | 0 | 1 | 0 |
| (4) a Dead | – | – | – | – | 2 | 3 | 2 | 1 | 1 | 0 | 0 | 0 | 2 | 3 | 3 | 1 |
| b Living | 7 | 6 | 2 | 5 | 11 | 5 | 7 | 7 | 8 | 3 | 4 | 4 | 6 | 2 | 7 | 2 |
| (5) Living | – | 15 | – | 15 | 1 | 23 | 2 | 18 | 1 | 29 | 0 | 14 | 2 | 10 | 1 | 2 |
| (6) Living | – | – | – | – | – | 2 | – | 3 | – | – | – | 1 | – | 2 | – | 3 |
| Total living strength | 10 | 21 | 5 | 21 Total 57 | 13 | 30 | 11 | 28 Total 82 | 12 | 32 | 4 | 20 Total 68 | 9 | 14 | 9 | 7 Total 39 |
| (Total clan strength, for comparison) | | | | 443 | | | | 365 | | | | 384 | | | | 89 |

For footnote, see previous page.

choice and as such represented less of a drain upon the resources of the group. A dash in the table indicates for past generations that there may have been members whom I did not record, and for present generations that there are potentialities which cannot be accurately estimated (possible marriages of young children or births to young married couples).

This Table, being an analysis of patrilineal groups, includes married women under their father's and not their husband's group.

Analysis of the Table allows certain general inferences to be drawn ; though the figures are small they cover the whole field and therefore represent the actual position (in 1929).

Comparing the strength of the four chiefly houses, that of Tafua is seen to be the greatest and Faŋarere by far the weakest. In labour terms this means that for immediate communal enterprises Tafua has the largest source of supply. Their position in this respect is intensified by the obligations which they can demand from the husbands of the women who have married from their house. In clan strength, however, Kafika is the greatest, so that for enterprises of the largest scale the Ariki Kafika is in the best position from the point of view of kinship. (Local ties of course complicate the situation.)

As regards command over land, however, the situation is different again. I have no complete records of the number, area, and quality of the orchards and gardens owned or controlled by all the chiefs, but from such data as I have, including statements of natives, it is possible to put the chiefly houses in a scale of land wealth. Roughly speaking, if the lands commanded by the Ariki Faŋarere be $a$, then those of the Ariki Kafika would be in the neighbourhood of $3a$, and those of the Ariki Tafua and Taumako would be $6a$ each.[1] The proportions of land available to a person in each of the four groups are then respectively :

in Kafika $\frac{a}{19}$, in Tafua $\frac{a}{14}$, in Taumako $\frac{a}{11}$, and in Faŋarere $\frac{a}{39}$.

The comparative wealth of Tafua and Taumako and the poverty of Faŋarere, however, is complicated by the land rights which custom gives to a woman on marriage. On the one hand, a man and his children acquire the usufruct of a certain amount of the

---

[1] This is borne out by the data I have given for the respective holdings of the chiefs of Tafua and Faŋarere, op. cit., 388–9. Cf. also material on Kafika, ibid., 360, 392.

lands of the woman's family while she lives, the precise amount depending upon the comparative wealth of the parties concerned. On the other hand, they suffer loss through any lands which they yield on the marriage of women from their house. Here the men of Taumako, and to a less extent those of Kafika, are in the best position, since against twelve men and ten men married respectively, they have to provide for only four and five women of their houses who are married. With Tafua and Faŋarere, however, this profit and loss account is almost balanced. In addition to this the obligations demanded of mother's brothers involve some considerable drain upon food and other resources, which accentuates the position.

On the whole, then, the chiefly house of Taumako is in the best landed position with Tafua and Kafika following in this order, and Faŋarere in much the poorest state.

Consideration of potentialities, however, indicates that this position may change in the next couple of generations. At the present time Tafua has the greatest number of young married men, and Taumako the greatest number of male children and youths unmarried. There is then a potentially greater pressure on Tafua in this present generation and on Taumako in the next generation. By the celibacy or overseas voyaging of some of these males this pressure may not be realized, and to some extent the Ariki Tafua has attempted consciously to meet it for his own house by encroachment upon lands formerly open to his clan. Reference to generation (3) of Taumako shows that no females married in this generation ; six of them, who were daughters of the chief himself, remained celibate, through fear of their father, so their brother informed me. Such a reduction of pressure upon the family lands might also be possible in the future.

### COMMAND OF FOOD RESOURCES BY INDIVIDUALS

We may now consider in general the command which ordinary individuals have over food resources in the existing Tikopia economy, in particular, vegetable products and fish.

Individual productive power is regulated in the main by the system of ownership and the associated code of social obligations and rights ; by the quality of technical equipment and by skill. These factors tend to operate with differential effect as far as land and sea products are concerned.

The traditional ownership of orchards and garden plots by

kinship groups means that a man has specific rights to land by patrilineal, matrilineal, and affinal connection. There are no landless Tikopia. In addition, areas held under the control of his clan chief are normally open to him for planting. A bachelor normally does not have separate plantations of food, but works in common with the head of the house in which he lives. At times, however, bachelors do undertake separate cultivations.

There are, however, limitations to these land rights. Certain portions of land, those surrounding temples and the *marae*, the open spaces on which important public religious rites take place, are reserved from cultivation. While I was in Tikopia the planting of manioc in a corner of the very sacred Marae in Uta, due to disregard of the *tapu* rather than to land shortage, caused an angry discussion, and the plants were allowed to remain only because they were not perennial. Again, certain garden areas are dedicated primarily to the provision of taro for ritual purposes, and are not always open for common use. One area is so sacred that until the chief is elderly he can allow it to be planted only two or three times (see p. 69). The withdrawal of such areas from cultivation for long periods does not represent a very serious diminution in the total quantity of cultivable land, but it is a factor. Again, while in general a chief displays considerable economic responsibility towards his clansfolk, there are times when his political power is abused in his own interests. When the Tafua chief, for instance, planted coco-nut palms in a large garden area which his clan normally used for taro growing, this caused them to resort to other areas which in native opinion had not stood vacant long enough to give a maximum yield in the crop. Such action, which was censured by other chiefs, can affect the economic welfare of a number of people.

Against such limitations there is, however, a compensatory factor. By Tikopia convention it is quite allowable for a man to plant temporary foods on the land of another, even without first asking the owner's permission, if he sees a desirable vacant plot. When the crop is lifted a basket of food is sent to the owner as compensation ; such use is for one season only, and involves no title to the land itself. If the owner wishes particularly to cultivate that plot himself or to keep it fallow, he sets up a sign of prohibition, which is respected. The effect of this convention is that the traditional standard system of land ownership is not allowed, as it might, to inhibit production, and the differential size of properties is thus, to some extent, offset. A wealthier man cannot either keep the majority of his land out of production for any length of time or exact a higher " rent " for the use of it. Again, this convention offsets to some extent the need for rigid foresight in the use of one's own individual and family land. There is a situation of total scarcity in the community but individual scarcity is relative to it. For the community the quantity of land is fixed, by social and ritual usage as well as by geographical limitations. For the individual there is a certain elasticity of supply which can meet his elasticity of demand—which varies according to ceremonial as well as alimentary commitments.

There is in Tikopia no purchase or exchange of land, and the transfer of land is rare. Changes of ownership are historical events, as at the marriage of a chief's daughter, or the settlement of a notable immigrant, or the dying out of a kinship group. There is, therefore, no exchange value for land, no price. One might try to assess the value of a plot in terms of the " rent " paid for its use for one season. But this would be meaningless to the Tikopia, and moreover would afford no basis for measurement, since the same payment (two bundles) is made in the case of plots of varying size or varying soil productivity, and only if the crop is very poor is the payment halved. This is still further removed from rent since the risk is partly shared by the owner. I am not arguing here against the classification as " rent " of such return, but against the possibility of proceeding from it to capitalization and reckoning the value of the land. It is a specifically socialized concept of participation of the owner in production.

It might seem that we have here a simple example of primitive communism. This is very far from the truth. There is no idealization of community rights, no attitude that the land should be the common property of all. There is a definite idea of private ownership by kinship groups and by individuals, evidenced by fierce quarrels over land boundaries and over the possession of orchards and garden lands, the title to which is disputed through the extinction of a related kinship group. At times these bickerings may even culminate into bitter cursing, the use of black magic, and fighting. Combined with this stark individualism is the recognition of standard communal claims, a recognition which is carried primarily on the basis of conventional norms of etiquette, and which demands some economic acknowledgment.

The question may be asked : Why does not an enterprising individual then plant large quantities of the vacant land of others ? Some of the restraining factors are the limitations of his own physical energy, his difficulty in mustering constantly large supplies of labour to assist him, his difficulty in accumulating a sufficiency of seed tops, and the competition of other planters. Of another type are such factors as social disapproval at his grabbing so much more than his normal area, and the repercussions of the chiefs' interpretation that he was intending to elevate himself at their expense. But again, to the Tikopia such a question would be without significance, for to them greatly increased production must be motivated by some definite ceremonial requirement, and they fail to see how excess accumulation can be utilized. Within their social system some sort of equilibrium has been established between production and social requirements, and they fail to appreciate the pressure of the abstract drive to economic gain which operates—or is said to operate—in our society. In the absence of a price mechanism to provide a common denominator of values, of a convenient store of wealth given by money, and of a wide range of objects for individual consumption, unlimited acquisition is debarred. The general social equilibrium and the specific organization are against it. Moreover, there is no socially recognized mechanism for the display of quantities of accumulated goods—as is offered, for example, in the Trobriands. The Tikopia are not without the desire to increase their wealth or to see that reciprocity is obtained for a gift. In some circumstances, as in the acquisition of European goods, they display a keenness which amounts even to greed. But this desire for acquisition operates within the sphere of their social values. Put another way it may be said that the particular code regulating their use of material goods inhibits to a considerable extent the profit motive *per se* and limits the extent of production.

As regards Tikopia flesh food the situation is somewhat different. The island is remarkably deficient in mammalian life. The only types (apart from man) are rats and bats, which, however, are not regarded as edible, partly from æsthetic and partly from religious reasons. Birds of a number of species exist, but again because of their religious affiliations very few of them are eaten. Even the pigeon, consumed by most Polynesians, is eaten only by members of a few kinship groups, and then rarely. The small swift (*Collocalia francica*), a noddy, and a petrel are the only birds deliberately and periodically sought by netting. They are not regarded as the property of any individuals or groups, and the catch depends on personal skill and initiative. They are not an important element in the food supply. Of reptiles there are lizards, never eaten, and turtles, usually eaten.

Of fish there is a vast variety, ranging from the salmon-like *kiokio* of the lake to the small fry of the reef, and the many varieties of off-shore fish, including such large types as *Ruvettus*, bonito, and shark. With fish as with birds there is not complete utilization of resources offered. The eel in its various lake and reef forms is never eaten, a restraint which is justified by the natives on grounds of repulsion to its appearance, as well as its religious associations.[1] Eating shark is a matter of individual taste. Some people hold that they do not like shark's flesh because the shark eats man. Others maintain that since the shark eats man it is only fair that man should eat the shark ! In fact, though all types of shark are consumed by some people if caught, the majority are probably not man-eaters. Aversion from shark's flesh can take the form of a physical reaction. A small shark of the *kaukaunaea* type, three " cuts " long (about four feet), was caught by Pa Nukureŋa. It was taboo to him and his kinsfolk since his dead father had been a noted shark fisherman. Hence, the fish was given to Pa Niata, younger brother of my neighbour Pae Sao. The latter, who might have shared in the gift, was indifferent : he explained to me that he could not eat it ; it was distasteful (*faufau*) to him. He added " when such a thing is distasteful, one spits and spits saliva, and then vomits ".

Distribution of resources in fishing is of a different order from that in the case of land. At first sight the resources of the sea are unlimited, but in fact the shoals of fish (not to mention crabs) vary considerably in different seasons of the year. Some fish like the bonito appear off the coast only for a short time about March, and others like flying-fish and the lake fish are available only in greatly diminished numbers in April, May, and June. Again, deep-sea fish are not to be caught all around the coast, but only from local fishing banks. Apart from the limitations imposed by nature there are those which hamper human application. The size and capacity of the canoes, a major item in productive equipment, is one conditioning factor in the situation,

[1] For further analysis see my " Totemism in Polynesia ", *Oceania*, i, 1930–1. It may be noted that the eel is eaten with avidity by the Maori.

while another, allied, to it is the restriction imposed by the
necessities of the crew who feel obliged to return on shore at
the end of the day or night for food and relief from their cramped
quarters. All fishing tackle is individually owned, and canoes are
titularly owned by the heads of kinship groups and actually by
the members of the group as a whole. But there is no monopoly
in the use of them. A man without a canoe, as a younger brother
of the kinship head, normally goes out in one of those belonging
to this head, or is welcomed in making up a crew in the vessel
of another group. He may even take the initiative in borrowing

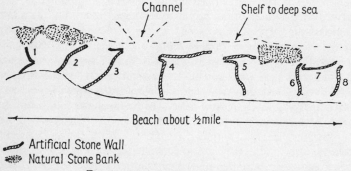

Fig. 1.—Fish Corrals on Raveŋa Reef.

a canoe from any owner, who may not necessarily go out in it
himself. Some data on number of canoes available is given on
pp. 245–7.

And unlike land, fish sources are not owned ; the banks are
free to all, though if a man discovers a new one he takes cross
bearings from it on the shore, keeps its position a secret, as far
as he can, and tells only his kinsfolk. But if he makes good catches
he is soon followed and others share in the spoils. Men and women
wander as they will up and down the reef and there are no proprietary rights in those portions of it which front villages, or even
the residences of chiefs. Low stone walls are built as corrals to
assist in retaining the fish when organized drives are made as
the tide recedes (see Fig. 1). Though these are utilized by their
builders, other people also use them. The builders have no
proprietary rights in those portions of the reef on which they
build. The lake which provides valuable fish is theoretically the.
joint property of the four chiefs, with the Ariki Kafika as the
principal suzerain. But in fact, any one at all sets his nets therein

at will, and the competition is not keen enough to cause dispute over the most favoured spots. There is a great deal of ritual to attract fish to the coastal waters and to the hooks or nets of individual fishermen, but the concept is one of inexhaustible supply and there is no attempt to isolate by magical means any portion of it. The situation is then that the ownership of the sources of fish production is communal, though the ownership of the productive equipment is of a group and even individual kind. Details of catches of fish are given in Appendix I.

Taking the three factors of differences in ownership of natural resources, in technical equipment, and in human skill, they have a different degree of importance in giving a yield from land than in giving a yield from the sea. Every man is a taro planter, and many women also have their own plots, brought into cultivation to some extent by the assistance of their menfolk. But not every man is a deep-sea fisherman and no women fish except with scoop nets on the reef. The minimal role of individual aptitude in agriculture, as compared with its larger role in fishing, is reflected in terminology. The term *mafi* means an industrious person, particularly in taro planting, but there is no term for a skilled, knowledgeable taro planter ; the term *tautai*, however, means a skilled expert fisherman, and there is no word for industry, as such, in fishing. There are canoes at the command of would-be fishermen, just as there is land at the command of would-be taro planters. But individual skill is much more of a determining factor for the result achieved in the former than in the latter case. This differentiation is not, however, reflected in distribution. Skill as such does not entitle a person exclusively to his individual product, any more than industrious labour. (Compare material on apportionment in Chapter VII.)

A word may now be said about water supply. The rocky slopes of the extinct volcanic crater provide a water catchment which drains partly into the lake and partly down the sides to pools or springs. These give fresh water for drinking and for rinsing down after sea bathing, and also for the manufacture of sago and turmeric flour. To some extent the position of these *vai*, " waters," has determined the settlement sites, though water is sometimes brought from some distance in the coco-nut bottles which serve as household carriers and storage vessels. The manufacture of sago and turmeric, however, is directly dependent on a copious water supply, and is localized at the " waters "—or the places to which they are led by aqueducts. The titular ownership which individual chiefs and a few other men of rank exercise over these sources becomes actual at this time, and they assume leadership in these industries partly because of this ownership, which has a religious aspect. The lake is too brackish to serve as drinking water or as a means of extracting turmeric, but it serves for washing, for transport, for steeping foods such as *soi* to remove their astringent properties, or *masoa* to extract the starch,[1] and as a source of fish. Despite titular ownership of it by the four chiefs it is in practice free for the use of all in the island. Incidentally, there is no attempt to use the roofs of buildings as catchments, nor to store water in any quantity.

## CULTIVATION OF THE MAJOR FOOD PLANTS

The relation of physical factors, technical methods, and social conditions to the cultivation of the major food plants may now be considered in more detail.

For agricultural purposes a distinction may be drawn between the lands on the hillsides and hill-crests surrounding the ancient crater, which are primarily of volcanic character ; and the flat lands to the south of the crater, which consist partly of light sandy material near the coast and partly of heavier alluvial material farther inland. I have no data on soil fertility, though it would seem that the presence of a certain amount of coral sand in the soil of the flat area probably means that a reasonable calcium content at least is secured. All the land is under production except the ledges of the rocky cliffs. Coco-nut palms, sago palms, and the *pulaka* (*Alocasia* sp.), allied to taro, grow more freely on the flat lands and lower slopes than they do on the hills, but with this exception the major food plants are found fairly well spread over the island.

As far as cultivation proper is concerned the amount of labour and attention devoted to the major food plants is not in each case proportionate to its role in consumption. The extent to which the plant is self-propagating is one factor in the situation ; another is the way in which the plant is organized into the religious system.

In terms of relative amounts consumed, the staple vegetable

---

[1] The *masoa* of Samoa is an arrowroot (*Tacca pinnatifida*), and the starch is prepared from the tubers, as in Tikopia. Since the name of *masoa* is a modern one in Samoa the Tikopia plant is probably recently introduced, though I was told it was an " ancient food in Tikopia "

food is the taro, termed by the natives themselves " the basis of food ". Secondary to it in importance are the breadfruit (known metaphorically as *te urufena*, the " head of the land "), banana, and coco-nut, the last sometimes being used alone and sometimes in conjunction with the others. Of lesser importance, quantitatively, are the yam, sago, and *pulaka*. The taro, the yam, and the pulaka are planted and cultivated with care ; as also the coco-nut, though because of the long life of the palm no great quantity is ever set in at one time ; to the other plants little or no attention is paid.

A correlation might be expected between the relative importance of these foods for consumption and the relative degree of attention they receive in the scheme of productive ritual. This is not the case. Among the major vegetable foods four, the yam, the coco-nut, the taro, and the breadfruit, are linked with the four clans, Kafika, Tafua, Taumako and Faŋarere respectively, in this order of preference as far as their religious affiliations are concerned. The food is considered as the head or body of the principal clan god, and the chief of the clan has the ultimate responsibility for its fertility. A fifth plant, the sago palm, stands in a similar position to the "house" and elder of Fusi. Yet the ritual performed over them is unequal in importance (see Table IV).

TABLE IV

COMPARISON OF ECONOMIC AND RITUAL VALUES OF MAJOR FOOD PLANTS

| Quantitative Importance for Consumption | Labour expended in Cultivation | Attention in Cultivation Ritual | Attention in Harvest Ritual | Associated Clan and Deity (Numbers indicate general ritual precedence) |
|---|---|---|---|---|
| Taro . . | Taro . . | Yam . . | Yam . . | Kafika (1) |
| Breadfruit . | Yam . . | Taro . . | Taro . . | Taumako (3) |
| Coco-nut . | Pulaka . | Coco-nut . | Breadfruit . | Faŋarere (4) |
| Banana . . | Coco-nut . | Banana . | Sago . . | Fusi (house of Tafua) |
| Pulaka . . | Banana . | Breadfruit . | Coco-nut . | Tafua (2) |
| Sago . . | Breadfruit . | Sago . . | Banana . | (none) |
| Yam . . | Sago . . | Pulaka . | Pulaka . | (none) |

*Note.*—For each particular aspect mentioned the foods are arranged in roughly decreasing order of importance. The last two columns go together.

The banana is the object of no ritual at all, as also the pulaka, though they are important elements in the food supply. The yam bulks far less in the Tikopia diet than any of the other foodstuffs mentioned above, yet ritually it is the most important of all with a disproportionate expenditure of time and labour on the purely formal aspects of its cultivation.[1] It is difficult to explain a religious affiliation which runs so counter to economic interest. A theoretical interpretation in terms of the value of symbols, and tendencies to institutional efflorescence seems necessary. There is no special desirability attributed to the yam as food.

The Tikopia agricultural system is socially rather than technically complex. The people do not use a shifting system of cultivation, with destruction of wild vegetation by fire, and subsequent abandonment of the site, which would create difficulties in such a small island with its dense population, and which is also unnecessary in virtue of the high soil fertility. They follow a rotation of cultivation areas, this practice being based on an empiricism about crops, and sustained to some extent by the religious importance of the areas known as *mara* (see later). But they do not follow any conscious rotation of crops as such ; areas are planted over and over again, after due fallowing, in taro or yams as the case may be.

The principal cultivating implement used is the digging stick. Some details of the cultivation of taro and yams will indicate how technical methods and social conditions may affect the amount produced.

*Taro.*—Taro matures in four or five months, and can yield a crop at any time of the year. As a rule, a man has four or five plots of taro at different stages of growth at a time ; if he is a *mafi*, however, an industrious cultivator, he may have as many as ten or twelve. The fresh " seedlings " planted are the tops removed from the mature corms used for food, so that harvest and planting are intimately connected. The soil is prepared by cutting the brushwood, a process termed *autaru*, and then breaking up the ground to a depth of about nine inches with the digging stick. This is termed *raŋa*. As the digging proceeds the tops of the brushwood are piled on one side and then laid over the dug earth. This process is known as *ufiufi* (" covering "). Only in gardens used for the ritual planting of yams, which need no mulch, is the brushwood burned off when dry. This must have some effect

[1] A detailed analysis of the yam ritual will be given in the *Work of the Gods.*

in facilitating the entry of its mineral salts into the soil, but involves loss of the organic matter it contains. In no case is there any turning of vegetable matter into the soil as green manure.

In planting the " seed " tops of taro the digging stick is driven into the soil, the hole is enlarged, and the stick is then dibbled in the bottom of the hole to make a soft bed for the plant. The seedling is put in, the stick is again dibbled in the bottom of the hole to cover the base of the shoot, and the earth pressed down firm around it with the hand. The seedlings are put in singly, from eighteen inches to three feet apart (measuring by the feet of the planter). The brushwood is then laid firmly round the plant " so that it is not destroyed by the sun ", that is, as a mulch. Conservation of moisture is of the greatest importance. Loads of grass are often brought in, carried on the backs of women, to provide an additional mulch. To some extent the mulch must add organic matter to the soil, in which in such a climate it is continually being reduced by bacterial action.

Next comes the weeding (*sua*) This is done by the women of the household, when the plants h ive been observed to have put out about three leaves apiece. T e rubbish furnished by the weeding is left *in situ* to protect further the growing plant. While weeding the women press dow the base of the plant into the soil, a process termed *aku*. A second weeding is carried out later, in the same manner as before. Later again a third weeding of the plot may be thought necessary. This time the rubbish is not used as a mulch, but is thrown away " because the taro has become mature ". A last process is to dig earth from near by the plants and dump it into the holes in which they stand, thus burying the corm, which has begun to show. This is the *tanu matua*, the " mature burying ".

In harvesting the taro crop portions of it are dug as required ; unlike the yam it is never stored in any quantity, since if left uncooked for more than two or three days it goes rotten.

Some estimate of the amount of land devoted to taro cultivation has been given earlier (p. 49). But not all the taro lands are open to use in the same way. Ordinarily, after a crop has been secured, the land must lie fallow for several seasons until the brushwood has once more grown high. But ritual practices limit the use of those areas known as *mara*, which are sacred, and are controlled primarily by the Ariki Taumako in the name of his

principal deity or of his ancestors. In general terms the whole of
the taro of Tikopia is under his ægis, and he is responsible for its
fertility, but specific ritual is performed only in connection with
that section of it which is grown in the *mara*. Not only do these
ritual requirements limit access to the sacred cultivations, but
they influence to some extent the distribution and consumption
of the crop.

An important feature of the taro cultivation of the Ariki
Taumako is the planting of the *mata pupura*, the " foremost
seedlings ", which symbolize the vegetable as a whole. They are
dedicated to the deity Taromata, son of the principal deity
of Taumako, who is associated particularly with the " house " of
Niumano. If the ground of the *mara* selected for the planting of
the *mata pupura* is adjudged good after the preliminary clearing
of the brushwood (a judgment largely based on its height) then
the chief performs a rite. A large digging stick, sacred, and em-
blematic of the ordinary cultivating implements, is kept in the
important clan temple of Taumako, the building called Resiake.
This sacred implement " belongs " to the deity Taromata. On
this occasion, after a kava rite in the temple, it is carried
ceremonially to the cultivation and set up there. Before the
planting begins the chief takes it, makes a feint of driving it into
the soil, and calls on the deity.

> " Taromata ! Turn to your body which is
>     about to be planted on this morning.
> Send down the sheltering cloud.
> Spread out your leaves above."

Each of the men who have taken part in the preliminary clearing of
the ground has cooked food in his household the night before and
has brought a basketful with him to the site. It has been set
down by the spot where the taro of the chief is to be planted.
The food is termed the *kava*, though no actual kava root or stem
is used as in ordinary rites of sacralization. The food is spoken
of as " the vivifying of the taro ". It provides the material
basis for the rite of appeal to the deity, and is then eaten on the
spot.

The *mara* of the Ariki Taumako are not all equally sacred ;
this is reflected in the varying extent of their use, and in different
destinations to which the crop from them must be taken. A list
of the most important *mara* is as follows :—

" Foŋa Raveŋa "   This is a very sacred area in Raveŋa. As it was said,
" Great is the *tapu* of the *mara* planted to the god."
While the chief is a comparatively young man (perhaps
for a couple of decades) he allows this to be planted
only two or three times. He uses it selectively (*fakata-
ratara*), not continuously in turn with the other
areas. It is permissible for a chief when elderly to
have it cleared and planted more frequently. When
the crop is lifted it is taken to the temple of Resiake,
a kava rite is performed to the principal Taumako
deity Sakura, and a huge ceremonial taro pudding,
6 feet or so across, consuming the whole of the crop
of the *mara*, is made and eaten. This is described as
" the food portion of the deity of Taumako ", and is
named the *pora*.

" Samea "        This area, in Te Roro, is dedicated to the chief ancestors.
" It is sacred, yet good " as compared with Foŋa
Raveŋa. That is, the taboo on it is lighter, and it may
be used more frequently. The crop from it is carried
to the clan temple named Taumako. From it is made
the ritual food gift " Te Ara o Pu ".[1]

" Vaotapu " and   These two areas are both in Rakisu. The crop from
" Matamata "      them is carried to the canoe-yard of the chief's sacred
vessel, Te Rurua.

" Fininamo "      This area is near Namo. The crop from it is carried
to the canoe-yard of the chief's vessel, Tukupasia.
On neither this nor any occasion except the celebration
of the crop from Foŋa Raveŋa is the crop converted
into the ceremonial taro pudding.

Taro may also be planted in these sacred cultivations without
the full set of rites described above. This lies primarily at the
discretion of the Ariki Taumako, and the most important element
affecting his decision seems to be the prospect of a good or a
poor yield. In the latter case the crop is not dedicated to the
deity. The sacred digging-stick is not set up in the cultivation.
The crop, again, is simply carried to the chief's coastal temple,
Raniniu, a less important sacerdotal building than the others ;
it is not even carried to the canoe-yard.

On the mountain, Reani, are two other cultivations,
" Rereŋaturi " and " Roto Reani ", in which formerly the *mata
pupura* were planted. From them the crop might be carried to
either of the clan temples in Uta, or an oven prepared for cooking
it on the mountain side itself. An old oven site is there, by the side
of " The Stone of Taromata " (the deity) which stands in one of
the cultivations. But since the death of the grandfather of the

---

[1] Presented to the Ariki Kafika in virtue of an ancestral kinship connection.

present Taumako chief, these areas have been abandoned as sacred cultivations and are used for ordinary taro planting. At a later time, however, they may be re-consecrated.

The existence of the *mara* means on the one hand that the land they comprise is not free of access to all comers, as other lands are, nor are they used so frequently. Moreover, they demand the expenditure of a considerable amount of time, and some extra labour, for the performance of the ritual. Again, the crop from them is not distributed through the ordinary channels piecemeal, but must first be ceremonialized, with the immediate consumption of at least a part of it by the persons participating in the rite ; with some portion going to the chief, before the remainder can be taken to the households of the planters. But the situation is not static, since the full rites need not be carried out in all cases, and it is possible for some of the cultivations to be converted to ordinary use, at least for a time.

*Yam.*—The cultivation of yams is in many respects similar to that of taro, though a much smaller quantity is planted. There are several varieties of yam in Tikopia, as well as the *taumako*, an allied species with a prickly vine. Only one type, the *ufi tapu*, the " sacred yam ", has ritual associated with its cultivation, and this ritual has pride of place in all the religious institutions of the Tikopia. Strictly speaking, the " sacred yam " is not a separate variety at all, but merely the product of specially reserved seed of the variety known as *ufi vaea*. It is dedicated to the principal deity of the Ariki Kafika, who is also the premier deity of the whole island.

Like the taro, the sacred yam is planted in sacred cultivations known as *mara tapu*. But whereas in the ritual planting of the taro men of clans other than that of the presiding chief may have plots in the cultivation, in that of the yam only a few families are represented ; namely of Kafika and the chiefly house of Faŋarere, which is allied to that of Kafika in many ritual proceedings. Some of these sacred cultivations, like those of the taro, are worked only infrequently. The most sacred of all is that known by the name of " Penusisi ", which is cultivated only two or three times during a chief's whole reign, on account of the weight of ritual connected with it.

I attended the sacred yam planting on two occasions, and observed the air of solemnity which surrounded all the work, and the way in which it was closely regulated by the religious sanctions.

One cultivation, named " Matatoa ", on Mauŋa, measured about 120 ft. by 100 ft. It was divided off into six major plots and one smaller one, each being the ground of a separate kinship group. In that of the house of Kafika, containing the " sacred yam " proper, thirty-nine hillocks were made, and several pieces of seed yam were planted in each.  In all there were twenty-six men engaged, some of them being of Taumako and Tafua clans. These were brought by kinship or friendship ties to help in the work, but none of them planted for themselves.

Little need be said here of the more technical aspects of yam cultivation, save that the seed is planted twice a year, and the crop is harvested in one cultivation at the same time as the other is planted.  No mulch is used for the yam, since it requires less moisture than the taro, and this obviates the need for much assistance from female labour.  Because of its greater resistance to dry weather the yam is drawn upon when taro tends to run short.  I have no reason to think, however, that this accounts for the greater respect paid to it in the ritual scheme of the Tikopia.

*Other Food Plants.*—Comparatively little labour is devoted to the cultivation of the other food plants, and there are no lands specially reserved for them, as with taro and yam.  Banana and breadfruit suckers are sometimes planted out, as also sprouting coco-nuts, but they are then left to fend for themselves, with perhaps some weeding in the early stages.  Manioc, which has been introduced recently, and is of value because its tap-root enables it to obtain moisture longer than the taro or the yam in times of drought, is cultivated from slips, as also the *vakiri* (un-identified), which gives a red root when cooked.  The sago-palm is allowed to propagate itself, as also are the pawpaw and other fruiting trees or plants, such as *soi*, *kafika*, *vere*, *voia*, *natu*, and plants such as *masoa* (arrowroot) and *ti* (cordyline) whose roots give food.

The planting of banana, breadfruit, and especially coco-nut palms, all of which bear perennially, immobilizes the land on which they stand for other cultivation.  For this reason a different convention obtains than in the case of taro, yam, and manioc ; anyone who plants them on another person's land gets not the yield but a reputation from them (see p. 263).

For the breadfruit there is practically no ritual of planting, but there is a harvest ritual of some magnitude, primarily under the ægis of the Ariki Faŋarere. There are four or five crops of breadfruit in the course of a year, and towards the end of January, six months after my arrival, the third crop was just beginning to mature. A crop lasts, as a rule, for about two months. The initial harvest rite, termed *poroporo mei*, is accompanied by a ceremonial levy upon the crop in all orchards. Two or three fruit are taken from each, without distinction of ownership. Thus sa Faŋarere have no orchards in quantity in Raveŋa, but they take toll therefrom just the same (see *Aru*, p. 260). It is said that the breadfruit ripens earlier in Faea, and that in olden days when the people of Faea were still heathen, they would pluck their quota and carry it to the Ariki Faŋarere for the rite to be performed, or that the people of Raveŋa would go to Rakisu and Rotoaia, say to those of Faea : " We are going to pluck breadfruit," and go through all the orchards without objection being raised.

It was said also in olden days that any person who plucked breadfruit before the ritual would find it bad for his belly ; it would make him ill. Even now in Raveŋa the new season's crop is not supposed to be interfered with before the ceremony. But it is admitted that some people do not wait, but pluck their crop secretly. If the chiefs delay in performing the rite the people may murmur : " The breadfruit is ripe ; why don't the group of chiefs go and *poroporo* the breadfruit ? "

Since the technical methods of planting are simple, and the skill required is small, fluctuations in all crops depend upon meteorological changes and the presence of animal pests.

Weather variations follow a seasonal course in the change from the period of the trade winds from the east and south-east, which last approximately from April to October, to that of the " monsoon ", characterized by variable winds mainly from the north and west which alternate with calms, which last from November to March. Since the island is well within the tropics— 12° 18′ S. latitude, in 168° 48′ E. longitude, according to the *Pacific Islands Pilot*—the temperature has a fairly small range throughout the year. The usual figure recorded by my thermometer about midday was slightly above 80° F. for most of the year, but it rose to 90° F. in the middle of December. Changes in the daily rhythm of labour can be linked to some extent with changes in rain and wind conditions : a rough windy day may keep people from fishing and send them to their cultivations ; a very wet day may keep them indoors. On the other hand, after a period of rough weather they flock to the sea and the reef to get fish to enliven their diet, while after a rainy spell they proceed to plant taro. In this way indirect fluctuations in the crops may occur.

Direct fluctuations are caused by severe gales which occasionally come in the early part of the monsoon season, and last several days. Such gales, especially when, as seems to happen about once in a decade, they rise to hurricane force, damage the vegetation greatly and reduce the food supply for months to come. Variations in the rainfall affect the taro in particular, which needs much moisture. In ordinary years there is little overt anxiety concerning the rainfall, though appeals for rain are commonly included by the chiefs in their ritual invocations to their gods and indicate a latent fear. From native statements, however, it appears that droughts periodically occur. In one of these the shortage of food was so severe that a man took his sons and went off with them to sea to perish in despair.[1]

Animal pests are responsible for some reduction of the vegetable food supply. The rail, *karae* (*Porphyrio* sp.), the paroquet, the fruit-bat, and the rat attack bananas and other fruits, as also does a kind of caterpillar (*unufe*). A grub (*kasoso*) attacks the taro, and another insect, the *kama*, devours coco-nut leaf. Any of these may perceptibly reduce a crop to a limited extent. The rat is trapped, and the rail trapped or shot with bow and arrow, but the bat, primarily for religious reasons, goes almost untouched. There is no effective method of dealing with insect pests.

## VARIATIONS IN FOOD SUPPLY, 1928–9

It is now desirable to give some more concrete information about the manner in which the elements of the Tikopia food supply vary, and the reasons why this happens. The appended Chart (Fig. 2) indicates in a broad way the fluctuations which occurred during the year of my residence on the island. This should be compared with the synoptic chart of seasonal and other activities in Appendix I.

Two points must be noted in qualification of Fig. 2. The chart does not represent an exact quantitative record of community supplies or consumption—which would have been impossible to obtain—but is a condensation of rough daily

---

[1] There is a specific Tikopia word for extreme food shortage or famine, *oŋe*.

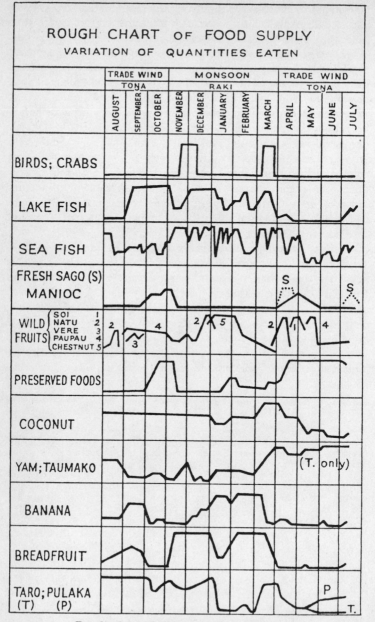

FIG. 2.—Seasonal Changes in Food Production.

notes of the occurrence and preponderance of foods eaten by myself and observed by me in native houses and at ceremonies. In my constant visits to houses on both sides of the island, and attendance at most of the ceremonies performed, it was easy to record the abundance or scarcity of the different types of food and native conversation about them. I made, however, no actual measurements of quantities. Again, the rise and fall in the line of each type of foodstuff represents an increase or decrease in the amount consumed, but indicates only approximately its proportion in the total food consumption. It is not possible, for instance, to say just what relation the quantity of crabs eaten at the end of March bore to that of taro and coco-nut, though they were important at that time as a food item, and vanished from the menu almost immediately after.

However rough the material on which the chart is based a few broad generalizations emerge.

An inverse correlation is shown, as might be expected, between the consumption of fresh vegetable foods on the one hand and of preserved food, together with manioc and *taumako*, which can be kept in reserve in the ground, on the other. The preserved food is provided partly by pastes (any excess of mature taro, breadfruit, and bananas over what is required for immediate consumption being laid down in pits) ; partly by the flour of sago, turmeric, and *masoa*, kept in bags ; and partly also by Canarium almonds, yams, and mature coco-nuts, stored in racks or piles as the case may be. Neither birds nor fish are preserved for future use, as they are among the Maori.

The consumption of vegetable foodstuffs can be seen to be on the whole more steady than that of fish and birds and crabs. This is what might be expected from the greater degree of control of the conditions of production in the former case.

A marked scarcity of almost every kind of food is seen for May and June. The year 1929 may have been abnormal in this respect, but I gathered from native opinion that such scarcity is not uncommon at this time owing to an interval between crops, assisted by a lower rainfall. This shortage was beginning to be perceptible about the middle of April, when it was mentioned to me that " Raveŋa is steeping *soi* ", meaning that the people of that district were short of cultivated food. *Soi*, *masoa*, and *vakiri* are among the foods described as " ancient foods of Tikopia, foods when the famine has come indeed ".

An examination of the individual lines in the chart shows in them a considerable amount of variation. Fluctuations in the supply of sea-fish are naturally the most severe, the principal causes being bad weather, or moonlight which restricts the use of torches. It should be noted that the monsoon season is the better for sea-fishing. But while the trade wind sometimes causes such a heavy surf on the reef as to bar the canoes from going out, such weather causes more keen combing of the fringing reef and drives the people to secure varieties of small crabs and shellfish about which they normally bother little. I have not been able to list these separately, so that to some extent they tend to correct the fluctuations in off-shore fishing. A combination of heavy rainfall, high easterly wind, and a spring tide, again conditions unfavourable to canoe fishing, give a periodic opportunity to open up the channel leading from the lake to the sea and secure large quantities of fish. On the other hand the catch of deep-sea fish is augmented on very calm days (in the monsoon) by diving for green-snail and clams, an occupation pursued intermittently. Changes in sea life such as the seasonal appearance of the bonito and the fluctuations in the number of flying-fish may be related to temperature conditions, but of this I have no knowledge.

From the social side, funeral restrictions have also an effect since they frequently include abstention from canoe fishing. Lake fishing is not subject to these influences to the same extent, and the line is therefore less irregular. The two peaks in the lines of birds and crabs represent the only occasions on which these creatures were caught in very large numbers, periods which apparently depended upon their breeding habits. The consumption of wild fruits also is seen to be sporadic, and on the whole tends to be high when that of taro and breadfruit are low. This is due as much to the fact that they are sought in times of scarcity as to their maturing more freely on such occasions. The line for breadfruit shows on the whole more severe but less frequent fluctuation than that for taro. This is probably due to the fact that when the breadfruit is in season it matures rapidly and if not plucked falls to the ground to rot.[1] It is therefore utilized as far as possible to the limit of capacity as long as it is there, while taro, the other staple, which can afford to be left in the ground for a short time after maturity, is drawn upon to

[1] If stored as a paste in pits in the ground, this means more labour.

a less extent.  The line for coco-nut in actuality should, perhaps, show greater fluctuations than are indicated here.  But its smoothness is at any rate partly due to the fact that coco-nut provides not only fresh but also preserved food.  When taro or breadfruit is short there is a tendency at least for a time to use coco-nut cream in larger quantities in combination with sago and other flours.

The description of the food situation in Tikopia given in this Chapter, and how it is met, has been primarily factual. But it has involved reference to matters outside the province of nutrition—a labour supply ;  conditions of ownership of resources ;  technical methods of production ;  a ritual organization and concepts of a social interest in property.  We may first examine the knowledge of resources possessed by the Tikopia and the technical means they have for the utilization of them.

## CHAPTER III

# KNOWLEDGE, TECHNIQUE, AND ECONOMIC LORE

IN ordinary economic analysis there is no need to describe the technological system, the material equipment, and body of knowledge at command of the participants in the economy. These are " given factors " in production, and for the industrial communities are well enough known, while specialist studies are available for documentation of the position. From common knowledge it is evident that our complex industrial technique demands to a high degree whole-time specialization of labour ; a complex combination of labourers ; technical direction in each branch ; and in combination with the elaborate marketing system, a special management function. This last co-ordinates production for any unit as a whole, and arranges for the inflow of materials, the apportionment of tasks and the disposal of the product.

For the study of a primitive economy this is not so. Already it will be evident that in Tikopia these are not the conditions of production, and that the system of organization stands upon a different technical basis. Technology must not be confused with economics. But some outline of the level of technical achievement which the Tikopia have reached ; the kind of rules which they formulate to guide them in their technical procedure ; and the manner in which their body of practical knowledge is treated as a cultural possession for transmission to their descendants is relevant to our inquiry. In the first place it will help to make the economic analysis more intelligible to those who have no knowledge of a Western Pacific community. In the second place it will show some of the reasons why the type of productive organization in vogue has this particular structure.

## THE LEVEL OF TECHNICAL ACHIEVEMENT

The culture of the pre-European Polynesians is generally described as being neolithic in type. In the narrow sense, relating to the manufacture and use of polished stone implements, this term hardly applies to Tikopia, where the use of such stone tools was rare even before contact with Europeans, and where it is doubtful if they were ever manufactured, owing to the scarcity of workable stone. To-day there are only about half a dozen stone adze blades, cherished as valuable objects, and probably imported. A century ago the most accurate description from the point of view of the working tools used would have been a " shell-wood " culture. The material for adze blades was clam shell, and for borers the pointed *Terebra* shell ; while wood was extensively used for other tools. In addition, the fibres of coco-nut, paper mulberry, and hibiscus were drawn upon for many secondary purposes.

In the broader sense of neolithic, however, as an economy of food-producing in contrast to food-gathering or foraging, the term is more applicable. Though the pottery-making, weaving, and domestication of animals of the classical neolithic economy did not exist, agriculture was one of the two main techniques in the production of food, and the culture may therefore be classified as being of a " limited neolithic " type.[1]

In Tikopia, though wood and fibre have retained much of their old use, nowadays the material for working tools has largely changed from shell to steel. The change has made for greater efficiency in two directions. Firstly, there has been a saving of time in the work of cutting and hewing (according to native state-ment it takes now only two or three months to build a canoe instead of ten or twelve) ; secondly, much harder timbers can now be utilized for canoes than previously was the case. But the general form of the culture appears to have remained the same. The forms of material goods—houses, canoes, clubs, bark-cloth, mats—retain what is said to be their traditional style. The forms of economic organization appear also to be of the same nature as before, and there has been no diminution in the extent of co-operation, a phenomenon which has not characterized the culture contact process in some other Polynesian communities. Ritual forms, again, maintain their ancient character ; so much is this the case that in the ceremonies of re-consecration of sacred

---

[1] V. Gordon Childe has recently stressed the need for the broader connota-tion of the classical terms " palæolithic ", " neolithic ", etc., and has suggested that consideration be given to the economic and social revolutions that accom-panied revolutions in technique in each case. (" Changing Methods and Aims in Prehistory," *Proceedings of the Prehistoric Society*, 1935, 7–8.)

canoes, the adzes used have the antique shell blades.[1] The advent
of the new material goods, principally tools, has, however, had
the indirect effect of causing a change from the worship of the
old gods to Christianity on half the island.

The correlation of the material culture and technology of
the Tikopia with their natural environment is very close. They
have utilized the properties of the available substances for
appropriate ends—the harder timbers for canoes, beaters, bowls,
spears, or clubs ; the softer for canoe and net floats and dance
bats ; the brittle sago leaf for thatch, the more pliant coco-nut
leaf for fans and baskets ; the longitudinal fibres of the hibiscus
(possessing great tensile strength) for cord and pads for wringing
out coco-nut cream.

The coco-nut palm, for instance, provides a great variety of
objects ; from its fronds are plaited roof-thatch when green,
and torches when dry ; appropriately cut they are made into floor
mats and baskets ; a pair of pinnules are a chief's necklet ; the
rib of the frond makes a food pounder, a stirrer, or a pair of tongs ;
strips torn from it are used as temporary lashing. The nuts
provide drink and food at their various stages of growth and
maturity ; empty they make water bottles, or if small, lime-
containers ; their dry spathe serves as a torch or to kindle a
fire. The coco-nut shell itself gives a cup for liquid of any kind,
including kava and tattooing pigment ; serrated it makes a
grater for attacking a sago trunk ; cut small it is converted
into beads. As an example of how the productive needs of one
industry regulate activity in another may be mentioned the use
of whole coco-nut fronds. When green they are laid over the
sago thatch of house roofs to hold down the thatch sheets in
the wind. But torches for flying-fish netting are plaited from
the dry fronds. These are taken from the roofs, so that the
constant demand for torches means an automatic replacement
of roof covers at a time when, being dry, light, and brittle, they
have lost much of their efficiency.

In the extractive processes they employ, as in the securing
of arrowroot, sago, and turmeric flours, the Tikopia show an

---

[1] It is interesting to note that the term for an adze blade, *toki*, is the same as
that for the clam. The name of the latter is probably derived from the former use
of its shell, since *toki* is the general Polynesian term for an adze, irrespective
of the material from which the blade is made. But nowadays when the blades
are of steel they still share the name with the clam, thus originating a pair of
homonyms.

THE MANUFACTURE OF SAGO FLOUR

The boy is water-carrier to the two men kneading the sago pith.

PLATE I.

MAKING A FILTER-FUNNEL FOR TURMERIC MANUFACTURE

The Ariki Tafua, standing, directs the work. A stand for a second funnel is on the left.

PLATE II.

unexpected insight into the possibilities of the raw material. Not only do the grating, filtering, decanting, washing, and baking of the turmeric, for instance, demand considerable technical skill, but these techniques rest upon a perception that the latent properties of the root can be resolved into two useful commodities— an edible extract (*tauo*) of a light yellow colour, and a pigment (*reŋa*) of a blood-red hue.   These are separated by making use of their different specific gravities after suspension of the filtered matter in water. Granted that this knowledge is traditional, it is nevertheless applied with a clear realization of the technical problem.

Another example of the ingenuity of the technical devices of the Tikopia is seen when they dive for green-snail from their canoes in fine weather.   To help them in locating these large molluscs they chew the flesh of the mature coco-nut and spray it out over the water to the lee of the vessel, thus giving by the thin film of oil a smooth clear surface through which they can gaze.

It should be clear that simple materials worked up by simple technique do not necessarily mean that wants are satisfied on a crude level of physical needs alone. The Tikopia in some respects have elaborated from the one source a series of artifacts of similar general function, but each item in the series is correlated with some specific physical or social convention. For example, consider their containers. They have no metals and as far as I am aware no suitable clay for pottery and no animal skins which are convertible into vessels.  The gourd (*kapia*) is used to hold lime or oil, but it is not common. But from the coco-nut they make cups, lime containers, and water bottles, and from the rough fibrous material around the base of the fronds they make bags for flour or nuts.  Baskets, plaited from the leaves, are of four kinds ; openwork *popota* for bulk foods ;  closer mesh *kete* for fishing tackle ;  fine mesh open-mouthed *loŋi* for household food packets ; and small close-mouthed *taŋa* for small personal goods.

Leaf of the cordyline provides wrapping for fish roasted over a fire or for packing up lime or small articles.  Leaf of the giant taro (*pulaka*), gathered together and tied, is used as a container for semi-liquid material such as fish paste or sago pudding to be cooked in the oven.  For pudding, again, and for liquids, wooden bowls are used.  Very large bowls, more properly to be called troughs, are employed for turmeric and sago making ; they are about six feet long. At times the hull of a small canoe, stripped of its outrigger, serves as a substitute, being of the same shape.

But the function of some of these articles is not highly specialized. If the fibrous material which, gathered together, forms a bag for holding nuts is laid out in a sheet instead, it gives a filter which can be used in one of the processes of turmeric manufacture. A basket of plaited coco-nut frond, ordinarily used for carrying water bottles, can serve as a sieve for the manufacture of sago. It is obvious then that a single form of object may serve more than one function, and for the understanding of its place in the native culture it is essential to consider this multiplicity of functions.

The highest level of technical achievement of the Tikopia is reached in their canoes. The canoe is formed of a dugout hull, made more seaworthy by the addition of washstrakes and bow and stern covers, with a single outrigger to give stability. Its manufacture is primarily the work of master-craftsmen (*tufuŋa*) whose functions are described in Chapters IV and VIII.

In their technical devices the Tikopia make no use of wheel or pulley and only to a small degree of the lever. The wedge, however, they employ not for splitting but for holding firm a joint by driving it beneath a lashing. Their cardinal method of securing objects to each other is by lashing, or where necessary boring and lashing. The nail or spike is not used. In house-building they hollow the top of a post on which a ridge-pole or side-beam rests to hold it steady, and I have even seen a roughly made mortise and tenon to join the tops of rafters over a ridge-pole. The ordinary principle was modified here by making the mortise a slot and straining the rafters slightly apart so that they were held firm by the pressure of the tenon at an angle to the mortise. The hinge is not used but the same purpose can be served by straps or ties of fibre, which allow some freedom of movement. Normally the Tikopia do not use such a device as a hinge substitute, but when I wanted a window for light to my house the builder at once adapted the ordinary thatch-tie to my problem and gave me a sheet of thatch held loosely from above so that it could be propped open. There is no suspension of thatch sheets or wooden slabs from the side after the fashion of doors.

Mechanical aids in wood-working are few and simple. The major tool is the adze. A slot cut deep into a length of timber serves as a primitive vice to hold firm a slab that is being dressed ; it is termed *fakanapara*. If the upper part of a canoe is being worked then this principle is extended by setting the keel in notches cut into two skids and then jamming the bow up against a sinnet cord which has been wound round a pair of sticks set close together in the ground. While the washstrakes of the canoe are being lashed into position, a piece of wood jammed between them holds them firmly apart.

The Tikopia distinguish two kinds of slot in wood-working, as shown in the diagram. That with square corners is termed *tu pau* (or *tu fakapaku*) ; that with oblique sides *tu fakakai*—this according to the Ariki Kafika,

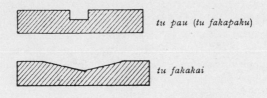

tu pau (tu fakapaku)

tu fakakai

Fig. 3.—Types of Slot in Wood-working.

In repairing a large house a simple form of ladder is some-times used. This is termed *kakeŋa*, " something to climb on." It consists of a large forked limb of a tree with vine tied across it at intervals to form steps. One man climbs up it and lashes on the fresh sheets of thatch while another holds it below.

In filtration of the turmeric ingenious use is made of the tripod principle to provide support for the filter. Three poles are set up and lashed together at the top ; a cord is run round the middle and on this banana leaves are thickly hung. These are gathered in by a network of sinnet cord to form a funnel, which is lined with corrugated leaves of the umbrella palm. Across the top of the funnel a sheet of coco-nut fibre is spread as a filter cloth. The whole apparatus is rough in appearance, but quite efficient for the work it has to do. (See Plate II.)

In some communities a considerable amount of the time of a craftsman in wood is absorbed in the æsthetic elaboration of the object he is making. The delicacy of the work gives opportunity for greater specialization, tending to create a class of master-craftsmen, and *ceteris paribus*, demands a longer time in the production of the object.  In Tikopia elaborate art forms comparable to the carvings on canoe stem and stern pieces, wooden bowls, or houses of men of rank, such as obtained among the Maori or the Marquesans do not exist.  Nor does the printing of bark-cloth which characterizes Central Polynesia.  Houses and bowls are plain, simple geometrical forms adorn canoes, and bark-cloth is either plain or simply dyed with turmeric.  Fans, pandanus mats, head-rests, betel mortars and clubs are sometimes worked in simple geometrical motifs, but little extra time is spent upon them.  Only in tattooing is the craftsman primarily interested in the ornamentation of his subject, but even here the complexity and delicacy of design, characteristic of so much Samoan, Marquesan and ancient Maori work is lacking.[1]

## INVENTION AS A CULTURAL PROCESS

Comparison with other Polynesian communities shows that much of Tikopia material culture and technology cannot be an original mode of coping with their local environment, but must have involved the application of already known processes to the materials and conditions of the island.

Some of these items and processes they do recognize as specifically of foreign origin (apart from recent introductions due to European contacts).  The Canarium almond (*voia*), for instance, is said to have been brought by an ancestor of the Ariki Taumako[2] from Vanikoro; and a few varieties of coco-nut and taro are named as having been introduced from Anuta and other islands.  The bow and arrow are regarded as native to Tikopia, but one type of arrow head is described as *fakaFiti*, of the style of Vanikoro and the other islands to the north-west.  The large concave net known as *parae* is said to have been adopted from Anuta, and the pole-net for catching flying-fish is said by tradition to have been introduced from Nanumanga (Ellice Islands) by a man named Vaoroa.  This man, who lived in Faea on land belonging to the house of Fasi, is also stated to have introduced the sinnet-noose method of catching large sea-fish, known as the *sere para*.  The practice of tattooing, again, is said to have been introduced by an immigrant from Rotuma about eight generations ago.  The authenticity of this tradition is doubtful, since a century ago

[1] A description of Tikopia tattooing designs has been given in *Man*, Oct., 1936, 236.

[2] Matakai II, mentioned by P. Dillon as a visitor to Vanikoro prior to 1827.

European visitors recorded Tikopia tattooing in a form practically identical with that of to-day. Since every Tikopia adult is tattooed, and apparently was so even then, it would seem that the art had a more ancient vogue in the island.

So closely have the Tikopia identified themselves with their present form of culture that they attribute the majority of their items of material culture and technical processes to local sources, even though in some cases this is difficult to credit from a comparative survey. The netting-knot they use, for instance, is of a type commonly found in other parts of the world, but they regard it as their own product. The *tiri*, the large net set in the lake or used in a smaller form for reef fishing, is held to be a local object—" because its basis is the lake and the sea ; the *kiokio* (the salmon-like lake fish) and the fish of the sea grow in this land. The *tiri* was made among the gods or was made among men." This opinion ignores the similar nets and similar conditions of other Polynesian groups. It is true that according to a well-known myth the *tiri* was brought from the realm of the gods by the deity Rata, who is given a spiritual dwelling-place in the islands to the north-west, but it is held notwithstanding to be a characteristically Tikopia product. So also with the curious dance-bat (*paki*), which closely resembles that of Uvea, or some of the elements in canoe-construction, such as the flanged method of attachment of wash-strake to hull, or the pyramidal bow and stern ornamentation which present obvious affinities with Samoan and Ellice Island practice—these can hardly be local inventions.

The major cultural items of the Tikopia are treated as "given" as it were, by the nature of things. In a few spheres specific invention is recorded, particularly for individual dance songs and new variants of design in string figures. Such are known by the name of the person who first composed them, even after several generations have passed, and some people are remembered as having been especially fertile in such invention. But even here the general pattern of dancing, and the art of making string figures, have as a whole no story of origins. For the native technical processes it is usually quite impossible to obtain any information about inventions. For the extraction of turmeric, for instance, there is no traditional body of knowledge regarding the discovery of the two substances in the root, nor the invention of the process of separation. There is merely a statement that the premier deity of the island was responsible for initiating the manufacture of turmeric as a whole, and that hence it is now under his super-natural control. It may be that this process was introduced from another island group, colonized earlier during the Polynesian settlement of the Central and Western Pacific (possibly Samoa, where in a slightly simpler form it is still current). The Tikopia are cognisant that the extraction of turmeric is practised in other islands, and mention specifically Rotuma and Anuta in one of their ritual formulae, but while recognizing the sharing of the practice they do not regard it in their own case as having been introduced from abroad.

This lack of tradition concerning the adoption of technical implements and processes does not rest upon a simple ignorance of the existence of other island groups, or denial of past contact with them. There is, on the contrary, specific citation of many of the ancestors of the present kinship groups in Tikopia as having come from Tonga, Samoa, Rotuma, Uvea and other islands. But it is the bare record of arrival that has been preserved, and each such ancestor is treated as having come into an already fully equipped Tikopia culture. The items already mentioned as acknowledged introductions are accredited either to voyaging Tikopia themselves, or to casual immigrants whose descendants have played no important part in the social structure. The Tikopia have formulated no particular doctrine of technical invention, but in a negative way in their traditions and myths have turned their backs on a thesis of fusion of a mixture of cultural elements (which must in fact be the explanation) in favour of an insistence on autocthonous technology. This can be linked with their emphasis for purposes of social and religious prestige on descent from " soil-sprung " ancestors.

Put another way, it may be said that their interest is in cultural origins rather than in technological origins. Attention is concentrated on the mythological adoption or emergence of processes out of a pre-existing matrix rather than on the human invention or introduction of them. In the present-day culture, for instance, the plaiting of sinnet cord by men and the beating of bark-cloth by women are two of the primary features in their technology and economic life. But there are no traditions as to the discovery or invention of these crafts *per se*. In the origin myth which is the basis of the Tikopia explanation of their social and material universe it is said merely that when the land was pulled up from the sea the progenitors of the people were discovered upon it, in the act of practising these employments. They are part of the assumptions of Tikopia culture. Again, a series of most important myths of the people, which serve as the validation for their basic ceremonial and religious performances, are concerned with the doings of the Deity of Kafika, a culture-hero described as having been first a man and a chief and later a god. It was he who dictated many of the basic ritual patterns which characterize the present culture—including the manufacture of turmeric. But the stories concerning him are essentially myths of achievement and adoption, not of invention. People of other clans than Kafika tell with some pride and even a little bitterness how he took over from them the most important items in his repertoire, such as the ritual of yam planting and the sacred dances he sponsored. But of the ultimate origins of these institutions no account remains.

The lack of technological curiosity concerning the past is seen also in the present-day attitude towards invention. The Tikopia discuss their current techniques a great deal, canvassing the relative merits of variants in style, and the grasp of a craft shown by the makers of specific objects. But they do not speculate to any extent upon the possibilities of finding new techniques, or of improving the processes they already employ. They accept the body of their culture, and do not see themselves as always on the brink of some fresh technical discovery, or indeed, as seriously hemmed in by their admittedly simple technique. They exhibit no constant search for new objects and new processes with which to amplify their control over their environment, such as characterizes our modern civilization. Though they are aware of some of the complex mechanical constructions of the white man, and modestly deprecate their own material achievements by comparison, they do not speak as if they envisaged one day being equipped themselves with any of these advanced techniques. There is no resistance to the acquisition of knowledge, implements, and technique from outside ; on the contrary the Tikopia are very eager for steel tools, calico, European beads, new food plants, and new technical methods where these seem to be of advantage to them. And when occasion arises they are capable of efficient adjustment of their technique. They fit plane irons to handles and use them as adzes ; they borrow a brace-and-bit for their canoe work ; they even converted my composition tooth-brush handles (which they certainly had never seen before) into ear-rings by the method by which they treated turtle-shell. Again, the builder of my house provided me with a rough but effective window by an adaptation of thatch technique. But these things are done and received within the framework of the present culture ; the impetus to them comes from without, and not as part of any thorough-going and persistent attempt of the Tikopia themselves to master their environment more effectively. In brief, the Tikopia may be said to lack technical ambition.

This may be regarded as a natural feature of the primitive character of their way of life. But it must not be simply inter-preted as a gap in their mental endowment, a prime cause of their economic backwardness. Technical experiment and intellectual exploration are promoted by appropriate social conditions, and the relative absence of them must be sought first of all in the general framework of social relationships and ideas current at the time.

For the Tikopia, the absence of any systematic marketing organization of their products, and of competitive relations between producers to obtain a share of the market, means that this stimulus to cheaper and more efficient production, and to the search for variety to catch the consumer's attention, is lacking. More important, however, is their theory of natural resources. This may be described briefly as a theory of the human utilization of resources under supernatural control, which governs not only their fertility, but also the social and economic relationships of those who handle them.

It is not possible here to examine in detail the Tikopia theory of society. But a few words on some of the native categories of rank and of ritual will illustrate how the technological system tends to be controlled by a more general ideology.

In modern European society political and economic power is given to a large extent by control of the means of production, divorced for most people from ideas of any religious title to this control. (The idea of wealth as a trust from God is no longer an operative factor of any moment in economic relationships.) In Tikopia, on the other hand, the control of production is to a large extent in the hands of chiefs whose political and economic influence rests in the last resort on a religious basis.

The Tikopia theory of class relationships assumes the pre-existence of social categories of chiefs and commoners, the former being the prime representatives of the gods and intermediaries with them, in economic as in other affairs. There is no theory that chiefs originated as the heads of their respective families—which is the position as the anthropologist sees it—although it is recognized that accretions to the ranks of commoners are made from time to time by offshoots from the chiefly families after several generations have passed.[1] There is also no theory of the historical emergence of suzerainty over land or grasp of power by the chiefs, though traditions of struggles between prominent men can be interpreted as competitive, and more than simple attempts to defend existing and acknowledged privileges. On the other hand, there is a very definite theory as to the interlocking relationships and privileges of chiefs, and the obligations due to them by members of their clans. This appears very prominently in the use of canoes and land. Concerning the latter a common type of formulation is " Cultivations which stand there are cultivations of ours, but indeed they are cultivations of the chief ".[2] This is not a simple statement of joint ownership, but of rights and privileges, the operation of which is governed by rules of loyalty and etiquette and in the last resort by ideas of supernatural power and religious office.

The close relationship between the productive system in fishing and agriculture, and the control exercised by the chiefs as a basic feature of the social organization, tends then to concentrate attention on the maintenance of the *status quo* rather than on a search for changed forms of production.

Moreover, the ritual ideas of the people tend to reinforce this.

The Tikopia theory of the universe comprises not only a set of ideas as to physical relationships of cause and effect but also beliefs in the stimulation of such relationships through non-human intervention. Natural phenomena work as they do in a normal course to a large extent through the *manu*, the supernatural power of spiritual beings, stimulated and canalized through the qualities and acts of chiefs. Many Tikopia generalizations are then of a pseudo-empirical order resting, as it were, upon a strongly held prior belief in powers which can be to some extent controlled by human agency but lie ultimately at the arbitrary discretion of beings of a super-human order. This pseudo-empiricism does not remain simply a matter of speech. It affects

---

[1] *We, The Tikopia*, 355–7.
[2] For further material on the role of chiefs in land ownership, see *We, The Tikopia*, 376–385.

the behaviour of the people in most of their institutions and controls to a considerable degree their economic behaviour. The chiefs are bound by this system of ideas as well as their people. Any radical departure from the traditional system of technology and production runs the risk, then, of alienating the favour of the gods, to the detriment of the *manu* of economic undertakings. Moreover, to some extent the religious beliefs and ritual themselves act as a substitute for research into technical improvement.

A couple of illustrations will make this point clearer.

In their agricultural system the Tikopia have formulated the simple thesis that rain is necessary for taro to grow, and they plainly see that at times the crop suffers from drought. I did not hear them discuss plant growth in terms of water or moisture in general, though doubtless they could have formulated their generalization in such wider terms. But in any case, though taro is a plant that needs considerable moisture, they have made no attempts to improve their cultivation of it by irrigation, nor did I ever hear the possibility of such a process mentioned. Yet they already flume water from springs to convenient points on lower levels for drinking purposes, bathing, and the extraction of sago and turmeric flour. I have insufficient information to estimate the amount of irrigation they could do, but it seems possible that some effort could be made to organize the surface drainage and divert it through their gardens on its way to lake or swamp or the sea. A tradition of discussion of the possibilities of technical improvement, and the formulation of a set of propositions on the value to the crops of a system of artificial water supply might act as a stimulus in this respect.

But the position is complicated by the religious factor. Invention and technical control can only take maximum effect where they do not run counter to other established formulations. In Tikopia, rain is believed to be controlled by the spirit beings, who are appealed to in verbal formulae and by offerings. On the whole the tendency is for the Tikopia when faced by a drought to intensify their efforts to placate and cajole their gods rather than to seek methods of water conservation or diversion.

Much the same is true in turmeric manufacture, which is always an enterprise of great tenseness, because of the considerable chances of a poor yield, and failure in the baking. Further research into the conditions of maturity of the plant, quality of the soil, temperature of the extraction and other possible factors which may govern the amount of pigment obtained from the roots, as into the optimum conditions which give a hard-baked cylinder from the oven, is limited by the thesis that turmeric can be " stolen " magically during the process of manufacture, and that breach of taboo spoils it in the baking. The human hopes, fears and disappointments which find institutionalized expression in a theory of magical control of turmeric-making, and are linked with the general native theory of magic and religion, thus act as an inhibiting factor to the pursuit of technical research and invention.

A theory of magic sponsored by Malinowski, and generally accepted, is that appeals to supernatural agencies such as those mentioned above act as a supplement to technical knowledge, filling the gaps in it, so to speak, and do not displace this knowledge. In any specific undertaking this seems to be true ; the native does not lazily substitute a magical operation for a craft operation which is part of his cultural equipment and tradition. But from the wider point of view of possible change in technique, the question of the relation of magic to practical knowledge must be posed afresh. Granted that magico-religious beliefs and practices fill in the gaps in practical knowledge, how far does their existence prevent the extension of knowledge and control, by giving traditional explanation of disasters and failures which might have been avoided by inventive adaptation, by directing human behaviour on the assumption that only by rite and spell can certain forces be controlled, and by implanting not only confidence in success but also passive resignation to failure ? How far, in human history, research has been held up and invention stultified in this way it is impossible to say. But it is clear that so far as Tikopia is concerned, the possibility of experiment and invention is limited by their acceptance of a traditional system of magico-religious interpretations. This point which is essentially a restatement of the views held by E. B. Tylor and Sir James Frazer has tended to be overlooked in recent theoretical work on magic which has stressed the socially useful and integrative functions ignored by the earlier writers.

It has not been my purpose here to analyse the nature of the inventive process as such, to discuss the relationship of the components in the subtle fusion of thought, word and act, which gives the impetus to technical change. I have tried merely to stress the fact that the Tikopia economic system is not characterized by a conscious impetus to invention, and that this is due not apparently to the lack of inventive faculties as such, but rather to the nature of their closely integrated culture, which puts no premium upon technological advance, and lays the emphasis upon conformity to the established rules.

This is not to say that the religious and magical ideas and practices of the people are simply a hindrance. From the long-period view they may be regarded as so much cultural lumber, a drag upon productive energy, and an impediment to increased control over nature. But in the short run they have a positive cultural function in integrating activity and providing a stimulus with which the community in its present state could hardly afford to dispense. There is no assurance that if deprived of such a system of beliefs and rites, the Tikopia would at once utilize their time and speculative energy in more efficient production and technical discovery. What I have said here poses in effect the problem considered in Chapter V.

Moreover, the traditional formulations which to a large extent define the modes of practical adjustment of the Tikopia are not only of a magico-religious order. Principles of kinship association, views on the social order, canons of etiquette and hospitality, just as dogmatically held, condition their technical operations and the economic organization.

## REASON AND RULE IN TECHNICAL PROCEDURE

A further problem for consideration is, granted the matrix of social and religious ideas in which the Tikopia technological system is embedded, how far do they proceed by rule-of-thumb methods, or by blind adherence to traditional forms, and how far can they formulate clear and logical reasons for their procedure ? Again, to what extent have they reduced these reasons to rules of a more abstract order, capable of being applied to all situations of the kind ? On the whole, it may be said that clear reasons can be usually given for a technical act, and that such reasons are often embodied in the form of more general rules. In practice, as distinct from the imparting of information to an anthropologist, these rules are cited in a fragmentary manner as a guide to behaviour and a correction of errors actually being committed. There is no institutionalized education by the teaching of these rules when the activity is not under way ; in ordinary conditions linguistic and manual demonstration go side by side. Some of these technical rules have an obvious practical utility ; others are justified by traditional practice ; others again rest upon an agreed set of ritual relationships. Some are couched in the terms of ordinary speech current in many other situations ; others employ special terms which subsume a complex of manual acts and can be understood only in that specific context. In some, again, categories of general application are combined metaphorically with other factual terms to describe particular technical objects, substances or processes.

A simple example from Tikopia agriculture will show the kind of rational approach which these people take to many of their technical problems. I saw a man cutting down a tree in his orchard, for no apparent reason that I could perceive at the moment. When I asked him why he did it he replied : " I am cutting it out that the coco-nuts may live." I then noticed a number of young palms that he had planted, and which needed room to grow. These are set about twelve feet apart, and the natives are quite aware that they need such space between them in order to bear well ; and are prepared to sacrifice other useful vegetation to them.

The practicality of the Tikopia observation of natural processes and the type of limited abstraction which they formulate is well illustrated by their generalizations concerning the growth of taro. It is held that the quality of the crop stands in direct relation to the height of the brushwood on the plot before it is cleared. A plot where the vegetation is low and poor is known as *tarutaru maru* (or *tautaru maru*), an immature plot ; that where it is well-grown as *tarutaru : ao matua*, a plot of mature brushwood. The first statement I received on this point arose from a discussion of the rotation in planting a number of different areas. The reason given was that the brushwood in each could not attain its full height in a single season, and that *tarutaru maru* was unsatisfactory. " If taro is planted in a *vao tarutaru maru* it is good and yet bad ; but if it is planted in a *vao matua* it is good." It was explained in illustration that the taro of the favoured garden-area Rakisu had been poor of recent years because the brushwood had not been left to reach any height. In later discussion I was told : " If when the brushwood is *tarutaru maru* it is cleared away, and taro is planted it is bad. If the brushwood goes up above (grows high) then the taro goes up above." Here then, the

Tikopia have formulated a correlation empirically observed. How far have they integrated it into a scientific agricultural explanation ? That they use this principle as a basis for action is shown by the fact that they adopt different styles of planting for ground which has stood in immature and in mature brushwood. The term to fakavava, " plant gapingly," means to plant at wide intervals, three feet or so apart ; to ki muri ŋao ma mata ŋao, " plant to heel and toe" (of opposite feet) means to plant about two feet apart. When the brushwood has been mature the former style is used since, it is said, the taro will be large-leaved, and the wider spaces are left for the leaves to touch. But after immature brushwood, the taro is planted closely, in the latter style, so, it is said, that the leaves may still touch and will force each other upwards. The plants are set close together because it is realized that they will not grow tall and their leaves will therefore occupy less space. This shows that the Tikopia are not considering soil nourishment but an overt growth-parallelism. I questioned people to find if the judgment of future crop quality by height of brushwood embodied any idea of any magical contagion between them. But I could not get the formulation beyond the equation of the states of brushwood and taro. The Tikopia have clear ideas on the importance of rain to the taro crop, and the value of using the cut brushwood and other vegetable material as a shelter round the root of the taro to conserve moisture. But the equation is not in terms of quantity of material as a mulch but of the standing brushwood. They realize also that the taro derives its growth from the soil. When they mould up the earth around the root at a later stage they speak of heaping it together to " feed " (faŋai) the plants, using the same term as is used for the feeding of a child by its mother. But they have not linked up these separate propositions ; they have not attempted to translate the value of a mature brushwood into terms of soil recovery, nor have they any theory of how rain and soil properties combine to make taro grow.

From the examples just given it is evident that the existence of such technical rules in agriculture must have certain effects on the economic organization : they are one of the factors governing the use of resources in land, and they have repercussions on the labour organization, if only by setting a point in the time schedule for the distribution of labour between different employments. The way in which such economic effects are produced will be realized more clearly if an example be taken for consideration in some detail : the process of net-making. This material will give some indication of the relation between the native theory and their practice, and will also show the manner in which they deal with quantitative problems. The data here given may also be related to the case material on the organization of net-making given in the following Chapter.

The net-making apparatus employed is very simple. It consists of a thin slab of wood about two feet long, the *tama varu fau*, on which the hibiscus bark (*fau*) is scraped with a shell to remove the outer cortex and leave the strong inner fibres ; the resulting cord (*uka*) produced by rolling the fibres ; the netting-needle (*sika*) a shuttle-like wooden implement about ten inches long on which the cord is wound and carried ; and the wooden gauge (*afa*) about six inches long on which the meshes are constructed.

As a preliminary to net-making the hibiscus bark is stripped off the bushes by men of the household and brought back in baskets. It is then scraped by a woman of the house on the *tama*, laid across her thigh, and the result is a thin, silky fibre, extremely tough. This is rolled into cord by the men on their thighs, and then wound on the netting-needle. The end of the cord is slipped through the hole and knotted, and the cord is wound first through the " lips " of the needle (see sketch) and then in a figure-of-eight movement. It is important that the cord should form a clean string, without loose ends of fibre sticking out, which would give the net a " cobwebby " appearance.

A number of netting-needles full of cord are assembled, and the work begins. The net-maker takes a needle charged with cord, ties a loop round his left big toe, makes a loop in the cord, and with the gauge begins to run a line of meshes. The technique used is illustrated in the accompanying series of sketches.

In constructing each new mesh the middle finger of the left hand is stretched up and catches down the next free mesh in the line above. The forefinger and thumb are used to hold fast the knot while the gauge rests in the fork of the thumb. The netting-needle is held in the right hand, near its lower end, the cord is passed up over the face of the gauge, then down through the free mesh, and then the knot is made as shown. As the gauge becomes full with a set of meshes it is slipped out, then inserted again, from underneath in the last mesh of the set, and the work carried on. When the net-maker comes to the end of a row he gives the

## NETTING TECHNIQUE

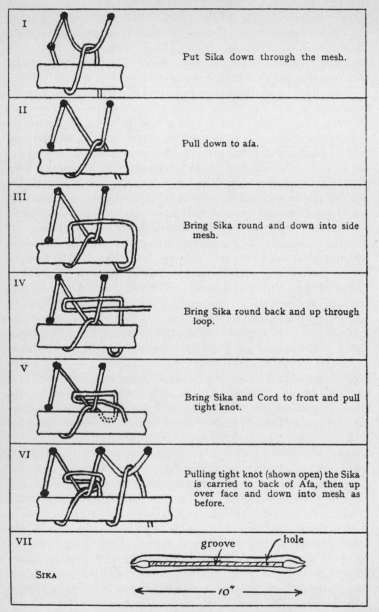

I    Put Sika down through the mesh.

II    Pull down to afa.

III    Bring Sika round and down into side mesh.

IV    Bring Sika round back and up through loop.

V    Bring Sika and Cord to front and pull tight knot.

VI    Pulling tight knot (shown open) the Sika is carried to back of Afa, then up over face and down into mesh as before.

VII

SIKA

groove    hole

10″

FIG. 4

net a twist over, and begins again in the reverse direction, thus still proceeding from left to right. When the cord on a needle has almost run out the knot holding its end is untied, the needle is put aside and the work is finished by hand—as deftly as with the needle.

So much for the actual process, each step in which can be described by the natives accurately. As a whole the technique of making a net is described by the term *tia*. (In contrast to the technical processes so symbolized is another set of processes described by the phonetically allied word *ti*, which means to gather a net on to the poles used for carrying it, or in other contexts to put on a cord, as in stringing fish together. " Nets are spread out on the shore ; we say ' Go and gather hither the nets. Rain has come, run quickly and go and gather hither the nets.")

The apparatus used in making the net, simple as it is, does not depend for its form merely upon chance, or tradition. Each feature in it has its technical reason, of which the Tikopia are conscious, and they discuss the variations in these features in terms of their technical efficiency. Thus the gauge has the primary function of ensuring uniformity in the size of the meshes. Of the different types of net, some like the bag-net and scoop-net are intended to hold the fish in the enclosure ; others, like the seine-net are intended to catch them fast in the meshes. The gauges vary in size correspondingly. Discussion is common about the precise size of gauge to be used, and also about its thickness. In one such conversation I heard the expert give it as his opinion that the gauge should not be too thin, but that it was better for it to be a little on the thick side, for ease in working the cord. Again, the netting-needle varies also according to the net to be made. Its primary function is to hold the cord in a convenient manner, but the use of it facilitates insertion of the cord through the meshes. Hence one hears such instructions as this given by the expert to a boy : " Go, reject the small needle, and bring me the large needle." Or one sees a net-maker about to begin a small-meshed scoop-net finding his needle too large, and quickly fashioning one of appropriate smallness from a reed.

For the net to be efficient it is essential for the knots to be tight. Hence during the work a watchful eye is kept on the operator, and the injunction is frequently addressed to him : " Pull tightly," or " Tie it tightly ; tie it tightly first, that it may be first tight ", or " Pull the cord tight that the knot may bite fast ". Again, for proper work it is necessary for the operator to have a full arm swing. I once saw a boy enter the house and sit at the back of the operator, thus cramping his action. He was at once ordered away, and went, laughing. " Laugh ! Laugh ! " said the operator fiercely to him.

All such incidents show the keen sense of the technical require-ments of the task that the Tikopia have, and their perception of the need for attention to detail to secure efficient results.

When the netting is done the new portion is joined to the old, and the floats and sinkers are attached. The floats are of light wood, and the sinkers of cowrie shell, and since the life of both is considerably longer than that of the cord of a net, they are transferred from the discarded section. The joining of the sections of the net is done by lacing the meshes together with a doubled cord, working backwards from the top of the net. This job is done by the specialist. The sinkers are threaded on a sinnet cord, which is then threaded through the bottom meshes of the net, or caught up and knotted to them. The attachment of floats and sinkers is closely watched by the specialist if he himself does not do the work.

The manufacture of a net is interspersed by ceremonies which place the net under the tutelage of an ancestor or deity, and which have the effect of lengthening the time taken in completing the net, and of linking the technical processes with the organization of food supplies for the ceremonies. But no more need be said at this point about the way in which the technical rules for the treatment of materials are qualified by the ritual setting of the activity, or the way in which the organization and personnel of the working group is governed by the ritual factor. These problems are dis-cussed in Chapter V.

There is now the quantitative side of the craft to be considered. What ideas have the Tikopia as to the appropriate size for such a net ? And what notion have they of how much material is required ?

As regards size of the net there are three elements involved : the depth of the net, its length, and the size of the mesh. The last-named is determined primarily by the size of the fish to be held or enmeshed by it, and this the Tikopia can discuss in great detail. Incidentally, I was told : " The mesh of the net in former days was large ; to-day it is not so, because the fish have become smaller in these latter days." This statement I could not verify, and it sounds like a pious exaltation of the " good old days " rather than an item of fact. To measure the gauge of a large net for comparative purposes the human arm is used. It is thrust through the mesh until this fits tightly, and is then described as fitting the forearm, fitting the elbow, or fitting the upper arm. The Ariki Kafika tested the new net of the Ariki Taumako in this way, and was satisfied to find that it was of the same gauge as his own.

The depth of the net is determined primarily by the conditions in which the net is set or dragged. That pulled through the shallow reef waters is naturally less deep than that to be set in the waters of the lake.

For nets to be set in the lake the depth usually adopted is somewhere in the region of fifteen feet, though there is variation according to the owner's estimate of its efficiency, the resultant weight, and the labour and materials he has at his command. The initial row of meshes run, the " beginning " (tamata) determines the depth of the net, and these are carefully counted in units of ten. Some nets are approximately fifty meshes deep, others sixty, or even seventy. The net of the Ariki Taumako that I saw made was sixty-six meshes deep—" six units and six remaining in the seventh unit ". Considerable interest is taken by people of other clans and villages in the depth of a net that is being made, as also in the number of fathoms of the net made each day.

The length of a net varies considerably, but a fair-sized one is perhaps forty to fifty feet long. Large nets are made in two sections, which are then joined together by lacing the meshes with a double cord. Not infrequently, however, to avoid labour, a new net is not constructed as a whole, but a torn or rotting section is replaced by a new one of appropriate size. By this process of partial replacement a net can be regarded as of long ancestry, though in fact there may be no portion of it which is very old. The process of using floats and sinkers from the old net to equip the new also tends to promote the idea of its continuity. This idea is partly due to a sentimental attachment to ancient things, which have some prestige, but also to the ritual side of net-making and utilization ; each net is dedicated to an ancestor or deity on whom its success is held to depend. I was told by a kinsman of the Ariki Taumako that the net of this chief was the only one on Raveŋa of any antiquity. " Indeed it is an ancient thing." It was " the same net " as was made by the chief's grandfather and great-grandfather. It was explained that as one part got into bad repair it was replaced but that the net as a whole was never cast aside. The net of the Ariki Kafika, however, was begun afresh by him ; the original net of his family was rejected by him on his father's death. Here is to be seen the convention of continuity which operates for nets as for canoes, houses, sacred spears and other Tikopia material things—a convention bound up with the ritual affiliations of these objects.

There is still the question of how far the Tikopia are competent to estimate the amount of raw material required for the finished product. In general they do not reckon exactly what amount of cord they will need beforehand, and accumulate it before starting work. " They net blindly only," that is they prepare a quantity of cord, begin to work, and if the cord is insufficient, they prepare more. As a rule, four or five *sika* are got ready in advance, each holding about 10 *kumi* or 100 fathoms of cord. But though the Tikopia do not prepare the full quantity in advance they can make an estimate of the amount needed to make a given length of net. Pa Fenuatara said to me " Three hundred fathoms of cord, that is a net of three fathoms." His father the chief who was listening said, " Oh ! three hundred fathoms will give a net of two fathoms." A rough calculation in terms of a 3-inch mesh of fifty or so meshes deep shows that the chief's estimate is more accurate. This conversation took place while one of their kinsmen was actually measuring the amount of cord that they had in hand. He counted it in full arm-stretches (" fathoms ", termed *rofa*), while Pa Fenuatara paid out the cord from a roll. The chief sat near with a bunch of areca nuts, and as the counter reached each unit of ten fathoms he murmured " ten " and the chief dropped a nut. At the end of the cord the counter said " Remains four in its ten " that is there were four fathoms over from the last ten. The chief then counted the nuts he had dropped and announced, " Two hundreds, and there remain two individual *kumi*." A *kumi* is a unit of ten fathoms, so that the total was 200 fathoms and 2 *kumi* ; that is, 22 *kumi*, or 220 fathoms in all. (The four fathoms at the end were disregarded.) According to the estimate of the chief mentioned above this would give a portion of net less than 9 feet long, and as seen in G. ii. of the case material (p. 135) the net-making had to be suspended for more fibre to be collected. In fact, the net remained unfinished during my stay.

From all this it can be seen that the Tikopia envisage clearly the technical ends they pursue, have ideas about the efficiency of the processes they use and quantities required, formulate these ideas in speech, and use this speech to further the ends of production. This is only what might be expected of any community, primitive or civilized, but it is necessary to demonstrate it for primitive communities, if only to show the importance of language as a " carrier-medium " for the craft tradition.

Examination of fishing technology, house-building, canoe-building and other crafts would show the same features. Even in such an apparently simple technical process as cooking there is a body of generalizations which regulate the work. Quantitative estimate such as " For every single ten packages of taro paste one bundle of ten nuts will be creamed with it " shows the existence of technical standards and an appreciation of what is necessary to attain the desired result.

A word may be said here about the linguistic aspect of the material given in this section. We have been interested primarily in the analysis of technical rules as expressed in language. But the expression of knowledge in verbal form is not a mere casual reflection of the degree of technical achievement reached. It is a means for the communication of this achievement from the more to the less skilled in an activity ; it serves to transmit the body of recognized and proved technical principles from one generation of workers to another ; and it acts as a goad to activity within the technical situation. The importance of the verbal element in regulating a piece of work, and in handing on craft rules has been seen already ; its role as a stimulus to activity is discussed in Chapter IV.

Linked with technical manipulation and speculative interest language can play a further part, in changing the way of handling the material environment. In general, language functions as a cultural determinant, moulding behaviour as well as expressing or symbolizing it. As such, linguistic formulation of experience or speculation, by giving a basis for comparison or a challenge to perception, may well be an important factor in stimulating invention. To express a relationship between things in speech may lead to the establishment of a relation between them in technical process. The plasticity of the spoken word is so much greater than that of the manual act ; changes in verbal expression involve so little energy in comparison and themselves do not alter the material environment ; experiments in words are much simpler than experiments with the hands.

Yet this hypothesis of the importance of the verbal formulation of relationships in stimulating the degree of technical advancement has its qualifications. Clarity of expression in itself can involve labour of a kind, and the formulation of general principles demands an effort of comprehension and synthesis to which not everyone will lend himself. Moreover, intellectual exploration may form part of the tradition of one culture, but not of another—a fact already noted.

As Malinowski has shown by a meticulous analysis of the linguistics of Trobriand agriculture, the examination of the place of language in a technological study cannot be restricted to a simple citation of a list of terms for parts of objects and for the processes of making them ; the whole problem of the categories of knowledge is involved, as well as that of the use of language as a mode of action.[1]

## The Distribution and Transmission of Economic Lore

A further question now to be considered is how the body of knowledge used in technical and economic affairs by the Tikopia is held between different individuals and sections of the people, and the effects of this on their command of resources and their income.

In some spheres there is little scope for the accumulation and use of differential knowledge. In agriculture the techniques employed are so simple and so few that knowledge of them is shared by all the people. It is significant here that there is no special term for a skilled agriculturalist, but merely a term for an industrious one (*te mafi*). On the ritual side differential knowledge is exercised by the chiefs and a few elders ; they assume the direction of the major ritual of planting and harvest, and are credited with general powers of controlling rain, sunshine, and storms. But it is not so much a matter of the possession of special knowledge *per se*, as of the upkeep of this knowledge, because of the functions with which they have been endowed by the ritual system itself.

In fishing, especially deep-sea fishing, and in some other crafts, knowledge of the technical processes and of the associated

[1] *Coral Gardens and Their Magic*, vol. ii, 1935.

ritual is unequally distributed. As could be expected, it is linked with special manual aptitude in them. Here are terms not for industrious persons as such, but for skilled, knowledgeable persons, such as *tufuŋa* (expert craftsman), *tautai* (sea-expert), and *taŋata o atu* (man of bonito) (see later). One effect of the possession of such knowledge lacking in others is the opportunity of enlarging one's resources. This is done by resort to fishing banks not commonly known, or use of a special technique at times when the fish refuse all others ; or, in the case of a craftsman, by more prompt replacement of his implements, or by gaining goods in payment for his work for others ; or to a small extent by the securing of a material return for the imparting of his knowledge to others.[1] Important as an inducement to the acquisition of such personal knowledge, however, is the prestige that it obtains.

I did not obtain any accurate measure of the possession of economic lore by different sections of the population. But on the whole chiefs are more knowledgeable than commoners. This is due in the first place to their superior opportunities for receiving instruction. A young man who is regarded as the probable heir to the chieftainship is told by his father and by other elders a great deal of ritual information which is not imparted to others not in the line of succession. Again, the context of chieftainship itself tends to promote a more elaborate equipment of information because on so many occasions the chief must take the initiative and must recite the appropriate formulae. Hence if he succeeds to the chieftainship without having received from his father a proper store of knowledge, he will apply to his father's brother, or even his father's sister or to another chief who is known to have been well instructed. A basket of food is the appropriate introduction to such request. On the whole, too, elderly men are more knowledgeable than younger men, if only for the reason that they have had many more opportunities of exchanging opinions, hearing traditional stories, correcting ideas and filling in the gaps. Again, a younger man of rank will not normally know as much as his father because in native belief if a chief or elder imparts the last vestiges of his ritual knowledge to his son, then the gods regard that as a sign that he is

---

[1] An interesting case of this last was the custom of labourers who returned from the sugar plantations of Fiji and Queensland divulging their stock of pidgin English in response to a customary present of food. The value of this English as a commodity is that it facilitates—or is held to facilitate—trading intercourse with the rare vessels that call.

finished with the affairs of this world and will soon make him die. Only when he is very old or ill does he divulge the information.

The Ariki Kafika gave me a formula designed to bring about the punishment of men who cut coco-nut fronds for thatch in defiance of a *tapu* consequent upon the roofing of the Kafika temple. He said that this formula was kept hidden by the chief from all but his eldest son and that in his own case it was still concealed from his son Pa Fenuatara. The reason he gave was that it was one of the few items he was keeping back lest his gods should say among themselves, " Now indeed his things there have been made known completely to his son. He there, is he dead ? " He added that when he would be old and no longer able to walk about he would tell his son to come and pillow on his arm, would cover him with his own blanket and tell him all the formulae of the kava and his complete set of ritual knowledge. Then he would say, " Now you speak to see if it is complete, that I may listen." His son would then repeat all he had learnt and he would correct him and make additions. When he was satisfied he would say, " Now your things have become complete." He could then prepare himself for death. This system obviously means that there is considerable possibility of a failure in the full transmission of lore.

But it is recognized that there is considerable variation in the knowledge which individual men of rank possess. Some, like the father of the present Ariki Taumako, were renowned for what they knew, and other people went to them to fill in gaps for use in their own ritual. Others again are credited with having a great store of knowledge, but with being somewhat erratic. Such is Pa Torokiŋa. A few others again are recognized as having bad memories—*roto ŋaroŋaro*, " losing insides " as the Tikopia put it. Such a man was the elder, Pa Farekofe, who acknowledged to me that he could not remember the names of his ancestors properly and got them out of order in the kava invocations— he mixed them up thoroughly, though honestly, on the several occasions he told them to me. The Ariki Taumako, a much younger man, told me in fact that before performing a kava ceremony, Pa Farekofe went to him to have the names of his ancestors recited to him so that he could hold them in his mind for a brief space. One further factor which makes for differentiation in knowledge is the refusal by some men to acquire an elaborate store of ritual information, holding that this would be infringing upon the position of their relative, the chief. Such a man was Pa Tarikitoŋa, the noted Taumako craftsman.

What has been said above refers primarily to the knowledge of ritual procedure, names of the gods and the like. To some extent the distribution of purely technical knowledge follows the same pattern, though here there is more tendency for younger men to acquire a fund of information which they can put to immediate practical use. But on the whole I found, naturally enough, that elderly men had a much greater range of knowledge and were much more conversant with precise details than the younger men. Moreover, there is no rigid separation between technical and ritual knowledge, and the recognition of certain men, either chiefs or commoners, as experts means that they are not only skilled above the average in the actual performance of a craft, and know more about its technical details, but that they have a greater body of knowledge about the ritual which pertains to it.

I am able to say very little about the distribution of knowledge among women. Certain women are credited with special skill in crafts and can explain the technical details better than others. On the whole women in Tikopia know very much less about the ritual side of institutions than do men. But they have some definite ritual functions to perform. Again, although a woman is not the normal repository of the ritual lore of a kinship group there are occasions when she is made so. If a man who has no brothers is contemplating an extended sea voyage, and is leaving his young son behind, he may instruct his sister in the essentials of the family ritual. It will then be her duty to pass on this knowledge to the boy when he is of an age to retain it.

On the whole, the effect of this unequal distribution of " immaterial resources " is in the direction of maintaining the control over the material means of production by the chiefly families on the one hand, and by the senior members of the commoner families on the other, against the commoners as a body, and especially the more junior members. As far as income and standard of living are concerned (not using these terms in a very precise sense), however, differential knowledge and capacity have freer play, and even a young bachelor of a minor commoner family can increase his economic position thereby. In general the social organization is such as to secure these benefits only indirectly to women. It must be emphasized, however, that as discussed later, there is no conception of exploitation of commoners by chiefs, or of women by men in Tikopia.

A further point to be briefly mentioned is the way in which the mass of economic and technical knowledge accumulated over generations is handed on, and the advantages or losses to individuals resulting from this.

The mechanism of transmission of this body of economic lore is not highly organized. There is in Tikopia no guild of craftsmen for any activity as there is a guild of builders in Samoa ; nor is there any institution for the transmission of ritual knowledge in any way comparable to the " House of Learning " among the Maori. Transmission of economic lore is usually done on a kinship basis, a parent, a grandparent or a mother's brother instructing a person in some particular craft. Children usually learn by accompanying a working party, and being taught on the spot. A former Ariki Taumako when young was taken by a noted fisherman, Pu Niukapu, to sea and instructed in fishing lore. " He was carried to each fishing bank, and told of its markings in the ocean, and of its markings to shore "— that is its bearings for future identification. In this case the lad was an " adhering grandchild " of the fisherman.[1] There is no closely defined set of conditions attaching to this transmission and usually no specific payment. Certain times and places are more appropriate than others, but use of them is a matter of convenience rather than prescription. Seremata, a keen fisherman, insisted on making known to me the formula for deep-sea line fishing only when we were actually in a canoe at sea. This, he said, was the appropriate occasion. But other people made no such stipulation. Knowledge of fishing practices and formulae does tend to be imparted mostly in the immediate context of situation, which is obviously most suitable.

To some extent transmission of ritual and economic lore is made in recognition of services rendered. Thus after Pa Raŋi-maseke had given me the formula for deep-sea line fishing he said that he had learnt it from his " brother ", Pa Veterei, who was a noted fisherman. " He made known to me the variations in sea craft," he said. He added, " If a man looks well upon another man who has filled his water-bottle (that is who has made him gifts of food) then he makes known to him some ancient things." He said that this is done as a favour and not for special

[1] See *We, The Tikopia*, 203-6, for explanation of this term.

payment.  In his case Pa Veterei had built his canoe.  Some time after this Pa Raŋimaseke invited the builder to his house and prepared an oven.  When the food was ready they ate and then the host asked his guest about fishing formulae.  Pa Veterei gave him the information which he described as " my own speech in my own canoe ".  He said too that this practice is especially common among chiefs.  If a man keeps on bringing the chief gifts of food then one day the latter will make known to him some piece of ritual knowledge which he can turn to account in his work.

The kinship principle thus does not apply in every case in the transmission of knowledge.  To give an example from a specialized craft—the Ariki Tafua is a noted expert in the manufacture of turmeric.  His grandfather was an expert also, but his father was not, having voyaged abroad before he had learnt the art.  The chief told me that his grandfather died before he could receive the knowledge from him, and that he had acquired it from an old man, Pa Retiare, not a close kinsman, not even on the mother's side.  When turmeric was being made on one occasion in Te Roro the Ariki had taken part in the work and the old man had then taught him the details out of good will.

The absence of any well defined institutionalized transmission of knowledge must have meant considerable inefficiency in Tikopia life, since on many occasions elder relatives must have died before they had handed on to their descendants their own theoretical and practical equipment.  These people must then have had to apply elsewhere.  The Tikopia themselves are conscious of this defect and also of the liability of memory to failure.  One of them, contrasting European accuracy with the native defects, said neatly :  " Tikopia here has its paper in lips," meaning that the records were verbal only.

I have no record of any crafts or technical processes of which the knowledge has now been lost, but the memory still held.  The existence, however, of archaic speech, of terms not in common use nowadays and preserved in the memory of old men alone, shows the possibility of the decay of knowledge.

This question of the transmission of knowledge brings up again the problem of technical progress.  It is clear that in such conditions changes in technical processes and in economic organization have probably been small and slow.  In the short time at my disposal it was not possible for me to detect any definite advancement, or whether in fact such advancement was taking place. But it is a fair inference that the economy of the Tikopia is not retrogressive, and not even purely static. What I have said earlier goes to show not that the people are prohibited by custom from invention, but that the integration they have achieved between their technique, their economic organization, their social structure and their social ideals is on the whole satisfactory to them. They have not what may be called an ideology of invention, and no moral quality attaches to any increased utilization of the earth's resources. The *auri sacra fames* which has led European civilization to disturb to the roots native communities in Australia, Kenya, and elsewhere would have no meaning for them. As to most other native peoples, the idea that it is a duty laid upon man to utilize to the full the resources of nature would be incomprehensible to the Tikopia. The society is characterized then rather by an absence of interest in invention than by an absence of the potentialities for invention.

## CHAPTER IV

# THE LABOUR SITUATION

WHILE the problem of production is a concrete one to the Tikopia they have definite ideas about the general use of land, labour, and productive equipment, and the organization bringing them to bear on one another for the satisfaction of their wants. As far as the aims of production are concerned not only have they a clear realization of short term situations, but they are also capable of envisaging one productive act in terms of another in a longer sequence. This planning of productive effort is not restricted to individual ends alone. The issues are realized as affecting to some extent the resources and satisfactions of the community as a whole, and in some spheres control vested in a few individuals of rank amounts to a form of embryonic social planning (see Chapter VI, *tapu*).

The general problem of this chapter may be stated as follows : Given certain material resources, technical methods and instruments of production, and a system of control of them (see Chapters III and VII), what is the system of utilization of labour resources, and how far is the system efficiently directed to secure the ends desired ?

The total labour supply available has been calculated in Chapter II (Table I). There it is shown that the proportion of workers of maximum efficiency in the whole Tikopia population is about 38 per cent ; the widest available labour group is about 65 per cent ; and expressed in terms of adult working power the labour supply is somewhere in the region of 50 per cent of population. This labour supply is divided on principles of sex, age, and specialist skill, also to some extent on the basis of rank. On the other hand it is integrated for different types of task, partly by reason of the technical requirements involved, and partly by reason of certain social conventions. Granted these qualitative principles there is then the question as to how far the type of organization is effective in securing maximum efficiency within the scheme adopted.

By the idea of a scheme adopted is meant not only the conventional organization of labour but also the structure of the work situation itself, and the ideas that the people have about its nature.  The Tikopia have a general term *fekau* which can mean work in general as opposed to rest, recreation, and other activities such as those of sex.  It applies to participation in ceremonial and ritual activities as well as to acts of ordinary production where the immediate economic imperative stands out more clearly.  The reality of the compulsive force implied in this concept is indicated by the fact that the most popular name for a seasonal cycle of ceremonies which are the apex of Tikopia religious performance is the " Work of the Gods ", or in the specific context " the Work ".  Expressions such as " The Work of the Gods is only to be done correctly " imply the strong ritual backing for the conduct of the procedure. In its ordinary specific sense *fekau* refers to any task that is being undertaken.  It can imply that there are time limits to the task, that there are definite aims for it, and that it may progress by stages and involve differential contributions by the personnel engaged.  Attached to this concept are judgments as to the burdens or disabilities of the task.  " Great is the work " is an expression often heard in respect of the daily calls upon effort in the period of yam planting and harvest, the sweat of paddling a canoe through a hot day's fishing, or the length of time taken in building a canoe. But this concept of the disutility of labour cannot be a simple one, since, as discussed later, labour in Tikopia can be a social service as well as a purely economic contribution.  The difficulty of measuring pains and satisfactions of such different order against one another complicates the situation of reward, and the possibility of relating actual disbursements to marginal quantities of labour supplied, and to efficiency obtained in the undertaking.

The material of this Chapter comprises : first, a factual description of division of labour according to the principles of individual endowment ; second, an account of an observed complex labour situation to give a detailed example of one important type of co-operative activity ; third, a selection in summary form of case material on typical undertakings to indicate particularly the quantitative aspect of the Tikopia labour situation ; and fourth, an examination of the factors, apart from the technical requirements of the task, which determine the native co-operative productive organization.

## DIVISION OF LABOUR

Description of various activities (pp. 134–8) shows several features in differentiation of employments. A sex basis in the division of labour can be seen in the performance of activities such as bark-cloth beating by women, and flying-fish netting by men. Hardly ever here does a member of one sex intrude into the sphere of the other. Very occasionally, either for the sport or to make up a crew, a girl will go out as paddler on a flying-fish expedition. But she never wields a net, and the native convention does not allow a married woman to participate in this work at all. On the other hand, no case is known to me of a man beating bark-cloth. Each sex has its own way of bearing burdens—men from a pole held on the shoulder, women with the load held on the back with strips of bark-cloth. There is no stringent taboo of the male back as was the case among the Maori, however, and I did see once a well-known craftsman who could not find a pole laughingly tie his burden on his back, to the great amusement of those present. Certain crafts such as plaiting of mats are practised exclusively by women ; a man, however, may plait fans or the small basket used by men as a personal bag. In agriculture men and women both take part, but their spheres are to some extent separated. A woman does not often break up the ground, though she may plant and dig out taro. One of her main functions is to weed the growing crop and normally no man carries the grass which is used as a mulch around the roots. And while in a household men and women co-operate constantly, in agriculture social convention allows only a few specified ways in which a married woman of one household may work together with a man of another (see Chapter VIII).

Ritual factors also play their part in defining the respective roles of men and women. The peculiar association of certain male deities with sacred canoes debars women from setting foot in them or even approaching them too closely. On the whole, too, they are excluded from the technical activities in immediate association with ritual performances, though there are certain compensatory spheres where they play the principal role and men may not enter (as in some rites of the Work of the Gods). They take part in such preliminary operations of turmeric making as the digging, washing, and grating of the roots, but they have no hand in the more delicate operations of filtering and baking. Moreover, the degree of their participation varies with the ritual situation. For instance when the Ariki Tafua was directing the manufacture of turmeric on the first day when it was his own material that was being filtered, women were excluded from the enclosure ; on the following day it was the turmeric of commoners that was being filtered and women carried in the water for this. In neither case, however, did they manipulate the turmeric itself nor take part in the subsequent operations.[1]

Traditional validation of two most important tasks belonging to men and women respectively is given by a myth of origins mentioned already (p. 86). Other myths embodying references to crafts, to carrying burdens, and to common tasks perform a similar function.

There are no rigid principles of division of labour according to age in Tikopia. As one might expect, children participate from an early age in the work of their parents and kinsfolk, performing subsidiary tasks, and gradually working in to the more important technical processes. At the other end of life there is diminishing participation in economic activities, but old people never retire at any given stage. Old men go out occasionally to their cultivations, and old women plait mats. Feebleness and sickness are the only factors which debar people from work.

Principles of division of labour according to rank are discussed in detail in Chapter VI. There it will be seen that only the chief and the obvious heir to chieftainship, the eldest son, are debarred from participation in certain tasks. All commoners, including close relatives of the chief, such as his brothers, and ritual elders who are heads of families take part in such work as kindling and tending the oven, which is the nearest approach to a menial task in Tikopia.

## OCCUPATIONAL SPECIALISTS

Within these broad lines of employment there is great homogeneity. Every Tikopia man is an agriculturist and a fisherman, and to some extent a worker in wood ; every woman weeds plantations, uses her scoop net on the reef, beats bark-cloth and

[1] The general principles of sex division of labour in Polynesia are discussed by Thurnwald, *op. cit.*, 112–13, 212. Cf. also Margaret Mead, *Social Organization of Manu'a*, 66–70, and my *Primitive Economics of the New Zealand Maori*, 194–200.

PLATE III.

A. Carrying a Log through a Taro Field

The timber is for the washstrake of the canoe Sapiniakau.

B. Preparing a Sago Oven

The stones are being spread to receive the sago slabs. The intense heat causes long poles and rakes to be used.

PLATE IV.

FILTERING TURMERIC

At one stand, Pa Nukunefu pours water on to the grated turmeric, at the other Pa Tekaumata kneads the mass. In the background is part of the fence which isolates the workers.

plaits mats. Such specialization as exists is the development of extra capacity in a craft and not the practice of the craft to the exclusion of others. Differentiation of function is merely temporary, and when a man has completed a particular task as a specialist he turns again to the ordinary daily work such as his fellows perform. He may in fact put some ordinary task such as planting before a specialized one such as canoe building. There is no institutionalized mechanism of hiring labour to perform one's domestic occupations while engaged primarily in one's own specialized craft. Strictly speaking, though I use the term specialist for those experts for whom the Tikopia have specific names, it is of comparative proficiency rather than specialization that one should speak.

Experts are distinguished in a number of branches of activity. There is the *tautai*, sea-expert, a term which includes proficiency in fishing as well as in seamanship and does not mean any high degree of specialization. As a sub-species of this is the *taŋata o atu*, " the man of bonito," who is distinguished by his having taken ten bonito on a single expedition. But this does not mean that only such men go out for these fish. The term *purotu* applies to a particularly skilled dancer and has its economic connotation in the payment made when such a man is invited to introduce a specific dance. But there is no particular point at which a man gains the title nor is the introduction of dances left to these men alone. The term *tufuŋa* is a generic title for a skilled craftsman and has attached to it a number of explanatory expressions indicating proficiency in tattooing, plaiting of sinnet, net-making, working of bowls or building of canoes. Here again there is no specific quantitative point of achievement at which the title may be attained and it is a matter of degree of activity and quality of the product rather than of specialization in the craft. But there is one difference to be observed. Whereas every man engages to some extent in agriculture, fishing, sinnet-plaiting, dancing and minor wood-work, only a few are tattooers and canoe architects, though not exclusively. Women are also admitted to have special proficiency in crafts, particularly in the plaiting of mats. But the term *tufuŋa* is never applied to a woman. We have here, perhaps, another aspect of the dominance which convention, though not necessarily actual practice, gives to males in Tikopia society.

A close relationship is conceived to exist between theory

and practice : a person with a wide grasp of the theory of a craft must also be an expert practitioner of it. If information is imparted to the anthropologist by someone who is not a practical expert then his competency is denied as well as his privilege in giving the information. I remember telling the Ariki Taumako and some of his kinsfolk, all expert fishermen, that I had received from Pa Nukutai the formula used in bonito fishing. They all laughed in scorn at this, exclaiming, " How could he pretend to give the formula when he was not himself a ' man of bonito '." In fact, as I found, the formula he gave was practically identical with that which I received from expert bonito fishermen, and there is no reason why if a man had a good memory it should not be so since as a member of a crew he could have heard it shouted aloud many times in the course of bonito fishing. The relevant fact here is that knowledge, whether of technique or of ritual, is a matter of pride to individuals, to families and to clans, and is regarded as receiving its proof in achievement. A man who has not demonstrated his prowess cannot therefore according to Tikopia ideas be properly equipped in the theory of a craft.

This point is also seen in the manufacture of turmeric and sago, where the chief technical operator is also the chief performer of ritual.

In the emergence of a specialist craftsman individual training plays some part, as when a father makes for his son a model of a house lashing in order to demonstrate the peculiar technique involved, or has the lad at his side when he is engaged in woodwork, or in fishing. But here the personal factors of individual interest and aptitude are paramount and there is no attempt to force the child into following his father's special craft. Since every specialist also takes part in the general productive activity in other fields there is plenty of scope for any member of a family who shows no particular bent for a specialized craft. Some children appear to develop as specialists at quite an early age. Seuku, a boy of about twelve, was a wood-worker to whom other boys went to get heads for their darts. These were quite passable specimens, as was also a model of a club which he made for his own interest and which I bought from him. Again, when some children imitated a current activity of their elders and began to remodel the bow of a small canoe, it was Seuku who acted as *tufuŋa* and directed the work. Seuku appeared to have developed

largely on his own initiative ; neither his father nor his elder
brothers had any special proficiency as wood-workers. On the
other hand there is sometimes a continuity in the practice of a
craft by members of a family, as in tattooing.[1] The house of
Niukapu has an ancient tradition of seamanship ; and the
chiefly house of Taumako a reputation for skill in all the major
crafts. A man of Tafua, who could be expected to belittle rather
than praise their accomplishments, said to me, " They are the
*tufuŋa* house in this land ; they are expert indeed in all
things."

## TYPES OF CO-OPERATION IN WORK

The type and the extent of co-operation in work are determined by a number of factors, some of a technical order, others of
the nature of social conventions.

In the technical sphere there is first the character of the
natural resources. When a sago palm trunk has been felled and
stripped for grating it must be attacked soon lest the pith turn
sour ; hence the labour of the person wanting the flour is supplemented by that of a large number of his kinsfolk and neighbours.
When a tree-trunk has to be brought down to the lowlands for
conversion into a canoe a mass of man-power is required for the
hauling or carrying. Secondly, co-operation is dictated to some
degree by the nature of the technical instruments employed.
Filtration of the sago flour at a trough needs only two or three
workers, with a child or .two to carry water (see Plate I).
Efficient handling of a Tikopia canoe in torch-light fishing requires
at least three people—a man wielding the net, a torch-bearer,
and a paddler-steersman, but the craft cannot accommodate
adequately more than four or five workers. Thirdly, the delicacy
of manipulation required in the different processes of the work also
dictates to some extent the character of the personnel of the
group engaged. Efficient utilization of differential skill allows
children to be co-opted into a working party which is filtering
sago, but tends to exclude them from a torch-light fishing canoe.

The social conventions involved are complex. There are those
which make for co-operation as such—as ties of kinship ; there
are those which control individual contributions in relation to
each other while the work is in progress—as rules about working

---

[1] For some details see *Man*, 1936, 236.

hard or resting ; and those which exclude some types of person from given tasks—irrespective of their skill—as debarring married women from fishing in canoes at sea, or chiefs from helping in the preparation of an oven. An example of the effect of such social conventions is seen in the way in which the practice of rewarding labourers by a meal brings into many co-operative activities a set of people, including women, whose role is not to participate in the technical act of production itself but to prepare the food for the workers. Moreover, since some of the workers themselves may take a hand in this food preparation the tendency is for a larger number to assemble than is strictly required by the technical operation. A fuller discussion of this aspect of co-operation is given later in the sections on the ideology of production and conventions of work.

The advantages of work in co-operation are clearly recognized by the Tikopia, not only from the point of view of the technical assistance gained, but from that of the general efficiency of the work. One man said to me : " When workers are plentiful then the work is light ; we are not hurried. When the crowd is large they joke together, they converse, the work is vigorous. If they do not converse the work is weak." The two terms which I have translated as " vigorous " (*maroro*) and " weak " (*ŋaeŋae*) are those ordinarily used for physical health and sickness respectively. These statements put in a nutshell a most important point about the efficiency of primitive labour.

It is not necessary to document in detail the various institutionalized forms of co-operative work in Tikopia. I therefore give as an empirical basis for the later generalizations one description *in extenso*, as I observed it, of the working of the organization for the repair of a canoe of a chief, followed by a set of skeleton examples, also from my own observation, of the organization of ten other activities, of varying degree of complexity. These can be taken as a fair sample of Tikopia co-operative production—though it must be remembered that a great deal of work is done by individuals alone, or with one or two members of the household to assist. The first example shows in particular how the integration of the different phases of the task proceeds, and how the economic aspects of the work are linked with other social and particularly ritual aspects ; the others show primarily the size of the labour supply assembled, the basis of co-operation, and the division of the task between the workers.

## STUDY OF A WORKING PARTY AT THE REPAIR OF A CANOE

A brief note may first be given on the Tikopia canoe. These vessels, which are all of the single outrigger type, are divided from the social and ritual point of view into two classes, *vaka tapu* and *paopao* (including *tovi*). *Vaka tapu*, " sacred canoes," have each a set of tutelary deities and ancestral spirits, are owned mostly by the men of rank and are under the formal control of the clan chief in each case. They are intimately bound up with the native religious system and have seasonal reconsecration ceremonies performed over them, severally and collectively.[1] *Paopao* are more ordinary craft, not specifically dedicated to any spiritual beings, and have no ceremonies connected with them. They are owned by men of rank and by commoners, and nearly every independent household has one or more. Some of the *paopao* are identical with the *vaka tapu* in size and structure ; they have simply not been consecrated, but they are used for deep-sea fishing in the same manner. Others, the majority, are inferior vessels, lacking wash-strakes and bow and stern-covers, figurehead and ornamented stern ; or it may be, fully equipped but old or cranky craft withdrawn from active sea service. Such *paopao* are used only in reef waters or on the lake. The term *tovi* is commonly used for canoes of this inferior type, especially those with the simple dugout hull and no ornamentation. *Tovi o te roto* is the usual expression for a lake canoe.

Even the humblest *paopao* or *tovi* is regarded as a valuable piece of property. " It is termed the orchard of the commoners," the natives say, meaning that from it they derive sustenance at sea equivalent to that which they draw from their lands. But *vaka tapu* are much more valuable partly because of their greater efficiency as productive instruments, and partly because of their ritual associations.

In March, 1929, the Ariki Kafika decided that repairs were necessary to one of his sacred canoes, by name Sapiniakau. It was necessary to replace one of the wash-strakes. First a *fetau* tree was felled by the chief and Pa Niata, brother of Pae Sao, who lived in the village next to that of the chief. The tree was the property of the house of Samoa. The usual custom when timber is required for such a purpose and is not available on the property of the canoe owner is for him to take a coil of sinnet cord,

---

[1] I hope to describe the ritual of the sacred canoes in detail in a publication on the *Work of the Gods*.

present it to the owner of the tree and with his permission go and fell it. On this occasion the day after the trunk had been felled I asked one of the workers if such equivalent had been given. He said : " I don't know ; it depends on father and son of Kafika." As a matter of fact it transpired later that no such return had been given, and it was said that the owners were annoyed.

The day after the felling a crowd of men assembled about mid-morning to carry the timber down to the coast, at the invitation of the chief and Pa Fenuatara. There were about twenty altogether : men from clans other than Kafika, who came because they were neighbours to the chief, or kinsfolk of himself and his son's wives.

The trunk was roughly dressed, and Nau Kafika and other women carried off the waste material for firewood. The men cut poles and inserted them under the trunk, assembled in pairs and bore it off (see Plate III). They carried the timber from where it was cut in Rakisu to the coast at Ratia, a distance of about half a mile, in four stages, with a rest of a few minutes between each. At the beach the timber was put into the sea and floated round by one man to the village of Sukumarae where the canoe lay.

This portion of the work was done with celerity although the trunk was heavy. In such a simple task, involving a minimum of skill, the two critical phases are the collective lifting and setting down of the burden. One might have expected a specific leader, but actually there was no one man in command of the party and each member gave his opinion amid a running fire of comment as the carrying proceeded. As the tree was lifted a shout was given by all together. This, it was said, helped to render the trunk lighter. Often if such a timber is heavy a song is chanted. On this occasion it was omitted " because the pair of brothers stand badly ; they are *pali* ". A pair of the working party were in mourning and so could not participate in any dance song which is the form of chant used. Moreover, the typical work song is of a special type known as *feuku*, involving bawdy reference, citation of sex members, etc., which would be peculiarly inappropriate to any such situation of restraint. All the party therefore refrained. Normally the rhythm of the song in itself helps to set the pace for the activity and indicates appropriate pauses. But in this case the initial wordless shout and the subsequent exchange of opinion had to suffice.

The Ariki Kafika did not help in this work but went with two other men to one of his orchards near by to pluck green coco-nuts for a later ceremony. His son, Pa Fenuatara, and Rimakoroa, son of the Ariki Taumako, took part in the carrying, although both were heirs to chieftainship.

People who do such work receive payment for their labour in food. Either an oven is prepared and they are given a meal or, as far as I remember in this case, large quantities of coco-nuts are plucked and given to them.

The economic situation here is bound up with ritual concepts. Of the coco-nuts plucked some were set out on the sacred side of the house, pierced, and libations poured from them to the tutelary deities of the canoe. This was an " announcement " to the gods of the timber to be used in the canoe repairs. Hence the ceremony is termed *fakaari o te rakau*, announcement of the timber,

The full details of canoe ritual and the esoteric beliefs attaching to these craft cannot be given here. It is sufficient to say that " Sapiniakau ", the second sacred canoe built for the Ariki Kafika, had three tutelary *atua*, supernatural beings. One of these was Pa Veterei, a maternal nephew of the chief, who had been the builder of the vessel, but who had since died ; his spirit had its post at the bow. At the stern were the spirit of the dead father of the chief, and the father's own deity, the god of Faea, who is incarnated in the octopus. One of the names of this deity is Sapiniakau, which gave the name to the canoe.

An indication of the importance of the canoe work was given by the blocking of the path by coco-nut fronds to bar the casual entry of outsiders.

The working party formed a fairly definite group to which the addition of a newcomer was welcome, but the presence of mere onlookers was discouraged. The leaf barrier was of the kind known as *pipi*, a bar which etiquette respected, but not a taboo proper (see p. 203). Similar but more stringent barriers screen off the people engaged in the extraction of sago or turmeric.

Before the work could be begun next morning a ceremony known as *fakauviuvi o ŋa atua*, " lifting down of the gods," had to be performed. Since the canoe was to be tampered with by alteration the gods had to be removed from it lest they resent the interference and visit the workers with illness or misfortune. Early in the morning an oven was prepared, the canoe was carried out into the open, and a kava rite was performed. In this the ordinary list of clan gods of the chief was invoked. After the kava the chief went with a piece of bark-cloth over to the stern of the vessel, draped the cloth over it with a movement of obeisance, and recited a formula in a loud voice. He said :—

> " You jump on to your valuables
> In order that your timber may be first got ready."

Then he dragged the cloth away.

The chief himself explained to me shortly afterwards that when he lays the cloth on the side of the vessel and takes it off with a dragging movement the deities rise and jump on to the cloth, are borne upon it back into the house and remain there while the work is in progress. They are later restored by a reverse rite, of spreading the bark-cloth again, when the chief says :

> " I eat ten times your excrement, deities of the canoe
> Come hither and climb on your bark cloth
> Your timber has been renewed
> The handling of it has finished."

It has been mentioned that one of the tutelary deities of the vessel was Pa Veterei, dead builder and nephew of the Ariki Kafika. On this occasion the chief, from affection it was said, desired that the dead man should be present in spirit form. He said : " Tell Pa Veterei to come and chew a wad of betel for himself." A spirit medium who was present became possessed and chewed betel which was offered him in the ordinary way. There was no particular demonstration of interest—for such possession is a frequent phenomenon on these occasions—but Pa Fenuatara said to his father, " You have speech with . . . .", not mentioning the spirit by name. But the attention of the Ariki had been diverted elsewhere, no conversation took place, and shortly afterwards the spirit left. This incident illustrates the close relationship which the Tikopia maintain between this world and the after world, technical affairs and spiritual interests. It is difficult in fact to find what may be called a purely technical or economic activity.

Present at the ceremony were sixteen men comprising neighbours of the chief ; his patrilineal kinsfolk ; one of his ritual elders ; and the specialist in charge of the work. Immediately after the rite the work began. The canoe was stripped to the hull. The lashings of bow and stern covers were cut and the covers laid aside in the canoe-shed. Fresh sinnet cord had been prepared

by the chief and a couple of helpers in the early morning for later
use. The lashings of the old wash-strake were cut and the timber
lifted off. It was seen at once that it had been attacked by borer,
and so it was discarded. I was impressed by the careful attention
shown in the examination of the timber ; any slight defect was
immediately noted, and it was evident how much value the
Tikopia attach to the soundness of their canoes. When the wash-
strake was removed anxiety was shown by all as to whether
the hull had been also attacked, and in particular whether the
borer were still alive and at work. The borings were examined
and a few flakes of the wood were tentatively shaved off by the
chief—under protest from several people who feared he might
do damage. Then he handed the adze to the expert, Pa
Tarititoŋa, brother of the deceased builder, who had been invited
to replace him and conduct the repairs. The expert cut gently, but
a little deeper into the edge of the hull with the adze, which was
of a light single-handed type known as *toki fakatu*. At first he
seemed to think the borer was dead. Then with a shout of " *It is
alive* " he dropped the light tool, seized the heavy adze, and cut
deep into the timber. " Look you hither on the canoe that I
am handling here," he murmured. This was an appeal to the
deities of the vessel to become aware of what he was doing and
why. People crowded round and there was a dramatic scene.
One of the chief's young kinsmen dropped his head on to the side
of the vessel and began to wail for the body of the canoe that was
being wounded. The Tikopia express this attitude of solicitude
and emotion towards their canoes in a variety of verbal images.
The Ariki Kafika explained to me, " the canoe is the head of the
deity, the body of a deity." Another man said : " It is held that
the canoe is a child ; it is warm in the belly ; if the canoe is
wounded, one wails then." It turned out later that the damage
done by the borer was less than was at first feared, and by means
of carefully cutting the wash-strake to shape, the hull would be
made sound again.

Technology again comes into relation with the religious ideas
of the Tikopia. The borer, it is believed, can be coped with
not only by physical means but also by the power of the gods.
Adzes of a size for hewing out canoes are scarce in Tikopia and
each is a most prized possession. That which belongs to the chiefly
family of Taumako is especially valuable. When the chiefs of
other clans wish to build their canoes they invite the experts

from this family as a rule to come and perform the work. It is an old custom since their skill in canoe building is traditional. But there is an additional reason. Their adze is believed to have the power of killing any borer that may be in the timber and stopping decay. Like other valued property it has its own tutelary deity, in this case Pusi, whose incarnation is the grey reef eel, noted for the sharpness of its teeth and its ferocity. When the adze is struck on to the wood the deity is invoked :—

> " Thy friend, Pusiuraura
> Let it be bitten by thy sacred tooth."

Then, say the natives, " the decay and the borer disappear. He eats them on the instant, they vanish, and the insect dies." Because of the power of this adze it is not as freely lent as those of lesser importance are. " It goes only with the men of their chiefly family, it is not handed over loosely, it goes only with them. It is not given to the clan, it is *tapu*, because it is the tooth of the deity," said the Ariki Kafika. Before using the tool the expert, Pa Tarikitoŋa, dedicates it in a few words to his dead brother as former user, and to the deity.

Acknowledgment must be made to the deity for this specific type of service. I was told that when the food portion of the expert would be given to him at the first meal he would say " Tie it up ! Tie it up and carry it to the chief." It would then be carried to the Ariki Taumako, who would throw offerings from it to the deity of the adze. If this were not done then Pa Tarikitoŋa himself would throw offerings, saying as follows :—

> " Recite a formula hither Pa Taumako
> For the food of Pusiuraura
> Light be your premier adze
> Light be the path of your adze
> Anything destructive for the timber here
> Let it be eaten by you, Pusiuraura."

Moreover, later a basket of food and a bundle of green coco-nuts were carried to the Ariki Taumako as " the payment for his adze ", meaning for the use of it. I have mentioned that the adze is spoken of as the " tooth " of the deity. I was told that if the god is angered by some action or negligence of the expert who is wielding the tool he will cause it to slip and cut his foot. Here is a special sanction for care in the work, and an explanation of accident in supernatural terms.

After the damaged wood had been cut away attention was

turned to the making of thè wash-strake. The baulk of timber was propped up on edge and four men with adzes were set to work at thinning it down. Pa Tarikitoŋa was in charge of the party and I noted the decisive strokes of his adze, firm and sure. After a time he got the old strake brought up and set against the baulk, so that he might scribe the rough dimensions from it with charcoal. This was done in the style of a European carpenter.

The expert justified his position by his technical competence. He obviously " carried the job in his head " as a carpenter would say. He made his adze strokes, then glanced sideways, measuring by eye sizes and lengths and the extension of his cutting. He clearly was calculating the effect of his cut on the set of the timber at any particular spot. When the two timbers were put together for marking they were held by the whole crowd of men while he ran round with his charcoal stick drawing his line.[1] He himself began the dressing of the timber from the mark. He was assisted at first by Pa Taramoa, a son of the Ariki, who asked his advice. " Pa Tarikitoŋa ! I shall strike on the charcoal there ? " wanting to know if he should cut away the mark itself. The expert answered with an affirmative jerk of the head. " Cut." An energetic man, he did not waste words. Pa Taramoa was told how to strike the correct type of blow by his brother, and this was confirmed by the expert.

In the late afternoon another ceremony was performed— the kava of the canoe. Food from a large oven was brought into the chief's house, a series of libations poured, and offerings made to the gods of the vessel and of the chief. About a dozen men were present inside, but the expert and some of the workers refused an invitation to come in. " He eats at the side of the timber ; he sits and throws his offerings there," was the comment when I asked why the expert did not enter. Such is the usual custom, it was said. The convention of work is that the expert should remain by his job. This is a moral imperative which has the general function of maintaining economic efficiency. Kindred obligations are to be at the scene of work at or soon after day-break ; not to leave the work to get on with other tasks ; and not to dally in eating meals.

[1] To assist in fitting wash-strake to hull on another occasion the expert made a mark with a pencil of burnt stick on both timbers and then reinforced it with an adze cut. For later fitting the edge of the adze blade was held in the cut on the hull, and the corresponding cut in the strake was moved up to it so that the two timbers were in exactly the same relative position as before.

The following day the work of fitting the new wash-strake was begun while it was still far too thick for final use, so that there would be plenty of room for adjustment. The edge of the hull was not even, so to avoid leaks in the canoe the fitting had to be made with the utmost exactness. This necessitated many trials, and the closest attention of the expert. The timber was lifted up and held on the edge of the hull by half a dozen men. To afford handholds for them nubs of wood had been left on the sides in the preliminary trimming ; when the final fitting was complete these were chopped off. They were termed *pukeraŋa*, " holds," or *sauaŋa*, " lifts." Under the expert's orders of " Hold you the timber down ", and the like, they kept it firmly in position while he took a chip of wood, dipped it in a bowl of thin mud, examined the joint carefully for chinks and uneven fitting, inserted the chip and marked the gaps. Then they lifted the timber down again, turned it up and removed protuberances where the mud did not show. Again and again, every few minutes throughout the day, this was repeated, until the fitting was very close.

The next day the same task was continued, while in addition the other wash-strake was removed for cleaning and then relashed. This lashing process will be described later. On this day there were about a dozen men seated around the work, relieving each other at the various jobs. Other men were engaged at the oven, and from time to time people rose from the working party and went to assist there in different capacities, later returning again. The expert, by custom, took no part in the task of cooking. At this stage of fitting he was the sole craftsman ; the other men simply assisted him in the subsidiary items. The same simple technical means of a mud smear was used as on the preceding day, but as the fitting became closer its application was changed. Now the whole length of the hull-edge was smeared with the mud paint by a brush of coco-nut fibre tied on to a stick, the slab was fitted, then removed, and the mud smear showed where wood had still to be taken off. The expert sat down during the fittings, then got up, ran his eye over the slab, shaved it down where it was needed and sat down again.

The fourth day of the actual wood-working was a continuation of this, until at midday the final fitting was made and the adjustment pronounced accurate. As the oven had been uncovered by then the food was brought out to the scene of the work and all the men knocked off and ate. There were then twenty-six in all, several newcomers, as Seremata of Taumako clan and Tai district, and Pa Mea, of Faŋarere clan and Te Roro district, themselves craftsmen, having come to help Pa Tarikitoŋa. After the meal, however, I noted that a number of the men disappeared on various pretexts, and took no further part in that day's work. By the time the meal and the subsequent gossiping was over it was well into the afternoon, and the rest of the work was done quickly. The slab was prepared for lashing on to the hull by having the outer face roughly trimmed down once more, and then was lifted into position. Little sticks dipped in charcoal paste were pushed up the holes already in the hull-edge to mark with black dots where the corresponding holes were to be bored in the edge of the wash-strake. The boring was done with a European brace-and-bit, of which there were only a couple in Tikopia, and which were eagerly borrowed for all such work. In olden days, it was said, the long pointed *Terebra* shells were used. The boring was done carefully, so as not to break out to the surface of the wood ; the holes were completed later. Then came the removal of material from the inner side of the slab to thin it to the requisite breadth, but leaving a shoulder at the lower edge to facilitate attachment. Pa Tarikitoŋa seized his adze and made a series of cuts along the inner side of the timber (*e toŋi saere*) to assist this process and indicate the depth of wood to be removed. Four men were then put on to clear off the waste material, which they did in half an hour, working rapidly. All through this day and particularly as the goal came in sight the tempo of work was quick, and there were no intermissions except for the single meal.

The reasons for haste can be summarized thus. There is the ritual drive—a canoe in pieces is in a sense an offence to the tutelary spirits who have charge of it. There is the energy of the expert himself, who in this case was a bustling person in all his activities. Such an attitude towards work in progress is common. It is associated with the possibility of going off to another task on the following day. Claims of the cultivations and of fishing or of other woodwork may press, not least upon the expert himself. There is also the stimulus given by the chief, partly due to his own wish to see the task finished and partly, though not obviously expressed, to the fact that he will then not have to feed the workers for a further day. All this of course contradicts a popular notion that the savage treats his work like play and is incapable of haste.

During this work a packing for the joint was prepared from bark-cloth, laid on the hull-edge and cut to shape with appropriate holes. The new strake was now lashed on to the hull. The other had already been relashed, as mentioned already. First a thin layer of mud was spread on the edge of the hull, and then a layer of gum (*piki*, " a sticky thing ") from the breadfruit tree ; then the *kuru*, the layer of felt-like bark-cloth, and then another layer of gum. The wash-strake was then set carefully on this packing. Lengths of *kareva* fibre, torn from coco-nut frond spathe, had been poked up through the holes in the hull-edge and then up through the holes in the strake and made fast. This assisted the final lashing by ensuring that the holes in the two timbers were correctly opposed. The proper lashing was done with thin sinnet cord, prepared while the woodwork was in progress. To avoid the exasperating difficulty of poking a fuzzy end of cord through the holes the cord was doubled, the end made fast to the bight, the doubled cord pushed through and the bight pulled after in a kind of endless chain movement until it was tight. The process was then repeated, to leave finally a single cord as lashing. Sometimes the lashing is assisted by attaching a short length of fish-line to the end of the stouter sinnet cord, and to this again a piece of *kareva* which by its stiffness can be poked through the holes easily.

The fifth day was the most spectacular to the observer. Not only was the final dressing of the timber completed, but the covers and outrigger of the canoe were relashed in place, the vessel was decorated, and payment was made to the workers.

The outer face of the wash-strake was dressed *in situ* so as to bring it back flush with the hull. Asked why they did not adze it on the ground, with possibly less disturbance to the lashing, the workers said that they could see the required dimensions more exactly when it was in position. At this task sometimes three, sometimes two, adzes were engaged, but Pa Tarikitoŋa and Pa Fenuatara remained constantly at work. This finishing is a job for skilled men, and has its responsibility. Earlier, while the slab was still on the ground, Pa Vainunu, ortho-cousin to the Ariki Kafika, was dressing it across the grain and split it slightly. After it had been bored and lashed in place the chief came and saw it. He was angry. " What do you mean by splitting our canoe ? " he asked. Pa Vainunu was, however, supported by other men, who argued that it was the fault of the timber, and the chief passed the matter over.

The oven was prepared as usual during the morning, but " was divided into two ", as the natives said. The ordinary oven in the cooking house had its complement of food, while another was dug outside close to the canoe. Not only did this serve as an overflow for the extra food required on this day, but hot stones were taken from it to heat water for cleaning the hull of the vessel. A large bowl was filled with salt water by balers and the stones were slid in. It was a busy scene. Two people pushed over the stones in the oven to enable the best to be selected, three others carried them to the water, three more took up the hot water in coco-nut cups and poured it over the upturned hull while four others rubbed over the timber with scraps of coco-nut husk. The object of this cleaning was to rid the hull of its accumulation of dirt and fungoid growths. Meanwhile, green food was brought from the orchards, and fish were sought on the reef. The women of the party hunted for small fry while eight men with a net of small mesh had a fish drive on the rising tide. When the catch was brought in it was cooked at an open fire by the fishe folk.

At the same time the expert was busy. He went around the newly lashed topstrake with a little sharpened stick which he drove under each lashing and broke off, thus making tiny wedges to hold the lashings firm. Such a wedge is termed *matarafi*. The bow and stern covers were then lashed in place by the same method as described before, but in addition a couple of ropes of bark-cloth were bound tightly round each to hold them firm while the lashing proceeded. The canoe was then dragged out from under the trees and the outrigger lashed again in position. The vessel was now completely repaired.

But there were two phases of the activity still to take place : the payment to the expert, and others who had assisted, and the resacralizing of the vessel. Although the first was an economic transaction and the second a ritual procedure they took place in combination.

The whole crowd of workers and food providers clustered around. The baskets of food from the oven were stood outside the sacred side of the house. That basket which was to form part of the payment to the expert was set apart from the others ; it was not put where the chief sat, but a little distance away. The food of the expert, who was technically a commoner, could not have a ritual position beside that of the chief.

The first operation was the decoration of the newly restored vessel. Two pieces of bark-cloth were laid down and the canoe set on them. The hull of the vessel was then marked along the starboard side with a running zig-zag line and a few extra touches in

FIG. 5A.—Decoration of the Canoe Hull. Bright red turmeric is applied in a zigzag line to the hull.

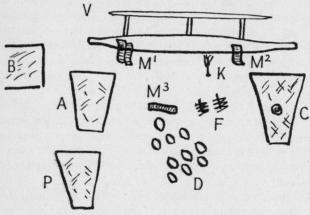

FIG. 5B.—Plan of Canoe Ceremony.

| | | | |
|---|---|---|---|
| V. | The canoe. | A. | Seating mat of the chief. |
| B. | The canoe shed. | P. | Seating mat of the elders. |
| K. | Stem of kava. | C. | Kava maker. |
| D. | Baskets of food. | F. | Bunches of ripe bananas. |
| M1. | White bark-cloth. | M2. | Orange bark-cloth. |
| M3. | Bark-cloth payment to the expert. | | |

bright red turmeric which was applied dry (v. Fig. 5A). The turmeric design was pure ornamentation, described as " the turmeric of the canoe which has been damaged to be bad ". But whereas the ornamentation was termed " the valuables of the vessel ", the bark-cloth had another function. It was " valuables of the vessel spread, because it had been taken down ; the making of it *tapu* ; not a person may go and strike at it again ". This was in effect a ritualization of the completion of the work, imposing an esoteric bar on any further tampering with what had been done. For instance, it would inhibit anyone from taking up an adze to trim off some protuberance that he had just observed. This ritual seal on the work has the effect of imposing a standard upon the expert and his assistant so that when they declare the job is done they know that they cannot make up any deficiencies by further tinkering. Put in terms of the native religion, when the canoe is laid on the bark-cloth this effects the re-entry of the gods into the vessel—just as before the work began they were removed from it by the bark-cloth. The desacralized piece of timber on which the people were working has now become recharged and is a sacred craft once more.

When the decoration was finished a kava rite was performed, in accordance with the general rule. Seating mats were laid out and the chief took his place by the stern of the vessel, the bow of which pointed seawards. This orientation is significant ; the canoe is once more ready to go forth to its work. The elders of the chief sat near him, various ritual objects were put on the mat, and the food was set in the centre of the gathering. The *maro* which was to be the payment to the expert was laid there also with his basket of food (v. Fig. 5 B). The *maro* consisted of about eight pieces of plain bark-cloth in a bundle with an orange piece on top.

The first element of the ceremony was the anointing of the canoe and the spreading on bow and stern of the sacred pieces of bark-cloth which represented the deities of the vessel. Then came the kava ceremony, in which acknowledgment was made to the expert with a portion of food. A special element on this occasion was the ritual " lifting down " of the gods from the expert, a ceremony somewhat akin to purification. Since he had cut the body of the canoe the gods had, as it were, hung themselves upon him, and had to be removed. Hence it is said, " the expert is rid of the gods." This is inconsistent with the explanation that the gods had been removed from the vessel prior to the repairs being undertaken, but it represents a kind of double insurance against misfortune which might be incurred through their anger. The expert came to the chief and knelt before him. The chief took two pieces of bark-cloth, one plain and one orange, from the head of his mat, made obeisance with them to the canoe, then swung round and passed them several times backwards and forwards over the expert's head to the accompaniment of a murmured formula. The bark-cloth was then taken back to the canoe shed, rolled up, and put away for future use. A leaf of *ti* (*Cordyline terminalis*) was taken by the chief, twisted, and tied around the expert's neck. The rite with the bark-cloth was the desacralization ; that with the leaf was the investiture with an amulet to give protection and welfare. The expert was now free from any consequences of his interference with the sacred vessel.

The chief then gave instructions to carry off the payment to the households of the expert and other outsiders who had assisted. " Come and take away the *maro*, that mother and daughters may come hither to carry them," he said to some of the men. This was to allow the women of the household to take up their burden without approaching too near the canoe. In addition to the bark-cloth for the expert, a piece was sent to Pa Niata, who helped the chief in the first instance to fell the tree for the wash-strake. Baskets of food were also given to each of the members of the working party who were not close relatives of the chief, and a large food portion to the man whose brace-and-bit had been borrowed. With the carriage of these gifts the proceedings ended.

A number of points of general economic interest for the theory of primitive production can be seen in this typical example of a working party. The factors which determine the assembly of the working group may include the prospect of the food provided. But of more overt importance are the recognition of ties of kinship and neighbourliness, the code which demands that commoners should cluster round a chief, and the convention that a piece of productive equipment should be kept effective. The evaluation of the weight of these respective factors in the case of any single worker is not possible, but it is clear that they must operate differently in the case of the expert, say, than of the chief's son.

In the organization of the work the expert stands out. For an unskilled activity such as the initial carrying of the log there is no leader, but during the repair work the expert is definitely in charge. The Tikopia make a specific point of securing control by a single individual over the group as a whole. It is to be noted that from the expert is demanded not only specialist knowledge and manual skill, but also control of the total activity. It is obvious from the description how considerable is his technical competence, and how he regards the repair problem from a plain, practical attitude. He gives in addition his personal energy, which he is expected to display. It is the tradition of canoe-making that the expert shall be on the job every day as soon as the sun has risen. By this demonstration of responsibility and keenness, which is in part dictated by the code of his craft, he is enabled to set an example to the others.

The owner of the vessel, even though himself a canoe expert, is never the controller. His task is to provide food for the workers ; he does, however, give assistance from time to time and his sons, if skilled, may be there constantly. But he does not interfere with the technical direction of the expert.

Apart from the authority of the expert and of the owner, if he be a man of rank, there are other factors which contribute to the organization of the group. One is the imperative of the situation itself, the overt recognition by most, if not all, of the workers that there is a positive value in completing their task. In other words, the job is done not merely because the chief wants it, but because it is recognized as being itself worth doing. This is helped by the fact that many of them in the ordinary way may use the vessel and receive advantage from its fishing. There is also the ritual imperative ; the close integration between work and ceremonial shows how the canoe is not simply a material object devoted to practical ends, but linked with beliefs about the gods and to be treated as the property of powerful beings. Protracted idleness or careless workmanship become then religious as well as social offences. Even the implements used have an extra-technical side, as when an adze is credited with the property of destroying borer.

The parallelism of the ritual organization with the economic organization thus assists the performance of the task. Not only does it provide an imperative for work, but also to some extent inspires the worker with belief in his own competence, as when the expert dedicates his adze to the appropriate gods. On the other hand, much of the ritual cannot be said to supply any positive contribution. Attention to it in fact takes up time that might otherwise be employed on the job and to that extent it must be regarded as a drag upon the economic situation. It is highly codified and can only be understood by reference to a wider scheme of beliefs and activities. As such any positive function that it may have must be sought in the analysis of this wider situation.

## THE ROLE OF LANGUAGE IN WORK

A brief observation on how far language is effective in providing incentive and control in the work may be given here.

I take these examples from my notebook. As Pa Vainunu is trimming the edge of the plank he puts one foot in line with the blow of the adze, to steady it. The chief and other men warn him " Your foot, son ! " " Adze is sharp, cut gently ! " and the like. Such injunctions are repeated several times ; nevertheless he only smiles and continues. Pa Fenuatara, as he is cutting at one topstrake, calls to Pa Mea, " Run here and hold the other side." The man does not move, but Pa Tarikitoŋa goes and sits on it to keep it firm. Another time Pa Tarikitoŋa sees a man whom he thinks should be working instead of watching two others. " E ! You, sitting and staring at the pair ! " One of them, Pa Fenuafuri, a son of the chief, chimes in " Staring he sits there ! " But the man does not stir. Again, Pa Tarikitoŋa calls out to Pa Vainunu and Pa Fenuafuri, " You watch, thud, thud ! Why don't you do it quickly ? " They are working on the bow-cover which he has left to them, and he is getting impatient. He calls excitedly again, " Hey ! Do it properly and quickly ! " Again, Pa Tarikitoŋa, ever-watchful and energetic, calls out to a couple of men who are lashing the stern-cover, " Married couple are working at the stern there ! Married couple, married couple, married couple ! " This is a jesting taunt to make them hurry up. The suggestion is not that a married couple are lazy, but that meta- phorically sex activity has replaced other activity here. The epithet is applied in other contexts also, where the reference to sex is obviously inappropriate to the situation in hand. " Why don't you do it quickly ? " he says again. It is the ethic of such jests that they be taken in good part ; they are usually answered merely with a grin, or a joke in kind. " In this land if a man makes a joke, and the other man sits and does not laugh back, that is a bad man," said the Tikopia, in comment on this particular example, which provoked merely an answering smile.

It may seem from these examples quoted that the effect in economic organization of such speech imperatives is practically nil ; that they are not a factor of any importance in regulating behaviour and in stimulating men to work against their wish. Such a conclusion would be superficial. In the first place, the effect of such orders and jesting goads, reiterated as is the Tikopia style, is cumulative. There may be no response the first time, but after a series of such pricks the person addressed usually responds. Moreover, the nature of the response varies according to the nature of the situation. If it is merely a question of greater speed, or doing something which can wait, or which someone else can equally do, then the response is often nil, or delayed. But it is hardly ever negative, a direct refusal. And if it is a question of immediate action necessary to retrieve a situation, or guard against accident, there is usually a quick response. For example, when the hull of the canoe was being turned over for washing, a hole was dug to accommodate the projecting bow ornament. People handling the canoe called out to Pa Mea : " Pa Mea E ! Stand up and level off the place," meaning the spot where the topstrake was to rest. This he did at once, since instant action was needed.

In quite another context, in comment on a dance song, I was given some observations on the use of the verbal medium in lightening heavy work. Pa Fenuatara said : " If it be a ridge pole, or a canoe which people have gone to drag hither, and they pull, pull, pull in vain, then some man becomes annoyed. ' What is it ? Why is there no *tauraŋi* then for the timber ? ' Then the *tauraŋi* may be made simply by a yell. When the yell is omitted people will say to each other, ' What is it ? Pulling a timber ? ' But if the *tauraŋi* is made with a dance song then the dance song is stood up. When the dance song of the land stands, the timber is taken, it is merely light. The speech is ' To *tauraŋi* that the timber may hear '. It is held that the timber hears its song or the yell which is produced, and thereupon becomes light."

The *tauraŋi* is the linguistic medium, either the conventional whoop of " *Iefu* ", or a chanted song. The Tikopia explain its action in terms of response of the timber itself ; but it is clear that the concerted action of the workers in this way does give a co-ordination which enables them to cope more easily with the weight, and probably lends them also encouragement in their task.

Apart from giving a possible incentive to labour, speech is of the greatest importance in the use of technical terms. These, acting as symbols for objects and actions, allow an economy of effort without which such complex productive efforts would be practically impossible.

### CASE MATERIAL ON SPECIFIC UNDERTAKINGS

In the following Table I give some data on the organization of production in different activities, of an ordinary economic type and of a ritual type.[1] Although no systematic series is presented the data indicate some quantitative aspects of the labour situation. The description may not be complete in all cases as there may have been women and children assisting in the preparation of food in the background whom I did not always include.

## SPECIFIC CASES OF ECONOMIC ACTIVITY

A.  *Activity* : Taro-planting of Ariki Kafika.

*Personnel and Organization* : Seven persons engaged—Ariki Kafika, wife, son, son's wife, son's " adopted " son (who is also a grandson of the chief), kinswoman married into Taumako chiefly house, and Pa Porima, chief's ritual elder.

This is a typical planting group, assembled primarily on a kinship basis. In the middle of the morning they stop to drink green coco-nuts, provided by the chief, who first pours out a libation to his chiefly ancestor whose stone stands in the cultivation.

B.  *Activity* : Removal of bark from paper-mulberry trunks for conversion into cloth for initiation ceremony.

*Personnel and Organization* : Three persons engaged—sister of initiate, and two young men co-opted by her father. Girl cut slit down trunk, and she and young men each prised bark from trunk with wooden levers. Lad assisting by cutting fresh levers as others broke. Several children impressed to help by holding trunk, pulling bark free, and rinsing bark in sea-water. Children later went off playing with discarded rind as a sledge.

This group typical of many domestic, semi-skilled tasks. (Semi-skilled, since one young man had to be instructed by other in procedure.)

C.  *Activity* : House-building, on old site.

*Personnel and Organization* : Six men engaged. Owner and neighbour prepared timber a week before. On day of building, owner, two neighbours, brother, brother-in-law, and father-in-law assembled. No expert craftsman among them. Posts set in early in morning ; frame up by early afternoon. No recompense in goods, but meal prepared in houses of owner and one neighbour furnished common meal.

D.  *Activity* : Repair of fishing canoe, bow-piece being re-shaped.

*Personnel and Organization* : Work done by original builder of vessel. Screen of coco-nut frond erected by owner to shelter him from sun. Food prepared by owner in his house, with assistance from others who form ordinary crew of the vessel. Majority of fish from catch of previous night kept back from distribution for this.

---

[1] I have used the term entrepreneur here in default of finding a better. It must be taken in its simplest sense of the person primarily responsible for an undertaking, and is not intended to imply propositions about risk-taking or profit-reception. For the Tikopia economy the term covers ownership of the final product, responsibility for payment of the workers if such has to be made, and usually some actual participation in the work.

E. *Activity* : Repair of shed of sacred canoe of Mapusaŋa house of Kafika.

*Personnel and Organization* : Posts re-dressed, two beams replaced, and new thatch put on. Work done by Ariki Kafika, son, two owners of vessel, two ritual elders of chief, son of another ritual elder, and six other kinsfolk. No specialist builder, but son of chief in nominal charge of work. About six men at work at any one time, others rising from resting to replace them from time to time. Grandson of chief acting as errand boy to fetch cord, etc. Food cooked for workers in ovens of owners. Two bowls of pudding and three large baskets divided among twelve men ; another large basket as ritual gift to chief. Following day, Ariki, six men and children at work ; fed on large fish caught by canoe and some vegetable food.

F. *Activity* : Sago filtration of house of Kafika.

| *Entrepreneur* : | *Personnel and Organization.* |
|---|---|
| Ariki Kafika | Eight men and three women engaged on extraction of sago, all kinsfolk of Ariki Kafika. In addition, small group in cook-house preparing food. Among these, eldest son of Ariki, who explained that he as chief's heir did not take part in actual work of sago. Work begun in late morning, carried on in rain, and finished about 3 p.m. Two large troughs used alternately to hold filtered liquid, with canoe used as water-trough. Sediment poured off from troughs into three medium-sized bowls. Rite performed over bowl of fresh sago when work done, and meal taken. |

G. *Activity* : Net-making. Preliminary stages begun about middle of January, to prepare nets for setting in lake in *toŋa* season—about end of March. Hibiscus fibre collected by men, scraped by women, rolled into cord by men.

| *Entrepreneur* : | *Personnel and Organization.* |
|---|---|
| (i) Pae Sao | Five men engaged—owner, brother, two neighbours, and expert friend. Owner, brother, and one neighbour roll cord, on shuttle borrowed from fellow-villager ; other neighbour and expert first roll cord and then make net. New portion joined to old, since working group small. Owner said if his kin group had been large different sections of it would each have made new portions of net, which would have been joined to make completely new net. Net finished towards end of April ; floats and sinkers attached a month later, and payment given to expert. |
| (ii) Ariki Kafika | Seven men engaged on first day—Ariki, two sons, and four other kinsmen. Work of making net begun about middle of February. Ariki himself makes net, others roll and wind cord. Ritual performed with libation to gods. Work continued for three more days by Ariki, with smaller party. |

|                      | On fifth day he and son went to woods to collect more fibre. Net left unfinished. . . . |
| (iii) Ariki Taumako  | Cord began to be rolled about middle of January, by chief and party at a song practice for a dance ; continued spasmodically ; towards middle of February six men spent a day rolling cord in chief's house. That evening three kinsfolk of chief and three women brought loads of food for oven ; net to be made on morrow. Net-making—nine men and two boys engaged ; chief, two sons of father's brother ; brother-in-law, three sons, three other kinsmen, and a ritual elder. Ariki expert at net-making but delegated job to Pa Kamota and Pa Tarikitoŋa. To begin with, Pa Tarikitoŋa makes net, Ariki winds cord on shuttle, boy sent for larger shuttle ; two men rolling cord, others lying down. Later two men work at net, one at each end. Work continued next day ; by midday nearly eight fathoms completed ; this constituted one section, and another begun. Next day more fibre collected by chief and party. After break of three days, new sections joined to remainder of old net, floats and cowrie-shell sinkers put on by Pa Kamota. Present—chief, two experts, two sons, two other kinsmen and Ariki Kafika. All participate in stripping old net of floats, etc., or assisting in equipping new one. On next two mornings new net dragged in lake, getting eight fish and no fish respectively. Kava ceremony performed second afternoon in chief's house over net. |

A feature of Tikopia industry, in the absence of a contract system of hiring labour on a time basis, is the fluctuation in the number of workers engaged at the different stages of the activity, and even during the same stage. The return to the workers in the form of meals and betel materials is broadly speaking the same ; I did not hear of any differentiation on the ground that any person did more or less work than another. But the practice, with its interspersing of personal tasks with work for others, allows of easier acquiescence in the obligation to assist, and also relieves the entrepreneur of having to organize the work very closely in order to keep in occupation those workers temporarily free.

As an example of this fluctuation I quote from a record I made of the number of persons engaged on different tasks in connection with the turmeric extraction of the Ariki Tafua. (See Plates II and IV.)

H. *Activity* : Turmeric Extraction.

| Day and Time. | Stage of Work. | Persons Engaged. |
|---|---|---|
| First Day | Erection of grating shed . . | Ariki and 4 sons |
| Second Day | Transport of turmeric in canoe of Ariki. | 2 men |
| Third Day | Digging turmeric . . . . | 1 man, 4 women |
| | Building enclosure; sewing filter-cloth. | Ariki and 4 men |
| | Cleaning turmeric . . . | 12 women, 12 children |
| | Washing turmeric in sea . . | 6 youths and girls |
| | Scraping roots . · . . . | 1 woman |
| | Washing bowl . . . . | 1 man |
| | Washing graters . . . . | several owners |
| Fourth Day | | |
| 7 a.m. | Grating turmeric . . . . | 1 man, 19 women |
| 10 a.m. | ,, ,, . . . | 5 men, 28 women |
| | Erecting filter-stand . . . | 6 men, 2 boys |
| | Preparing food . . . . | 20 men, 2 women |
| Midday | Pause for refreshment . . . | — |
| 1 p.m. | Filtering turmeric . . . | 9 men |
| 2 p.m. | Meal. | |
| Fifth Day | | |
| 6 a.m. | Meal. | |
| 7 a.m. | Construction of second enclosure . | 8 men |
| | Work in first enclosure . . . | 6 men |
| | Grating turmeric . . . . | 1 man, 9 women |
| | Making covers for turmeric . . | 2 men |
| 7.30 a.m. | Pouring off troughs . . . | 8 men |
| | Filtering turmeric . . . | 5 men |
| 9 a.m. | Filtering turmeric . . . | 6 men |
| | Grating turmeric . . . . | 1 man, 19 women |
| 10 a.m. | Shelter from rain . . . . | — |
| 11.30 a.m. | Preparation of bowls . . . | 3 men |
| 3.30 p.m. | Preparation of food . . . | 12 men |
| | Separation of pigments . . | 4 men |
| | Decanting from troughs . . | 9 men |
| | Filtering turmeric . . . | 4 men, 4 women |
| | Procuring food for morrow . . | 1 man |
| Sixth Day | | |
| Dawn | Meal. | |
| 7 a.m. | Separation of pigments; decanting from troughs. | 4 men |
| 10 a.m. | Collecting breadfruit . . . | 1 man |
| | Cooking food . . . . | 6 men |
| | Cleaning out turmeric oven . . | 1 man, 1 boy |
| | Preparing turmeric baking cylinders | 5 men |

| Day and Time | Stage of Work. | Persons Engaged. |
|---|---|---|
| 11 a.m. | Meal. | |
| noon | Preparing turmeric oven    .    . | 2 men |
| 1 p.m. | Filling baking cylinders ;  blowing cylinders. | 6 men |

A few simple empirical generalizations may now be given as to the quantity of labour engaged in different employments.

(i) A general norm of labour supply can be seen for different types of activity. Reference to Table III in conjunction with the case material shows that the labour assembled for a large scale activity is only from five to ten per cent of the maximum labour power available in the community, and that for the enterprise of a chief not more than about one-third of the total clan force is mobilized. Tikopia generalizations that " the whole clan " assembles at whatever a chief undertakes are therefore an exaggeration.

(ii) The quantity of labour tends to be determined to some extent by the technical requirements of the task and the possibilities of efficient co-operation.

(iii) There are frequently rapid fluctuations in the number of persons immediately engaged in different stages of the work. (See especially Case H.) This can be correlated with the Tikopia household system of ordinary production which allows of irregular application to domestic tasks.

(iv) Casual labour is often pressed into service, with no specific reward, especially in the case of the unskilled help of children and young people.

(v) The social status of the entrepreneur is one factor which conditions the supply of labour in a given activity.

(vi) The efficiency of the organization provided by the entrepreneur is also to some extent a determining factor (compare Cases G ii and iii).

(vii) There is a tendency for the optimum labour supply to be assembled for large scale undertakings, thus allowing of leisure to some participants and for a rapid substitution of fresh for fatigued workers.

(viii) As a source of the labour supply the local group is most important. Neighbours and fellow villagers usually participate whatever be their kinship connection.

(ix) The concurrence of social obligations has a considerable effect upon the labour supply. But the treatment as a unit of the labour and capital resources of a household, and even of the combined households of a larger family group, tends to obviate any serious inadequacy.

## LABOUR SUPPLY

We may now consider more directly what determines the amount of labour used for an undertaking, particularly that sponsored by a given individual who may be called for convenience the entrepreneur. Any discussion of the quantity of labour is rendered difficult by the fact that one cannot relate it to calculations of output per head, for which there is no index in the Tikopia economy. A measurement of the results of an individual's work over a period can be made, but an average of the total result obtained between the total number of labourers engaged is not very satisfactory, and the Tikopia themselves make no such calculation. A few general observations, however, will indicate the factors actually involved.

In gathering the working group together a specific invitation is issued to a few people, to close kinsfolk and neighbours, and perhaps to one or more specialist craftsmen. The principal factors influencing the decision of the entrepreneur as to whom to invite are the known requirements of the work and his estimate of his own resources available to meet his consequent commitments. But the convention of the *fiuri* (see p. 149) relieves him of the necessity of making any exact calculation of the relative marginal utilities of labour and food ; even if he tried to do so he would probably be defeated by the recognized conventions of assistance. The number of people on whom he can count is not rigidly defined, and therefore the general gossip about the event may bring additional people who interpret their kinship obligations more strictly than he himself is prepared to demand. Such cases of voluntary unsought help make little drain on the resources of the entrepreneur, and if the amount of labour already engaged on the technical side or the food preparation does not allow of the absorption of the extra hands then the volunteers can sit around and talk, or return home. More commonly, they relieve a worker for a short time and then go. The lack of a strict equation between service and reward also allows the entrepreneur to press into the undertaking a casual visitor. When I visited with Seremata the sago-grating of Pa Saukirima,

the latter said to him : " You are *maroro* (strong, vigorous):
go and grate," and he took part in the work for an hour or so
without reward.   The close integration of the whole Tikopia
economic system provides the possibility of a delayed reciprocity
for the exaction of such service, but there is no precise calculation.
A few betel materials or a scrap of tobacco at the time, and food
if the visitor stays on till a meal is ready give a rough immediate
recompense.

What are the factors which influence the decision of the
people choosing to participate in the work ?   On their part
the people who assemble do not necessarily weigh up carefully
the relative material advantages of working for the entrepreneur
or for themselves at that particular time.

At any given moment, in theory, the Tikopia has his choice
between employments in most of which he has some skill.   The
absence of a high degree of specialization means that a person
can transfer his labour easily from one sphere to another.   It is
true that in deciding on a certain day between different forms of
fishing, or bird-snaring, or of agricultural work, or manufacture
of a bowl or a net, or assisting at someone else's canoe building,
he may be guided by the comparative yield which they promise,
having regard to his individual capacity in each.   But it is equally
likely that other considerations will rule his choice—such as the
claims of ritual, of a chief, or of a brother-in-law.   The return
he may get for his labour may be considerably less than that which
he would have got by working for himself, but this does not
prevent him from deciding in favour of the social claims.   The
conventional character of the repayment for labour means that
he can expect no rise in the rate of reward to complicate his choice.
And even when the claims of his own immediate interests are too
strong to be neglected the choice is facilitated by the Tikopia
custom of sending a representative in the person of a son or
younger brother.   Even a brother-in-law, out of a sense of kinship
responsibility, may voluntarily assume an economic obligation
and disburse goods or labour for him without his knowledge.

In other cases, again, a certain undertaking may be virtually
prescribed for him by the canons of etiquette.   When people who
want a canoe built invite an expert from outside refusal would be
tantamount to an unfriendly act, and would have repercussions
upon him.

In general terms, social consideration rather than simple

economic advantage induce the volunteering of labour in the Tikopia productive situation. The social and not the economic definition of each man's position as a worker tends to assure an adequate labour supply.

But the response to an expressed desire for labour assistance is not automatic ; there is some evaluation of the event against other personal claims. Pressing occupations elsewhere—either economic or ceremonial—may be one reason, but personal disinclination or emotional strain between the parties may also be responsible. Thus when a brother of Pa Raŋifuri sent a boy as messenger to ask him to be a member of a fishing crew, he replied that his shoulders were weary from paddling the day before, and that his brother should seek a crew elsewhere. No further appeal was made to him. Again, Pa Porima did not participate in some of the work of his chief, the Ariki Kafika, in Uta at one period because, it was said, his kinsman Pae Sao had been insulted by the chief. Even between brothers-in-law such conditions are sometimes strong enough to outweigh kinship claims.[1]

So far we have assumed that every activity proposed receives its full complement of workers. The question remains whether this is always the case. On the whole the considerable amount of leisure available, the absence of contractual engagements for a period, the weight attached to requests for assistance and the customary reward for labour primarily in meals at the site do allow undertakings to be carried out. But the entrepreneur himself often has to judge the most appropriate time for the undertaking by reference to what is already in hand or proposed by others. During the season in which sago extraction commonly takes place, for instance, or during the ritual of the Work of the Gods, it is unusual to attempt to enlist workers for canoe building or other large-scale enterprise.

Occasionally all available workers are employed elsewhere. A man cannot get together a fishing crew in good fishing weather if he sends out invitations too late in the morning. Or a man who is late in deciding to fell a sago-palm may have to wait for assistants till the filtering by others is done. If food supplies have been accumulated for his undertaking there is no loss since they can be diverted to other ends—in gifts to a chief, or in wiping out old obligations.

Sometimes there is a deficiency in the supply of labour at

[1] *We, The Tikopia,* 217.

a task already under way. Even in the case of an enterprise sponsored by a chief there are sometimes too few workers (see p. 196). This results not in an increase of the remuneration to those labourers who come—except perhaps inadvertently through extra tobacco or betel materials on hand—nor in a higher inducement to others to participate, but in social reverberations of complaint, gossip, and bad feeling. Also, though the labourers may have to work for a longer time to complete their task their remuneration is not raised correspondingly in any single day.

It may be asked what happens if, for example, several people want canoes built or nets made at the same time, and there is a demand for more specialists than are free. The answer is that this is extremely improbable ; the quick passage of news round the island would warn men who intend to begin such work, and the tendency would be for those of lesser rank, or less immediate kinship ties with the specialist craftsmen, to postpone their plans. Since the time element as such is not so important as in our society (" time " is not " money ") they would not suffer to any extent by having to wait. In no case have I ever discovered any competitive bargaining, or any holding out for an increased rate of reward.

Since there is no floating labour supply seeking employment the introduction of an increased demand for labour must mean the diversion of some of the energies of men already engaged in work.

In the Tikopia economy of to-day a new act of production does not necessarily result in a dislocation of individual tasks because the extra time put into these is that which would otherwise be spent in leisure. The nature of Tikopia industry, lacking a concept of regular labour hours, results in minimal dislocation. But if, for instance, a new demand for labour came from white employers requiring regular periods of work and individual contract without the possibility of an *ad hoc* delegation or substitution of one labourer for another then the situation would be different. Considerable dislocation of the native productive scheme would be bound to occur. There is room for some absorption by Europeans, as of younger sons in a family. This is what happened when the inducements of whaling and plantation work were given in the nineteenth century. But an extensive new demand would tend to drain off more than these people.

## LEADERSHIP IN WORK

We must now discuss in more detail the integrative factors in Tikopia work—the reasons which bring them together and keep them together as an effective productive unit. Under this head the element of leadership or direction is frequently the only one examined in studies of primitive economics. The problem of integration, however, necessitates attention to the general system of what may be called the *ideology of production*. This is less easy to define than leadership, since it is expressed not in the advisory or controlling action of a single personality, but in the set of conventions which regulate work and the relation of work to other types of activity such as rest and recreation. Moreover, these conventions, which may be of a technical, a social, or a ritual order, are formulated in an elaborate set of linguistic idioms, the appreciation of which can only be gained by a study of the native language as a whole.

In conformity with the absence of a class of purely specialist craftsmen, there is in Tikopia no specialized function of leadership of an activity. Integration of work is accomplished through a diffused mechanism of discussion in which naturally the more skilled members of the group take the most prominent part. One man may assume primary control but this is always an extension of his position as an interested or a working member, and not the exercise of a directive function *per se*. It is thus difficult in Tikopia to separate the wages of management from the wages of labour when the distribution of the reward for work is made.

In an ordinary working group of young people, for instance, one of the seniors, using an authority which he has acquired by age, personality, rank, leadership in games, or any combination of these qualities, takes command, but obedience is not implicit and discussion is free. Quarrels in such working parties are not unknown. In one that I observed, a split occurred. The leader, Seremata, told the party to wait for him while he went to his house to fetch his knife. When he returned they had all gone except one. It turned out that they had gone round the lake to Mauŋa Faea. But, so he said afterwards, he had told them that the work was to be done that day in Mauŋa, a district somewhat to the east. He accordingly went on with a companion and collected on the way the owner of the orchard in which the day's work was to be done. The three arrived and began to work.

Meanwhile the others after waiting found that their leader did not join them and came over where he was. When they arrived they arranged among themselves to remain separate from the three, out of pique. Sia, an arrogant young man, was the head of the malcontents. Their defence was that Seremata had told them to go to Faea. This he indignantly denied, stigmatizing them as liars (though it seemed to me a clear case of verbal mis-understanding). The news of the separation was brought to Seremata by two of the others who refused to remain aloof and came to join him. Angrily he agreed. He was rendered still more annoyed by the fact that the party had taken his water bottle with them and drunk most of the contents, leaving him only a little for the heat of the day. The two parties worked separately until nightfall. In the meantime news went down to the village that the two parties had fought in the orchard, but this was, of course, an exaggeration, common when gossip gets busy with a quarrel.

This example shows how tenuous is the tie that binds the leader and others of a working group in such an activity, yet how they are kept together by ideological factors concerning the meaning of work, and also the tie to the owner of the plantation, despite the absence of any ritual association or co-ordination of specialist craft. It shows, too, how personal sensitiveness, concepts of dignity, and feelings of affront, all of which are derived from and expressed in social convention, act as factors of disintegration. The position is complicated by the existence of a definite system of rank.

Leadership in Tikopia co-operative work relies upon two principles, that of social status and that of skill. The most extreme example of the first is where a chief assumes command in such an enterprise as the production of sago or turmeric ; of the second where a canoe builder is in charge of the making of a chief's craft. In the first case men who have more technical deftness may be subordinate to the directions of their senior in rank ; in the second case the chief has his function as provider of food and future owner of the canoe but the commands of the expert are obeyed by him in all technical matters. These two principles are not exclusive ; the chief is himself frequently an acknowledged technician and so has a double right of leadership. Or conversely the canoe builder who is in charge may be himself a man of rank either in ritual affairs or in the political sphere.

Moreover, in a sense, acknowledged skill in the major crafts gives in itself the title to direction of the work and has a social value. The basis of distinction is the amount of proficiency involved, which is correlated with the liability to failure. In the activities which demand less proficiency and in which the range of technical competence from man to man is not so great, the possession of ritual status tends to be the determining factor. In the activities where this variation in technical competence is most significant, as in canoe building, the technician is for obvious reasons the leader in his own sphere. In some communities, as in Melanesia, he tends to be the ritual practitioner as well, thus controlling both sides of the activity. In Tikopia this is not so. When a chief is having a new sacred canoe constructed he cannot be the craftsman. He must enlist the services of such a man while the technical aspects of the activity are carried on within a ritual framework in which he himself has the directing voice. Even if he is himself an acknowledged craftsman he conforms to the division of function between provider of food and executor of the work.

## IDEOLOGY OF PRODUCTION

It has been shown that the level of technical achievement and complexity of processes in Tikopia do not in themselves alone demand the extensive co-operation which actually occurs. Nor can the labour situation be interpreted simply as a response to a system of economic reward. Workers are not drawn into an undertaking from a free reservoir of labour power, their choice determined by the wage-rates offered ; they come from groups attached by definite social ties to the entrepreneur. Social forces catch up and enmesh the economic factors in a wider net. In a summary way it may be said that the codes which govern the behaviour of individuals in this society are such that a great deal of economic co-operation is based upon a primary interest in the social aspects of co-operation for its own sake rather than in its economic advantage. This might be regarded as inefficiency in the application of technique to the problem of production, but as I see it, it is more satisfactory to consider it rather as an example of the preference of social advantage over economic advantage which is characteristic of the Tikopia economy as a whole. This point will be taken up later, particularly in the analysis of exchange.

The assembly, continued co-operation, and reassembly of individuals in a productive group are governed by a system of rules with a variety of sanctions. Considered from the individual point of view these rules might be described under the head of incentives to work but such a concept tends to be too narrow and to exclude a number of important governing factors. The rules may be described better as the *positive conventions of work*. They include ties of loyalty to kin, to neighbours, to bond friends, to a chief ; the concept of labour and its implications ; the explicit recognition of laziness on the one hand and of the need for rest on the other. In addition there are a number of modes of behaviour which are conventional in the sense that they generally follow and are linked up with traditionalized concepts. But they are not formulated so definitely and have not the same imperative character. They include firstly those with a positive effect upon work, such as emulation, which acts as a stimulus to productive effort ; and secondly, those with a negative effect, such as the perception of insult, or the fear of sorcery, which lead to a falling off in productive effort.

In the response to the positive conventions the more explicit formulation and the moral quality attaching to them bring in the weight of social opinion much more strongly and allow less scope for individual variation. For instance, it is held that a man should give economic assistance to his chief. If he feels that a chief has affronted him it is regarded by most people as natural that he should stay away, but there is no body of social injunctions to support him in this.

In all human societies language serves as one vehicle of transmission of these conventions from one generation to another, provides a norm by which the individual is guided, and is a link between the members of a working group whereby their co-ordination is more effectively secured. It is not necessary to analyse the linguistic apparatus of production in Tikopia ; the samples of speech of members of the canoe-repairing group cited earlier illustrate sufficiently the role of language during actual work. In using the term " linguistic apparatus " it is implied that language is not only a mode of thought of individuals or a medium of communication between them but is a mode of action in the speaker and of inducing action in others.[1]

---

[1] The use of this expression rests upon a theory of language which has been set out by B. Malinowski with elaborate documentation in " Meaning in Primitive

Exact analysis of the effects of the operation of these rules upon production in the individual cases would require psychological material which I did not obtain. It is not possible, for instance, to state the precise type of satisfaction which a person gains by conforming to these social dictates or by expressing his personality through them. But a general statement can indicate the type of regulation which is specifically recognized and formulated by the natives themselves. The case material given earlier gives an index to the effectiveness of these rules in practice.

Important among the positive conventions of production are obligations of kinship and neighbourliness, which are often difficult to separate. The manner in which these ties operate in individual cases has already been described elsewhere.[1] I may repeat here, however, the native saying, " The brother-in-law goes to seek his brother-in-law," put in another way by a man who said, " Anything done in the house of brother-in-law, I rise and go to look after it." Such expressions are cited to cover reciprocal assistance in work, and contributions of labour, food, and other materials on ordinary economic and on ceremonial occasions. Thus Pa Maniva, going to help in enlarging the house of his kinsman Pa Raŋimatere, carried with him a couple of light rafters, his contribution, cut from his own orchard. Such is the custom. Again, I met Pa Nukutauriri, of Kafika clan and Faea, carrying a large root of *pulaka* and a paddle. I knew he must be going to the marriage feast of Pa Roŋoifo (of Taumako clan and Namo), and asked him why he was going since I did not recognize him as a relative. He answered : " I am of the kin group through the woman who lives with me." His wife was a sister of a classificatory " father " of the bridegroom. The convention of the *soko*, whereby cooks are secured for all important feasts through affinal ties, is extremely important.[2]

The role of kinship ties in determining the quantity of labour is seen in the participation of women in many activities. They are drawn, not from any source of labour which happens to be free, but from the households of the men who engage in the work. This gives what may be termed a system of sex-joined labour

Language " (*The Meaning of Meaning*, ed. C. K. Ogden and I. A. Richards) and *Coral Gardens and their Magic*. See also J. R. Firth, *Speech*. Since language is a cultural item *sui generis*, to speak of linguistic " apparatus " is not to equate words with material tools, but to draw attention in a figurative manner to their activating function.

[1] *We, The Tikopia*, 56, 62, 67, 71, 189, 230, 304, 355.
[2] *Op. cit.*, 305–7.

supply. One type of kinship obligation may, however, sometimes outweigh another. Pa Fenuatara, for instance, instead of remaining to help his father, the Ariki Kafika, at his net-making, went with a contribution of food to assist his " brother ", Pa Nukutuŋasau, in repairing his ancestral temple Vaisakiri in Uta. In such case, decisions are taken by family discussion on the basis of individual choice and labour available.

At times, kinship obligations operate to the detriment of work in hand. Pa Tekaumata, working in Rakisu planting his taro, was recalled by a messenger who told him that an old woman of the house of Korokoro had just died. Her mother came from ŋatotiu, his own house, so in accordance with custom he left his taro tops to wither in the middle of the field and went straight away to join in the mourning.

Another element of great force in determining co-operation in work is loyalty to the chief of one's clan. Further material bearing on this is given in Chapter VI.

Such affiliations can be contrasted with the absence of any convention of hiring of labour. Contracting to work for another person for a reward specified in advance is not a Tikopia custom. When one person works for another their association is so governed by canons of etiquette that it assumes the form of partnership in a joint enterprise, and the ultimate reward for the labour takes on the external form of a gift. The examples of canoe-repair in this Chapter and of sago extraction in Chapter VIII show how these conventions operate.

An analysis of the principles of property holding and accumulation is given in Chapter VII. But a word may be said here of the way in which the differential ownership of the means of production affects the organization of labour. Individual ownership of goods definitely exists in Tikopia and is expressed in linguistic form. But the conventions of the society do not allow material goods to be withheld from production for any long time when they are required by other individuals, nor the possession of them to be used as a bargaining instrument to secure an abnormal rate of return. An extensive system of borrowing linked with a customary rate of repayment (which in some cases is given by future reciprocity and not by any immediate material return) means that these goods can be injected into the productive process by persons who lack them but have need of them and have the labour available to use them. The methods of dealing with

raw materials such as timber for canoes, or palms for sago flour ;
with technical equipment such as adzes, troughs, and seine nets,
and with the food which is one of the bases of productive enterprise, are seen in Chapter VIII. The conventions of this system
are obviously linked with the fact that the avenues of employment
for capital and labour are not innumerable but definitely limited.
Withholding of goods from production is, therefore, placed in
direct opposition to the social interest in the utilization of them,
and the possession of labour power serves as a stimulus to their
employment. On the other hand, labour itself can be stimulated
in like manner by the desire to use productive equipment.

A characteristic feature of much Tikopia co-operation is
the manner in which the distributive process follows directly
upon the act of production, and is linked with it. Because of this
dual aspect of the activity—the technical operations on the one
hand, and the preparation of food for the workers on the other—
a considerable proportion of labour expended by workers arriving
from outside often goes to provide their own reward. Moreover,
the convention is that they themselves bring along a contribution
of green food, such as raw taro, breadfruit, or bananas, to the oven.
This is known technically as a *fiuri*. How does this system work
from the point of view of the labourer ? The fact that the host
himself provides a considerable share of the food does doubtless
give some incentive to the workers to assemble by relieving them
in part of the necessity for collecting and preparing their own
food that day. But the convention that one does not go empty-
handed (" bare ", as the Tikopia put it) to assist a kinsman or a
chief means that the net gain in terms of food is not great. I have
never heard any opinion such as : " Let us go along to assist so-
and-so and get a meal." On the other hand, expressions such as :
" I am going to help so-and-so because he is my brother-in-law "—
or " father ", or " brother "—are commonly heard. And the
native feeling is that the service *plus* contribution of food are
considerably greater in value than the meal obtained. The
economic reciprocity which is contingent upon such relationships
does add force to the reliance which is placed upon them in
productive organization, though fear of the loss of these reciprocal
benefits is by no means a complete explanation of their power and
functioning. The real stress is upon the social advantage to be
gained by conformity rather than upon the economic advantage.

The fact of contribution to the productive fund of the

entrepreneur helps to assure not the economic position of the worker, but his kinship and social position. He is not given a job because he contributes to the productive fund ; he makes the contribution because he has accepted the obligation of the job. It is important to note that in much Tikopia industry the functions of worker and ally of the entrepreneur are combined.

It has already been mentioned that in canoe-building a conventional division marks off the work of preparing food for the labourers from the actual technical processes of the task. The same holds for the erection of a major temple. The potential owners, even if themselves expert builders, are expected to refrain from any very active participation on the technical side. This is justified by the Tikopia themselves on the ground of efficiency, though it would seem that there is operating here a principle of social linkage such as is to be seen in cases of ceremonial exchange, when it is regarded as proper that the goods should be transferred between distant, rather than close, kinsfolk, and people of different villages and districts rather than those in the same units. But *prima facie* it would appear to be true that the best work can be done by craftsmen whose attention is not likely to be diverted by food problems. The Tikopia say of canoe-building : " Our body of kinsfolk do not hew at the vessel ; we sit merely to prepare the food." This is borne out by the fact that in building an ordinary dwelling house, which does not demand such care and precision, no experts are invited if the owner himself is at all competent, but he erects it with assistance from his kinsfolk and neighbours (see Case C).

Ritual conventions are also extremely important in production. In some cases they dictate its ends as when flying fish and sharks must be caught for the performance of seasonal canoe rites, taro and coco-nuts must be secured for a specific ceremony to the god of the Taumako clan, or the cultivation of the yam must be pursued as a principal theme in the Work of the Gods. Failure to carry on production and obtain the appropriate quantity of foodstuffs is visited, according to native ideas, by misfortune, sickness, or death. Here an elaborate set of myths about the power of the gods, with complementary tales about the way in which they have treated human beings, act as a powerful sanction. Ritual enters again as a limiting factor in production. Sex taboos restrict the entry of women into certain crafts or assign to them specific tasks ; other taboos regulate the behaviour of individuals

while they are actually engaged in the work. The bodily movements of bonito fishermen, for instance, are restrained in detail
when they are on the fishing grounds by a series of rules which
have their sanction in religious beliefs and mythology. The
participation of workers in the cultivation of the sacred yam,
again, is most rigidly defined ; for some stages of the work they
must arrive at the plantation by sunrise and they may not talk
loudly, joke, or shout.

An instance of the barriers which such ritual applies to
production is given by the case of Pa Tauraro (of Taumako clan),
invited to go over to Faea and assist with the hewing out of a
canoe. He refused to go for a few days, since, he said, the yam
seed of the Ariki Kafika was still lying out of the ground, and it
was taboo for him to participate in this noisy task. If he went the
chief would think he were making sport (*fai takaro*) with the yam
rites.

Ritual regulations, again, dictate the organization of certain
important tasks such as the building of sacred canoes and the
repair of clan temples. Thus when the time comes for rebuilding
the temple Kafika all the clans assemble, and while the people
of Kafika and Faŋarere collect and prepare food, those of Tafua
and Taumako do the work, dividing between them by traditional
rule the lashing of the great ridge-pole to the main centre posts.

## ATTITUDES TO WORK

The social attitude to work itself is also a basic element
in the ideology of production. The Tikopia distinguish
linguistically as we do mere activity from purposeful economic
activity. The native term *fekau*, corresponding to our term
" work ", has attached to it a definite moral imperative. By this
I do not mean that work for its own sake is exalted as an ideal
by the Tikopia, but that every person in the community is
expected to show a normal measure of application. This attitude
is maintained by encouraging statements, often of a sententious
kind, exchanged between the workers, by various premial
sanctions, and by disapprobation of slackness or laziness.

Various factors of a positive order relate to an ideal of productive efficiency. The Tikopia are quite conscious that a good
output of work depends upon making an early start. It is said :
" The expert canoe-builder wakes in the night." In the early

stages of the work, before the hull has been properly shaped, the main body of workers expect to hear the thud of his adze on the wood before they arrive on the scene. Later when " the body of the canoe has fallen ", when the hull has taken shape, the stringency of this rule is somewhat relaxed and the expert arrives on the scene when the day has properly dawned.

Comment by other people may be scathing when this convention of an early start is not observed. When the net of the Ariki Kafika was being made I heard the Ariki Taumako and Pa Vainunu discussing it. The former asked when it was started ; with scorn the latter, who had been one of the participants in the work, said : " Not till midday," and went on to criticize the slackness of the proceedings. On another occasion I intended to be present at a ceremony of the Kafika people in their village about half a mile from where I lived. My neighbour, Pae Sao, remarked that I need not hurry. " The oven of some people is ready quickly, but not so that village ! It will be dark before they make the kava."

The Tikopia frequently urge haste upon their fellow workers, though such injunctions are often disregarded. Usually they consist of phrases of the " hurry up " variety, but occasionally take on a more formal character. I heard such an expression during the sacred work of Somosomo. " Slope the back of your head, and let your forehead appear," was what one man called out to another going on an errand. The idea is of a person bent forward in haste as he leaves, and his forehead seen as he quickly returns. Unlike the Maori,[1] the Samoans, the Hawaiians, and many other Polynesians, the Tikopia have hardly anything that can be technically called a proverb. A few formal expressions of this kind were the nearest approximation to proverbs that I heard.[2] Another similar expression is " Paddle away, paddle hither ; the bird is going to be netted ". This was explained as " hurry up and return ; we are going to begin eating ". This expression is often used in short form to hasten a person. " Paddle away, paddle hither."

There is also a group of terms relating to men who are industrious, properly instructed, or technically expert. The use of any one of them in reference to a man is a sign of praise in the

[1] For the use of proverbs in Maori industry see my " Proverbs in Native Life ", *Folklore*, xxxvii, 1926, 138–142.

[2] The phrase " *manu kavea i te rakau*, bird carried away on the timber " is used to refer to a visitor who will soon depart—by ship, of course.

moral category of what is " good ". There are terms also for inefficient workers, as *te seva*, a bungler, for a man who is unskilful in the use of the paddle or the flying-fish net.

Men who are generally recognized as appropriately described by such terms sometimes bring such recognition to public expression by composing dance songs, lauding their own virtues and achievements. Such songs are received by the community at large as appropriate compositions and come into general currency through being chanted by groups of people while dancing. A man who is recognized by his fellows as inefficient would have to face ridicule if he ventured to extol himself in this way and I have no record of such songs by economic nonentities.

An example of such a song may be given. It was composed by Pa Rarovi in praise of his own hard work. In a time of famine his children and his brother were still young, and he alone supported them all. I give here the translation only :—

> " I died from my preparing of food like an orphan.
> My orchard consisted of my hands.
> I prepared my food, alone in the work.
>
> I look and look at them
> I envy the numerous hands
> Helping in the work."

The term " died " in the first line is a common native exaggeration equivalent to our own expression " it was a killing piece of work ". The second line means that the supply of food for the speaker and family depended only upon his own manual labour. The term " orchard " is used metaphorically by the Tikopia for a food source in general ; this man had of course ordinary orchards and taro gardens to use.

There are not so many songs in praise of hard work as for prowess in fishing and other activities. I was told : " People are ashamed to compose songs to their own industry. It would be held that they wanted to boast of their industry, it would be held that they wanted to rejoice in it." Special skill rather than hard work as such gives a title to assertion of personal pride. But the reputation for industry is a useful one.

To be known as an expert or an industrious man has the advantage for a bachelor of helping him to secure in marriage a woman whom he desires. The provision of an adequate food supply for the rest of her life is an important consideration to a

Tikopia woman and it is specifically stated that women prefer to marry such men. In one case a woman, Nau Vaṇatau, still living, has composed a song of praise to her husband, who is a recognized canoe-builder, mentioning the amount of goods that has flowed into their household through his labour. The song is as follows :—

> " Friend ! walk in the doings of men.
> You are the expert who brought me property,
> Valuable property, to me a commoner.
> You brought me food
> From which I eat, with my people.
>
> I rejoice in the *maru* here,
> The wealthy man standing fixedly.
> When he is ended, and disappears, I shall be orphaned,
> With my flower ornaments.
>
> *Iei !* stand hither together
> With your flower ornaments ;
> Grasping together in the hewing of canoes,
> Going walking about."

The first stanza lauds her husband for his craftsmanship and the recompense from which his wife and her kinsfolk benefit. The second stanza expresses appreciation of his wealth, which gives stability to her and her children, and laments the poverty that will follow his death. This is a poetic exaggeration, frequent in Tikopia songs. The " flower ornaments " are their children. The third stanza rejoices in the fact that these children (who are grown-up sons) assist their father in his work, going throughout the island and building canoes.

The " doings of men " referred to in the first line are the male crafts—as seamanship, fishing, and woodwork—in which Pa Vaṇatau is notably skilled. As the brother of the late chief of Taumako and father's brother of the present chief he is a *maru*, an executive official of standing. The reference in the first and last lines of the song to " walking about " implies that the services of the expert are in great demand ; he is not merely recruited for work in his own village.

The use of the neutral term of address, *Soa !* Friend ! by the wife to her husband indicates that the song is of the type known as *soa*, funeral dirges chanted by a spouse and his or her kin over the body of the deceased partner. As such this song will appear at Pa Vaṇatau's funeral and will proclaim his merits to the assembled crowd. Such songs must have some economically stimulating effect upon the young people who participate in the funerals.

There is not the same range of special terms of approval for women as for men, but it is stated that men desire as wives women who are skilled in plaiting and other crafts. " The desire of a man is a woman who is industrious, industrious in work, and a woman who is skilled in the plaiting of bed mats—that is the woman, a woman who knows all minds, all practices of this land." There are of course other factors which are involved in the choice of a wife, such as pleasantness of feature, sexual desirability, etc. Indeed the concept of industry as a desirable quality in the choice of a wife seems to be more articulate among the older and more responsible members of the community than among the young men actually seeking wives.[1] Young men object to women who are ugly, whose bodies are disfigured by ringworm, or who are known to be of loose morals, and it is said that a man will even spit in the face of such a woman who pursues him. While I did not hear of a young man objecting to marrying a woman on the ground that she was lazy or unskilled in feminine crafts, I did hear objections raised against young women who had been too free with their favours, " embraced by many men." One reason for this may be that a certain level of technical proficiency is reached by every girl, who cannot escape learning the elements of plaiting, garden work, bark-cloth making and cooking, and that interest by men in the quality of these achievements tends to come only later when a man is settled down in his own household.

As against the positive convention that work in progress should be carried through, are certain recognized factors of limitation. The need for periodic rest is admitted and has its linguistic expression in the term *manava*, which generally means breath, but in this economic context can be translated colloquially as " a breather ". Members of a working party appeal for a *manava* to their host or leader and the justification for such an appeal is usually admitted. At such a time the milk of fresh coco-nuts is often drunk, betel chewed, or tobacco smoked, the materials being provided by the host. On the other hand the host himself or another member of the working party often urges a rest upon the workers. When a net of the Ariki Taumako was being made everyone worked at high speed. Two of the younger men in

[1] *We, The Tikopia*, 538.

particular worked on in rivalry, each looking from time to time to see the progress that the other had made. Each man normally does an hour or so at the net before being relieved. When told to stop and eat they took no notice and continued. Someone said to them, " Brothers-in-law, stop." Then one of the other people went forward and took the needle from one of the net-makers with the words, " Come you and rest hither " (au ke o manava mai). Then he yielded.

The rest-periods which frequently occur during funerals and other ceremonies are often used for the plaiting of sinnet for fish-lines or water-bottle slings, the preparation of coco-nuts for water-bottles, the carving of head-rests, the dressing of timber for shelves. But there is no systematic utilization of spare time, and in particular, considering the amount of sinnet needed for ceremonial exchanges, it is curious that Tikopia men do not make it more regularly at such times.

Against the urgency of work is set also the need for sleep. Tikopia are used to sleeping at odd hours during the day and have not that traditional association of daylight with working period and night with sleep period which obtains in European communities. Their attitude towards sleep is governed greatly by their night fishing. Men who go out in the canoes may get a lot of sleep by the me afiafi, the evening sleep, but some go for several nights without sleeping. " When torchlight fishing has struck in this land, men do not sleep." A man may spend the night fishing, come in with his canoe in the morning, go off to the garden, work all day, and go out fishing again that night. This may go on, it is said, for three, four, or five nights. Then he feels a constriction above his eyes, a headache, and a great desire for sleep. It was explained by one man : " The desire for sleep has dwelt there " —pointing to his eyebrow. The man may say : " My eyes indeed, they are aching dreadfully." " Aching from what ? " someone may reply. " I don't know." " Did you sleep last night ? " " I did not sleep last night, and the night before I did not sleep ; the torchlight fishing has struck." But though they admit the value of sleep after prolonged activity the Tikopia do not regard it as entitled to any great consideration. They have no compunction about waking a man, however tired (or sick) he may be, to take food or to talk. Why should they, when there is no specially allotted time for sleep, and one can always drop off again ? The practice is to lie down and cover oneself up because one is sleepy and not because it is time to go to bed. The ease with which these natives can go without what we would consider to be a good night's rest is to be explained largely by their habit of dropping off to sleep intermittently as occasion offers, while waiting for the ovens to be ready, or for ceremonies to be performed. This ability to snatch short periods of sleep may mean that the natives' statements of going sleepless for three, four, five nights are not to be regarded literally.

Weather affects the efficiency of work, as when taro ground is difficult to dig after a drought or when bark-cloth is beaten on sunny days which dry it easily. Rain tends to diminish the amount of work done. Generally speaking the Tikopia are very susceptible to rain. When the day is thoroughly wet most people do not stir out of their houses. Only when there is no food at home, or the claims of ritual have to be met do people go out, carrying over their heads leaves of banana or of the umbrella palm.

On the other hand the people do not allow their dislike of bad weather to prevent them from accomplishing an important task. If a man desires to go on a fishing expedition or if the claims of ritual are to the forefront as in turmeric making (which takes place in a season of rain and wind) then no fuss is made. Moreover, in fishing out on the reef, or hauling in a canoe, objection is rarely raised to getting the body and clothing wet, though the garment is always changed for a dry one on shore. When there is a sudden tropical shower in the warmer monsoon season children rush out, dance up and down naked in the rain, make puddles with their feet, and enjoy it thoroughly.

The claims of weariness are also given some place in regard to compulsion to work. The usual question addressed to a man whom one wants to make up a fishing crew is " Are you *maroro* ? " a term covering a range of ideas from physical health to freshness and willingness. It corresponds roughly to our concept of " being fit ". The reverse of this takes in such terms as *ŋaeŋae* meaning sick, and the obviously related term *fakaŋaeŋae*, meaning tired and unwilling. The answer to the inquirer of " I am not *maroro* " or " I am *fakaŋaeŋae* " is frequently sufficient excuse for non-participation.

It is of course a matter of opinion in many cases as to whether refusal to work is due to physical weariness or mental distaste. In this latter sphere there is a specific term *kea* used for a lazy

person. It is definitely a term of disapproval and can be used as
a spur when people are engaged in work together. Expressions
such as these can be addressed to a man who is not doing a fair
share. " You there, are you merely bone-lazy ? "  " The lazy
one ! He does not cope with the work."  " The lazy one ! He
does not know the planting of food." Such expressions are called
*taraŋa fakaoso*, " speech causing to rush on." They are intended
as a verbal drive or stimulus, not an insult. They come in the
category of " good speech " (*taraŋa laui*), that is, they may be
used between kin who are in a relationship of constraint such as
father and son, or brothers-in-law. Lazy people are not reproached
by other folk in general, but only by fairly close relatives. Thus
during a kava rite Pa Fenuatara carried round areca nut and
coco-nuts. He then remarked to his brother Pa Taramoa, " Why
don't you do something ? You are sitting there like one who is
merely looking on at the kava." No reply was made at the time
but soon after Pa Taramoa was to be seen washing out a wooden
bowl. A chief does not normally rebuke a member of his clan for
laziness. The reason is given as being " because of his reputation
in the land ", meaning that the scoldings of the chief are reserved
for those occasions when he is really angry, lest they lose their
effect. It is said that the shame at being called lazy is not great.
" The person is ashamed, but it is all right ; he laughs. If he is
annoyed he is annoyed, but if he laughs, he laughs. He wants
to laugh at what one has said."

Frequently the spur is applied without actually calling a
man lazy. People say to him " Hi ! What are you sitting there
for ? Why don't you go and work ? If you sit there, what will
there be for you to eat ? " Or again, " He there, why does he sit ?
Why does he not come and do some work for himself ? " A kinsman may say to him, " You, why not come that we two may go
to work ? " The man replies, " O, I do not want to go and work."
The other retorts, " There you are, you will keep on sitting there
and what will you eat ? Now, are you going to commit suicide ?
What are you ? A spirit that you will sit there and not eat ?
We men—it is well for us to be industrious, to rush off to the
middle of the woods to plant food for ourselves that there may
be plenty. If you keep on sitting there you will go and steal·
It is not good." He may add " you who are lazing there, aren't
you a man with children ? What will your children be fed on ?
Will you go and steal to feed your children ? " The appeal to

theft brings in a whole range of moral concepts and that to children invokes the family sentiment which is held to be basic in the Tikopia kinship structure. I have never heard any questioning of the validity of the concepts embodied in both these categories. The sanction here is the ridicule and disapprobation of kinsfolk and neighbours, rather than the fear of actually going foodless.

Statements on the value of enlisting active workers to help are easily obtained. Pa Raŋifuri said, " If you see people who are industrious, carry them off ; but if you see a lazy person, you do not want him." And again, " Our own desire is only for the industrious man, because the lazy one simply eats ; he will come merely to eat from one." The reference here is to the custom of enlisting labour in work and of rewarding the labourer with food, giving thus a rough balance of work obtained with expenditure. The Ariki Taumako said to me, " If I see a man who is a hard worker, I say to him ' Friend, we will go and work '. But if I see a man who is lazy, I don't want him." In further illustration Pa Raŋifuri gave me a sample of the kind of dialogue that sometimes takes place between a man for whom a group of people are working and members of the party. A lazy man in the party seeing the host departed says, " What's the use of rushing to die of work ; let us work temperately and have a breather." But the host on his return may say, " Now you are lazy. You are not skilled in the work to plant food properly to be plentiful for us."[1] One of the group answers, " O, friend, great is the work ; the sun still stands above. Let us rest first." The host replies, " O, do not rest friends ; the sun will sink, plant properly some food for us that it may be plentiful." Or he may spur them on further by adding, " You, friends, exercise your skill on my work to do it well."

When scolding is used in the attempt to speed up work it follows a conventional form ; it is sententious, and is expected to be received equably. The issue is in practice largely expletive and though a flagging or lazy person is kept at work by the verbal stimulus his rate of work is not necessarily increased thereby.

[1] The expression " for us " is worth noting here, since it is very common in Tikopia discussions about work and property. It does not mean full joint ownership, but is a verbal socialization of individual rights. It implies, however, a code of etiquette and usages of reciprocity in drawing upon other people's resources. (See Chapter VII.)

The situation is complicated by the Tikopia code of etiquette. When a party of people works for a man, relations between them are governed by rules of courtesy in addition to the economic relationships involved. As an example may be cited the grating of taro and bananas for a feast. It is the custom as each hundred leaf packets of grated material are prepared for the workers to give a *forua*, a loud whoop of " *Iefu !* " This announces to the assembled crowd that the " century " has been reached, and is a token of their industry and speed. But it is more. " The *forua*, its thought is, that the man who is giving the feast may have a good face ; his feast is a large one." The expression " good face " (*matamata laui*) is used in many other situations ; it refers to the preservation of *amour propre*, the inducing of an agreeable state of mind. And acts of politeness are frequently done in order to induce this state.

On the other hand, the entrepreneur is by custom expected to thank the workers for their services and praise them. In canoe-building this expression has a set form, and embodies the anxieties of the canoe-owner as well. It is said, " The man who owns the canoe comes to give thanks to the experts ; he comes to laud his canoe and the experts." When he comes on the scene at some stage of the hewing out of the hull he recites formally :—

> " Thanks ! Thanks ! expert builders, expert builders.
> Expert cutting, expert cutting,
> Cut, adze ; cut, adze.
> Cut, but in leisurely fashion.
> I eat ten times your excrement.
> Do your work quietly.
> Though you desire food, yet do quietly your work.
> Bind your loins with your sinnet belts ;
> Wake, and do your work."

This recital contains three elements of the owner's attitude— his formal acknowledgment of the service being done ; his injunction to the builders to work ; and his wish that the work shall be done carefully, without haste. The expressed " eating of excrement " is a metaphorical abasement known as the *oriori*, used also in giving thanks for a feast (see p. 224) and in invocations to ancestors and gods. At the end of the recital the builders politely reply " *Tapuraia* ", a formal acknowledgment in particular of the *oriori*.

The *fakaaueaue*, the " giving of thanks " as it is termed,

is often not recited in full, but the owner contents himself with the opening phrases " *Aue ! Aue ! tai tufuŋa, tai tufuŋa* ".

Allowance is also made in the Tikopia economic scheme for the desire for recreation. There is a convention that the appropriate time for dancing and games is at night, and in the ordinary way only children play during the day time. Periodically, however, there are specific dance festivals and dart match competitions, and it is expected that large numbers of people of both sexes and all ages will attend. The affair is not purely on a voluntary basis since clan and district structure and often ritual affiliations are the basis of the organization, and people attend in response to these obligations. The preparation of food which is consumed and frequently exchanged formally at these gatherings is a definite task. In a sense then the dance festival or the dart match is an economic activity affecting productive organization. On the other hand these periodic gatherings interspersed at times when the pressure of seasonal work is at a minimum undoubtedly have an important effect in providing an outlet for recreational interests and so preventing them from impinging too strongly on the working life.

We have now to mention a group of factors which, though not expressed in such clearly defined concepts, nor the object of the same kind of moral opinions, have some power as stimuli to work.

One of these is the interest in technique and in the work of a man's hands. I cannot be dogmatic on this psychological point but from observation of the activity of such men as Pa Tarikitoŋa and Fakasiŋetevasa in woodwork, the Ariki Taumako in setting his nets in the lake, Seremata in his sea-fishing, and the Ariki Tafua in the making of turmeric, I received the impression that they took much more than a perfunctory interest in the actual operations involved and in their handling of tools and material, as distinct from the end which they wished to attain. As a further instance may be mentioned the carving done for me by Pa Fenuatara as a parting gift. He explained that it was his first piece of wood-carving and I could see from the interest he took in it that he wanted to see what he could do. The result was quite effective.

On the other hand there does not seem to be much interest in the purely æsthetic side of work in Tikopia. Appliances are rough but serviceable, and, as mentioned in Chapter III, little time is spent on any fine elaborations. The æsthetic interests of the Tikopia appear rather in the preparation of their foods and the high degree of elaboration of the details of their ceremonial.

A factor of a positive kind in stimulating industry is the spirit of rivalry between individuals and between social groups. Individuals on their own behalf and as heads of their groups boast of the power of their respective gods, lay claims to greater antiquity of descent than others, compete against each other covertly in making cures for sickness or in producing conception in women. This emulation can also be a powerful factor in the economic sphere. Individuals, clans, districts strive to excel in flying-fish netting, in wood-working, in turmeric making, scoff at the pretensions of others in the same pursuits, and exaggerate their own achievements. Thus Pa Roŋonafa said of his fellow woodworkers of Raveŋa, " It is held that in this district there are the experts of chiefs, but that in Faea there are the common experts." By this he meant that the former were more proficient and were therefore more likely to be called upon by the chiefs, whereas the latter had talent of no outstanding order. Pa Fenuatara went fishing on the lake one night and caught a single *kiokio*. He asked the wife of a neighbour how many this man had taken. The wife answered, " Two, like yours." " Where are those he boasted about ? " exclaimed Pa Fenuatara in a slighting way. It is quite usual in comparing the haul of canoes for a man to say, " If such and such circumstances had not been the case, I should have made a great catch," taking for granted his own skill and attributing that of others to good fortune. On one occasion Pa Raŋifuri told me that he was ignorant of the " clamshell formula " used in shark-fishing But a few moments later he said, " I don't want to boast to you, but of the younger fishing experts the fish are greatest with me." And later he added that when he went fishing he made the *fakaariki* constantly, that is, sent large fish from his catch to all the chiefs, whereas other people did it only occasionally.

It is a commonplace that this attitude of rivalry and championing one's own claims to technical proficiency can be found among the artisans of a Western industrial system. From the comparative point of view what is interesting in the Tikopia expression of it is the absence of a convention of modesty. Boasting about proven ability is not subject to the same social criticism as in our society ; where the sensitiveness comes is in suspicion of display or boasting about wealth.

Another feature of Tikopia assertion of technical prowess which is in strong contrast to our own is the expression of it in song. An expert fisherman, for example, may compose a dance-song about his own achievements, and this, so far from being looked upon with scorn by people at large, is seized upon and chanted in chorus on public occasions. As such, it tends to lose its personal character and become merely a vehicle for rhythm. I give one example here in translation of a song composed by the grandfather of the Ariki Kafika, a noted sea-expert and fisherman. It is composed in commemoration of his prowess as a " man of bonito ".[1]

> " My rod stands in the channel,
> Stands twice, four times in the channel.
>
> The crowd of people rushed to see
> The bonito O ! that I hooked.
> The *varu* O ! that I carried to shore."

To some extent this spirit of emulation rests content with mere words, with building up an imaginative superior edifice on the basis of standard performance. Claims to superiority sometimes lead to no special effort to attain it ; but in many cases such as in the seasonal shark fishing or the attempts by a canoe crew to attain the premial number of 100 flying-fish in a night rivalry undoubtedly provides a spur. Again, to take an individual case, the serious attempts of Pa Fenuatara to gain a mastery of a number of technical processes were undoubtedly motivated to some extent by his high personal pride which would not allow him to acknowledge inferiority to the craftsmen of Taumako. This was evident from his frequent comparisons of his work with theirs. On the other hand when it was a question of district comparisons he championed the abilities of the Taumako men against those of the people of Faea.[2]

This jealousy between craftsmen commonly takes the form of belittling other people's work, and assertion of their ignorance of technical detail and ritual knowledge. It receives most frequent expression not in slighting statements about a particular man,

---

[1] For similar songs of prowess in dart-throwing see " A Dart-match in Tikopia ", *Oceania*, i, 1930.
[2] Cf. *We, The Tikopia*, 72–5.

but in assertions of the speaker's own competency contrasted with the lack of it by " the crowd ", " other persons ", or " the land as a whole ". He is thus able to vaunt his own pride at a minimum cost in social repercussions. Even when the rivalry has received specific formulation, as between the chiefly families of Taumako and Tafua, it can be submerged by conventional modes of behaviour. Thus the sacred canoe of the Ariki Taumako, built by men of the Tafua family, failed to reach the standard catch of 100 flying-fish one season. It was taken round to Faea that its builders might test it out in fishing—and was soon returned, having attained the goal. Such invitations to rival craftsmen are always issued and received with great politeness.

As far as I know, there is no term in Tikopia for " rivalry " in general, though there is an expression *tautau ka*, which might be translated as " equally burning ", which signifies immediate competition, as in a race, in grating taro, in hauling in fish, or in net making.

Of a negative order, tending to mar productive efficiency, are such factors as the fear of sorcery, or the reaction to an insult. Here are two examples of the former. When the Ariki Tafua began to resort to an orchard of some of his clansfolk on Mauŋa Faea, they deserted it because they were afraid that if they persisted in taking food from it he would bewitch them. Again, when Pa Raŋimaseke saw the Ariki Tafua standing in a swamp on the boundary of his Tafua lands and those of Kafika, and heard him repeating words which he thought were those of sorcery he immediately left his work, went home, and performed a rite to avert any evil consequences. Here a whole set of ideas about the existence of evil formulae, the powers of men of rank to use them, and the ill effects that follow from their use, can serve as inhibiting factors to economic activity.

If a man feels that he has been insulted then he may refuse to work and retire to his house to brood. On one occasion Pa Fenuatara took no part in the preparation of a marriage feast because, so I was told by others present, although he was the principal man of rank among the cooks, they had not waited for him to arrive before lighting the oven. Again, Pa Raŋifuri went to borrow an axe from his father the Ariki Tafua in order that he and his wife might cut down trees for bark-cloth, but, offended at something his father said, he retired to his house in a very emotional state. The better part of the day was spent in resolving the difference between them and Pa Raŋifuri did not begin the task until the following day. The same point is illustrated in Chapter VI, in the incident of the Ariki Taumako retiring in anger because of an insulting protest against work he proposed to supervise.

### EFFICIENCY OF THE TIKOPIA LABOUR ORGANIZATION

As a conclusion to this lengthy Chapter some of the general features of the Tikopia labour situation may be summed up, with particular reference to the question of the efficiency of the organization in attaining the ends desired. I am aware that these generalizations about efficiency must be tentative, especially in the absence of detailed comparative material from other primitive societies, but they may be useful as suggestions for further investigation.

I have shown that labour in Tikopia is on the whole socially controlled. For nearly all individuals mobility of occupation is high, in that a person can turn easily from one type of activity to another—from agriculture to fishing, house-building, cooking, plaiting sinnet cord, or helping in the making of a net or a canoe. Each day a choice of such employments is open to every worker. His decision between them is determined in part by the comparative yield which they offer, but in part also by the wants of the household of which he is a member, by the traditional dictates of seasonal occupations, by the special claims of ritual, or by other social obligations. Greater specialization of individuals in particular crafts would probably mean more effective utilization of comparative skill, and of the variety of natural resources ; but on the other hand the existing system of mobility allows of easier conformity to changes in weather conditions, and to the seasonal variations in resources, and also by allowing the required labour to be injected into any undertaking with facility, makes for a more efficient system of total co-operation. Decisions as to the application of one's labour to one undertaking as against another are made by the individual, but in a sense the traditional common sanctions provide a kind of " final organizer ", though the operation of these sanctions is not automatic.

For single undertakings involving co-operation the principle of scarcity of labour operates, in that anyone wishing to command the services of others cannot rely without question on getting a full complement of workers for his task. Again, there is a relative scarcity of specialists in some crafts, particularly woodwork. To some extent the higher payment given to these specialists, contrasted with that given to the comparatively unspecialized workers engaged, is a measure of this relative scarcity, and acts as a limiting factor in the effective demand for their services. But with them, as with those of recognized less proficiency, the system is essentially one of *diffuse reward*, not to be calculated solely in terms of the immediate material return. Here the native theory of social obligation acts as a mechanism promoting the efficiency of the work.

Moreover, the mobility between the functions of individuals in the productive process is also high, in that there is no entrepreneur class solely and consistently occupied in initiating undertakings, organizing them, and taking the risks and concomitant profits of production. One day a man may be a worker for someone else, the next he may be employing his erstwhile host at some other task, or even one of the same kind. Hence there is no deepseated clash of interests between " workers " as a whole and " employers " as a whole ; such clashes as occur can be but temporary. There are no strikes of labour in Tikopia.[1] There may be failure of workers to appear. But this is regarded not as a breach of economic contract, but of social contract. Labour for others is essentially a social service, and work as a whole is explicitly given a socialized character. Moral imperatives, dictated by the traditionally approved canons of the society, play a large part in both the qualitative and the quantitative aspects of labour.

This also affects the system of reward (see Chapter VIII). The absence of a cash-nexus and a price system of reward does prevent an entrepreneur from gauging very accurately the relation of his outgoings to the final product of the work, and robs him also of one direct control over the labour supply. Threatened loss of wages is not an effective medium in Tikopia for governing the actions of potential participants in work ; and labour that appears superfluous cannot be simply turned away with lessened reward. On the other hand, the system, by calling on other

---

[1] In Samoa such strikes do sometimes occur, when house-builders are not supplied with food on what they consider an adequate scale. See P. H. Buck, *Samoan Material Culture*, 89.

sanctions than that of money reward, does manage to secure effective production, makes for the provision of at least a minimum labour supply, and has the advantage of not imposing great strain either on the physiological and psychological capacity of the workers, or on the relations between them and the owner of the goods produced.

## CHAPTER V

# RITUAL IN PRODUCTIVE ACTIVITY

## THE GENERAL PROBLEM OF RITUAL AND ECONOMICS

ONE of the characteristic features of a primitive economic system is the close association between technical processes and ritual activity. Without attempting to give any exact definition of what is meant by ritual it may be described roughly as activity following a set form and pursued for a definite purpose but appearing to the external investigator to lead *in itself* to no demonstrably practical results for the attainment of that end. A distinction is frequently drawn between those set forms of procedure which are not bound up with ideas of the supernatural —of a magical or religious nature—and are commonly termed ceremonial, and those which are, for which the term ritual is often reserved. Since it is often difficult to decide in practice at what point the association with magic or religion stops, and since there is no general agreement even about the precise connotation of these two terms, the distinction between ritual and ceremonial can be but a rough working hypothesis. Broadly speaking, in a society such as Tikopia, one can distinguish those types of ritual practice which are not governed by express beliefs in the participation of spiritual beings in the activity—such as the transfer of goods at initiation or marriage—from those so governed—as in fishing, agriculture or canoe-building—where invocation of such a being is a part of the practice.

I propose to discuss in this Chapter practices of this latter type. On the whole they can be easily distinguished from rules of technical procedure, where a sequence of activities is followed leading demonstrably from our point of view to the attainment of the practical end desired.

Most accounts of ritual in relation to primitive economics emphasize, often in great detail, the close connection which is manifest between them in practical activity. But the economic problem so raised is frequently not faced ; there is little systematic attempt to analyse the effects of the performance of the ritual upon the organization of the work, and upon the volume of production. Occasionally a writer is so impressed by the interpenetration of ritual and economic activity that like Hocart he maintains that to single out the economic sphere for special treatment is a fallacy. A more positive contribution has been made by showing that in a normally functioning native society the ritual system associated with the economic system provides a stimulus to this. The most elaborate and systematic examination of the relation of ritual to economic production has been made by Malinowski as part of his general analysis of magic.[1]

The principal problems which he has formulated and considered from his Trobriand data are :—At what point does magic enter the productive field ? What is its essential and fundamental feature ? What is its role in the productive process ?

In the first place Malinowski has drawn attention to the distinction between " independent " and " systematic " magical rites and formulae, the former being used as a free individual act, whenever the need arises, the latter consisting of a connected and consecutive body of spells and concomitant performances, each of which can only be performed in sequence with the others.[2] He has shown clearly how the performance of magic rites of this " systematic " type in particular, and the belief in their power, tend to promote the systematization of the purely economic effort of the natives, and further their productive organization. Malinowski has drawn attention also to the fact that the point at which magic enters the productive field is on the whole that where human knowledge is least, and consequently where the liability to failure in the activity is greatest. The less the possibility of human calculation, the greater the tendency to rely on extra-human factors. Magic then does not replace technique and knowledge, but has the function of giving confidence to the worker, of acting as a supplementary sanction for the performance of the task. As such, it contributes towards economic efficiency.

The central problem of this Chapter is to a large extent a re-examination of Malinowski's generalizations, framed primarily

---

[1] See his " Economic Aspect of the Intichiuma Ceremonies," *Festskrift Tillägnad Edvard Westermarck*, 1912, 81–108 ; " The Primitive Economics of the Trobrianders," *Economic Journal*, Mar., 1921, 1–16 ; *Argonauts of the Western Pacific*, 1922, 392–427 ; *Coral Gardens and Their Magic*, 1935, i, 55–289.

[2] *Argonauts of the Western Pacific*, 412–13.

from Trobriand material, in terms of the data from Tikopia.[1]
Considering the totality of the activity expended by the Tikopia
in any undertaking, to what extent do their ritual performances
affect their economic efficiency ?    How far may the ritual be
regarded as part of the technique of production ?    What is its
effect on the individual worker ; and on the organization of the
activity ?    To what extent does it influence the rate and manner
of carrying out the work ?    And what result, if any, does it have
on the yield from the act of production ?

## SOME GENERAL PROPOSITIONS FOR TIKOPIA

Analysis of the relation of ritual to technology and economics
could be made over a wide range of Tikopia activities.  Not only
do the types of ritual tend to vary according to the nature of the
situation in which they are performed—whether raising crops,
securing fish, extraction of sago and turmeric, or manufacture of
canoes and other goods—but other cross-classifications can be
made.  Tikopia ritual with an economic bias can be divided on
the basis of intent into four categories :  (a) ritual of production
of goods ;  (b) ritual of general conservation or increase of
resources ;  (c) ritual of specific protection of resources ;  (d)
ritual of destruction of resources.  Then again, one may speak
of the sub-categories of ritual of immediate production, and ritual
of deferred production.  It is not always easy to classify any
particular ritual act under one or other of these heads, since sometimes a dual intent is manifest in the one rite.  But, broadly
speaking, under (a) may be classified such rites as those performed
for fishing, for the making of a net or canoe, or for the extraction
of turmeric ;  under (b) those which are directed to maintain the
fertility of the sago palm, or the desired equilibrium of rain and
fine weather, under (c) those designed to protect taro land from
planting or coco-nuts and other crops from untimely use or theft ;
and under (d) rites intended to destroy the crops of others or
nullify the results of their labour.  The first two categories are
not differentiated as such by the Tikopia—their rites are described
either by individual names or by some qualification of the general
term *tarotaro*, which means primarily a ritual formula.    They
will be the subject of examination in this Chapter.  Rites of type

---

[1] A similar examination of Maori material has been given in Ch. VII of my
*Primitive Economics of the New Zealand Maori ;*  see also my article on " Magic "
in *Encyclopædia Britannica*, 14th ed.

(c) are mainly of the order of *tapu* and their economic effects are examined in the following Chapter. Rites of type (d), known to the Tikopia as *tautuku*, are discussed in this book only incidentally.

The point of this classification is to split up the problem of ritual in relation to economics, and to allow it to be seen that whereas in one type of ritual, that of protection, the result intended and the actual result practically coincide, in the ritual of production and conservation they diverge widely. Moreover it will show that the economic function of all ritual practices ostensibly connected with production is not necessarily identical.

In a general sense, however, all economic ritual in Tikopia helps in the perpetuation of the system of production and distribution in vogue in the society, and in particular, in the maintenance of the economic position of people of rank. Ritual is essentially a conservative force. The titular ownership of lands, springs of water, and canoes by the chiefs ; the assistance that is given to them in many of their undertakings ; the gifts of food brought to them, hang upon the belief of all the members of the community that the chiefs are the representatives of the gods and ancestors in whose power the fertility and efficient functioning of the system of production lie. These beliefs, in their turn, are sustained and expressed by the system of ritual practices. The same principles are responsible for the subordinate control exercised over production by the heads of the kinship groups known as " houses ", who have customary ritual functions to perform.

This maintenance of the economic position of the chiefs and men of rank by the ritual system in which they take a leading part has been demonstrated for primitive society as a whole by Paul Radin.[1] But he has distorted the situation by laying the primary emphasis on the element of exploitation. The maintenance of a social fabric does not necessarily mean this fabric is composed of a consistent set of relationships whereby the fruits of labour of one class are diverted to the use of another. " Exploitation " is a term usually given a moral connotation, and is best replaced by a more neutral set of expressions. The question for Tikopia may be put in such terms as : how far do the chiefs and other men of rank enjoy a higher standard of living than their fellows ; do they labour less and get more ; does their income received through the ritual system exceed their outgoings

[1] P. Radin, *Primitive Religion*, 1938.

under this system ? Or again, does the control which the ritual system places in their hands result in a higher level of consumption for them or simply in the power to direct production into channels which may seem to them most advisable ? These questions are taken up in some detail in Chapter VI. But a summary answer with regard to the ritual side of their functions can be given here. The performance of the great part of ritual practices with which they are traditionally vested, and which is not challenged by the commoners, and their clansfolk, does not give them an appreciably higher standard of living, nor allow them to accumulate large stocks of goods without the obligation of disbursing them again through similar channels. It does place in their hands the power to direct much production, and here the checks upon them are provided to a considerable extent by their individual conformity to a theory of responsibility and to the opinion of the body of the commoners. But even here they are not in a position of being able to turn resources to their own profit to any large degree ; they can hold back production much more than they can divert it to their own ends. In terms of income they do reap certain differential advantages. But here, too, they are bound to contribute something to the productive fund from which they receive these benefits, and not infrequently the heavier share of the burden of the supplies accumulated for the ritual falls upon them. In terms of labour performed, again, they cannot rest in idleness while others work. An interesting generalization by Viljoen for primitive society as a whole calls for comment here. He states " social and economic inequalities appear not so much in the form of differences in the standard of living as in the amount of work performed and the security enjoyed by the different classes." [1] In throwing the weight off the differential level of consumption this is a suggestive statement, and may well represent the situation in many primitive societies. But for Tikopia it is not true. The ritual system does not give chiefs and ritual elders relief from labour, but if anything calls for a greater amount of work to be performed by them. Not only do they work in the cultivations, go out fishing on the reef and engage in crafts like other men, but they have also to spend a considerable amount of time and energy on carrying out rites, sometimes alone, sometimes as the head of a group of

[1] S. Viljoen, *op. cit.*, 1936, 255.    Cf. Margaret Read, *op. cit.*, 20–1 for the Ngoni of Nyasaland.

other people. The physical labour demanded by this is not great, but the cumulative effect is considerable, and is regarded by the men themselves as work—rightly, as it seems to the observer. I judged that the Ariki Kafika was the hardest working man in the community. He was constantly in demand for ritual practices of one kind or another, he had to rise at a very early hour on many mornings, before most of the people were stirring, he had to leave off his conversation or resting to go and perform the kava, to be responsible for collecting others and to take charge of the organization of affairs, and to have quantities of food on hand from his own labour and that of his family to meet, almost daily, a diversity of ritual claims. In addition, in his own mind and those of the people at large, he had to bear the brunt of responsibility to the ancestors and gods in the event of failure to make the appropriate offerings. No wonder he said to me at one stage of the six weeks' cycle of ceremonies of the Work of the Gods : " Great is the work, friend ! "

## DIFFERENT FORMS OF RITUAL OF PRODUCTION

The ritual associated with production in Tikopia is not of a uniform character. Differences in structure occur, from the recital of simple formulae, with the technical procedure itself serving as the " rite " for transmitting the words to the object, to the performance of a complex set of acts involving libations of kava, dedication of working implements to spiritual beings and offering of food and bark-cloth to them, accompanied by long and involved formal utterances. The ritual of the first type is essentially individual in character and may be carried out by any person in the community. Such is the case when a man is planting banana suckers, or fishing with rod and line at the edge of the reef. Ritual of the second type demands the participation of a set of persons, though the core of the rite itself is controlled and manipulated by a single individual whose position is defined in terms of a wider social status. Such is the case in the extraction of sago, the making of a net, or the repair of a chief's canoe. A further difference lies in the fact that some of the rites, such as those for line-fishing or banana planting, are not integrated into a wider system of beliefs in spiritual beings, but are directed immediately on to the object concerned, the fish or the banana plants as the case may be ; while the majority of the rites, on the other hand, are appeals to spiritual beings, and are conceived in terms of an elaborate system of belief backed up by mythology.

Space does not allow of a detailed presentation of my material on all these forms of ritual. But I give one example, the ritual associated with the manufacture of an important instrument of production, a net, for which the technical processes involved have already been described in Chapter III, and the organization of labour given summarily in Chapter IV. The description of the repair of a sacred canoe in Chapter IV has also shown the type of ritual performed there, and the generalizations from these examples are brought into relation with those concerned with other forms of ritual at the end of this Chapter.

## Ritual of Net-making

The major problems to be considered may be again brought to mind : how far the ritual is believed by the Tikopia to be part of the technique of production ; what ends it is expected to achieve or facilitate ; at what points it enters into production ; and where, if at all, it affects the efficiency of the productive process.

The answer to the first three questions is fairly easy to give, and will be seen from the factual description. The answer to the last question is more complex and abstract. The reader may be disappointed to find how little relationship there seems to be between the rites of net-making and the economic organization, strictly conceived. It will be seen that whereas the performance of the ritual as a whole must have a positive effect in stimulating production, in much of its detail the ritual is quite neutral, and at some points is even of negative value. In brief, it is difficult to prove that the immediate efficiency of the work and the level of subsequent output gain to any appreciable degree from the rites.

Nets for setting in the lake or dragging on the reef are not owned by every household in the island, but mostly by the senior households of family groups, the junior members borrowing them when desired in accordance with the ordinary principles of Tikopia ownership. Such a net is a valued piece of property, analogous to a canoe. It is in fact referred to metaphorically as *te vaka o ŋa uta*, " the canoe of the shore (waters) "—" different from the canoe of the ocean which is drawn up in the canoe-shed here." People may say of a house where a net is being made, " the house there is building a canoe." In this connection " a new canoe " means a new net ; " an old canoe " an old net.

As with other instruments of production, the net of a chief is of special importance. It is not necessarily larger or better than that of a commoner, though the chief's greater command of resources does mean that this is sometimes so. But its significance is primarily ritual. It is known as a *mata kupeŋa*, an expression which may be translated as " foremost net ". I was told by Kafika people that in former times only the net of the Ariki Kafika was so described, and that the nets of the other chiefs were known by the names of their respective temples ; that of the Ariki Tafua being " the net in Motuapi ", and that of the Ariki Taumako being " the net in Raniniu ". Even these were titles and not simply descriptive terms. But nowadays the nets of the four chiefs all bear the title of " foremost net ". When such a net is taken out of the house for the first time a floor mat is laid down in the doorway as a mark of respect to it, just as such a mat is laid down for a person of rank to sit upon, or coco-nut fronds for a sacred canoe to rest upon.

Each net is dedicated to a spiritual being. " One man makes his net to his grandfather, another makes his net to his father," that is, places it in charge of this ancestor. But the net of a chief is placed in charge of a superior spirit, a deity of non-human origin. Thus the Ariki Taumako told me that his lake-net was consecrated to a deity called Manumanu-ki-raŋi, which is the Taumako title of the Eel-God Tuna. The son of the Ariki Kafika told me that his father's net was under the control of a group of deities, ŋa Ariki, " The Chiefs," and Te Atua Fafine, " The Female Deity," who are the prime gods of the Kafika clan. Hence the net is known as " the foremost net of the Chiefs ". Pa Raŋifuri told me that the net of his father, the Ariki Tafua, was dedicated first to Tufaretai, a deity of his mother's family, and spoken of as " the deity owning the net " (*te atua tau kupeŋa*), and then to Kere-tapuna, one of the many names borne by the Eel-God, who also " goes to it ". The net was also in charge of Foki-mai-Niteni, the chief's dead father. It is a Tikopia custom that chiefs and elders invoke in their list of gods the premier deity of the family from which their mother came, and this deity is often put in charge of the net, as in the case of the Ariki Tafua, and the Ariki Taumako. But the Ariki Kafika, though from the family of Taumako on his mother's side, does not follow this practice, since his net is ritually at least believed to be that of greatest antiquity, " the ancient foremost net," and so remains constantly in the charge of the premier deities of the Kafika clan itself. The net of each chief is the " foremost net " in his clan, not merely because of his position, but because it provides the link for all the nets of the people with the important deity or deities which control it and net-fishing as a whole. Thus when a commoner has caught an abundance of fish in his own net, controlled immediately by one of his own ancestors, he carries part of the catch to his chief, for the chief to recite a formula over it to the prime net deity, to ensure the net's future success.

This brief description of the beliefs connected with the ownership of nets shows a hierarchy of these instruments of production, linked with the hierarchy in the social structure and in the pantheon of spiritual beings. Resulting from this is also a grading in the extent and intensity of ritual practices. Nets of commoners are made with small ceremony, whereas those of chiefs are made to the accompaniment of a series of rites. The aim of these rites is to secure the efficiency and success of the net and not its technical perfection. For the strength of the cord, the uniformity and correct size of the mesh, and the tightness of the knots reliance is placed upon purely technical skill ; it is for the presence of fish in the net that the action of the ancestors and deities is invoked and the ritual performed.

The initial rite is performed after the first few meshes of the net have been run. As the craftsman bends over the work the chief recites a formula :—

> " Be netted with efficacy thy foremost net, Sea-expert chief.
> Thy foremost net which is being begun on this day
> Be firm thou in thy sea-expertise
> Towards thy canoe of the shore (waters).
> Light be the eyes of the fish to thy foremost net."

The term translated as " with efficacy " is the word *manu*, conveying the idea of success and a proper yield. The " sea-expert chief " is the principal net-deity, who performs other marine functions. The expression " light be the eyes of the fish " is an appeal for them to be attracted by the net, on analogy with the way in which men's eyes are caught by a light.

Formula and offering usually go together in Tikopia. After a time a bunch of green coco-nuts is brought in, and some cooked food. From these a libation is poured and token offerings made, with a recital of similar phrases as above.  If the chief so decides, the ritual may be made more elaborate by the performance of the kava ceremony.

The final rite takes place when the actual construction of the meshes of the net is done, and when the floats and sinkers are being attached.  This operation is regarded as an important one, to be done with care, and is performed by the expert.  When it is the " foremost net " of a chief, it is carried into his temple, together with the old net.  The wooden floats and the sinkers of cowrie shell are stripped from the section of the old net to be discarded, the new section and the old section that is being retained are joined together with a double cord of sinnet, and the floats and sinkers are reattached.  At the beginning and at the end of this work libations from green coco-nuts are poured on the floor mats and over the net by the chief.  As he does so he recites :

" Sprinkle with efficacy the floats, Sea-expert chief.
Thy foremost net is having its cowrie shells attached on this day.
Its vivifying is first done on the float in front here.
Now, the fish which darts,
Whence come his eyes
Divert him to thy broad net to enter it."

Here again the injunction of the formula is to the guardian deity of the net—whose name is usually introduced into the recital—to lead the fish into the net.  The " sprinkling " and the " vivifying " refer to the libations of coco-nut milk.  Here again, the technical efficiency of the net is taken for granted, guaranteed by the care of the expert, and what the ritual is expected to secure is the appropriate behaviour of the fish, which is not under human technical control.

This description of rites and account of formulae are the result of my observations in the house of the Ariki Taumako and of subsequent conversations with Pa Fenuatara.  They represent the minimum ritual on such an occasion.  At an earlier period I observed a more complex rite in the house of the Ariki Tafua, and was given the formulae involved by his son, Pa Raṇifuri.  Here the old chief, nominally a Christian, was a well-known spirit medium and the affair was made more complex by his becoming possessed by the guardian spirits of his net, the deity Kere-tapuna and his dead father.

The old net, before being partially stripped of floats and

sinkers, and joined with the new section, was laid on the father's grave ; offerings of bark-cloth and areca nut were prepared for the spirits, and portions of food were also laid out on the grave mats of other ancestors.  As the chief set out the bark-cloth he murmured :

> " Thy offering, Foki-mai-niteni, will be spread out.
> Turn to your offering
> You give hither properly
> A fish to my net."

The details of the act of spirit possession cannot be given here.  But one incident, mentioned to me afterwards by Pa Raŋifuri, is relevant to our problems.  When the chief was possessed by his father the spirit addressed Pa Raŋifuri : " You do it quickly ; walk to the sea "—meaning, " finish the work and go and try out the net."  Pa Raŋifuri answered the spirit : " Grandfather ! You look after the fish, that they do not dash off ; that they may stand firm."  To this, said Pa Raŋifuri, the spirit replied : " O ! they will not run away ; the fish will stay there."  And he said, " he was right ; when I went they had not gone ; the fish had stayed there. The fish had been worked on by the spirits ; they simply stayed."  As the result of this intervention, though some time elapsed before the net was ready, when it was dragged along the reef there was a shoal of fish available, and about twenty were caught.  In fact, so I was told, the fish rushed so hard against the old portion of the net that they broke through it. If not, " we had died from the fish," that is, the weight of them would have been terrific.

This formal consultation of the spirits through the medium is a frequent phenomenon.  In this case it served as an augury of a good catch, and alleviated the anxiety of the workers lest the shoal which had been seen would disappear before they were ready to net for it.

After this rite the chief ceremonially cut the sinnet cord at the bottom of the old net, and the work of joining and fitting was carried out.

Before the net was carried down to the reef a further rite was performed, in which the chief aspersed the net with water, reciting as he did so a formula to the deity Kere-tapuna to " turn to the net ; that the net might be *manu* ; and fish come to it ".  And after the catch had been obtained still further ritual was performed to celebrate it and, as it were, to fix the success of the net.

It is now possible to give an answer to the problems posed. The ritual of net-making is hardly to be described as part of the technique of production. It is not intended to assist the manufacture of the net itself, but to help the net to fulfill its proper function afterwards. It may be described as a rite of deferred production, not a rite of immediate production. It contrasts in this respect with the fishing ritual mentioned earlier. Again, the ritual is performed at strategic points of the work of the net—the very beginning, the final fitting-out with floats and sinkers, and the moment when it is about to be used.

As far as its effects on the efficiency of the process of production are concerned, the ritual does not challenge the autonomy of the technical processes for the work as a whole. But the ritual has certain positive effects. It is a material expression of the dogmatic background of net-making and net-using, and as such reinforces the atmosphere of the significance of the task. It consecrates the instrument of production, investing it with importance as the property of a deity. Again, some phases of the ritual may allay anxiety, as when Pa Raŋifuri was assured by the spirit medium that the shoal of fish would await the coming of the net —though such confidence may prove ill-founded. The assumption of supernatural control of the net provides also a theory of occasional failure in fishing. Seasonal absence of fish is recognized, and for this the gods are not blamed ; canoes are not even taken out at such a time. But if at the change of the seasons the normal supply of fish should not appear, then explanation of the failure of the productive instruments is given in terms of the activity and disposition of the gods and ancestors. Again, to some extent the ritual acts as a stimulus to the productive process, as when the spirit through the lips of the medium issued the injunction to hasten the work and take the net down to the sea. Further, the ritual and its associated beliefs give a basis for the assembly of labour at the work ; it is a unifying factor, drawing the people together to their priest-leader. It is impossible to estimate the exact quantitative effect of these psychological elements, but it is a reasonable inference that they exert such effect.

From another angle, however, the ritual is of neutral or even negative value for the productive process. It occupies time which might be spent on the technical processes—about fifteen minutes were taken in attending the Ariki Tafua when he became spirit-possessed though a shoal of fish had been perceived on the reef—

small quantities of food, areca nut, and coco-nut milk are thrown away ; and the preparation of food and ritual serving of it takes up labour and time. It might be argued also that the concentration of interest on the supernatural control of the net tends to inhibit research into the technical conditions which are responsible for failure to make the catch expected.

But in the Tikopia economic system as it stands, in the absence of contractual wage-labour and of work for an external market, the time and labour consumed by the ritual are not necessarily a loss to the productive organization. The ritual tends to be performed at just those points in the technical activity when there is most free time. Again, the close connection of the ritual with the preparation and consumption of food means that the rite provides a cradle of organization, marking the points for rest, discussion of the further technical operations, and partaking of food. It helps to provide a framework for the organization of this subsistence economy, and to assemble people at appropriate times. In all this, the effect of the ritual is to maintain the association of the major instruments of production with the group of persons of higher social status, especially the chiefs of the clans. It is a conservative force, orienting the productive system towards the interests of the privileged group. But these interests are not simply those of economic exploitation and the accumulation of wealth. The strength of the kinship ties which bind chiefs to their people, and the theory of responsibility which dictates much of the activity of the chiefs, mean that their gain is in terms of social rather than economic privilege. In the manufacture of a net the ritual position of a chief helps to secure to him the services of an expert and a sufficient supply of subsidiary labour. But he makes a return for this labour in the same way as does a commoner—if anything on a higher scale—and the food supplies which have to be provided for the ritual come in a large measure from his own resources. Thus for the ritual at the attachment of floats and sinkers to the net the Ariki Taumako provided a bunch of bananas and a bundle of green coco-nuts from his own store ; and the Ariki Tafua a bowl of sago pudding and a bunch of areca nut likewise. And for a rite which followed the first dragging of the new net of the Ariki Tafua the food consisted of nine bowls and several baskets of food, the major portion of which came from the orchards of the chief, and from the catch of twenty fish obtained in the net. About fifteen men were present at the rite, and afterwards the food was divided among them, each eating a part of his share and taking the rest home to his family. On balance, then, the chief is maintained in his leadership by the ritual of production rather than enlarged in his wealth. It is important to recognize that the ritual performed over his net is not designed to bring fish to it alone, but to all the nets of his clan ; it is a token performance of which his people also are expected to reap the advantage. Thus the day after the net of the Ariki Tafua was completed, a shoal of mackerel was seen off the reef, and not only the net of the chief, but also three other nets in the village were taken down and dragged with a common set of beaters.

## EFFECTS OF RITUAL ON PRODUCTION

We may now carry the analysis into the more general field, and compare the position in different activities.

First let us consider the extent to which the performance of ritual acts as an incentive to undertake production. In the case of individual ritual for line-fishing or banana planting there is no effect of this kind. The rite is an accompaniment, almost of an incidental kind, to the technical act, not a spur to it, as is shown by its frequent omission. But in other cases the obligation to perform the ritual provides a direct incentive to undertake the work ; the periodical building and replacement of sacred canoes, the cultivation of taro by the Ariki Taumako, the yam planting, turmeric manufacture, shark-fishing, and repair of temples of the seasonal Work of the Gods are all examples of large-scale production in which the belief that the ancestors and gods have certain needs, and are interested in seeing that these are met, is overtly responsible for the initiation of the work. Moreover, the ritual imperative often dictates the most appropriate time, as when canoes are overhauled as part of the Work of the Gods at the beginning of the fishing season.

For the same reason these types of complex ritual also serve as an incentive to carry on production. The traditional sequence of rites of necessity involves a corresponding sequence of technical operations, as when the obligation to restore canoe deities to their vessel hastens on the work of repairs. But the ritual incentive is not absolute, as is shown by the net-making of the Ariki Kafika, which was left in suspense owing to insufficient raw materials, despite the uncompleted ritual.

As far as the organization of the activity is concerned the obligation to perform the ritual is one of the factors helping in the assembly of personnel; continual neglect to attend the rites and play one's part in the contributions of food and labour is thought in a general way to render a person liable to the anger or cold-shouldering of the deities, with repercussions on his prosperity. But there is a difference here, in that this factor is more important in the case of the chief or ritual elder than in that of the assistants. In one important respect the ritual helps in the integration of the work by prescribing quantities of green coco-nuts or cooked food at various stages, to be " announced " to the gods and ancestors. This is then available for the workers, to the undoubted benefit of their physical and technical cohesion.

In all these respects the imperative of the ritual provides a safeguard to production. This generalization could be confirmed if it could be shown that with similar environmental, technical and social conditions, work of this kind is performed with less regularity, secures a smaller labour force, and is integrated less effectively where it is not accompanied by such ritual. These conditions might be looked for in the district of Faea, in which the people are nominally Christian, and with their chief the Ariki Tafua have abandoned the performance of the traditional kava rites. The majority of their temples have been allowed to fall into decay, their sacred canoes have been " reduced to the ranks " and are classed as *paopao*, and they no longer attend the Work of the Gods. But comparison of their activities with those of the people of Raveŋa and Namo, who still hold the ancient ritual, is obscured because beneath the veneer of Christianity most of the old beliefs still hold sway. Men still address the fish when they use rod and line, the Ariki Tafua still performs all the essentials of the ritual for the manufacture of turmeric and of a new net. Again, the existence of the cycles of ritual on the other side of the island, with which there is constant communication and institutional co-operation, still acts as a time-signal and a stimulus to the people of Faea in their technical operations such as the repair of canoes and houses and the manufacture of sago and turmeric. When the whole island has been Christian for a generation it will be more possible to make a valid comparison. From observation by writers on other Oceanic communities it is clear that decay of production has set in with the abandonment of the ancient ritual system.[1] As might be expected, this has been mainly in the large-scale co-operative activities, while individual and household production appears to go on at much the same intensity. Moreover, one important factor is the suddenness of the change. If, as in Tikopia, it is not the ritual system root and branch that is superseded at a blow, but simply the more obvious features, and then only in a part of the community, there is more opportunity of an effective substitution of other sanctions for large-scale production. Among the Maori, where the abandonment of the traditional ritual system was fairly rapid and complete, it has taken the best part of a century for a communal spirit of co-operation to be built up again out of kinship and local forces of integration into an effective mechanism capable of large-scale organization for economic ends. In theory, the replacement of a native ritual system by Christianity should be able to supply an effective scheme of religious sanctions for co-operative production, and examples of this can be seen in various mission organizations. But often the new type of Christian organization aimed at or set up fails to withstand the rationalism by which the native is confronted among lay Europeans, the sectarianism among the Christian body itself, the inability of missionaries to realize their problem as one of social and economic reconstruction as well as of mere proselytization, and the conflict of interests that arises between natives and Europeans as a whole.

After this general digression we may return to examine the relation between ritual performance and the time occupied in production in Tikopia. It has already been shown that certain types of ritual do make for conformity of the work to a time schedule, and so help to safeguard the task from miscalculation and inertia. In so far, however, as some of these performances are dependent upon the decision of a single individual, usually a chief (but in the case of the traditional manufacture of sago, the ritual elder of the house of Fusi), there is a danger. If the performer at the core of the system of rites is lagging in his duty, then the economic activity as a whole may suffer, and belief in the efficacy and the necessity of the ritual may be a drag upon productivity. I saw no case in Tikopia where production actually suffered from this cause, but I was witness to the anxiety of the people of Raveŋa,

---

[1] E.g., for the Maori see Firth, *op. cit.*, 471 ; for Eddystone Island, see W. H. R. Rivers, *Essays on the Depopulation of Melanesia*, 1922, 102, 108 ; for San Cristoval, see C. E. Fox, *Threshold of the Pacific*, 1924, 315 *et seq.*

upon practical as well as ritual grounds, when the Ariki Kafika delayed the preliminary rite of " Throwing the Firestick " which had to open the season of the Work of the Gods and give the signal for harvesting and repair of canoes.

It is obvious that the performance of ritual does occupy a considerable time. In the repair of the canoe of the Ariki Kafika there were six rites during the period of five days, taking up altogether, at a conservative estimate, about forty man-hours. To some extent this is a drain upon the efficiency of the technical side of production. But there is no guarantee that the disappearance of the ritual from the scene would mean a corresponding increase of output. Granted the technical methods in vogue, and the existing system of wants, the practice of the ritual is *de facto* in part a social elaboration of the technical activity rather than a direct diversion of productive energies. Moreover, as mentioned in the case of net-making, the ritual often takes place at the end of a stage in the process, and provides a convenient rest-pause for the majority of the workers. Not infrequently a few of the party occupy this time in accumulating raw materials or preparing the scene for the next stage.

One further economic effect of the Tikopia ritual system is in increasing the demand for certain types of goods—especially bark-cloth and food, but also, in smaller quantities, coco-nut oil, turmeric, fresh coco-nut fronds, and seating mats. In this way it gives an additional stimulus to the production of these articles. From the point of view of distribution of resources to meet individual wants, there is a small waste—green coco-nut milk poured out as libations, scraps of food thrown away, lengths of bark-cloth kept as ritual offerings. But in terms of the net economic effect, this is unimportant, because of the native custom of putting ritual objects into general circulation again. If anything, the tendency is for the individual standard of consumption to be increased thereby.

Something may be briefly said now about the attitude of mind of the individual worker while the ritual is being performed. Malinowski has stressed here the importance of the psychological stiffening which the ritual gives to the person engaged in perform-ing it, in what may be called the " confidence-theory " of magic.[1] According to this view, by his ritual act man is endowed with the conviction that he can master the obstacles which nature

[1] *Magic, Science and Religion*, 1925, 73–4, 82–3.

presents to him, and therefore is equipped to undertake tasks from which he would otherwise shrink. That the ritual system as a whole has this general function is undoubted, and it has been part of Malinowski's brilliant contribution to the theory of ritual to show that it has such independent positive functions, and is not mere false science. But I find it difficult to estimate how far this confidence element is operative in any given Tikopia rite. In many cases it seemed that the rite was performed in an attitude of acquiescence in traditional forms ; it was " something from of old ", usually done, and if omitted, the technical activity *might* be less successful. From this angle it might be said that it is not the performance of the rite which gives confidence in the face of the incalculable powers of nature, but that lack of confidence in nature and in man's power to grapple with his problems is engendered by the ritual system itself. All that the rite does, then, is to fill a self-created gap. Again, certain of the Tikopia ritual performances are of an experimental character. Natives have said to me concerning a fishing formula : " We do not know if the fish hear and respond or not ; it's a practice of olden times indeed." And often a fisherman will withdraw some phrases from his formula and insert others, hoping that he may thereby be more successful ; his immediate attitude is here not one of confidence in his powers, but of trial and error, seeking results. Furthermore, in the recital of some formulae the prevailing temper of mind appears to be that of finding an outlet in words for the nervous energy and emotional tension of the worker—as expressed in injunctions to the fish to bite—rather than any process of building up confidence in the technique. Malinowski has emphasized the importance of the emotional element in magical rites, and has built it up into a plausible hypothesis of the evolution of magic from baffled desire. This, however, seems to be the result of introspective rather than of observational analysis. It may be necessary, then, to distinguish the generic elements of magical psychology, as he so well describes them, from the specific elements which may be present in any single magical act.

In conclusion, it is clear that in Tikopia, granted the present technique and knowledge of resources, the ritual system is a positive factor in the situation of production, contributing directly to the organization and indirectly affecting the output. In this sense it might be classed as part of the technique of production, being one of the given factors in the total situation. But ritual is more accurately to be regarded as an autonomous element, parallel to technique, linked with the general theory of resources, and their bearing upon human affairs. From this point of view, though not to be described as an inefficient or wrongly oriented branch of technique, the ritual beliefs and practices may have some negative influence upon technical advance. By insisting upon the truth of certain false propositions, and by treating failure as an event of a non-technical order, to be corrected by further ritual rather than by experiment, beliefs and practices such as those described may immobilize some of the forces of invention and hamper more efficient adaptation.[1]

[1] This point is well discussed by Viljoen, *op. cit.*, 32 *et seq.*

## CHAPTER VI

ECONOMIC FUNCTIONS OF THE CHIEFS

IT is very evident from the material of the foregoing chapters that all Tikopia do not participate in economic affairs on the same level. The differential economic position of individuals is due in part to the differences in their command of productive resources, but also in no small degree to the differences in their status which rest upon supra-economic factors. The recognition of these is dependent upon the traditional organization of the

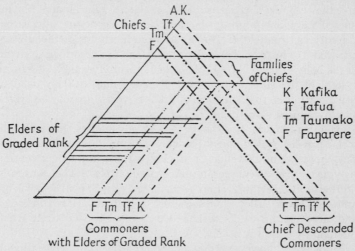

FIG. 6.—Grades of Tikopia Society.

society. Leaving aside the factors of sex and age, which have been discussed earlier, the symbolic representation of the grades of Tikopia society may be given in a diagram (Fig. 6).

The broadest distinction is between commoners (*paito fakaarofa*) and chiefly families (*paito ŋa ariki*). Some of the former are descended from chiefs, but through length of time have lost their superior status. The other commoner families have as their ancestors immigrants or men said to be autochthones. These families are aggregated into a set of major kinship groups each headed by an elder with important ritual functions.

As regards the members of his own kinship group the elder stands in relation to them much as a chief does to the members of his clan, though on a much smaller scale. He takes a prominent part in the organization of production for the group, acts as leader in many of their co-operative affairs, has a prime voice in the distribution of their goods, and, most important from their point of view, is primarily responsible for the ritual contacts with their gods on which their prosperity depends. When illness or failure of crops or fishing threatens any part of the group it is to him that appeal is usually first made. *De facto* he is normally in personal control of larger quantities of wealth than the other members of the group.

In each of the four clans of Tikopia there is a single chief, and the term *ariki* is restricted to designate him alone. For his immediate kinship group he acts in an economic and ritual capacity as ritual elder. But in addition he stands at the apex of the affairs of his whole clan, in ways which are described in detail in the body of this chapter. The chiefs themselves have a definite system of precedence, the Ariki Kafika being at their head in ritual matters so that the form of Tikopia society may be described as a pyramidal structure.[1]

Members of the *paito ariki*, the chiefly houses, have certain social privileges as against the commoners : deference is shown them in economic as well as in other situations, and by convention they may exer ise force in personal quarrels. The sons and brothers of a reigning chief form a body of executive officials known as *maru*. They have some responsibility for law and order, and carry out the chief's wishes on occasions of social strain when disciplinary action is needed.

Sometimes, however, they act on their own initiative, though the chief usually later asserts his control. I have given elsewhere [2] a case of a protracted quarrel over an orchard, culminating in the decision of one of the contending groups, that of Mataioa, to go off to sea. One of the reasons which led to their decision was that

---

[1] In the course of Tikopia history a process of centralization of ritual functions has apparently taken place, so that the Ariki Kafika has emerged as religious leader among a number of groups of immigrant stock. But his position is supported by a myth of his autochthonous origin, and the situation is by no means clear. The structure of kinship grouping and the line of division of chiefly families is discussed in *We, The Tikopia*, ch. x.

[2] *Op. cit.*, 395–6.

two brothers in the house of Morava, connected by birth and marriage with the Ariki Taumako, had intervened. The orchard concerned at one time had belonged to their ancestor, Pu Oliki, three generations before, and the brothers, objecting to the quarrel about it, " bound " it with a *tapu*, thus excluding it from the contestants. The chief, himself hearing of the intention of the Mataioa group to flee the land, then took a hand. He sent for the wife (his own sister) and the son of one of the Morava brothers, and upbraided them—he could not do so to his own brother-in-law. He said that if the house of Mataioa, who were of his own clan, had not sent him the customary presents of food constantly then there would have been some grounds for barring them from the orchard, but they had always behaved properly and contributed to his kava. Moreover, what was his " father " going to do ? This was a reference to his father's brother, old Pa Vaŋatau. This man had protested, saying that the folk of Mataioa, his neighbours, were " his commoners ". He had done nothing to the commoners under the protection of the Morava brothers in Potu sa Taumako, so why had the two brothers interfered with his commoners, who brought him presents of food constantly ?

The result was that the Mataioa group were reinstated, and the Morava brothers snubbed.

This example shows members of a chiefly house taking a protective attitude towards commoner groups on the basis of their economic assistance, and clashing indirectly with one another, with the chief as the ultimate resolver of the situation.

In the economic field it is the eldest son of a chief who is of special importance.

## Economic Position of a Potential Chief

The native economic organization is conditioned by the fact that to some extent the children of a chief share in the restrictions and privileges which attach to his position. In the general social field they have something of his *tapu*. They may not be insulted with impunity, nor may they be struck by commoners. Even between themselves these rules are observed. I once saw a son of the Ariki Kafika rate soundly a number of children who had been obstructing an activity. He then observed that one of the younger sons of the Ariki Taumako was among them and said : " What I said was not meant for you, friend. I was talking to the children here."

In the economic field, however, it is the eldest son who is of special importance. He takes a prominent part in the productive activities of his clan, or of his village. Like his father, he does not participate as a rule in the actual oven work on a ceremonial occasion, although he attends and helps in directing the activity, and in his own home does take part in cooking. But he assumes by right the leadership of many co-operative activities, as a communal fish drive, or the preparation of a sago oven. Again, he imposes economic *tapu* of a wide range and assumes responsibility for the welfare of his whole clan (see p. 208). This his younger brothers do not do.

In the sphere of distribution he is equally prominent. He frequently takes up the role of director in allotting shares of a co-operative product, or of food from an oven, or tobacco or betel nut. He is also a specific recipient of goods in many types of ceremonial exchange, in addition to his father, whereas his younger brothers are treated as appendages to their father. For other than chiefly families such a dual presentation of goods to a single family is not the rule. Moreover, his clansfolk carry to him gifts of food from time to time, explicitly because he is the potential chief.

Finally, by his acts he may give a stimulus to the economic activity of his clan, as by taking a mistress, when the clansfolk, anticipating his marriage, begin to plant extra quantities of taro to prepare for the marriage feast.

Special terms such as " the growing chief " and " the seed of the gods " are indicative of the unique position that he occupies. As he himself becomes older and more mature, and his father more aged, there is naturally the tendency for him to assume more control in economic affairs. There is, however, no system of retirement of chiefs in Tikopia, and while his father is alive he can never supersede him in any ritual functions.

The economic position of the chiefs is so outstanding that the remainder of this chapter is devoted to a definition of their role.

## THE ROLE OF THE CHIEF IN PRODUCTION

In Tikopia a chief has normally a greater command of economic resources than others of his clan. In his position he is overlord and principal owner-holder of clan lands, and of clan canoes.[1]

---

[1] v. *We, The Tikopia*, ch. xi, for an analysis of chieftainship and land tenure ; and Chapter VII of the present book for a summary of land and canoe ownership (also end of this chapter, p. 218).

In relation to his clan he stands at the focal point of distribution in addition to being the prime mover in production.

In his productive role the chief works himself and makes his family work for their own subsistence, using the instruments of production which they own individually or in common. Most of their food comes from their own exertions. The essentially domestic character of the consumption of the chief's household has been stressed in *We, The Tikopia*, as also the emphasis upon exchange between the chief's household and other groups. The major obligation of providing the chief's household with food falls upon the chief himself, his sons, brothers and other immediate kin, since the " tribute " received is essentially in the nature of gifts which must be reciprocated later. There is no permanent and institutionalized court surrounding the chief, as in some of the larger Polynesian islands, which relieves him from ordinary labour.

Apart from his own work and his productive role in directing that of his household, the chief sets an example to his clan not so much by the moral effect of his industry as by the sphere to which he directs his productive attentions. Members of his clan, seeing their chief breaking up an extra piece of ground, begin to do likewise, since they know he is probably planning some ceremony which will need large quantities of food to which they will have to contribute. Again, the chief has an important integrative function because as primary intermediary with the clan gods he supplies the initiative and controls the correct utilization of most natural resources. Not only are the ceremonies he performs the pivotal points of the seasonal economic cycle, but by his imposition of taboos on crops and land he can make his people change their sphere and locality of production.

Although the chief, like other men, is expected to take an active part in the productive activities of his household, certain ceremonial and magico-religious restrictions, depending on his rank, are imposed upon him in this respect. Unlike other men, he should not carry burdens ; his adze, his staff, his fishing tackle, his little bag of betel materials should constitute all his load. Coco-nuts, bananas, taro and whatever he may wish to bring from his cultivations should be borne by others. Travelling alone with the Ariki Kafika on one occasion I was even given coco-nuts to carry by a man we met in an orchard, with the remark that " the chief does not shoulder burdens ". He may take part in the preparation of food for the oven, but not in the actual work of cooking. Like everyone else he is subject to the obligations incurred by marriage but when such obligations would require him to cook, his son or his younger brother goes in his stead. If he is a young man the chief may attend the kindling of an oven and sit down modestly to help. He will begin, for instance, to grate taro. But he is never left very long at such work—soon one of his people comes up and replaces him.

The restrictions to which the chief is subjected in productive activity are expressed in general terms as part of his *tapu*. And here we see the concept of the chiefly function as being conferred upon a man by the community. There is in Tikopia no automatic process of succession to chieftainship, even if there is an obvious heir in an adult eldest son. The chief must always be elected, and formally installed by being raised in the arms of his supporters in the midst of a concourse of people from all clans. The Ariki Tafua discussed with me the bar upon the carrying of burdens by chief's from this point of view. He said : " The chief is made *tapu* indeed by the body of the land, not to shoulder burdens." By " the body of the land " is meant the mass of people as a whole. He explained it thus, " The *tapu* is one thing, but the making *tapu* of a chief is different. The expression is used ' the Ariki is *tapu* ', an expression from the body of the land. When the body of the land assembles then it is said ' the eyes of the chief are *tapu* '. When a chief is elected of course he has been made *tapu* by the body of the land. While he lives as a commoner he lives as a *maru* (an executive official, brother or son of the reigning chief) but when he has been elected as chief he is now *tapu*. When the chief is to be elected the whole land gathers together ; and so the expression is used ' he is made *tapu* by the body of the land '." This statement seems somewhat involved but I have given the full translation of it as an example of the kind of formulation which the Tikopia themselves make on the subject. It shows that although expressed in esoteric terms there is this definite idea that the chief owes his special position ultimately to social creation.

Though we might regard such restrictions as on the whole advantageous to the chief he at time finds them irksome and disregards them, to the annoyance of his clansfolk. A Tikopia saying is " *Te ti o fenua sise e poi ki moana* ". The *ti o fenua* is the *ariki tu o fenua*, the " standing chief of the land ", that is the Ariki Kafika, the premier chief. The saying " the standing chief of the land does not go out to sea " refers to a prohibition that applies to the Ariki Kafika but not to the other chiefs. Since he is in supreme control of the fertility of the land and of the ocean, his duty is to stay on shore during the night's fishing and invoke the gods for a successful catch. If the fish are plentiful then he may go out with the canoes for a night or so, but not continuously throughout the season ; if the fish are scarce he should not go at all. A breach of this rule, it is believed, will result in poor catches. The present Ariki Kafika has " overturned " this rule. Being a sea-expert and an active man he goes fishing consistently, to the indignation of some people. His *tautau laui*, his brothers and mother's brothers, seeing him out at sea exclaim jokingly : " Husband of a she-devil ! Why does he not stay on shore ? " They jest, because he is the chief, but they are really annoyed. This I was told by Seremata who commented on the fact that the Ariki had gone out the night before, when there were only two canoes at sea ; his canoe had caught ten flying-fish, the other had got five. " It is bad," said he. The fish were not plentiful, therefore the chief should have stayed at home.

This example shows the chief in the position of a man whose personal inclinations are constrained, or at least criticized by public opinion. In the case of the Ariki Kafika this opinion is not restricted to members of his own clan—for Seremata is of the Taumako group.

These specific restrictions upon the activity of the chief, however, do not mean that he is idle or that he is confined to priestly functions. If he is alone in his canoe he paddles it himself and when he lands he pulls the craft up himself. If he is a member of a crew he participates both in the paddling and in the hauling up (there is no " state barge " in Tikopia as in some communities with sacred chiefs). On one occasion the Ariki Kafika strained his back in hauling up his canoe ; he preferred to try to do the job himself instead of calling for assistance. But when heavy communal work is under way the chief usually finds scope for his energies elsewhere. For instance, when the canoe-shed of a vessel of the Ariki Kafika was being rebuilt, the chief did not take part in the hardest tasks of lifting timber and digging post-holes but took the lighter work of rolling coco-nut fibre into short lengths to make ties for the timbers, and was prominent in the direction of the whole activity. Work with the adze is recognized as appropriate to a chief. When the vessel itself was being repaired the Ariki Kafika spent some time in dressing timber for an outrigger boom ; driven indoors by the rain he came out again as soon as it ceased and continued his work. He sent a young kinsman off to find the length of the old boom and the amount to be allowed for the seat across the gunwales. The lad came back with a stick, the bark of which he had scratched to show the correct points. The chief cut the stick appropriately, laid it on the timber to gauge its lengths, and carried on busily.

Moreover, in connection with his ·place in the productive scheme of his household, to which reference has been made, a chief works in his own cultivation, breaking up the soil with a digging stick and planting taro or banana shoots or plucking breadfruit like any other man ; he grubs grass round his house ; he fishes on the reef with rod and line or puts down his net in the evening to catch *kiokio* in the lake ; he directs the manufacture of sago and turmeric, and with his helpers fills and empties the bowls. If he is an expert in making nets he does this work whenever he wishes. For instance, the Ariki Taumako began on a net for his young son, a boy of about ten years old. The latter had rolled the cord and put it on a netting needle. This needle was too large for the mesh required so the chief got the lad to bring a dry reed stem, which he cut and used instead. A Tikopia is rarely at a loss in practical situations of this kind. He usually gets something, however rough, to serve his purpose. The cord was badly rolled with many ends of fibre sticking out. " *Taraŋa, taraŋa* " said the chief, " Speech, speech " (an abbreviation of " speech of the land "), a testy exclamation equivalent to " my word ". He told the boy that his net would be all cobwebby. Such a domestic scene could be found in the household of almost any commoner. Sometimes a chief enlists the services of a skilled net-maker when he is having a new net repaired, sometimes not. When the Ariki Kafika was directing the manufacture of a new net no special expert was engaged. His son said to me that where a chief is competent in the work he does it himself—meaning that he acts as controller and one of the main participants. This remark had a backhanded implication, since at that time the Ariki Taumako was also having a net made, but had engaged two experts to take charge of it.

The pinning of sago leaf thatch, a common but necessary kind of work, may also be done by a chief.  At the Resiake ceremonies of Taumako ten men cut sago leaf in the orchard of their chief close at hand.  When they returned the work of preparing it for thatch began, in two adjacent houses for shade. In one dwelling five men were busy ; in the other eight.  The chief took his place as a worker in the former group, his father's brother Pa Vaŋatau tearing out the midrib while he pinned the fronds together in sheets.  (The accompanying plan, Fig. 7, shows

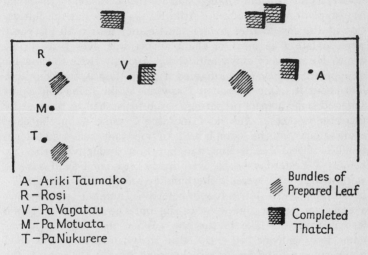

A – Ariki Taumako
R – Rosi
V – Pa Vaŋatau
M – Pa Motuata
T – Pa Nukurere

Bundles of
Prepared Leaf

Completed
Thatch

FIG. 7.—Plan of Thatch-making Organization.

how the workers were seated.)  At one stage the chief called his son Rosi to come across the house and drag the pile of prepared leaf over to him.  After about an hour Pa Vaŋatau faced about and began to pin the leaf prepared by the two workers on the other side of him.  The Ariki continued to use the pile got ready for him by Pa Vaŋatau, and going ahead steadily completed six sheets of thatch in about one and a half hours.  This was at least as fast as any other worker.  It will be noted from the plan that the chief is seated alone at one end of the house.  This is his normal position ; even although he is a simple participant in communal economic activity, he is not thereby denuded of the ordinary privileges and restrictions which surround him in social intercourse.

When the chief as a worker is dependent upon the voluntary co-operation of others, the organization usually works smoothly enough.  But evidence that his people are not constrained to assist him in any absolute sense is given by the following series of small incidents of economic dislocation which I casually observed. The day after the pinning of the thatch just mentioned saw the actual re-thatching of the house. The chief arrived early on the scene but his people were late. He made some complaint about this, though when they actually did begin work he merely sat by, looking on and talking.  On another occasion at the ritual of yam planting at Kafika the Ariki Kafika arrived at the cultivation at the agreed time before sunrise, but nearly all his party were so late that most of the planting was over before they came.  He was very angry and whooped loudly twice to show his disapproval.  They were ashamed, though they later joked with him about it.  One afternoon I saw the Ariki Tafua, his eldest son, and some helpers preparing thatch for a shed to be used by turmeric workers.  The next morning I came upon the chief again alone and he complained to me that some additional bundles of leaf beside him had not been brought in the day before. " Yesterday people were many ; to-day I shall have to work alone ; why weren't the bundles brought in yesterday ? " he grumbled.  In June, 1929, the Ariki Taumako got together a crowd of people and went to dig out the channel in Namo leading from the lake to the sea.  When they arrived it was found that someone had excreted in the channel bed.  The chief was very angry and finally left the scene, leaving the work to the other people.  The act of excretion there was regarded as an expression of disagreement by someone who did not want the channel dug at that time.  There was much speculation as to who it could have been, but the culprit was not found.  The chief was angry, especially with the local people in Namo, though they denied complicity.

The fact that the chief in such cases is frequently first on the scene of operations indicates how his sense of responsibility is apt to be keener than that of his people.

The following account of the preparations for the cooking of taro for the first-fruits ritual of the sacred cultivation of the Ariki Kafika illustrates the part played by the chief in everyday economic life. Taro was brought in from the cultivation and put outside the house in a heap.  The crowd of people assembled, then sat around waiting, and in the general discussion there was some uncertainty as to when the Ariki Kafika would arrive. Someone said that he would come by canoe and when, some time later, a canoe was sighted, there were cries of " He has come ". The canoe did in fact carry the Ariki and his children, and one or two people went down to meet it, taking from him his taro grater, his kit with his water bottle and coco-nut grating stool. One man helped him to drag up his canoe, though the others, including his son, sat still.

The Ariki came up, with the flap of his waist cloth still tucked up after his work with the canoe. Pulling down the flap, he said " let us go ", and led the way to the front of the house. He pulled out the taro from the heap, bundle by bundle, and threw it towards the side of the house, where people seized the bundles and got them ready for scraping. After complaining that the taro was bad because of the lack of rain, the Ariki went off to bathe while preparations were made for the oven.

This simple example illustrates very well how the chief himself takes an active part in work, while playing a unique role in initiating and directing, in an informal way, the economic activities of his people.

To illustrate the variety and amount of work done by a chief I give in the following summary a list of the major occupations of the Ariki Kafika over a period of three months when I was in close touch with him. Each of the items cited was his main occupation for a day, but I did not record them all. Just previous to this time he had spent six weeks, until 25th December (a fortuitous coincidence with Christmas Day [1]), directing and officiating in the cycle of religious ceremonies, the Work of the Gods.

## OCCUPATIONS OF ARIKI KAFIKA

### After Work of Gods in December, 1928

December, 1928   Rested one day, did not go to dance festival ; made flying-fish net ; felled tree for bark-cloth for ceremony of recovery of one of his elders from illness ; went to Uta to pluck breadfruit ; worked timber for a house.

[1] The concluding rite was to have been performed the following day, but the chief decided to have it on Christmas Day, saying that the mosquitoes in Uta were too much for him.

January, 1929    Made *masi* in Uta ; staked up yams ; visited me ; indoors on wet rough day ; went to Mauŋa to get fibre for net ; attended illness rite of one of his elders ; attended dance practice ; attended dance festival ; presided over song practice ; danced at festival ; went to Faea to cut trees for bark-cloth for ritual purification ; visited his orchard in Faea ; led discussion about dance festival in Faea ; attended festival ; made adze handle ; stayed at home ; went out flying-fishing ; limed his head.

February, 1929    Making adze handle ; visited sick Ariki Tafua and slept there ; returned home ; went to Uta to cultivate in his orchard ; visited me ; making net (four days) ; visited Ariki Tafua with food ; got fibre for net ; rebuilding canoe-shed ; cut sago-leaf for thatch ; finished relashing of canoe ; made thunder kava ; superintended grating of sago in Uta ; slept most of showery day ; superintended sago extraction ; performed kava ritual in Kafika temple.

March, 1929    Thatched his oven house ; planting banana suckers in Mauŋa ; digging up ground in Rakisu for taro ; cultivating for taro ; mended acqueduct in Rakisu ; visit from spirit medium ; planted taro ; prepared bowstring ; superintended repair of sacred canoe (five days) ; went to sea in chase of bonito.

The amount of work done by chiefs varies with their status, age, and personality. As has been seen, the special position of the Ariki Kafika as premier chief of the land imposes special restrictions upon him which do not apply to the Ariki Taumako, who is also a sea-expert. The latter is about forty years of age, burly and virile, the youngest and most energetic of all the chiefs. The Ariki Kafika said of him in a tone of approbation : " *Matea tana faifekau ; siei se manava* "—" Great is his performance of work ; he does not rest." The Ariki Faŋarere, on the other hand, who is the senior Ariki in age, suffers from a diseased foot and does less active work, though he grates taro, and plants in his cultivations.

Finally, reference should be made to the energy expended by the chiefs in carrying out their non-economic ritual duties, which sometimes involve considerable effort. Thus in regard to the series of daily visits which formerly had to be paid by the Ariki Tafua to Uta during the Work of the Gods—to put marks of turmeric pigment on different parts of his temple, to participate in ceremonial food preparing, etc., the chief said to me : " It is all right for a younger man, but for an old man, no—he becomes sick of it. It is all right if he is living in Namo and can come by canoe, but when one is living in Faea—one becomes very tired."

It may be asked if these ritual obligations are treated seriously by the chiefs. In Tikopia they certainly are. For instance the Ariki Kafika, I noticed, was pale one day at a kava ceremony. He told me that he had fasted for two days and nights before the ceremony, and said that this was always the case before the seasonal Work of the Gods. He kept on thinking of the Work so that his food became bitter to him, there was no flavour and aroma in it for him. These statements fit in with my observations on his nervous disposition. I doubt if the other chiefs take their responsibilities so seriously, though they do conform to them regularly.

We have seen that in domestic affairs a chief is left to go his own way and is in fact expected to be ordinarily industrious. The nature of his activities is, however, a matter of public interest and a constant passage of people to and from their cultivations and an exchange of gossip render this simple enough. If a chief shows special industry in one field then people speculate, and his clansfolk may begin to follow his example. Not long before I left Tikopia the Ariki Tafua began to plant taro extensively in Rakisu. The Ariki Kafika commented on this, " Follow after the mind of the chief that has been made up—that is the custom of this land." He referred to the action of the Tafua people in planting taro likewise. The same idea is given in an explicit proclamation which in pre-Christian times was formally uttered once a year at Rarokoka. A section of this proclamation enjoined people who saw any special kinds of food obviously held in reserve in the orchards of their chief to go and set aside supplies likewise, so that when the time came they would not have to steal in order to bring along their appropriate contributions.

When a chief plays the part of economic agent by engaging the services of a number of people, including expert craftsmen, to prepare a piece of capital equipment, such as a canoe or a seine net, he reciprocates the services of these people by gifts of bark-cloth, etc., and food. In this he behaves as any other men of wealth in the community. The difference is that his reciprocation is apt to be on a more generous scale. In any case, social obligations require him to furnish a certain amount of this productive equipment for the service of his gods and the use of his clan. A man who wishes to go fishing and has no canoe of his own may borrow that of the chief after obtaining permission. When he returns he gives the catch to the chief, who distributes it, returning the larger portion to the canoe crew and keeping a little for himself. (The borrowing of a fellow clansman's canoe on the same principle is also common.) The chief's productive equipment stands as it were at the apex of that of his clan and to some extent is representative of it for esoteric purposes.[1] When a chief's net is being made or repaired the kava is performed daily ; so also with his sea-going canoes.

Allied to this last function is that of the chief as an integrator of production. Seasonally he performs ceremonies which are intended to increase the catch of fish and to some extent to serve as a framework within which people pursue their fishing. Each chief, moreover, has one of the major vegetable foodstuffs under his control and in the last resort is held responsible for its fertility.[2] The people of his clan do not plant or gather these foods only because they have to make contributions of them when the chief performs his ritual, but their obligation to make these contributions when required is one factor in the interest which they have in them. They do believe firmly that their capacity to use this foodstuff depends on the actions of the chief, his personal power and his feelings towards them and the community as a whole. For example, towards the middle of 1929 when the breadfruit showed signs of developing, people attributed it to the fact that dart matches had begun. These are held to be a positive factor influencing fertility. The Ariki Faŋarere was annoyed because he had already unfolded the special ritual mat to the god who is regarded as tutelary deity of the fruit, and he held that this was the true cause. Hence he said, " They say that the breadfruit has come on through this dart match. All right ! Let their breadfruit bear ! " The result was, according to the Ariki Kafika, that the first signs of fruiting disappeared and many trees would not bear at all. The Ariki Faŋarere had, in effect, thrown the onus of fertility on to the dart match, which was not powerful enough to bear it. The Ariki Kafika in telling me this said, " All the chiefs uphold the Ariki Faŋarere. Such is the custom of Tikopia."

[1] This applies particularly to his sacred canoes, the equipment for turmeric making and nets for lake fishing.
[2] v. " Totemism in Polynesia," 5–10, for an account of this.

## THE IMPOSITION OF *TAPU*

The term *tapu* in Tikopia, used as substantive or adjective, has a duality of meaning such as is found in other Polynesian communities. On the one hand it has the connotation of " sacred ", as applied to chiefs, temples and gods ; and on the other it may mean " reserved " or " prohibited " as when persons and objects are not to be interfered with. There is of course a direct relationship between these two meanings. Sometimes one or other meaning predominates almost completely to the exclusion of the other, as when a fish that is *tapu* is not treated with any special reverence but is not regarded as fit for food.

In its substantival form a *tapu* may be of two kinds. Some *tapu* are regarded as a constant and integral part of the social structure and are not subject to individual imposition or alleviation. The temples of the gods and the person of the chief, for instance, are always in a *tapu* state. This may be intensified by particular ritual circumstances, but not even the chief himself can free them from their state. These *tapu* may have definite economic effects, as for instance the prohibition which lies upon a chief not to participate in tending an oven ; which means that substitute labour power must always be on hand to fulfil this function. We are concerned here, however, with another type of *tapu* which can be directly imposed or removed by individuals and which operates only for a limited time. The economic effects of these prohibitions are more obvious and operate in a more concentrated fashion.

A classification of these *tapu* is not easy to make but the following table will indicate the principal features in connection with them. Broadly speaking they comprise restrictions dictated by basic social claims on the one hand, such as funeral taboos, and on the other hand more specifically economic restrictions, the aim of which is immediate conservation of resources, or provision of food for a future event. They are principally concerned with the sphere of food, perhaps because restraint in food consumption is the most obvious method of showing conformity to social dictates.

In the material which follows it will be seen that the term *tapu* is sometimes used to refer to the condition of restriction and sometimes in a more concrete way to refer to the object, such as a coco-nut frond, which is the sign or exemplification of the restriction. So also the expression " to bind the *tapu*" may refer to the imposition of the restriction in the abstract sense, or to the act of setting up the material symbol used. The expression " to make *tapu*" (*fakatapu*) is an equivalent for this in the abstract sense.

TABLE V

CLASSIFICATION OF TABOOS

| Type of *Tapu* | Social Context | Sanction | Economic Effects |
|---|---|---|---|
| Imposed by Throwing the Firestick. | Initial operation of Work of the Gods by Ariki Kafika. | Respect for the chief, the cycle of ceremonies and the gods under whose auspices it is imposed. | Inhibits the felling of sago palms in Uta for nearly two months. |
| Funeral prohibitions :— (a) on richer foods. | Kept by principal mourners, self-imposed | Kinship sentiment and general convention. | Diversion to poorer foods, accumulation of reserves to small extent. diversion of productive energies from sea to land. |
| (b) on plucking coco-nuts. | Specified areas, set up by chief. | Fiat of chief, fear of chief and of supernatural punishment. | |
| (c) on reef fishing. | Same. | | |
| (d) on canoe fishing. | Same. | | |
| Restriction of access to taro land or individual cultivations. | Imposed by individuals in their own interests or immediate interests of group. Restricted sphere. | Respect for individual wish and sometimes fear of chief and/or supernatural punishment. | Retention of individual advantage; limitation on general freedom of utilization. |
| Restriction on taking coco-nuts. | Applied over wide area, only by chief or by his eldest son, in anticipation of future feast or as a safeguard in a time of scarcity. | Fear of chief or son, convention of respect for his fiat, fear of supernatural punishment, recognition of general advantage. | Restraint on immediate consumption with increased future consumption. Immediate diversion in part to other foodstuffs. |

There are two types of restriction upon the use of economic resources which are not classified by the Tikopia as *tapu*. The first consists in a verbal prohibition such as a chief will utter against breaking up a certain area of land for taro planting

The sanction behind this prohibition is respect for him, fear of his anger and perhaps of supernatural punishment by his gods, coupled with the recognition that such a prohibition is usually dictated by common sense as when the ground has not lain fallow long enough to yield the best crop. But in the absence of any specific ritual performance and of any material token of the prohibition, it rests outside the *tapu* classification. The second type of prohibition consists primarily in a material token, but has no ritual to bring it into the *tapu* sphere. If, for instance, a man wishes to reserve the fruit of a few coco-nut or areca palms, or a Canarium almond tree for his own use, he lashes some sago fronds to the trunk. This is a sign to all that they should leave such trees untouched. It applies particularly to near relatives and friends who in the ordinary way might be expected to cull the fruit without first asking the owner's permission. This sign is called a *pipi*, being a form of the word *pi*, to block. It is really an indication that permission is withheld. It may be put up by any commoner or chief. The same aim is sometimes sought by laying branches across a path or by filling up the entrance in the hedge which surrounds an orchard.

Sometimes such restrictions are imposed where an owner has been annoyed by wanton damage or fears it. Thus, one man cut down saplings and blocked a path in Rotoaia because people going through had thoughtlessly hacked at his paper mulberry trees and spoilt their bark. I was with a party when inquiry was made as to the reason for the blockage. The answer was given " He is angry ", " Who ? ", " The man who owns the orchard ". On this occasion we went round by another way. But the restriction is not always observed, particularly where it is regarded as transcending the rightful claims of others. Thus on the same occasion a path in Rakisu had been blocked by boughs at a place where a man had planted taro, and feared that people might walk over it. One of our party smashed down the obstruction, saying, " I am annoyed. People do not fly above," meaning that he should not have been required to go out of his way up the hillside. In this case it was a main route (*ara matua*) that had been stopped ; the other was a side path. On another occasion I heard the Ariki Kafika complaining that the main path around the lake shore in Raveŋa had been blocked by a man because some of his paper-mulberry spars had been stolen.[1]

[1] *We, The Tikopia*, 404-5.

The restriction was observed for a few days—probably because the man concerned was a person of rank closely related to the Ariki Taumako—but it was soon afterwards disregarded.

The observance of a proper *tapu* is usually more strict, partly because of the rank of the person who imposes it and partly because of the supernatural sanction which usually attaches to it. But here too the observance is by no means complete, as will be seen from the examination of the cases given in the following pages.

*Tapu* proper are of several types. Only a summary description of them can be given here since it is impossible to explain the differences adequately without an elaborate analysis of the native religious beliefs.

The first type, according to Pa Fenuatara, is the plain *sakilo*, an immature coco-nut frond. This is the ordinary *tapu* for the orchards of commoners and draws its ritual value primarily from the rank of the person who sets it up. The commoner does not " bind " it himself but goes to someone of a chiefly house— as to the eldest son of a chief—to put it up for him. Or he may get an elder or a spirit medium to do it. The value of such an act lies in the fact that these people have special control over supernatural beings, though the *tapu* itself is not necessarily directly dedicated to any of these. A *tapu* of this type will be set up in an orchard if a man finds that his taro are being stolen.

For a second kind of *tapu* the bottom leaves of the *sakilo* are knotted or plaited (*e pini*) as a token that an *atua*, a spiritual being, is contained within. " He has been knotted inside." This type of *sakilo* is used particularly by those spirit mediums who control spirits of the kind who are believed to put coco-nut fronds as dance ornaments in the back of their waistcloths. These are the spirits of the *atu mataŋi*, regarded as being especially affiliated with the general northern direction. Such spirits are very powerful—they have great *vave*, supernatural speed. Pa Tekaumata, a well-known medium, used such *sakilo* ; one that I saw was dedicated to his deity Pu Vaiefu. Sons of women from the chiefly line of Tafua are also entitled to use this kind since the major deity of their mother's clan is the tutelary deity of the coco-nut.

A third and most powerful type of *tapu* is the *famatua*, the mature coco-nut frond. This is put on only by a chief and as a rule he reserves it for nut trees such as the Canarium almond, and the *vere* (an unidentified purple fruit). These are highly esteemed. The *sakilo* is " light ", as the people say, in comparison with the mature frond, the use of which is the prerogative of the chief. He wears it as his ritual necklet. In this case the *tapu* is associated with the chief's most powerful god and it is thought that breach of it will result in sickness or death. When a spirit is associated with a *tapu* sign the frond must be continually renewed. If the spirit saw that it had become dry it is said that he would wonder what had happened and would desert it. The renewal is termed *fakamatamata ŋa tapu*, " making it green."

The general method of setting up such a *tapu* is by binding some fronds of the coco-nut palm to the trunk of a tree in a prominent place in the orchard or to a stake in an open garden or on the reef. The native term is *fakatu te tapu*, to cause the *tapu* to stand, or alternatively *noa te tapu*, to bind it. For instance, soon after the death of his brother the Ariki Tafua instituted a ban on fishing and on the consumption of coco-nuts in Faea. I was present when he did it. He said, " We are going to set up coco-nut frond." He went with one of his elders and one of his sons to Potimua. Staff in hand—a sign that he was engaged in formal business—he walked along the beach greeting people as they passed. At the place appointed, near the large rock Faturoa, the son went into the bush and gathered a bunch of Cordyline and another of immature coco-nut frond. A small growing tree was stripped of its lower branches and at its foot were laid five green coco-nuts on some coco-nut frond. The chief took the immature fronds (*sakilo*) and splayed them out as a fan. Laying this upright against the trunk he tied the fronds round and lashed them at the bottom with the Cordyline leaves. As he did this he murmured a formula. Then he sat down at the base of the tree, opened one of the coco-nuts, and with another formula poured out a libation of the milk on to the frond. His recital was to his ancestors and gods and according to him consisted primarily of an invocation for plentiful shoals of fish to come. He tied another frond to a tree near Rofaea while two of his other sons tied them at additional spots in the district. Pa Korokoro, an elder of the chief, also affixed a frond on the beach at Tufenua. The land near the village of Matautu itself was free of *tapu*—the people said because of the sympathy of the chief for them. But the reef waters were forbidden.

The object of this *tapu* was primarily to enforce mourning

obligations, but its economic side was not disregarded. The formula for setting up the *tapu* included an appeal for fertility—incidentally the sons of the chief did not recite formulae since that of their father was deemed to be sufficient for all the fronds affixed. Again, it was recognized that modifications of the *tapu* might be necessary. While it was being set up members of the party explained to me that on request the people of the district would be able to get permission from the chief to go fishing on the reef occasionally. If they saw a shoal of fish coming right in shore they could go to the chief and say, " We are going for a stroll in the reef waters." He would then reply, " It is well." Such a practice is recognized by custom and there is a special term *asi* which applies to the temporary lifting of the *tapu*. It means a suspension for the single occasion and not the end of the restriction as a whole. It is designed to avoid waste but it is a conventional mechanism which allows of occasional relief from the pressure of obligations, and is in keeping with the general practical attitude of the Tikopia towards their ritual affairs. An actual breach of this particular *tapu* is described later.

Towards the end of my stay in Tikopia a *tapu* was set up by the Ariki Taumako on the coco-nuts and areca nut in his orchards of Taumako and Kamota in Uta. According to Pa Motuata it was actually set up by a spirit. Te Ararere, a " son " of the chief—in reality the product of a miscarriage—entered a man of the Kamota house, who in this state of possession went and " tied " the *tapu*, which then became that of the spirit. In course of time the *sakilo* used became dry, so a ceremony was performed to renew it. The old frond was replaced by a fresh one, the ground at the side of the Taumako temple was cleansed (the sign of an important rite) and kava was made. When the chief was reciting the formula over the kava stem the spirit named " Pu ", that is the ancestor Rakaitoŋa, entered Pu Niumano, elder of the Ariki Taumako and a noted medium, and said to the company that areca nut should be conveyed to the other chiefs. So after the kava was over a basket of food was carried as a gift to the Ariki Kafika and another to the Ariki Faŋarere, with a bunch of areca in each case. On this occasion the Ariki Taumako hung necklets of Cordyline leaf on a number of people, for welfare—Pa Nukura wore his for weeks after, till it had quite dried up. The bestowal of these necklets meant too that the rite was one of importance.

*Tapu* that are applied to a group of trees or to a single orchard do not attract much attention since they affect people's conduct very little. But when they are set up for a wider area they naturally become the object of much interest. The prohibition is obeyed not only by people of the clan concerned but by all who have land interests there. Others are not entitled to be on the land. Such *tapu* are set up only by a chief or the eldest son of a chief ; moreover, they seem to be always of a comparatively mild type. The man who institutes one relies for its observance on the respect which people have for him, or he dedicates it to spirits who are not specifically evil by nature, and who therefore will not inflict dire consequences upon a person who breaks it. This is in line with the feeling of responsibility for their people that such men of rank show. The general feeling to which they conform is that the life of a man should not be sacrificed merely for the sake of conserving food. It is thus clear that in Tikopia the imposition and operation of an economic *tapu* is not automatic. Personal initiative and variation of attitude play their part in adapting the prohibition to the circumstance of the case. The prohibition of greatest weight in Tikopia is that of the Ariki Kafika. " This land which stands obeys the one chief ; Faea which stands is *tapu* from the one *tapu*, the *tapu* of the Ariki Kafika." He can in theory set up a *tapu* over the whole island but in practice he usually restricts such a prohibition to the areas over which he has most control, that is, where his own lands and those of his clan are most plentiful. Thus Mauŋa-lasi is his province. If he desires food to be plentiful there he will institute his prohibition, which is known as the great *tapu*, or " the breathing space of the soil ". When this stands no one of any clan may go there to procure food. If anyone does so secretly then it is believed that in the night thunder will sound and the lightning will strike down on his house, breaking its beams asunder, or there will be a rock-slide from a cliff in his neighbourhood. Other people will not know that the man has gone surreptitiously to his orchard, but they will see the results and suspect the cause. After a time, if the chief sees that the food it was desired to conserve is so plentiful that it is starting to fall and rot on the ground, he appoints a day to *asiasi* the *tapu*, to lift it momentarily. He issues a general invitation to everyone and people come whether they have land in Mauŋa or not. They go where they will, but keeping as far as possible to their own orchards, and each gathers a load of food, bananas, breadfruit, and other products. Coco-nuts alone, the prime object of the restriction, are not touched. The Ariki Kafika himself gets his family to gather a few coco-nuts only and sends a contribution to each of the other chiefs.

About a year before my visit Pa Fenuatara had set up a *tapu* in Mauŋa. He said to me, " I bound my *tapu* to block the crowd, for the eating of coco-nut to be abandoned." He had observed that coco-nuts were getting scarce and so deliberately took this action. " I bound the Mauŋa ; I had sympathy for the people, therefore I bound it that the coco-nuts might grow and be planted in their orchards." People as a whole, he said, had planted no palms there for some time, and only the families of the chiefs of Kafika and Taumako and the allied house of Vaŋatau had nuts for planting. He set up the *tapu* without consulting anyone except his father. " I am going to block the Mauŋa," he said. The chief replied, " It is good that you shall go and set up your *sakilo*." He set it up also in Te Roro, the flat land beneath the cliffs of Reani. Then he called together the people of Raveŋa and Namo outside his house and explained to them what he had done. The expression is, he set up his *fono*, his proclamation. He continued his story, " Then when the people heard, they wished it and they said that I was correct. Some objected, but they did not tell me, they objected mutely only. Then I asked thus ' Who is the man who objects ? Let him announce it to me at this moment '. Then the people called to me ' O ! not a man objects. We say throughout that you are correct ! ' ". Later, when the restriction had been in force for some time he said to the people, " We will all go to-morrow, to Mauŋa, and you will bring back your food. Stop for two days and consume it, and I shall go to Mauŋa alone ". He did so and spent the whole day walking through the orchards looking for signs of plucked coco-nut. He found none at all. Later some of the dry coco-nuts which had fallen were taken away secretly by women in their baskets but on the whole the *tapu* was respected. People went even further. The prohibition applied only to coconuts, but many men observing fine bunches of areca in their orchards said, " Let them stand in the *tapu*," and took only poorer bunches. Thus a great amount of areca nut also came to maturity. The result was a considerable increase of the wealth of the community in these important fruits.

REPAIRING A SACRED HOUSE

This is the oven-house of Resiake, the Taumako temple.

PLATE V.

PLATE VI.

FOOD FOR THE WORKERS

At a later stage in the repair of the sacred oven-house (see Plate V). Sheets of thatch lie to the left, and while men prepare the ties, women are busy at the ordinary oven, protected from the sun by a special shelter.

The *sakilo* was " bound " without any formula for making a man ill if he broke the *tapu*. This was announced to the people by Pa Fenuatara. He said, " I have not made my *tapu* evil. Go you and take food ; the coco-nut only must no person touch ". Thus he made the weight of the *tapu* rest on his own personal prestige and not on any fear of supernatural consequences.

A *tapu* which has been applied over a wide area must be formally relaxed at the end of the period. Just as it was " bound " in the beginning so it is now " untied " (*vete*). The lashings of the coco-nut frond are removed and the frond itself thrown away. A collection of food from the freed area is made and a meal prepared. If spirits have been involved in the *tapu* then a ceremony takes place to give them formal notification of its removal. When the *tapu* of Pa Fenuatara was untied, portions of food were sent from the family of Kafika to each of the other chiefs. Such gifts are of the type called *fakaariki*, recognitions of chieftainship. In this case they included " sprouting coco-nuts, good coco-nuts, green coco-nuts, green food, sugar cane, and cooked food ", to quote Pa Fenuatara. The sprouting coco-nuts were planted in the vicinity of the houses of the chiefs.

The *tapu* vary in range of application and in intensity. The one imposed after the death of the brother of the Ariki Tafua applied on land, to growing coco-nuts. It was permitted to use nuts which had fallen but it was forbidden to climb the palms for the fresh fruit.

The observance of the *tapu* also varies considerably according to the occasion. In general it may be said that *tapu* which are instituted for ritual reasons such as mourning or the seasonal cycle of ceremonies are kept more strictly than the directly conservational ones. But a breach is not unknown in either case. After the Ariki Tafua had imposed a restriction on reef fishing, some of the people of Rofaea went out one day with a seine net in the forbidden area. They were observed by the chief himself, who was going down to bathe, before they began to fish. He made a most extravagant demonstration of anger which drew people from all sides of the village and sent the offenders scurrying to their houses. On another occasion Afirua, a young man living in the chief's village, and who was related to him through his mother, was wounded in the hand by a garfish when engaged in a fish drive at night. This was interpreted as a sign that he had encroached upon the forbidden ground. The eldest son of the

chief said to me in explanation, " It was done by the spirits.
I was standing on the beach.  I asked Afirua (in the darkness)
' Who is the person sitting there ? '  I spoke and spoke, but he
did not call out to me ; Afirua said not a word.  I went away,
and there, the fish pierced his hand.  Because he had made sport
of our ancestor.  Grandfather in consequence was angry with
him ; because he was his fruit.  He saw that he was not sensible.
He is a sacred child of the chief.  A man who wishes to go and
catch fish on the reef asks permission of the chief. . . . The
garfish which pierced him appeared because the coco-nut frond is
fresh.  It is good when the *tapu* has gone brown, when it is dry."

I asked whether the accident was not due to the utterance of
maleficient formulae (*tautuku*) by the chief or someone else.  The
answer was, " Not a man did *tautuku*, no ! Because the *tapu* was
there ; it was done by the spirit, because he was his sacred child."
By " Grandfather " and " the spirit " in this case is meant
Tereiteata, the grandfather's brother of the present chief, who
acts as his tutelary deity for many purposes, and to whom Afirua
as brother's son's daughter's son stood in a special relationship.[1]

This explanation draws attention first to the belief in the
direct interest of the spirit ancestors in the doings of their own
descendants, and secondly to the belief that the potency of the
supernatural sanction decreases as its material symbol grows old.
This explanation in esoteric terms marches with the actual
human tendency to respect a prohibition when it is newly imposed
and to begin to neglect it as time goes on.  It may be noted that
according to this incident quoted the man did not answer when
spoken to by the son of the chief because he was contemplating
a breach of the *tapu*.  In actual fact of course this may not have
been so.  But this type of explanation is common in Tikopia
after an event has occurred and has its place as a reflection of
native beliefs, and as part of the general sanction for upholding
the regulations.

Breaches of the conservational *tapu* are not always held to be
followed by evil consequences.  For instance while I was in
Tikopia Pa Fenuatara set up a *sakilo* in Nuku.  When the time
came for it to be " untied " he invited his father the chief to
come and perform the kava.  Not many coco-nuts had been saved
through the *tapu*.  Folk had gone and taken them regardless of
the coco-nut frond standing there.  The reason was that it was a

[1] See *We, The Tikopia*, Genealogies II and V.

time of distinct scarcity of food. Because of this Pa Fenuatara made no objection to their action when he found it out, and indeed removed the *tapu* earlier than otherwise in consequence. The Ariki Kafika was in full agreement with this. It was a *tapu* of fairly small range, being only on the orchards of Kafika and Faŋarere in that district.

On another occasion Pa Fenuatara told me how Rimakoroa, the eldest son of the Ariki Taumako, a young bachelor, had set up his *tapu* in Fatuvera, his father's orchard in Raveŋa, intending it to apply to the whole of that district. But he had not made it widely known, so people went as usual and took coco-nuts from their orchards. In disgust Rimakoroa abandoned his *tapu*. Although Pa Fenuatara did not say so it seems probable that people disregarded the *tapu* in part at least because the young man had no very assured personal influence apart from being his father's obvious heir. He was unmarried and had not as yet won for himself the reputation for skill in crafts, energy, or wise counsel which would have given it more weight. From this example it is clear how in Tikopia the imposition of a *tapu* may represent the endeavour of a single man to enforce his superior will on a section of the community. If his superiority is not already manifest in one way or another by ability or control of supernatural powers, then his attempt may fail. In the results which follow his setting up of a *tapu* an ambitious man can see how far he has consolidated his position in the eyes of his clan and others. Since a conservational *tapu* is never imposed without some adequate reason, then broad conformity to it is usual. But it is rare for there to be no evasion. If a *tapu* is nullified by frequent breaches then the man who imposed it becomes angry and ashamed, but he does not take any involved or serious action against the offenders ; the situation works itself out in minor displays of emotion and clashes of personality. A further indication that a *tapu* is not a regulation simply imposed and automatically obeyed is that the man who sets it up, even if he is a chief, goes from time to time to examine the locality and see that everything is in order. It is after such visits that he is apt to give vent to his feelings if he has discovered that sly breaches of it have been made.

But breach of the *tapu* is not the only method of securing an alleviation of it. Sometimes a person closely related to the chief, or of rank in another clan, may make a direct appeal to him to limit its range or lessen its intensity. For instance, after the death of the grandson of the Ariki Tafua a general *tapu* was imposed upon sea fishing in his district. After a while it was limited to the shore waters only. I was told that a son of the Ariki Kafika requested that the waters off the reef should not be prohibited in order that the fish which collected in safety on the reef might be taken as they returned to sea. This example shows how the Tikopia realize the economic incidence of a *tapu* imposed for non-economic reasons and may attempt to modify it to some degree accordingly.

In considering the differential economic effects of the imposition of *tapu* one must bear in mind on the one hand the different concentration of the productive factors concerned, and on the other the final incidence of the *tapu*. For instance taro gardens are scattered all over the island and there is never any occasion when the total quantity of land available is withheld from production at once. In any orchard there are always small patches of ground that can be turned to use. Coco-nut palms on the other hand, though scattered throughout the orchards, cannot be planted and used *ad hoc* ; a *tapu* upon them in one district means that a large quantity are withdrawn from consumption. With canoes the position is even more definite. The vessels of an individual, a family, a village are concentrated in the one immediate area, so that a *tapu* upon sea fishing means complete withdrawal of the people in the area from this form of productive enterprise, and from the consumption of all large fish and flying fish—except in so far as these may be received by gift from elsewhere. Some of the taboos examined then merely limit immediate production and consumption in specific places while allowing similar effort elsewhere ; others divert productive energies partially or entirely from one field to another. Most marked here is the effort of a chief or his son to take charge of the economic forces of his clan or district in the interests of the community, and limit present application of labour in order to get an increased product later. Such taboos are generally applied to coco-nuts because they are not the staple foodstuff but have their most important function in enriching other foods and providing a necessary item in large scale enterprises.

## THE CHIEF AS CONSUMER

So far we have dealt primarily with the ways in which a chief influences production. His role in distribution and consumption is equally important. Stated briefly, he is the recipient from his people of periodic gifts of food and special types of raw material which, sporadic in the case of any individual contributor, nevertheless form *in toto* a steady stream of additions to his wealth. But the position is not merely one-sided, for a great deal of what he receives he redistributes, and with his family's help he must reciprocate the initial gifts, though not necessarily to an equal extent. Here the important thing is the material acknowledgment of the contribution ; the exact amount of the acknowledgment is not of such moment. In Tikopia the chief is not in the position of a simple receiver of tribute, retaining a portion and redistributing the rest. His own orchards and other resources are drawn upon largely to the advantage of his people ; and his capital goods such as canoes are used to a considerable extent by them.[1]

These periodic gifts of food to the chief go under the generic name of *muaki kai*, or *muakai*, " the foremost food". In some contexts this is equivalent to the firstfruits of an enterprise or of a season's crop. But in general it refers to the fact that such gifts to the chief should be first claim upon the clansman's lands. This obligation is widely interpreted ; not only the chief's own clansfolk, but folk of other clans who live near him or are closely related to him take him gifts. These food gifts consist usually of a large basket (*popora*) containing a well-creamed pudding, or fish, or other delicacy, together with a mass of baked taro or yam tubers, breadfruit, or bananas. The principal item such as the pudding is of a type termed *kai ŋa ariki*, food of chiefs. This does not mean that such food may be eaten only by chiefs, but that it is of the quality fit for chiefs to eat. For instance, Pa Tekaumata made one day *roi futi*, a pudding of banana paste and coco-nut cream. His wife, a daughter of the Ariki Tafua, filled a basket with some and took it along to the chief. Pa Tekaumata said to me, " We are kinsfolk and so we put it in a *loŋi* or we put it in a *kete* " (both are types of small basket). Another man (not a kinsman) would take a large basket (*popora*). He said that the food would be reciprocated, not on the same day, but soon afterwards. The chief himself cannot of course consume personally all that he receives, and so distributes it

---

[1] This must be borne in mind in considering the generalization given by Thurnwald (*Economics of Primitive Communities*, xii) about the dominant economic position of the chief in Polynesia.

among members of his family, his neighbours, and his close kin. To some extent he reciprocates previous gifts in this way, so that he acts to a considerable extent as an agent in the circulation of food. But he reaps the benefit by being credited with generosity. His sons call him in formal terms " their orchard ". One of them said to me, " A chief is like an orchard, because food comes continually to him. When food comes the chief eats a little of it, but his sons eat a great deal. Therefore they speak of their father as their orchard, ' their orchard standing continually.' This is from of old, ancient speech from of old." The function of the chief as giver of largesse may be celebrated by the recipients in songs chanted on ceremonial occasions. Here is one composed in olden times by Pa Kavasa to his father, the then Ariki Taumako.

> *Tafito* :  Father ! Hasten to Uta,
> Celebrate your kava.
> I sit here.
> To me are carried
> My fish which have been strung separately, which
> Have been set apart and conveyed to me.

> *Kupu* :  My orchard is the *muakai*.
> Father ! My food portion
> I consume continually by your side.

This man lived in a separate house from his father, but frequently received food gifts from him, including fish specially set aside for him. Hence his gratitude.

Custom dictates that certain large fish such as shark, *varu*, and *para* should be given by clansmen to their chief. It is permissible for elders such as Pae Sao, Pa Rarovi, and others to cook such fish for themselves but even then they usually make a gesture and hand it over. It is believed that if an ordinary commoner keeps such a prize for himself the chief will be angry and will bewitch the man so that his belly swells and he falls ill. For this reason men are afraid to retain such foods. But evasion is practised. I was told that if a man hauls up a *varu* he will not wait till morning to come in with the fleet but will slip in during the night. The fish is hidden in his house and when the oven is prepared is secretly put into it. None but his family and canoe crew know and they will not tell. These fish, though somewhat rank to European taste, are highly esteemed by the Tikopia. They are termed " the fish of chiefs ", but again the frame of reference is distribution rather than ownership. As with the *muakai* the chief orders portions of them to be distributed to other people. Once when a *varu* was hauled up by my neighbour Pa ŋatotiu he presented it to me after some talk in his family. He said, " You are a chief, so that it is appropriate for you to have it." This was a good move on his part because my house had no oven and the obvious thing for me to do was to ask him to cook it for me. The upshot was that he and his family received the largest share. My servant Vahihaloa remarked cynically that this in fact was the object of the presentation. Otherwise Pa ŋatotiu would have had to give it to his chief, the Ariki Taumako.

Another type of customary gift is expressed in the saying " The border of the path is the orchard of the chiefs " (*Te vae ara te tofi o ŋa ariki*). This is not merely a rhetorical prerogative but an actual one. If, for instance, a bunch of bananas is growing to maturity near the edge of a path between orchards the kinsmen of the owner may say to him, " What are you leaving your banana bunch there at the border of the path for ? Why don't you cut it (and cook it green) ? Do you want to carry it to the chief ? " The operation of the convention is not automatic ; it rests at the discretion of the owner, not at the fiat of the chief. And the owner decides what to do in accordance with his relative desires for bananas, his relations with his chief, the periodicity of his gifts in the past, and whether he wishes something from the chief in the immediate future.

Gifts of food to a chief are also made as material expressions of specific kinship ties. Pa Niukapu was discussing with me how the junior descendants of chiefs become in time commoners. Now and again such a commoner will say, " I am going to prepare food for my father the chief." The food is got ready and the chief invited to the man's house. There a kava ceremony is performed with the chief as officiator, some food is eaten and then the chief goes. A large basket of food is then sent after him as a gift to his own house. The idea of this is that the commoner thus keeps up the ancestral connection—" He goes to the chief " as the expression is. Pa Niukapu said, " If it were I living here, if I do not go to the chief, it is bad. I go like a rat or like a swamp rail ; I go apart, there is no basis for me. But if I go to the chief, it is fine." He went on to say that this link is not kept up equally by all people. " People are many who gather around the chief ; but while one man goes, another man does not."

Such gifts are made to the chief especially when he has become the object of immediate social interest, as when he is ill, in mourning, paying a visit to another chief or receiving a visit from him. For instance when the Ariki Tafua stayed with the Ariki Taumako in the latter's house Raniniu, members of his clan came daily to him from Faea with presents of food. Such attendance is known as *sakiraŋa*, " seeking " the chief. In this case eight or ten baskets of food were received by the Ariki Tafua on each day of his stay. After the donors had made their presentation they were given areca nut from a supply put at the disposal of the Ariki Tafua by his host. The food itself was handed over by the guest to the Ariki Taumako, and when the people returned home in the evening they were given a counter present from the Taumako supplies.

When a person is in mourning, he is debarred from eating certain types of food. This restriction operates less to his disadvantage than might at first appear. Different members of his kinship group come from time to time according to their inclination, bringing with them creamed puddings or other food to " feed " the mourner. Strictly speaking this food is *tapu* to him, but on being pressed by the visitor he generally eats, so that the giver will not be ashamed—such being the official native explanation. In fact it is nothing but a conventional mechanism for lightening the mourning burdens. A chief reaps more benefit from this than do commoners, partly because of his wider kinship relations, and partly because his condition attracts greater attention. When the Ariki Tafua was in mourning for his brother he was frequently " fed " in this way. Two explanations were given me for this. One was " When the chief has dwelt long (in mourning) his people are sympathetic towards him, and prepare his portion of food ". The other was " Because he is an elderly person, he and mother ". " Mother " referred to his wife, who was included in the feeding as well. I noticed that the younger members of his family did not receive anything like the same consideration from their kinsfolk, and kept the food taboos much more rigidly. It may be noted that this " feeding " is analogous to the *asi*, the conventional breach of *tapu* imposed upon the catching of fish or the taking of coco-nuts. The Tikopia are no purists and have adopted recognized mechanisms to alleviate the burden of restrictions in the general force of which they believe.

An important part of the chief's income are the gifts of food that he receives from members of his clan and from other chiefs when they themselves have performed an important ceremony. Such are the *fakaariki*, an example of which was mentioned in describing the lifting of the *tapu* of Pa Fenuatara. Similar presentations occur frequently during the seasonal ritual cycles of the Work of the Gods. Then at the initiation, marriage, sickness, or death of a person of rank the chief also receives his present. For instance, when Pa Tavi, an elder of the Ariki Kafika, had a swollen mouth through a decaying tooth, a crowd of people, including the chiefs of Kafika and Taumako, assembled to wail over him. Large baskets of food were presented to each because of their attendance ; such is the custom when a chief visits a commoner on a ceremonial occasion. The gift to the Ariki Kafika is set out first—though it is not necessarily the best food from the oven. Precedence in distribution is. more important than quality here. Sometimes other goods are given in addition. The chief takes no present to the gathering himself, but some of his family carry a contribution of green food to the oven. This gift to the chief is of the type called *raŋoraŋo ŋa ariki*, " supporting of chiefs." The term has analogies with the lifting up of a canoe off the ground by means of skids, and means doing honour to the chief. Other increments to the chief's wealth come as *malai*, gifts of atonement. From the marriage of a clanswoman, from a detected theft of his property, from an apology for an insult to him, the chief receives a gift of food and valuables.

If a gift of food or valuables is sent from one chief to another then the recipient recites a formula to render the things " mild " (*marie*) ; coming direct from the donor they are " bitter " (*kona*). In this is implicit the idea of the contagious power of the touch of a chief. According to Pa Fenuatara his father renders the gift available for ordinary consumption by appealing to his two major deities Pu ma :

> " That is the food of you two, Pu ma.
> Let be made mild by you.
> The vegetation which has been plucked hither from
> Pa Taumako
> Be it brought down for well-being."

Pa Fenuatara said, " Vegetation which has been plucked and brought hither from another chief is a weighty affair. Therefore the chief to whom it is brought performs the kava over it that it may be mild."[1]

The concept of "the food of chiefs" has been discussed. Analogous with it is that of "the property of chiefs" (*koroa ŋa ariki*). This comprises articles which are not owned or used solely by chiefs but which are peculiarly appropriate to give to them, because of their value. In particular, they include hanks of the very strong sinnet cord used for catching shark, and bonito hooks with barb attached. Such are described as *araŋa vaka*, fittings of the canoe. A common type of statement about them is "They are there with the commoner, but they are fittings of the chief". For any important event the *malai* of atonement should include one or other of these articles. Gifts from one chief to another to obtain an important boon rely largely for their effect on the value of such articles. Other prized miscellaneous articles are also commonly put in this category. The Ariki Tafua and I were discussing the origin of the black stone adze blades of which there are a few in Tikopia among the generality of shell blades. He said that he did not know whether they were imported or made in the island but that they were valuable—"property of chiefs". In the same category come the cylindrical shell bead ornaments called *rei* though a few of them are owned by commoners too. Valuables of these latter types are rare with commoners, or where a commoner's house has one only, that of a chief will have a number.

The most developed form of this concept of delegated ownership is seen in the sacred canoes which are one of the most important forms of Tikopia property. They are described as being "canoes of the chief, but hauled up with the commoners". Actually they are built by the commoners' own resources and at their initiative; and they themselves use them. The function of the chief is to act as titular owner and perform the principal ritual for them. Some statements by Pa Porima will illustrate the point. In discussing fishing and canoe ritual, he said of a vessel of his, "My canoe, but the chief comes to perform kava for it; my own canoe which I have had built." He said again in general form, "The canoe of a man is hewn, hewn, and then

---

[1] I pointed out to Pa Fenuatara that there was among the Maori a custom of reciting a formula over a gift of food at a feast in order to remove from it possible evil influences associated with the donors. He agreed that the usage in Tikopia was somewhat similar, though here it seemed to be a question of involuntary powers rather than conscious witchcraft.

he goes to speak to the chief about the canoe of them both as to what may be his wish—as to who may be set up as tutelary spirits of the canoe. The sacred canoes are given, as big spirits, only the chiefs, the *kau firifiri* (that is, the line of dead chiefs). The chief may speak of their father or he may speak of their ancestor of old, whoever he may mention." By this he meant that it is the privilege of the chief to choose one of his own forbears as principal spirit guardian of the vessel. He gave as an example the canoe built by Pa Faiaki who went to the Ariki Taumako and asked him whom he would like to be the tutelary spirit of the vessel. The Ariki answered that he wished to have his father, the late chief, as the guardian spirit, so this appointment was made. The concept of ownership is based upon the thesis that while the material body of the craft is that of the commoner, the spirit guardian is that of the chief, hence the vessel is termed " the canoe of the chief ". The basis for this is that according to Tikopia practice the ancestor of a commoner cannot be invoked in the kava ceremony and so for any canoe which is important enough to be the subject of such a ceremony, an ancestor of the chief is essential. According to the Tikopia scheme of integration between ritual and economic affairs, kava ceremonies must be periodically performed over the larger vessels to ensure their success in fishing. In such a society, where the chiefs have not aggregated to themselves the majority of the lands and other material resources, it is not possible for them alone to undertake the expense of the construction of all the most important craft.' The solution has then been found in this system of joint or delegated ownership. Put another way the native statement expresses the situation thus, " A sacred canoe obeys the chief and the man with whom the canoe rests ; a sacred canoe obeys only its oven, the food which is prepared by the man with whom the canoe rests, but it is provided with spirit guardians, the spirits of the chief who came to perform ritual over it."

One important feature of the chief's role in consumption is the generosity that is expected from him. By convention he should send surpluses of food from his household to members of his clan, pass on to them baskets of food received from other sources, and always have on hand some tobacco and betel materials for distribution to those who call on him. The economic aspect of visiting and granting of hospitality is very marked.

I take from my notebook two sample instances observed when visits were paid to the Ariki Kafika one morning. One was made by Pa Tavi, an elder of the chief, who came with a basket of half a dozen seed yams. As he entered he called out " *E aue !* " (literally this means " Oh ! alas ", but the expression is often used as a sympathetic greeting). He handed the basket to the chief who took out the yams carefully. After they had talked a little, the chief told one of the women to produce food. Pa Tavi said, " No, leave it. I am full." They talked of fishing, and then the chief asked him if he was going to stay for the re-carpeting ceremonies of Nukuora temple which were due in a day or so. A little apologetically Pa Tavi said that he was going to work instead. " It is well," said the chief, " It is well. Wait until another time." He then took a piece of tobacco and handed it over, saying, " The payment for the yams." The Ariki then called for areca nut and a bunch of the smaller variety was brought. This he split and handed over half. It was taken without a word. The chief then told him to give half of his portion to a boy to take as a present to the Ariki Faŋarere who was in an adjacent house. Pa Tavi replied " Leave it, I'll take it myself ". Then he broke off a piece from his own remaining portion and handed it over to Nau Kafika. She protested, but he insisted and she put it into her basket. After a little more talk on fishing, he departed.

Another visit was paid by the Ariki Taumako to the Ariki Kafika. He really came for a talk, but the pretext was that he wanted some lime. He squatted outside the house for a moment until he was pressed to come in. He entered and was made to sit with his back against a post—a mark of respect. Both the chiefs talked freely to each other and to the other people in the house, joking together, which was proper since they were classificatory brothers. The Ariki Kafika played the courteous host, saying to a child who sat near the visitor " Eyes of the chief ", meaning keep away from the chief. The Ariki Taumako replied " Oh, he's all right sitting there ". The Ariki Kafika asked if his visitor had any betel materials—he produced a single areca nut, the only one he had, and promptly handed it over. The Ariki Kafika prepared it in his betel mortar. A discussion then took place as to where it came from—a temple ceremony which the Ariki Taumako had attended the day before. A few minutes later the host handed over a bit of tobacco to his guest and told him where it came from.  Discussion took place freely on the fish caught the night before, on areca nut, and on certain lengths of sinnet cord.  The visitor complained that no men had yet turned up to assist him in a piece of work he was about to do ; that so far only women were there.  They talked also of a dance to take place after all the ritual of the ceremonial season was over.  The Ariki Taumako proposed that the chiefs of Raveŋa go together to the Ariki Tafua and that they hold a collective festival in Faea.  At that time the Ariki Tafua was still barred from dancing because of the recent deaths of his grandson and of his brother. Then the Ariki Taumako went out, retreating stern first as a mark of respect to the Ariki Kafika.  The latter remarked when his visitor had gone " He's a chief who likes a laugh".

These two examples, which are typical of relations of hospitality, show the commingling of economic transactions and social intercourse which is so characteristic of the Tikopia.  It will be noted that in each case a gift or an article solicited received some material repayment.  Towards poor commoners, however, a chief is expected to be generous without necessarily getting anything in return.  On another occasion the Ariki Kafika commented on the Ariki Taumako, with a laugh, " The stupid, he asks me for tobacco leaf, like an orphan."

The following Table summarizes the principal ways in which the resources at the disposal of a chief are enlarged by gifts.

TABLE VI

CONTRIBUTIONS TO A CHIEF'S INCOME

(i)   *From commoners, usually of his clan or village.*

| *Gift.* | *Return Gift.* |
| --- | --- |
| Shark and other large fish | Basket of food |
| Bunches of areca, bananas, etc., from " borders of the path " | Tobacco, etc. |
| *Muakai*—periodic presents of cooked food | Basket of food |
| *Fakaariki*—share of food from important ceremony | Basket of food |
| *Vai* to chief on a visit | Basket of food |
| *Monotaŋa* of sacred canoe | Basket of food |
| *Monotaŋa* from funeral | Basket of food |
| *Fonakava* from re-carpeted temple | By re-distribution |
| *Monotaŋa* from initiation ceremony | Basket of food |
| *Malai* on marriage of woman of chiefly house | None |
| *Malai* for insult, loss of canoe, etc. | None |

(ii) *From other chiefs*

| Gift. | Return Gift. |
|---|---|
| Baskets of food on visit | Basket of food |
| Share of food from any important ceremony | Basket of food |
| Share of food at feast | Prior food |
| Food from temple rebuilding | Basket of food |
| *Monotaŋa* of *taumauri* canoes (to Ariki Kafika only) | Basket of food |
| " The path of our Ancestor " (from Taumako to Kafika only) | Basket of food |
| Goods for visit at sickness | Basket of food |

These items, taken together, do not represent a large accretion to the real income of a chief, since by prior contribution, by subsequent reciprocity or by redistribution he disburses nearly as much as he receives. But they do give him a command over wealth which is of great importance. In the recarpeting of temples in the monsoon season of 1928, for instance, the Ariki Kafika received eleven *fonakava*, and the Ariki Taumako seven, each consisting of a huge basket of cooked food and a supplementary basket of fish. These were redistributed on the spot to the principal kinship groups represented, including the donors. That of Nukuora temple was brought by the household of the Ariki Faŋarere, and handed over to that of Pa Tarairiki, of Kafika. But this man, in common with others of Kafika, had contributed a portion of green food to it.

## A Chief Gives a Feast

The chief also affects the economic processes of the community by the ceremonial feasts which he sponsors. One such feast is known as *aŋa*, a term applied also to the accumulations of food for initiation and marriage rites. The *aŋa* of a commoner is small compared with that of a chief, which mobilizes the economic life of the community on a large scale.

A first impression of such a feast as being a generous provision of food motivated by charity represents only one side of the picture. From the point of view of the chief the *aŋa* marks a stage in the progression of his reign. It gives an opportunity to display his food resources and to assert his rank ; it secures for him ceremonial expressions of thanks from his chiefly guests and of loyalty from his clanspeople ; and in the later stages demonstrates his own fidelity to his gods and thereby ensures their continued interest in him. The *aŋa* also has the general function of allowing chiefs to meet ceremonially and demonstrate their common interests.

The initiative for such a feast lies with the chief but he has a traditional obligation to have a certain number during his lifetime. Each feast has its own name and some have a definite order of precedence. The first is *te moriŋa*, " the conveying," and takes place soon after his election, and signifies the symbolic carriage of the new chief to his appropriate status. The next is *te puŋaumu*, " the kindling of the ovens," a generic name applied also to initiation and funeral meals. It takes place as a rule several years after the chief's accession. The third feast is *te fakataŋata* or *te aroarima* (or *te aroaroima*). The first name means literally " making a man " but does not correspond to any special maturity of status of the chief. This feast is of the type known as *aŋa soro*, so called because immense quantities of taro are grated (*soro*), so called because immense quantities of taro are grated (*soro*). By this time the chief is an elderly man ; his beard has begun to turn grey, " Its token is the jaw which has become grey haired." The last feast in order is *te fakamatua*, " the making elderly," the term again having no special significance. It also is of the *aŋa soro* type, and it takes place when the chief judges that the end of his life is near.

Another feast apart from the series mentioned is the *seru*. This is extremely important since it is the occasion of the first performance of sacred songs which the chief composes to his deities. It is made only when the chief is elderly, " When the grey hairs have sprung."

A chief will hold a feast only if the crops have been good that season, and if he has accumulated large reserves. The first three are regarded as obligatory but after the *fakataŋata* the others lie entirely at his discretion.

From Pa Fenumera and Pa Taraoro, leading men of Faŋarere clan, I obtained a long account of the *moriŋa*. When a chief dies and the new chief is elected he is " conveyed " to Marae, the sacerdotal centre of the island, by the medium of the *moriŋa* feast. It is the first large-scale public occasion on which he has ceremonial and economic relations with his fellow chiefs, and incidentally with his gods. Usually there is no long delay—the feast may even occur a couple of days after the funeral rites are over. If the chief is agreeable then he gives the word for the preliminary assembling of food, the *tokonaki* of the *aŋa*, a generic term for all such occasions.[1] Such work may take three days. Food of all kinds is brought in from the cultivations and orchards

[1] *We The Tikopia*, 436–9.

of the new chief and his clansfolk, while the other chiefs and their clansfolk send along contributions also.

For any feast of a chief all men connected with him by marriage to women of his kinship group and even of his clan go to assist as cooks.

At the same time messengers are sent from the new chief and the heads of families of his clan to invite the *paito* (kinship groups) of the other clans. Then in the morning baskets are filled with the food and carried to the house of the new chief. There they are exchanged between hosts and guests according to the plan of the invitations. After the exchange of food a rite termed *te kava taratara* is performed. The chiefs assemble in the house of their new fellow, he recites a formula over the kava stem, and libations are then poured to the gods. Cups of the liquid are carried to each chief in turn beginning with the new chief, as *ariki tau aŋa*, the chief responsible for the feast.

When the pouring of libations is complete there comes a formal recital of thanks known as the *oriori*, intended as a *fakaepa*, a mark of honour, and paid first by a representative of the host to each of the visiting chiefs in order of precedence, and then by each of their representatives to the host. The phraseology is conventional and a recital of similar name and in much the same terms is given by a man to the expert who has just made him a new canoe.

Pa Tarairaki of Kafika said that he recited as follows :

" Pa Taumako !
You excrete hither for me to eat.
You have brought in a mighty feast.
You have carried in sweet-smelling things completely in your
    feast.
You have turned up the continually standing stone.
You have lifted up the stone covered over.
You have brought together
Your death-causing feast.
The commoner people are smothered below,
They indeed who follow at the back of the chief,
And your clan there.
You excrete hither for me to eat."

As usual the formula contains a number of metaphorical expressions. The promised eating of excrement is a linguistic symbol of abasement. The " sweet-smelling things " (*manoŋi*) refers to the food of the *aŋa*. " The continually standing stone " is a reference to the yam, the food which more than any other is always available in the orchard. The " stone covered over " is the *masi*, paste of taro or breadfruit which is kept in a pit with stones on top. The suggestion is also, by using the word " stone ", that these foods are of a durable order. The epithet " death-causing " applies not, as might be thought, to any effects upon digestion but to the enormous labour necessary to bring it together.

When the *oriori* is finished kinsfolk of the reciter call out " *makona! makona!* " and again " *ku pi! ku pi!* " " satisfied, satisfied", " he is full, he is full", meaning from the excrement that he is alleged to have consumed. One informant said that phrases of the *makona* type are called out only by brothers of the reciter and men of equal status, since otherwise they might be insulting. The rest of his group merely call a general assent. When they hear the voice of the reciter say " Excrete that I may eat " they call out the phrases mentioned and also begin to whoop and shout so that the rest of the formula is never heard but is lost in the babel of sound.

Only a few people are competent to recite the *oriori*. In selecting a man it is said " there he shall *oriori* because he is a first-class expert ". As each chief hears the *oriori* recited to him he sends his special food portion, a large one, over to the reciter as an acknowledgment. The man's own chief also sends him a food portion with a gift of areca materials. At the time of the recital the speaker is standing outside the house while the chiefs are seated within. Each chief as he hears his name called sits with bowed head until the speech is over, then lifts his head and begins to eat. None of the food is consumed until the *oriori* is over.

The main meal of the day is prepared in the " great oven ". After the oven is uncovered large baskets of food are set out, one for each of the chiefs. Those for the visitors are topped off by two or three pieces of bark-cloth. The basket of the Ariki Kafika has an orange bark-cloth, the symbol of his god. Sprouting coco-nuts, bunches of bananas, and taro from the wall of food are added and also a branch of kava. The people of each clan with their chief in front have their own seating places in the host's house. Now comes a ceremony which is superficially a mark of honour to the new chief but is in reality one of making offerings to his dead ancestors. A procession of women enters, each bearing on her arm a pile of bark-cloths with a little package of turmeric on top. They come up behind the chief one by one to the tail end of his seating mat—the less sacred end—and he takes the gift from each and places it at the head of his mat. The women are representatives of the various ramages (*paito*), the *fuaŋa* of the dead chiefs, that is, their maternal kinsfolk in order of succession. Each woman smears her turmeric on the belly and arms of the new chief and retires. Baskets of food are brought by the women, too, and are later reciprocated from the supplies of the holder of the feast, but the bark-cloth is not. The cloths are termed *a noforaŋa*, seats, and are regarded as being placed for the spirits of the dead chiefs to sit upon.

After the women retire the kava of the " great oven " is made. A formula is recited by the new chief and he and the others pour their libations and make their offerings of food. Then the baskets are carried to the separate temples of each chief, who makes his own kava there with those people of his clan who have left and followed him. The passage of the food is called " *a morimori o ŋa ariki* " " conveyings of the chiefs ".

One further rite follows. The *aŋa* has been divided into three portions. One known as the *rau tapu*, the sacred portion, stands at the sacred end of the house of the chief. The next stands on the *mata paito* side, and is drawn upon for the gifts of sprouting coco-nuts, etc. ; the third stands on the *tuaumu* side, and is drawn upon for the ovens. The sacred portion is not touched until the day after the " great oven ". Then people from the visiting clans carry it with the remnants of the other portion and stand them at the bottom of Marae. People of the host's clan do not touch them. Then a " kava house " is built. This ceremonial operation consists in standing up a number of branches of kava to form a little erection. The work must be done by the two principal elders of Tafua—Pa Saukirima and Pae Sao. They are known as *a soka*, ritual workers. Then the four chiefs enter the sacred ground in procession according to precedence. Each chief goes to his seat in Marae. The host chief has brought with him four pieces of bark-cloth, which he lays on his seating mat. Then he rises, puts one on a *rau tea* leaf and makes a ceremonial presentation of it to the Ariki Faŋarere, after having made obeisance with it to this chief's god at Muafaitoka. He presents the next piece similarly to the Ariki Kafika and the third to the Ariki Taumako. The fourth remains on his own mat. These are

offerings not to the chiefs but to their respective deities.  This
rite is known as *moriŋa ŋa tapakau* " the conveying of seating
places of the deities ".

When this is over the Ariki Tafua, who is the chief traditionally
entitled to perform public ceremonial in Marae, goes to the little
" kava house ", places his hand on it, and recites a special form
of invocation used only in this sacred place.  When the kava is
over the food is carried inland where the chiefs' houses are and
is divided among them.  The host chief himself takes no portion
of the food.  Each chief divides what he has received among the
people of his clan.

The other feasts given by a chief follow the same general
form—a vast assemblage of food, a gathering of all the chiefs
together, a ceremonial mutual thanksgiving, some acknowledgment of the gods, and a distribution of the food.  The main
distinction is in feasts of the *aŋa soro* type.  Each chief gives
such a feast once or twice in his reign and for it he invites the
other chiefs to lend their *nafa*, huge bowl-shaped troughs, into
which taro is grated until they are heaped full.  The operation of
grating is termed *soro*, hence the name given to the feast as a whole.

When the Ariki Tafua held his *aŋa soro* some years before I
was in Tikopia the quantities of food were enormous.  According
to Seremata coco-nuts alone were brought in for two days and
were then followed by taro, yams, *pulaka* (giant taro), bananas,
*taumako* (pseudo-yam), breadfruit, and sugar cane.  Five troughs
were assembled and each was piled high with grated taro.  One
was from each of the other three Ariki, one from Pa Rarovi, and
one from Tafua itself.  Thus each of the five principal men of
Tikopia contributed a giant receptacle, the contents of which
were later allotted to him as part of his share of the feast.  As
each trough was carried to its place on the seaward side of Marae
the bearers emitted a series of whoops.  On the inland side of
Marae a great quantity of *masi* (fermented taro and breadfruit
paste) was accumulated.  " I counted the baskets," said my
informant.  " There was a complete hundred, and there remained
fifty in a second hundred."  After a meal together with their
guests the hosts distributed the food.  So great was the quantity
that it was said, " The Marae at Matautu, when the feast went
to it, disappeared.  Enormous was the amount of food indeed."
And again, " We who went to gather in the food came back killed
by the size of our shoulder-loads."

The economic organization of such a feast demands considerable forethought and preparations well in advance. Five months before I left Tikopia, the Ariki Tafua had begun to get ready for his *seru*. In the middle of February he and his sons began to break up the soil in their own and adjacent orchards in Rakisu for the planting of taro. As the days went by other people, mainly of the chief's district of Faea, began to follow suit. To some extent this was due to the arrival of the ordinary planting season but there was more than the ordinary concentration of labour. Every day from twenty to forty people were engaged. A fortnight later the planting of the Tafua family was complete and I was told that if the crop turned out well then it would be applied to the *seru* of the chief. As March went on the Ariki Kafika and his family also began to plant in Rakisu while the Ariki Taumako went to work in his cultivations on Reani. By the end of March planting was practically over. It was said at this time by members of the family of the Ariki Tafua that he had not yet begun to compose the songs for his *seru*, but that when the taro began to mature then he would " search " for his songs. By the beginning of May song practice had already begun in Matautu ; the songs tried out were some of those composed to the chief by members of his clan. At this time the women of the chief's household were preparing bark-cloth which was specifically said to be for the *aŋa*. A week later other families in the village had also taken up the work in large quantities. The preparations of bark-cloth went on all through May, that for the *aŋa* being merged with that for an initiation ceremony, and for a burial rite in the family of Tafua. Towards the end of June again the chief and his family began preparing more bark-cloth and pandanus mats, and their stimulus was taken up all through the village. By the beginning of July this work was in hand in many places through the island, including the household of the Ariki Taumako and those of other prominent people in Raveŋa. Song practice had now begun in earnest in Matautu. Unfortunately my departure from the island robbed me of the chance of attendance at the *seru* itself.

From various sources I was given an account of the organization of the *seru*. In quantities of food accumulated and the general character of the distribution among the assembled chiefs the *seru* follows the line of the feasts already described. The distinguishing feature is the chanting of a great number of songs.

Soon after I arrived in Tikopia I was told that the *seru* consisted in an assembly of people who sang songs in praise of one another. But later I realized that the motif of the *seru* is not so much the exchange of compliments between men as the paying of respect to gods.

Some of the songs are composed by the chief and his people to the gods of the clan, others to the chief by his clansfolk.

The co-ordination of the chanting of the songs is not a haphazard matter. The *purotu*, who are also practical experts in dancing, are expected to take the lead and are watched by the other dancers and the audience. They have the job of introducing songs and the responsibility for their adequate rendering. They are usually recognized composers as well. For these services they are rewarded by ceremonial presents of bark-cloth, *ufi*, " coverings ". The service for which they are specifically given is the compliment paid by the composition of a song to a chief or to one of his gods. Guests as well as host are involved in this, for the host chief has composed songs to some of the gods of the other chiefs. The limited number of these gods and the general recognition of their status by all gives a chief some idea in advance of what will occur. The visiting chiefs thus take care to provide themselves with bark-cloth and even pandanus leaf mats. If separate songs are sung in honour of several of the chief's gods then he makes a separate *ufi* for each. The gifts are made during the performance of the song, as soon as the chief recognizes its attribution, or immediately afterwards.

The songs of the *seru* are not lost after the completion of the ceremony. They are embodied in the permanent repertoire of the people by being used ceremonially in the Work of the Gods in the next and succeeding monsoon seasons.

A Tikopia chief plays an important role in ceremonial feasts outside the series specifically associated with him as just described. From time to time the childhood or adolescence of children of rank is marked by a celebration on the part of their parents. One such is the *pea*. It is described as *taumafa o ŋa tamariki* " food portions of the children ", and is performed only for girls. It consists of a feast, exchange of valuables, and dancing. The feast is termed *aŋa* as usual. Only chiefs, their near relatives and wealthy elders can afford such a gesture. As the *taŋata tau aŋa*, the primary feast giver, is thus usually a chief, he is able to command on general grounds a large supply of food and also reaps the major prestige of the event.

## SOCIAL EFFECTS OF FEASTS

In summarizing the social effects of this series of feasts there are three sets of personal considerations : as an offset to the expenditure of time, labour, and wealth the chief himself, the members of his clan, and his guests from the other clans must get some recompense.   The chief himself fulfils a traditional obligation, makes use of his command of wealth to maintain his reputation and sets the seal upon his status.  His people become a focus of social interest at second hand, indirectly acquire prestige through the size of the feast, and are able to demonstrate in a material way their fidelity to their leader.   The guests consume and take away quantities of food, more than they contribute, and receive wealth of a more permanent kind.  All alike share in the excitement which attaches to such a huge gathering and have a focal point for the orientation of their economic energies, and for their everyday conversation for many months.   Under the sanction of such strong obligations every person who takes part in the *aŋa* is impelled to participate in forms of co-operation which for the time being go far beyond his personal interests and those of his family and reach the bounds of the whole community.  Such a feast gathers together chiefs and their clansfolk who at other times are rivals ready to criticize and slander each other, but who assemble here with an outward show of amity.  The social forces and personal sentiments which lead them to participate in these activities are in some cases strongly contrasted, but harmony of action is secured by the unity of the common purpose in assembly, and by the recognition that certain common values at least are paramount. There are the explicit aims which can be translated into concrete linguistic expressions, bodily movements, and transference of material goods, as for instance when at the *aŋa* any member of a clan will describe his presence there and his contributions of food as tokens of loyalty to his chief.  In addition, such purposive activity subserves certain wider social ends, which are common in the sense that every person or nearly every person knowingly or unknowingly promotes them.  For instance, attendance at the *aŋa* and participation in the economic contributions does in fact help to support the Tikopia system of authority. Once, elected as chief, a man is able to control the behaviour of the members of his kinship group upon some of their most vital and personal issues, such as securing adequate food, freedom of recreation, and in the last resort even their right to live.

## THE CHIEF'S CONTRIBUTION IN THE TIKOPIA ECONOMY

In this chapter the chief has been shown to be the most important single human factor in the economic life of the Tikopia. Not only does he play a part as a producer within his immediate household, but by initiative and example he gives direction to the productive work of the community ; he is titular owner of the most valuable property of the members of his clan ; he imposes far-reaching restrictions on production and consumption and in many important activities he acts as a focal point in the processes of exchange and distribution.

But it should be clear that the role of the chief in the economic process is not that of an exploiting capitalist, taking in return for productive risks the profit of the enterprise. Every head of a household is to some extent an entrepreneur, and in the large scale productive undertakings initiated by a chief his people share in the benefits. The existence of chiefs may even prevent the rise of exploiting individuals in the society ; their social and ritual authority acts as a repressive factor on the emergence of authority due to economic power alone. Even though this may be simply in defence of their own class interests the effect is the same.

In view of the inequality of control over resources and of income between the chiefs and the commoners in Tikopia society one might expect to find some evidence of a clash between them, expressed partly in expressions of discontent with the existing state of things, and partly in attempts of the commoners to evade their material obligations. I have already given instances of clash between chiefs and commoners, and expression of opinion about the actions of chiefs.[1] And cases do occur where a commoner fails to render his due to his chief. But such criticism, evasion or failure to fulfil obligations is directed against the specific acts of chiefs in a defined context, and not against the system of chiefly rule and economic privileges as a whole. That the position is one generally accepted is demonstrated by the fact

[1] *We, The Tikopia,* 379–382.

that there is no real regimentation of the commoners to contribute to the chief's economic pre-eminence ; the forms of executive authority are vaguely defined, and come into operation only to cope with major breaches of the law, such as incest or direct insult to the chief. And even then, there are mechanisms to mitigate the final rigours of punishment. Failure to assist the chief in production or to give him customary tribute incurs his displeasure and grumbling, but involves no direct material sanctions against the defaulter, and is not backed up by any concensus of popular approval.

It is important to realize that in Tikopia the economic inequalities are mostly those of degree, and are often of small range of difference ; moreover, the economic position of one chief, the Ariki Faŋarere, is definitely and overtly recognized as being much less than that of some commoners. He is a " poor aristocrat ". It is in the social and ritual sphere that the inequalities are those of kind and are irreducible. They cannot be regarded as a simple outcome of economic differences.

However, if a chief is not primarily a capitalist may he not still be the final organizer of the economy, dictating the choices of his people as consumers and the spheres in which their activity as producers shall be applied ? To some extent this is so—by convention a commoner is barred from consuming the larger fish, and should render them to his chief ; and a commoner's utilization of his coco-nuts, certain taro lands, the reef waters and sea-going canoes may be governed by the fiat of the chief. But such a fiat does not normally operate to the chief's personal advantage ; if anything it may be to his disadvantage since the resulting diminution in quality and quantity of food obtained reacts upon the amount of " tribute " he receives. And in imposing such courses of action the chief usually shows himself distinctly conscious of his responsibility for the economic interests of his people. In so far as he takes a decisive part in the organization of the economy it is thus not directed to his own benefit. Moreover, in taking these decisions he is not simply following his own judgment—some of his taboos may be conservational in intent, but most are dictated by obligations of ritual such as mourning or respect for the gods.

This brings us to an important point—ultimately the mode of production is inherent in the social tradition, of which the chief is merely the prime agent and interpreter. He and his people share the same values: an ideology of kinship, ritual, and morality reinforced by legend and mythology. The chief is to a considerable extent a custodian of this tradition, but he is not alone in this. His elders, his fellow chiefs, the people of his clan, and even the members of his family are all imbued with the same values, and advise and criticize his actions. Moreover, the chief is bound in his own economic conduct by the system of *tapu*, which as we have seen is regarded by the people as essentially imposed by them, by the fact of their election of him. Even if their point of view should be regarded by the sociologist as a rationalization, by which the people ascribe to themselves an unreal volitional role in order to justify their own actual passivity in the system, it is undeniable that the acts of the chief are definitely so restricted, and that he himself shares the same point of view as his people about the derivative character of his power.

It is difficult to conceive what might be the economy of the Tikopia without chiefs. But it is fair to assume that production and consumption of households would be carried on much as at present, that co-operative undertakings such as fish drives, sago extraction, and canoe-building would still take place, as also the elaborate exchanges of goods and initiation, marriage, and mortuary ceremonies. But large-scale assemblies for ritual purposes would be absent, with the recreational facilities they offer ; and there would be no ultimate co-ordination of ownership of lands and canoes. There would be no " tribute " to be given to the central authority, but neither would there be any central source of hospitality and economic assistance. Nor would there be any ultimate authority for the adjustment of disputes, no personal rallying point for communal interests, no possibility of checking the emergence of power derived from differential wealth or exploitation by the seizure of the means of production. Moreover the economy would lack the system of co-ordination now provided by the ritual functions of the chiefs, the demarcation of spheres of interest among them and their precedence. At the present time the chief is a bridge between the kinship structure, the political organization, the ritual, and the economic system ; he is the prime human integrating factor in the society. That the co-ordinating value of the chief is a reality to the people is shown by the anxiety which they show when a chief goes off on a voyage. When several chiefs were absent simultaneously towards the end of last century, as native accounts tell, the people felt that the land was left leaderless, without proper direction.

No doubt, left to themselves the Tikopia could forge a system with a co-ordinated central authority, but it would take time, and might lack the precision and firmness of the present system. Moreover, it is quite possible that this co-ordination might be effective only at a low level of integration for the constituent groups of the community, and might fail to operate with any generally acknowledged sanctions.   If the breakdown of the chiefly system were due to the action of any external authority, such as a European administration, then the latter might easily be the case, the European government providing merely the façade of a central authority behind which in the everyday run of affairs the conflicting interests of individuals might be continually in active opposition.   If the intervening external authority is that of the church, then these conflicts of interests would tend to be resolved in terms of the Christian code.   But here the central authority would probably be in the hands of the Christian teachers whose position, not being defined in terms of seniority in the kinship structure, of the traditional code of hospitality, of the suzerainty over lands and canoes or of the recognized elective process, would lack the ultimate force of that enjoyed now by the chiefs, would be less smooth in its operation and would leave more room for conferring advantages on favoured individuals.

It seems probable that such will ultimately be the course of evolution of the Tikopia society.

We may now return to a consideration of present conditions.

In spite of the important relationship between chieftainship and economic life, it cannot be said that the position, activities, and prestige of the chief are determined by his economic functions alone. Though this statement may appear a truism, it nevertheless stresses factors sometimes ignored in those studies which derive political authority primarily from economic conditions.   Thus E. Kagarov says, concerning five systems of chieftainship in Melanesia : " The power of the chief is based on economic conditions and his authority is *entirely dependent* on the fulfilment of his economic and organizational functions." [1]  He presumably

[1] Kagarov, " The Ethnography of Foreign Countries in Soviet Science," in *Ethnography, Folklore, and Archæology in the U.S.S.R.*, published in VOKS, vol. iv, 1933, 95.   (Italics mine.)

would apply the same point of view to Polynesian chieftainship. To regard the facts presented in this chapter as providing evidence for such a view would mean ignoring the vital factors of a non-economic order which define the chief's place in the community. In the first place there is his position in the kinship scheme, as senior representative of his group.  The kinship bonds uniting him to other members of the community are, like those of commoners, developed largely upon a basis of sentimental attachment and residential associations, and have a complex ideology which cannot be reduced to economic relationships. And in the case of chiefs these bonds embrace a larger number of people than in the case of commoners, as is clearly seen for instance in the greater number of people who take an active part in attending his illnesses or mourning his death.  Secondly, there is the chief's magico-religious role as a link with the clan gods ; this emphasizes and gives expression to the sentiments of dependence of the people upon him, for through him they appeal to the most important of the supernatural beings upon which their welfare depends.  This dependence of the people upon their gods applies not only to economic affairs, but to such non-economic interests as health, safety at sea, destruction of enemies by black magic, the fertility of women and even such recreational activities as dancing and dart-throwing.[1]    Finally, his political power, though largely employed to regulate economic activities, extends to other fields also as, for example, intervention in disputes by the crystallization of public opinion against one of the antagonists or the punishment of murder and other flagrant offences against public order.

It may be argued that the role of the chief in all these spheres is simply an outgrowth of his economic position as controller of production.  But this would ignore the fact that while the chief is a most important stimulator of production and in theory is the owner of the most important sources of raw material and instruments of production, in actual fact he cannot withhold the means of subsistence from his people ; and that the ordinary productive routine of households goes on without his motivation or his sharing in the benefits.  It might equally well be said that the economic advantages of the chief are conceded to him by the people who have placed him in that position in order to bolster up his basic functions of regulator of public order and

[1] Cf. my " Dart Match in Tikopia ", in *Oceania*, i, 74–7.

intermediary between man and nature. In a society where the means of subsistence is already secured to every person by his own labour these must be regarded as primary and independent social determinants and needs. To substantiate this point a reference could be made to the disintegration of these primitive societies under European contact where the removal of the ritual and legal functions of the chief has robbed him of his economic position.

CHAPTER VII

## PROPERTY AND CAPITAL IN PRODUCTION

THE major problems of this Chapter will deal with the types of goods sought and produced in the Tikopia community, their amount, the mode of their accumulation and the extent of saving, the system of ownership in which they are held, and the function of property in production. The part played by property rights in apportioning the results of production will be considered in the next Chapter.

A question of classification may first be examined. How far is it appropriate here to speak of producer's and consumer's goods ?

Let us examine the furnishings and equipment of a Tikopia household from this point of view. An inventory of the kinds of material goods I observed in and around the dwelling of the Ariki Taumako comprised 62 types of goods in all, and though this did not exhaust the list of goods utilized by these people, it included the major types. Of these, 28 types were primarily those used to produce other goods, and 34 were types directly used for the satisfaction of the people's wants. A detailed indication of their nature can be seen in Table X which lists the kinds of specimens of native workmanship I obtained. In the category of consumer's goods for instance are head-rests, belts, dance bats, spears, and clubs, wrist and neck ornaments, kilts, food baskets, and turmeric. In the category of producer's goods are such items as nets, fishing lines, canoes, adzes, digging sticks, and coco-nut-grating stools. But this broad division of types mentioned above ignores the fact that a number of types of goods serve both functions.

A marked feature of the Tikopia economic system is the ease with which many goods ordinarily used for direct consumption are converted into goods used for production and vice versa. Pandanus mats, used for sleeping purposes, and bark-cloth, used for blankets and clothing, are employed to facilitate the production of such articles as canoes, troughs, and sinnet cord ; food, both cooked and raw, and food-plants such as sprouting coco-nuts, are essential elements in the maintenance and reward of producers. On the other hand sinnet cord, used in fishing and for the lashing of canoe and house timbers, and wooden bowls, used in the preparation of food, are sought and accumulated for transfer in large amounts on such non-productive occasions as funerals, marriage, and initiation ceremonies. Even such apparently fixed productive items as canoes, troughs, and bonito hooks can be handed over as indemnity for services of a non-economic kind. It is as if in our society clothing, bedding and plates and dishes were poured into the productive system to pay for the making of tables, chairs, boats, and motor-cars ; while on the other hand the habit of giving kitchen utensils as wedding presents were extended to embrace the presentation of ploughs and workmen's tools, and business men accumulated machinery partly for the purpose of meeting their social obligations.

What is the effect of this fluidity of function ? From the point of view of economic analysis it obviously makes definition in our terms more difficult. It is essential to insist upon a classification of goods by function and not by form in a community where there is no very clear distinction between working life and domestic or social life on the one hand, and between the home and site of production on the other ; and where the social conventions of the people explicitly provide that the uses of goods are not highly specialized.

As regards the native economy itself the result is that the resources of an individual are not easily immobilized, and that there is a minimal need for a loan system on the security of fixed capital to provide liquid resources, even though there are to some extent closed circuits of exchange (see p. 340). This multiplicity of functions, much more marked than in a civilized economy, is clearly to be correlated with the absence of money as a convenient means of expressing many kinds of obligations. It may in fact be argued that in such a non-price society this easy convertibility of goods from one function to another fills to some degree the role which the money medium serves in our own society.

A brief statement is now necessary on the principles which govern the quantity of goods produced in the Tikopia economy. In the absence of a price-mechanism individuals have to exercise their own judgment in calculating what is wanted, on a basis of personal and household requirements, supplemented by those of anticipated ceremonial and ritual. Here the fact that the amounts of goods transferred from one party to another are traditionally dictated is important. Another significant element is the idea of proportionate return, partly according to the service rendered, but partly also according to differential kinship status. Hence one factor in influencing the quantity of production is the actual number of kinsfolk of close and distant relationship—to be considered in relation to the small size of the community and the nature of the kinship structure.

On the whole, there is little attempt to engage in increased production for the sake of multiplying objects already possessed. There is little utilization of spare time in accumulating in duplicate or triplicate household implements of which one only is normally required.

But the popular conception of the irresponsible, hand-to-mouth existence of the savage makes it imperative for the anthropologist to study the extent to which the natives realize their economic responsibility ; the extent to which they foresee coming scarcity and plan accordingly ; and how they make allowances for any future disturbance of the usual routine which will call for unusual inroads on their stocks set aside or coming to maturity.

In Tikopia foresight is exercised by individuals and by households. This is shown in the planting of crops and in the restoration of depleted resources, by plaiting sinnet cord during periods of enforced inactivity at funerals, or beating bark-cloth in the slack period immediately afterwards. Periodically damaged or worn goods are repaired or renewed. In consumption, " saving " takes place by restraint in the use of green coco-nuts in order to use them more effectively when mature for the preparation of cream ; taro, breadfruit, and bananas in the time of profusion are grated and packed in pits against seasons of shortage. The propriety of such conduct is explicitly recognized in Tikopia opinion. Such an injunction as I heard in one family circle : " Go and catch fish that the food may stand in the cultivations," that is, in order to conserve the supply of vegetable food, is common. And at times a limitation on the size of ceremonial gifts may be agreed upon as a means of conserving resources.[1] This careful balancing of present denial against future satisfaction is governed not only by a simple desire to have food

[1] For an example of this see *We, The Tikopia*, 360.

for the future but by moral imperatives to meet social obligations, by desires to make a good show in ceremonial exchanges, and by pressure of public opinion. And apart from this regular cycle of replenishment, special events call for an urgent mobilization of the family productive effort ; for example, the anticipated marriage of a son who has taken a mistress, or the approaching death of a parent which will shortly imply the provisioning of a funeral. The occurrence of death should, in Tikopia theory, not find the family unprepared.

In addition there is planning of economic effort for a circle wider than the household or immediate kin. This depends largely upon the sense of responsibility by men of rank, especially chiefs, which has been discussed in the last Chapter. It is enough to mention here a couple of examples in which this attitude, either of care for the welfare of others, or of regard for traditional observances, operates from an economic angle. The Ariki Kafika on his way to Uta to " throw the firestick ", a ceremonial act which would close the district to tree-cutting and other loud noises, said to Pae Sao : " Go and fell a sago palm for your children ; the land is going to be made *tapu*." Pae Sao, who had an orchard near by, was not of Kafika clan, but as premier chief of the whole island the Ariki Kafika felt some responsibility for him. Again, the anger of chiefs and other men of rank at commoners who ate coco-nuts which, they held, should have been preserved for important ceremonies soon to take place, illustrates the feeling that resources should be conceived in relation to wider ends than those of simple household consumption. The planning of economic activity assumes its most marked form when an event of public importance is anticipated. When a feast is projected by the chief or when the economic demands of an initiation or a marriage ceremony are foreseen, special crops are planted months ahead, taboos are imposed upon the coco-nut, bark-cloth is cut and prepared, and mats are plaited. Even when a public event is not specifically envisaged, the extensive planting of taro by the chief may lead other members of the clan to follow suit, in order that when the time comes and his purpose is disclosed they may have the wherewithal to assist him to demonstrate their loyalty, and preserve his and their own reputation in the eyes of the other clans. Here the traditions of clan unity provide a powerful sanction for the sense of economic responsibility, but the productive effort initiated on such occasions

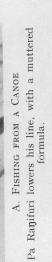

PLATE VII.

B. THE ARIKI KAFIKA IN HIS CULTIVATION

He is breaking up the ground for taro, with an umbrella-palm leaf at his back for shade. In the rear is a sacred stone on which one of his ancestors rested.

A. FISHING FROM A CANOE

Pa Ranjifuri lowers his line, with a muttered formula.

PLATE VIII.

A. Funeral Exchange—Loading up Bark-cloth

A woman is about to bear off a typical *maro*.

B. Funeral Exchange—Bowls and Sinnet Displayed

Set out in this apparently haphazard way, each has been allotted as an item of the *punefu*.

extends also to the other chiefs. They do not receive any direct intimation of his intentions but they begin to count supplies and act cautiously, to plant extra crops in order to be able to return adequately the presents which they know will be made to them.

Such extensive systems of economic planning are quite apart from that of the ordinary domestic economy of the household. Foresight in economic affairs requires that people should make provision for future events by keeping, where possible, several plots of taro coming to maturity at different stages. This means more or less constant cultivation—as one plot is exhausted another is planted.

A digression may be made here on the subject of what is in a way the reverse of planned activity—waste.

Waste has in popular speech an ethical connotation, but in objective terms it may be regarded as a less efficient use of means than is possible in attaining the ends desired. In this sense waste occurs in Tikopia if a man consumes his coco-nuts green instead of waiting till they are mature, when he would get more and better food from them. Apart from this, there are in some primitive societies forms of consumption which might superficially be described as " waste " but which represent real satisfactions consciously preferred. Instances which spring to mind are the Trobriander who allows quantities of food to rot in order to obtain prestige, even limiting his personal intake of food to this end ; the Tlinkit who finds satisfaction in the destruction of vast quantities of blankets and other wealth in the *potlatch*, or the Tikopia who cuts down coco-nut palms or breaks up a sea-worthy canoe on the death of a close relative. These represent a real or potential nutritional waste ; a sacrifice of future chances of enlarging the food supply. But this is not necessarily waste from an economic point of view. In the Trobriands, for example, part of the value of food, and part of the reason why it is produced, lies in its property of being able to rot.

Primitive societies differ in this last respect. In Tikopia there is no devotion of food to decay. If not eaten, it is handed on to other households, and warmed up by them so that they do not have to call on their own resources for that meal. As far as I could ascertain, no food is ever thrown away.

Reference may be made again here to the role of magic in

primitive economics. The fact that magical practices do not, *ex hypothesi*, produce the results directly attributed to them might lead us to class the energy expended upon them as " wasted ". Yet the fact remains that they do achieve beneficial results by assisting in the organization of production, by providing stimuli and sanctions for work, and by increasing human optimism and therefore psychological stamina. In this, magic presents close analogies with the use of rhythm in work. This illustrates very well the incursion of social factors into the so-called " purely economic " phases of primitive life. At first sight there is nothing further removed from the economist's province than the apparently futile manipulations and verbiage of the magical rite and spell. Yet the anthropologist is concerned to point out that these factors do actually increase the productive yield, and must therefore receive attention as relevant factors in the economic situation.

The question may now be asked whether there tends to be in Tikopia a concentration for a time on the production and maintenance of direct productive equipment to the detriment then or later of the community's needs of other goods. It may be said that the elements of this problem exist, because it is necessary at times to divert to the repair and production of canoes labour which presumably would otherwise be engaged in tasks more immediately related to consumptive needs. It is not actually a competitive relation. The fact that there is no production for sale in a market of uncertain potentialities means that there are no gross over-estimates of the amount of goods which the community can absorb, no over-loading or deserting of one field of productive effort in the wake of an elusive profit in another, and no piling up of productive equipment in the hope that there will be a field for its employment. It is theoretically possible that the diversion of some men's labour to canoe building might impair the production of food in the immediate small groups concerned but there is a specific mechanism which obviates this, namely the convention that a canoe shall not be built by the people who intend to be its owners. Their task is to provide food for the workers. The families of the workers find their own sustenance in the ordinary way during the period of the work but share in the food distribution at the end. If they built the vessel themselves, it is said, their need for food would make them hurry and perhaps spoil the work.

An example of the way in which the quantity of production may be affected by ritual claims may be given. When preparations for turmeric extraction were being made in June 1929, word went round that the Ariki Tafua had requested the other chiefs to limit the number of entrants to their turmeric groups in order that the work might be soon over, and his own ceremonial feast be the sooner begun. This meant firstly a decrease in the amount of turmeric obtained that season, and secondly some conservation of resources for the feast. As far as I know, the other chiefs acceded to the request, though I left the island before I could observe how this operated.

## ACCUMULATION OF SOME MAJOR TYPES OF GOODS

There are several limitations to the accumulation of large stocks of goods in Tikopia. The sphere of utilization of goods is restricted if only from the fact of the small population ; there are conventional standards of wealth which prevent a man from aspiring to enlarge his resources without limit, and extensive borrowing would tend to reduce fairly rapidly any stock which was very much in excess of that held by anyone else in the community. To some extent accumulation is reckoned as appropriate and is particularly associated with rank. Chiefs are recognized as being proper persons to control large quantities of food, to have a number of valued objects stored away in their houses. This allows them to pay the proper tokens of respect to one another and to lead their people worthily in large scale enterprises. Their retention of a number of items of a type of which other people normally have only one is assisted by the taboos surrounding their personal property and the general sanctity of their position. But the stocks which they accumulate are expected to be dispersed in a manner which will yield benefit to their people. Great accumulation by a commoner must also be followed by corresponding dispersal. But such a man would incur the charge from the chiefly families of *fia pasaki* " desiring to boast ", and would be watched by them lest he attempt to usurp some of their privileges. According to precedent in Tikopia history they would probably take an opportunity either to seize his goods or to kill him. Only a few commoners are wealthy by Tikopia standards and they are ritual elders whose social position is already well defined by tradition.

I omitted to make exact quantitative records of the property in Tikopia households. But some idea of the numbers of certain kinds of goods can be gathered from data given later in this Chapter. On the whole, of such items as bows, betel mortars, bark-cloth beaters, taro graters, ornamented kilts, and canoes, there is usually only one in a commoner's house, but two or three in the house of a chief. Of other items such as wooden head-rests, water bottles, wooden bowls, wrist and neck ornaments there are usually two or three in a commoner's house and half a dozen in the house of a chief, a ritual elder, or a craftsman. Differences in the quantities of bark-cloth, sinnet cord, and pandanus mats are greater.

Some of the features of the accumulation of canoes, mats, sinnet, and bark-cloth may be mentioned as being elements of great importance in furthering production.

### CANOES

Examination of some statistics of canoe ownership will allow us to realize something of the scale of inequality of wealth in Tikopia, the resources available to the various chiefs, and by comparison with the population figures the relation of these items of productive equipment to the available labour supply.

I took no complete canoe census in Tikopia, but with the help of native informants about the middle of my stay I made a list of the sea-going vessels in three districts, Raveŋa, Namo, and Rofaea, recording the names of the canoes, the kinship group which owned them, and the village in which their sheds were situated. The results for Raveŋa and Namo are given in the following Table. In addition, the people of Raveŋa and Namo possessed a number of small lake craft, which I did not record. In the Table I have distinguished " sacred " canoes, for which ritual is performed by the clan chief, and *paopao*, for which no such ritual is performed though the owners may appeal to their ancestors on their behalf. From my census figures I give also the number of males in each kinship group who might constitute members of the crew, taking for this purpose the widest age limits, from ten years upwards, which is about the time at which a boy begins to go to sea. In addition, I have given the numbers of similar males who do not belong to canoe-owning groups in the immediate vicinity, and who therefore form a source of extra labour for crews.

TABLE VII

OWNERSHIP AND MANNING OF CANOES (IN RAVEṆA AND NAMO)

| Kinship Group in Village | Clan | Sea-going Canoes | | Males of 10 years and upwards | |
|---|---|---|---|---|---|
| | | Sacred | *Paopao* | Owners | Non-owners |
| *Nuaraki* | | | | | |
| Torokiṇa . . | K. | 1 | | 4 | |
| Farekarae . . | Tf. | | 1 | 4 | |
| Retiare . . | Tf. | | 1 | 4 | |
| Fenutapu . . | Tf. | | 1 | 3 | |
| Raṇipaea . . | Tf. | 1 | 1 | 4 | |
| Tekaumako . | Tf. | 1 | | 3 | |
| | | | | 22+2 | |
| *Potu-i-te Ava* | | | | | |
| Saukirima . | Tf. | | 1 | 1 | |
| Niutao . . | Tf. | | 1 | 1 | |
| Torokiṇa . . | K. | | 1 | 3 | |
| | | | | 5+2 | |
| *Potu-i-Akitunu* | | | | | |
| Akitunu . . | Tf. | 1 | | 2 | |
| Nukufetau . | F. | 1 | | 9 | |
| Niumano . . | Tm. | 1 | | 3 | |
| Roṇoifo . . | Tm. | 1 | | 3 | |
| Raṇisaumako . | Tm. | 1 | | 2 | |
| Tekavamotu . | Tm. | | 1 | 7 | |
| | | | | 26+1 | |
| *Asana* | | | | | |
| Raṇifakaino . | K. | | 1 | 5 | |
| Nukufuti . . | Tm. | | 1 | 2 | |
| Roṇotau . . | K. | | 1 | 1 | |
| | | | | 8 | |
| *Potu-i-Fara* | | | | | |
| Kamota . . | Tm. | | 1 | 7 | |
| Mataioa . . | Tm. | | 1 | 9 | |
| Motuata . . | Tm. | | 1 | 3 | |
| | | | | 19 | |
| *Nuku* . . | | | | | +10 |
| *Uta* . . . | | | | | +1 |
| *Potu-sa-Faṇarere* | | | | | |
| Faṇarere . . | F. | 2 | 1 | 4 | |
| Tekava . . | F. | 2 | | 10 | |
| | | | | 14+9 | |
| *Potu-sa-Kafika* | | | | | |
| Kafika . . | K. | 2 | | 11 | |
| Vainunu . . | K. | | 1 | 5 | |
| Porima . . | K. | 1 | 1 | 4 | |
| Motusia . . | K. | | 1 | 4 | |
| Mapusaṇa . . | K. | 1 | 1 | 3 | |
| | | | | 27+9 | |

| Kinship Group in Village | Clan | Sea-going Canoes | | Males of 10 years and upwards | |
|---|---|---|---|---|---|
| | | Sacred | *Paopao* | Owners | Non-owners |
| *Faretapu* . . | | | | | |
| Rarovi . . | K. | 1 | | 2 | |
| Sarakivaka . | K. | | 1 | 1 | |
| Nukura . . | Tm. | | 1 | 2 (from  P.s. Tau- | |
| Aneve . . | Tm. | 1 | | 3 | [mako) |
| Kamota . . | Tm. | 1 | | – (from  Potu-i-Fara) | |
| Maneve . . | Tm. | 1 | | – ( : P.s.  Taumako) | |
| Fatumaru . . | Tm. | | 1 | 2 | |
| | | | | ——\|—— | |
| | | | | 10 | |
| *Potu-sa-Taumako* | | | | | |
| Taumako . . | Tm. | 2 | | 5 | |
| Avakofe . . | Tm. | 1 | 1 | 7 | |
| Vaŋatau . . | Tm. | 1 | | 3 (from  Nuku) | |
| Rimanu . . | Tm. | 1 | | 2 | |
| Raŋifau . . | Tm. | 1 | | 5 | |
| Faitoka . . | Tm. | 1 | | 4 | |
| Farekofe . . | Tm. | | 1 | 4 | |
| Maneve . . | Tm. | | 1 | 6 | |
| Sao . . . | Tf. | | 1 | 6 | |
| ŋatotiu . . | Tm. | | 1 | 4 | |
| | | | | ——\|—— | |
| | | | | 46 | |
| *Sukumarae* | | | | | |
| Sukumarae . | K. | | 1 | 1 | |
| Kafika . . | K. | 1 | | 4 | |
| Aneve . . | Tm. | | 1 | 1 (from  Raveŋa) | |
| Fetu . . | Tm. | | 1 | 4 | |
| Maniva . . | Tm. | | 1 | 1 | |
| | | | | ——\|—— | |
| | | | | 11 | |
| Totals . . | | 28 | 31 | 188+34 | |

*Note.*— (i) Under *clan*, K. represents Kafika ; Tf., Tafua ; Tm., Taumako ; F., Faŋarere.
(ii) Names of Villages are in Italic.
(iii) " Non-owners " in last column means members of kinship groups without canoes of their own.
(iv) Some canoes (of Nukura, Kamota, Maneve, Vaŋatau, Aneve) are kept in villages other than where their owners live.

The inferences from this material may be considered.  In the first place, the 59 canoes in Raveŋa and Namo—which, comprising nearly half the island, may be regarded as representative—are owned by approximately 85 per cent of the effective male population, 15 per cent of the males being not in possession of sea-going craft.  Moreover, among the kinship groups possessing canoes some are at a greater advantage than others : in some cases a single man is the owner, in others the vessel belongs to half a dozen, or in extreme cases to more men. As far as the three chiefly groups are concerned, Kafika, Taumako, and Faŋarere, all with headquarters in Raveŋa, the position is : the Ariki Kafika and his closely related kin have 6 canoes among 23 males ; the Ariki Taumako and his kin have 6 canoes among 18 males ; and the Ariki Faŋarere and his kin 3 canoes among 4 males.

But in terms of the efficient using of the vessels the situation is different. The people without canoes are not necessarily hampered in their fishing activities by this. Either they help to make up the crews of their neighbours and kin in their own village, or they join a crew in a village near by. And in such case they expect to use the canoes of their chief. In the village of the Ariki Kafika there are 9 males of his clan and kin without a canoe of their own, and in the village of the Ariki Faŋarere the position is the same. The clansfolk of the Ariki Taumako, however, are not lacking craft in the same way, and as far as command of equipment is concerned he is in the most favourable position.

But the situation may be viewed from another angle. A canoe is useless without a crew, and a single owner may find himself unable to utilize his craft. A Tikopia canoe can be managed at sea by two men, but for effective fishing, especially with torches at night, three are required, and four is a proper crew. If the number of canoes be compared with the number of effective males in the canoe-owning groups, the average is 3·2 males per vessel. If all the males available be included, from groups without canoes of their own as well, then the average is 3·8 males per vessel. From this it is obvious that if all the canoes of the district were taken out at the one time, there would be only bare crews for each, even when young boys and old men were all taken. In fact, at the height of the flying-fish season, when fleets from all round the island are out in strength, it is sometimes difficult for a few craft to whip up crews from the laggards, and occasionally a vessel is left in its shed despite the owner's wishes, through his inability to muster a crew. He himself then usually joins another craft. Sometimes, though rarely, an adventurous girl will be taken to ply a paddle ; this is said to be possible only in Christian Faea, where I saw it, and not in Raveŋa. On the whole, then, there can be no very strong competition for canoes, leading to the exploitation of canoe-less men by " capitalist " canoe-owners. Nor, on the other hand, does there seem to be any special inducement offered to labour in securing canoe-crews. There is no competitive bargaining in material terms ; the inducements come in the sphere of personal preference, kinship ties, and the like.

For the community as a whole, the demand for canoes seems to be a satisfied demand. With this is probably to be correlated the system of distribution whereby the members of the crew and the owner receive approximately equal shares of the fish obtained. But on occasions when the supply of canoes available is reduced, there is not a proportionate increase in the reward obtained by the owner. There are several factors leading to an occasional reduction in the supply of vessels. Occasionally a canoe is withdrawn from service for a time and laid up in its shed. The Tikopia call this giving it a " breathing-space " (manava). No repairs may be made to it, but the idea is that the craft, like man himself, is the better for a rest. If the craft is a sacred one, then a kava rite is performed when it is laid up and when it is taken out again. (When such a rite was performed for the vessel Karoatu, belonging to the Ariki Kafika, there were present the chief himself as officiant, a son of his, six other kinsfolk and neighbours and several children.) Again, after the death of a man of rank several canoes may be broken up, or left to decay, though in the latter case they are sometimes rescued by others and transferred to different ownership after a time. Thirdly, instead of the destruction of canoes, they may be withdrawn from active service owing to a taboo on sea-fishing. This, however, does not materially alter the ratio of craft to labour, since the people of those villages are inhibited from participating in canoe expeditions of all kinds for the period.

The question may be raised as to what determines the size of and number of canoes. In the first place the material factors of size of tree trunks and degree of technical capacity of the Tikopia are obviously important. But without much development of technical methods the Tikopia might have built up larger vessels from planks as did the Samoans, and other peoples to the east. It seems that they preferred for ease of manipulation in fishing, and facilities in getting a crew, small craft which three or four men could manage. For oversea voyages larger craft are more valuable and to some extent were built specifically for this purpose. But even here the Tikopia craft which voyage abroad are very much smaller than the Samoan, Fijian, and Gilbert Island vessels used in this way. It would seem as if the Tikopia are content to apply their energies to building vessels with a dual function rather than to do as other Polynesian peoples and to have two types, one for fishing and the other for travelling. In a sense they have preferred to take personal risks rather than economic risks, by using their fishing canoes for voyaging abroad. The effect is that there are no large specialized vessels laid up for occasional use, but every craft is in more or less constant employment.

The canoe is undoubtedly the most important object of productive equipment in Tikopia. But there is no attempt by any member of the community to build up any stock of canoes, establish with them a large-scale fishing industry or dispose of them to other people either by exchange or by hiring them out. The rare occasions when a canoe is transferred from one kinship group to another have a ritual setting (p. 345).

It is not possible for me to say what is the average life of a Tikopia canoe—perhaps fifteen or twenty years might be near the mark. The most important reasons for the building of new vessels are the replacement of those which have been lost at sea, damaged, or are worn or decayed ; and what might be called the statutory building of new craft by a chief at various times after his accession. In addition there is the construction of new vessels for young married men who are founding families which are beginning to be substantial offshoots from the parent kinship group—though this is rare ; and the building of a canoe by someone who wishes to have not only the convenience of a personal craft but also the prestige of an owner. The canoe built by Pa Roŋotau, financed largely through the resources accumulated by his payment as a mission teacher, comes in this category. Pae Sao, again, gave as his main reason for pressing me for the gift of an adze that he had marked down a tree and intended to build a vessel for his eldest son, then a lad approaching maturity.

There is one further factor which, perhaps, tends to maintain a fairly constant number of canoes in being. This is the ritual aspect of canoe ownership. A large number of the vessels—twenty-eight in Raveŋa and Namo alone—are classed as sacred canoes, have tutelary spirits appointed to them by the clan chief, and are seasonally resacralized by them. Thus there is a strong motive for continuing this ritual association by maintaining a canoe which has once been the object of it even when, as in the case of Roŋoifo or Rarovi groups, the immediate man-power of a kinship group would not seem to justify it. This factor too, by providing a stimulus to a considerable number of individual canoe owners, tends to minimize the possibility of the emergence of " canoe-capitalists ", who could derive profit from large-scale ownership. With the breakdown of the native religious system, which seems to be threatened, one may find that more specialization in canoe ownership may arise.

One further point may be considered in connection with the ownership of sacred canoes. In Rofaea, owing to the profession of Christianity, there were none of these vessels. In Raveŋa and Namo there were twenty-eight. One-quarter of these were held by the three chiefly groups of Kafika, Taumako, and Faŋarere, and nearly all the remainder by the most important kinship groups of their clans. Their distribution is of some importance economically, since the clan chief as part of his control over these vessels receives periodically a large present of food (the *monotaŋa* of the canoe) from the owner. The Ariki Kafika controls seven sacred canoes ; the Ariki Taumako thirteen, and the Ariki Faŋarere five. The Ariki Tafua nominally controls three in Namo, but since his adherence to Christianity the ritual and gifts connected with them have been transferred to the Ariki Taumako, whose interests in Namo are strong. These figures may compare with the material in Table III, and show that the strength of the Ariki Taumako in land is manifested also in canoes.

## PANDANUS MATS

Pandanus mats are an important property in every Tikopia household. Their use is twofold ; they are a major item in bedding, and they are employed largely for ceremonial gifts.

As bedding there is one mat to each adult, reserved for him or her personally ; children share the mats of their elders. These mats are very durable. I have no data as to how long they last in the island, but they are welcomed as floor mats by the Europeans of Tulagi because they wear better than any mat which one can obtain from the nearer Melanesian islands. Some of these mats which I myself used constantly as floor covering for three years did not then show great signs of wear. As bed mats in the Tikopia style they would have lasted much longer.

When a mat is given as a present or in exchange it must be

unused, that is, either newly made or from stock.    It may have
passed from hand to hand through having been received at a
funeral or an initiation ceremony, but it must not have been used
for domestic purposes.    Once it is used as a bed mat it is never
put into circulation again.

Such a mat of good workmanship, about eight feet long by
four feet wide and composed of quarter-inch strips, takes approximately three months of spare time work of a woman to plait—
according to native statement.    The mats of the best quality,
those for special gifts at initiation and marriage, take longer.
Considering the durability of these mats it is possible to accumulate a stock of them in each household without too much strain.
Usually half a dozen or a dozen in the wealthier households
are kept tied up in a bundle ready for contingencies such as a
funeral.    Sometimes a mat has to be plaited in a hurry owing to
an unexpected death, or a death followed closely upon an initiation
or other ceremony.    Rarely but occasionally an unfinished mat is
handed over in exchange.    This is accepted as if it were complete,
and is finished by a woman in the recipient's household.    Variations in the stock of mats held by a household occur, but depleted
stocks tend to be restored in part by immediate reciprocity and
in part by delayed reciprocity at a future ceremony.

Since plaiting is the work of women large stocks are
not found in the possession of bachelors, and comparative
wealth in this sphere will depend considerably upon the
number and industry of the women in a household.    But since
wooden bowls and sinnet cord are given in ceremonial exchange
for mats it is possible for a wood-carver or other industrious
man to accumulate a stock of mats irrespective to some degree
of the feminine industry he can command.    Skill in plaiting is
important for the saving of time it implies rather than for any
differential advantage to be gained by it directly.    Provided that
the mat conforms to certain specifications of size and ornament
according to class, variation in quality is immaterial as far as the
return for it goes.    Mats of poor quality may be commented upon
with a sneer, but there is no rule that they are matched in
reciprocity.    It may be noted that no correlation can be established
between the greater stock of mats on hand with chiefly families
and any greater leisure of their women.    Since the ordinary
distribution of tasks is the same in all types of household, chiefly
or commoner, they have no more spare time than anyone else,

but they probably have utilized this spare time more constantly in building up stocks of property, and have been able to draw upon a wider field of labour. This position once attained, the constant influx and outflow of goods tends to keep their supplies on hand at a fairly high level.

### SINNET

A coil of sinnet cord ten to twenty fathoms long takes at least five or six weeks to make. It is the work of men, done like plaiting by women, largely in their leisure time. Half a dozen coils are usually kept on hand for purposes of ceremonial exchange. In addition there may be a coil or two of the much heavier and more valuable sinnet used for shark fishing. This is usually made by a man who is a known expert (p. 296). These shark lines are found mostly in the houses of chiefs and deep-sea fishermen. A commoner who is not a skilled fisherman may have none.

The position with sinnet is different from that in the case of pandanus mats in that sinnet is acceptable in exchange when it has been in use for fishing. But it is interesting to note that the convention of exchange is somewhat different here. Whereas nominally one mat is as good as another (provided that both are unused) coils of sinnet are carefully matched. The recipient of one goes to his house, takes down his bundle, and selects from it that coil which is most nearly the same to the one he has received. This obviously gets over the possible difficulty that exists in the use of worn sinnet for exchange purposes.

### BARK-CLOTH

To prepare a piece of bark-cloth takes about three days. The advantage of it as an item of exchangeable goods is that it can be prepared rapidly for any social event which has not been announced long beforehand. Hence for a week preceding any important ceremony the sound of the wooden beaters is heard in every village. Bark-cloth is not an equivalent for pandanus mats but it supplements them and is given in large quantities even when mats are not. The extensive demand for it for ceremonial exchange and the consumption of it as wearing apparel means that a larger stock of it tends to be kept on hand than of pandanus mats, even granted a probable higher velocity of circulation.

The demand for bark-cloth is very elastic since not only is

there a steady consumption of it for wearing apparel and in blankets, but it is used as a ritual offering to gods and ancestors and it can be added to almost any type of ceremonial gift, in indefinite numbers. There is frequently no exact specification of the number of pieces required for a standard gift, and if his supplies at a moment are plentiful a person may " stick it on " (*fakapiki*) as a supplement to the conventional quantity. No exact return is given for this supplement. The reckoning is made in terms of the *maro* as a whole, that is, of the bundle irrespective of whether it contains half a dozen or two pieces of bark-cloth. In this respect it is similar to quantities of food transmitted in baskets. Bark-cloth is then a prime standby in the resources of a person wishing to demonstrate his liberality, or to implement any sudden demand.

A distinction must be drawn between the accumulation of goods for immediate disbursement and their accumulation for future commitments.

Some idea of the quantity required for a ceremonial disbursement of the first type is seen from the initiation of the boys Munakina and Seuku.[1]

The food accumulated comprised seven stakes of dry coco-nuts (300 to 400 nuts in all), 200 baskets of taro, about 30 baskets of yams, a dozen bunches of bananas, and a large pile of *pulaka* (*Alocasia*). There was a supply of fish in addition. The goods, apart from several paddles, a quantity of fish-hooks, and a few fathoms of calico, consisted of 60 pandanus mats and 100 pieces of bark-cloth. In the distribution there were four principal bundles for the close maternal kin, 30 other bundles apportioned between 60 other maternal kin, and 8 bundles for the cooks. A basket of food went with each bundle. Because of the anomalous position of the father on this occasion (a native from the Banks Islands) the contributions were made by one section of the maternal kin, and apportioned among another. In each case a reciprocal gift was made, principally in the form of sinnet cord and fish-hooks. Thus in one instance Pa Saukirima gave a bark-cloth blanket and a waist-cloth for distribution by the father, who allotted them to Pa Niukaso. This man returned through the wife of the donor a hank of sinnet cord, a fathom of calico, and a pipe. Reference to the summary in Appendix I will show the number of births, marriages, initiations, and funerals which

[1] *We, The Tikopia*, 433–463 and genealogy 7*a*.

occurred during the year and will allow the general momentum of this aspect of the economic situation to be seen.

It was not possible for me to calculate exactly the amount of goods accumulated from time to time against future commitments, but reference to the turmeric-making of the Ariki Tafua (p. 276) will show that such accumulation is often considerable. It is not possible either to determine what proportion of different items is so held by different individuals, but in general such proportion is determined by the estimate of requirement ; this appears to operate on the side of outflow rather than inflow. I heard expressions of opinion on the need for preparing for the initiation of a growing boy and the approaching demise of an ageing man, but at no time did I hear any calculation of the effect of probable receipts from a ceremony at which a man would benefit. Another factor is the working capacity of the women of the household—and it may be noted here that bachelors do not initiate large-scale enterprises. One important element in the situation, however, is the potentiality of borrowing or " bespeaking " specific items from close kin to make up the quantity or proportion of goods desirable and the voluntary action of such kin. Alteration of the proportion of one's resources by pure exchange is rare.

A definite replenishment of resources after a heavy drain upon them is frequent ; bark-cloth is beaten, sinnet is plaited, after a funeral or initiation is over. In the last resort the necessity for accumulation is modified by tempering the distribution according to the quantity available. There is a *pro rata* diminution in the size of the *maro*, and marginal cases in terms of kinship or assistance tend to suffer. In an extreme case there may be a substitution of goods, as for instance in the traditional case of the man who divided his daughters among the builders of his canoe because he had not the property to reward them (p. 302). But the unusualness of this case has made it a matter of amused and somewhat contemptuous narrative, though it occurred some generations ago. It is also difficult to say how far the accumulation of goods represents any permanent increment to the resources of an individual or family. At times the production of bark-cloth, pandanus mats, and sinnet is at a high rate, and the goods then dispersed throughout the community raise for the time being the general standard of property holding. The fairly slow rate at which they are finally destroyed would indicate a gradual rise in the volume of possessions. But against this must be offset some increase in population. Moreover, there is the possibility of a cycle in the rate of production ; the conventionalized size, number and occasion of many Tikopia rewards and gifts means that there is a limited incentive towards a higher rate, and a restricted outlet for goods accumulated. Hence when production has reached a certain level it is possible that there is a pause for the time being, but this I cannot document and it remains as a hypothesis.

To give some content to these generalizations I have attempted to estimate the amount produced per annum of the types of goods just described, and what this represents in terms of the working time of individuals. One method of doing this would be to follow the activities of a number of persons day by day, noting what time they spent. Another way, that which I have adopted here, is to calculate from the amount of goods in being. I have first estimated the quantity of such goods required for ordinary domestic purposes by the community, and the turnover of them on ritual occasions, economic reciprocity and the like. This turnover I have reduced by an arbitrary figure representing their respective velocities of circulation, since some of them are undoubtedly used several times for different ceremonies in the course of a year. The figures I have taken are : 1·5 for pandanus mats, 2·0 for bark-cloth squares, and 4·0 for sinnet, bowls, and bark-cloth strips. The last appear to change hands more rapidly, being in more constant demand. Judging from my impressions at the different ceremonies, they may be somewhat of an overestimate. The resulting totals, divided by an estimate of the average life of the different types of goods, show the numbers of each type which must on the average be replaced annually. Considering these in terms of the average time needed for the production of each (see pp. 251–2), a total time may be calculated, and this, compared with the numbers of the working population given in Table IB, gives an estimate of the average time demanded in such work for each individual. This means, of course, not as a sole occupation from dawn to dark, but as a major task.

Such an estimate is distinctly speculative, but it is based upon empirical records which, though incomplete, are significant (see Appendix I). If anything it is on the low side. According to the calculation, something like one-fifth of the working time of each woman is spent, on the average, in plaiting

mats and preparing bark-cloth ; and about one-ninth of the
working time of each man in the plaiting of sinnet cord and

TABLE VIII

ESTIMATED LEVEL OF PRODUCTION OF SOME MAJOR TYPES OF GOODS

| Goods in Use | Numbers in Use (reduced by velocities of circulation) | | Estimated average life | Average Number replaced per annum | Time demanded per annum | |
|---|---|---|---|---|---|---|
| | | | | | Total | Indiv. |
| | Total | | | | | |
| Pandanus mats. | | | | | | |
| Bedding | 900 | | | | | |
| Ritual, etc., | | | | | 600 | 2 |
| transfers | 100 | 1,000 | 5 years | 200 | months | months |
| Bark-cloth. | | | | | | |
| i. Strips : | | | | | | |
| clothing | 450 | | | | | |
| sacred | 300 | | | | 1,590 | |
| ritual, etc. | 315 | 1,065 | 2 years | 530 | days | |
| ii. Squares : | | | | | | 10 |
| clothing | 400 | | | | | days |
| bedding | 900 | | | | 1,965 | |
| ritual, etc. | 10 | 1,310 | 2 years | 655 | days | |
| Floor mats. | | | | | | |
| domestic | 2,000 | | | | 2,250 | 6¼ |
| ritual | 250 | 2,250 | 2 years | 1,125 | days | days |
| Women's craft Work. | | | | | | 2¼ months |
| Canoes (for 222 males) | 59 | 59 | 15–20 years | 3·5 built plus 3 days repairs for all | 1,050 days 660 days | 8 days |
| Sinnet cord. | | | | | | |
| domestic | 1,000 | | | | 330 | 1 |
| ritual, etc. | 125 | 1,125 | 5 years | 225 | months | month |
| Wooden Bowls. | | | | | | |
| domestic | 1,000 | | | | 28 | 2½ days |
| | 120 | 1,120 | 20 years | 56 | months | |
| Men's craft Work | | | | | | 1¼ months |

assisting in the building and repairing of canoes. In addition,
one man in six spends a fortnight each year, on the average, in
the making of wooden bowls, an occupation in which there is

some specialization.  Unfortunately I have no data from which to calculate the amount of time taken up in other craft work, which does occupy a considerable part of each man's labours. But the figures given in the Table show that, despite the great amount of time that must be given to the production and preparation of food, and that devoted to leisure, no inconsiderable drain upon labour power is represented by other technical occupations.

Having considered the types of goods sought and produced, and the stocks of them that are held, we may now proceed to examine the principles which govern the holding and use of them.

### Concept of Ownership

Examination of the principles of ownership in a primitive community is beset with difficulties.  In the absence of documentary records registering titles or defining the relations between persons and things the anthropologist must rely on more diffuse data.  A preliminary approach through language is less valuable than it seems at first.  It is easy to get statements from natives in which possessive pronouns are applied to things, and which even the anthropologist may regard as expressions of ownership.  In fact, they may indicate simply activity in connection with the object, or participation with others in a complicated scheme of activities.  Thus in Tikopia a pole has been pointed out to me by the lakeside as we were passing in a canoe, with the words " *Aku ne ta* ".  This translated literally is " Mine, did cut ".  This might mean " It is mine because I cut it " in line with a common concept of use giving title to property.  But in fact it means " I cut it ", an expression of the same order as " It was my axe-work that did it ".  The Tikopia frequently use possessives in this way to denote simple activity.  That in this case it is activity and not ownership as such that is meant is indicated by the specific form *aku* ;  the form *toku* [1] would have been used if the property concept was meant.  But even the use of the latter form of possessive does not mean exclusive ownership.  It may indicate simply that the speaker has a share in the rights to the thing.  Moreover, on the other hand, the use of a dual or plural possessive may be part of the Tikopia convention of etiquette, which includes a reference to the person spoken to without meaning that he has any concrete rights over the object of an equivalent kind to those held by the speaker.  The expression

[1] The addition of a particle *ke* would indicate greater exclusiveness.

*tatou tofi* means literally " our orchard ", including the person addressed, and was a frequent initial reply to a question of mine as to the ownership of ground.  This was primarily politeness ; I could, if I so wished, have taken coco-nuts from it, but that would have been a concession to my friendly relations to the " real " owners, and did not mean that I was regarded as having full rights to the use of the ground for planting, transmission to my heirs, or other social and ritual activity connected with it.

As Malinowski has pointed out so effectively for the Trobriand Islands, the anthropologist who has to define native property rights must rely not on verbal usage alone, but on the series of acts in regard to the object which represent immediate and ultimate control over it.

Primitive communities rarely have a simple linguistic expression for " ownership " which can be equated directly with our terms.  But they do have expressions which amount in effect to the same thing, if they be interpreted in terms of concrete behaviour.  In Tikopia the term *tau* in one connotation has this force.  Literally it means " linked ".  *Soa* is a friend, and *tau soa* are " linked friends ", that is, bond-friends.[1]  *Tau fanau* are persons of the same kinship grade, as brothers or cousins, " linked by birth " ;  *tau iŋoa* are persons bearing the same name, " linked names."  When this term joins a person to a thing then it conventionally expresses the idea of ownership.  *Taŋata tau vaka,* " man linked (with) canoe " is the owner of the vessel, and is equivalent to *taŋata ona te vaka*—" man his the canoe."  In concrete terms he is the man who initiated its building, who is acknowledged to have the primary right of disposal of it, who grants the use of it to others, who is called upon to distribute any catch of fish made from it, and on whom lies the obligation to perform the appropriate ritual for it and provide the baskets of food which are the material expression of its relations to the chief and the spirits.  Such an expression as *taŋata tau vaka* is not used of the younger members of a household, or of the members of the crew from other households.  The head of the household is the " man linked with canoe " for all practical purposes, and may be termed its owner.  This of course does not mean that he has the sole right to it ; the other members of his household and kin group, who have contributed to

[1] See my " Bond-Friendship in Tikopia ", in *Custom is King : Essays in Honour of R. R. Marett*, 1936, 259–269.

the building of it, have also their say in the use of it, and the chief of his clan is titularly its ultimate controller and can refer to it as " my canoe ", though his functions in regard to it are primarily of a ritual order.

Something may now be said of the empirical system of ownership of goods in Tikopia. The most important categories of property are land and manufactured goods. Property in persons does not exist ; there is no slavery or serfdom such as formerly existed among the Maori, though a chief may refer to a person in difficulties as " my man " (cf. p. 189).

## OWNERSHIP OF LAND

The principles of ownership of land in Tikopia rest primarily upon the bonds of kinship. The whole island is divided into orchards and garden plots, each of which has a name and is demarcated by natural boundaries such as trees or by paths and hedges. Each portion of land is held in immediate ownership by a patrilineal kinship group known to the natives as *paito* " house ". Every house owns a number of orchards and garden plots in different parts of the island though there is some tendency for immediate control in each case to be exercised by that branch of the house living most closely to it. In a wider sense these lands are spoken of as being the property of the various clans, with the clan chief as ultimate overlord. His position *vis-à-vis* the members of his clan has already been explained as a relationship of reciprocal obligations.

Titular ownership and actual use are not necessarily coincident. In the first place individual members or householders of the *paito* cultivate specific portions of the group territory for themselves and their rights therein are respected by the others. Secondly a woman on marriage is given certain rights of usage from her father's family which she, her husband, and her children exercise during her lifetime. When she. dies the land normally reverts again to her patrilineal kin. Thirdly, as has been mentioned in Chapter II, unoccupied land is available for planting purposes to any other person in the island, provided that the owners have not set an explicit prohibition against this. Such is usually done only when the owner regards the brushwood on the land as too immature, or when he himself is contemplating early use of it. Even here, however, no restriction may be imposed.

Fourthly, there are certain rights to cull from orchards a

limited quantity of produce for specific ceremonies or economic undertakings. These levies are known as *aru*. Those on a ceremonial basis are sanctioned by traditional usage and beliefs in the supernatural control exercised by spiritual beings ; those on an economic basis are sanctioned by tradition and recognition of the common benefits to be derived from the undertaking. Both types relate to large-scale activities sponsored by chiefs. An example of a ritual *aru* is that of coco-nuts and bananas levied from the cultivations of Rotoaia and Rakisu for the rites of Takarito (controlled by the Ariki Kafika) ; examples of economic *aru* are those which take place at the opening of the channel leading from the lake to the sea (controlled by the Ariki Taumako) and at the repair of acqueducts for turmeric-making (controlled by any of the chiefs of Kafika, Tafua, or Taumako).

In the *aru* the convention is that every orchard, whether of a member of the clan of the chief sponsoring the work or not, should be brought under contribution, but that only a small quantity of food should be taken from each. It is recognized that the levy of the *aru* is not in virtue of any right of ownership as such ; it is called metaphorically in fact *te kaia a ŋa ariki*, " the theft by the chiefs ". It is also described as " the food of chiefs ". It is said that no protest against the *aru* is ever made, whatever a man's personal feelings may be, and I did not hear of such. In reference to the levy in connection with the repairing of the acqueducts it was said, " If a man objects, from what will he drink ? " meaning that it is to his interest that they should be in good condition. After a levy in connection with the opening of the lake channel, however, I did hear objection from the Ariki Kafika. The chief was fulminating because coco-nuts had been taken from his orchard Porima. But this was not against the *aru* as such, but against the behaviour in this case. He said to me that it was correct for people on the opening of the channel to go to the low ground, which had been drained to some extent by the receding of the waters, and take *pulaka* which was growing there, but not to range over the higher lands, though he admitted that they had a free charter for all orchards. His warmth was probably due to the fact at this time coco-nuts were scarce. He described the taking of the coco-nuts as " theft " in angry tones. When I reminded him of the *aru* of Takarito, in which at his orders large numbers of coco-nuts had been taken, he laughed and said deprecatingly " The theft by the chiefs " then calmed down and explained to me that he did not intend to make a public protest against the *aru* or try to stop it. This example illustrates the fact that public acceptance of a convention need not coincide with private acquiescence in its individual application.

The conventions of the *aru* differ in detail according to its precise object. When the levy for Takarito is being made the correct procedure is for the collectors to go in silence, since it is believed they represent in their own persons the twin deities of the ritual. If they pass by a house its inmate may draw their attention by a " *sst!* " and when one of them turns his head he then points with his finger in the direction of a bunch of bananas or a coco-nut palm where appropriate food will be found. There is a complaint nowadays that these conditions are not strictly observed, and that the food-collectors go to houses and demand tobacco. For the *aru* connected with a sacred canoe of the Ariki Taumako the food-collectors must go with bare hands only, and take coco-nuts, bananas, and yams without the aid of a knife. The *aru* may be thus described as ceremonial licence, but controlled by ritual conditions.

As a sample of the Tikopia attitude towards the planting of land I give an account by Pa Taramoa, son of the Ariki Kafika, of what he said happened when a man cleared a portion of some-one else's land and then announced the fact to the owner. The latter says, " What ! You went and cleared the place I left for the insertion of my own seedlings. What's to be done ? "

" It has been cleared by me for the planting of my own seedlings." " Go then you and plant in that which you have cleared," says the owner, conceding the situation. Pa Taramoa held that the complaisance of the owner is due to the fact that he wishes his land to be kept in cultivation, and also that he knows he will receive a return at harvest. " When a man has gone and cleared in an orchard of another man, the taro stands, stands, stands, and matures. Then he goes to *poroporo* it. Then he goes and binds up his taro. He digs and digs, binds up two bunches, and carries them then on a pole to the man whose is the orchard. Because his taro were planted in the orchard of the other, he digs it and carries it to the house of the other. This is called *poroporo*."

It is explained that taro can thus be planted with impunity " because when it is dug it is finished ". Manioc is treated in the same way. But the custom with these crops, which are over in a single season, is contrasted with that in the case of coco-nut palms, breadfruit, and other trees, whose yield is perennial. Reference to some empirical material will show how the system of taro planting works in practice. In *We, The Tikopia*, Plan iv, I have given a rough plan of a large taro gardening area, with a list of the kinship groups recognized as owning the land in the various plots and a list also of the persons who planted taro in that area in April, 1929. By comparing this material with other data from census and genealogies some interesting figures emerge.

The distribution of land in this area is fairly equal between the people of the district of Faea on the one side and the allied districts of Raveŋa and Namo on the other. But in this particular season, partly because of estimated food requirements in the near future, and partly because of restriction of resources elsewhere by the chief of Faea, the people of this district turned out in greater numbers for planting taro than those of the other districts. The following table shows the manner in which the land owned was utilized for production.

TABLE IX
LAND UTILIZATION

| | Major Areas owned | | District | Plots in land of same clan | Plots in land of other clans | Total Plots |
|---|---|---|---|---|---|---|
| | Fallow | Planted | | | | |
| Faea . . . | 12 | 14½ | Same | 19 | 8 | 27 |
| | | | Other | 7 | 6 | 13 |
| Raveŋa and Namo | 13 | 16½ | Same | 15 | 5 | 20 |
| | | | Other | 0 | 1 | 1 |
| | 25 | 31 | | 41 | 20 | 61 |

*Note.*—Plots are subdivisions of major areas, and are of approximately the same size.

This shows that the people of each district resorted to the lands of their own house or their own clan, in their own district, to the extent of about one-half in the case of Faea and three-quarters in the case of Raveŋa. But the people of Faea used as one-third of their planting area land belonging to those of Raveŋa while there was only one case of the reverse. Moreover the people of Faea did not restrict themselves to the lands of their own clan when they went outside the land of the owners from their own district, but in 15 per cent of their planting utilized the land of people who were neither district members nor clan members.  Bearing in mind how strong are district loyalty, kinship ties and suspicion of other groups it is clear that the Tikopia concept of freedom in planting land belonging to others is definitely carried out in practice.  The fact that of the major areas left fallow practically half belonged to people of Faea shows that such resort for planting purposes to lands of others is not only due to land shortage.

There is a convention in Tikopia that coco-nut palms may be planted by one person on the ground of another.  But this planting establishes no right to the tree and its produce ; they belong to the owner of the soil.  It is said of the planter, " He plants for himself ?  No !  He plants for the man who owns the orchard."  In such case the planter may say to the owner, " My coco-nut palm there has been planted in your orchard—it is my speech, the lifting of my reputation ; while it stands as my speech, you then will garner from it."  The explanation of this cryptic utterance is that in the course of time people of the owner's house looking at the tree will speak about the man who planted it ; when he is dead they will say as they take its fruits, " O alas ! this is the palm planted by So-and-so who is gone."  It is then a kind of memorial to the planter, but since the records of a people without writing lie in their forms of speech it is appropriately spoken of by the planter as " my speech ".  So also with the phrase " lifting his reputation ".  The native word here is *roŋo*, the basic meaning of which is " to hear ".  His reputation lies in people hearing about him.  Breadfruit trees, *vere*, and other trees with a long life are treated in similar style.

This illustrates a number of points in the Tikopia economy.  There is a distinct concept of *meum* and *tuum* linked with the recognition that the product of labour need not necessarily belong to the labourer.  There is a verbal and conceptual distinction made not only in the actual planting situation, but in the description and explanation of this situation in terms of a generalized example, as the one given here, which is a direct translation of a native statement.  Five personal elements are distinguished in the example—the speaker, the listener, the planter, the owner, and the people who will later comment on the tree.  The native economic system is built up, operated and perpetuated in terms of such generalizations. Incidentally, the motive of self-advertisement given as the reason for the planter's action shows how extra-economic factors condition a situation of production and consumption.

## OWNERSHIP OF MANUFACTURED GOODS

The principles of Tikopia land ownership, based upon kinship with the clan chief as ultimate overlord, are in essence the same as those of the ownership of other types of material goods. But here, however, the less important the article, the narrower its range of satisfaction of wants, and the fewer its functions, the more does the tendency appear for it to be held as individual property.

A canoe, especially a sacred canoe, is held much like an orchard. It is in fact spoken of metaphorically as " the orchard of the ocean ". Such a vessel is controlled for all practical purposes by the head of a house, used by the members of his family, who all speak of it as " our canoe ". But from another angle it is " the canoe of the chief ", and is said to be " drawn up with So-and-so ", its *de facto* owner. The owner builds it and controls its use ; the chief performs the major ritual for it and receives the basket of food which is an expression of the fact that he has allotted to it its tutelary spirits, among them one of his own ancestors. But the ownership of sacred canoes presents one feature in contrast to that of orchards, in that the Ariki Kafika has an ultimate suzerainty through his premier deity over all the sacred canoes of the island. Nothing comparable exists with regard to land tenure.

Property in other goods shows more or less individualization. Certain items such as wooden bowls and other house furniture are best classified as household property. In others there is to some extent a sex specialization. Thus of the sixty-two types of goods mentioned earlier, thirty are associated with males in particular, seven are associated especially with females, and twenty-five are used by either sex. In the first category are sinnet beaters, betel mortars, turmeric baking cylinders, wooden head-rests, dance bats, sinnet belts, shark hooks, bows and arrows, spears, fish-lines, bonito hooks, and kilts ; in the second category are scoop nets, boards for plaiting mats, bark-cloth beaters, and in the third, property such as wrist and neck ornaments, beads, fans, taro graters, and pandanus mats. This paucity in women's goods is due to the fact that their main tasks—of procuring vegetable food, reef fishing, cooking, plaiting, and beating bark-cloth—demand few technical aids, but much hand-work, whereas those of the men are much more diversified and require much more technical assistance. The subordinate position of the women as property owners is then to some extent to be correlated with the type of technical equipment and system of production in vogue in Tikopia.

But this correlation cannot be carried too far. All the types of goods used by both sexes are not items held in common ownership. Thus a woman may own a knife, a fan, a sleeping mat, a blanket, arm rings, or other ornaments.

To some extent ritual conventions dictate the use and ownership of property on a sex basis. Thus the *fakamaru*, the long strip of bark-cloth, is the garment of men, and the *mami*, the bark-cloth square, is that of women. But both are made by women, and can be used by either sex in ceremonial gift or exchange. Male and female belts of sinnet cord differ considerably, however, that of women being much finer in workmanship, though less strong, and these are restricted in ownership to the respective sexes. Sometimes there may be a breach of the custom. Each sex has by convention its own type of leaf of the umbrella palm as a shelter from rain, that of females being smaller than that of males. They are specifically known as the " umbrella of the men " and " the umbrella of the women " respectively, and it is taboo to bear that of the other sex. Pa Fenuatara told me this while in fact holding over his head a female umbrella. He carried it about all one wet day, and the inconsistency did not worry him—these leaves are not too plentiful, and the convenience overcame what is really a very light prohibition. A stricter prohibition applies to the wearing of the pandanus mat kilt, the *kie*. This is in ritual terms the waist garment of the Atau-i-Kafika, the premier deity of the land ; the kilt of the women is another type of mat known as the *fakaro*. But I saw a young woman wear a *kie* once at a dance. This was disapproved of by the men, who said that her breach of custom was due to the coming of the *rotu*—Christianity—to the island.

Conventions of a ritual order also govern the use of other items of property.

Nau Fenuatara cut her hand badly while chopping chestnuts

with the large knife of her father-in-law the Ariki Kafika. The reason given for her injury by the members of her family was that she had committed a breach of *tapu* in handling the implement without first obtaining his permission. " It is taboo to grasp the knife of a chief." Other goods such as an adze or a wooden head-rest are similarly individualized by taboo. The son of a chief if asked about such an item will say, " Oh ! It is my father's." He does not go and take it unauthorized. It may be used by others than the owner if permission is first obtained. Then " it has been made correct ", and no evil consequences are expected to follow. In the case of commoners the taboo on such objects is not so strict, but the same principles apply.

An indication of the individualization of property is given by the way in which possessors of it, as against other people, spend time in caring for it. The Tikopia are very provident owners. Canoes are ordinarily kept each in its own shed, with hull and outrigger float raised off the ground on baulks of wood. They can explain the reasons for so doing, and the results which follow on neglect. Thus after I had acquired a small canoe the builders and other men kept an eye on it, and told me to keep it chocked up for fear of the float and its sinnet lashing rotting. I was rather careless about leaving it out in the open—not having a shed—and more than once a man sent children with mats and branches to cover it up from the sun. They told me that a single day's exposure would split the hull—I thought this an exaggeration, though I did not put it to the proof. The nets used in the lake are put out to dry after use, and taken in hurriedly when it rains ; and fish line is rinsed in fresh water, run out on poles to dry, and similarly removed if a shower comes. Wooden bowls also are rinsed each time after use, wiped out and put away on shelves in the house, bottom upwards. Pandanus mats are kept tied up carefully in bundles, covered in bark-cloth. On sunny days these are opened up and put outside, lest they become mouldy. The Tikopia were more careful about the mats I acquired than I was, and the wives of my friends inquired often whether they were kept properly sunned. On one occasion I came home to find that the wife of a neighbour had entered my house in my absence and got all the mats spread out for sunning and inspection.

A certain amount of care is also taken to preserve food from the depredations of rats and swamp rails. Occasionally a cone of sago leaf thatch pinned together with the midrib of the leaf itself is set over a food basket suspended on a wooden hook from the roof. This contrivance, acting like a food-safe, is termed *taoŋa*. In the cultivations, bunches of bananas approaching maturity are protected from the voracious rail by a sheathing of plaited coco-nut frond.

Distinguishing marks of ownership are rarely used in Tikopia. Apart from the special ties for hanks of sinnet cord, which help in their identification at funeral and other exchanges, the only instance of such marks I saw was at the baking of sago owned by different kinship groups ("houses") in a communal oven.

MARKS OF OWNERSHIP ON SAGO SLABS IN COMMUNAL OVEN

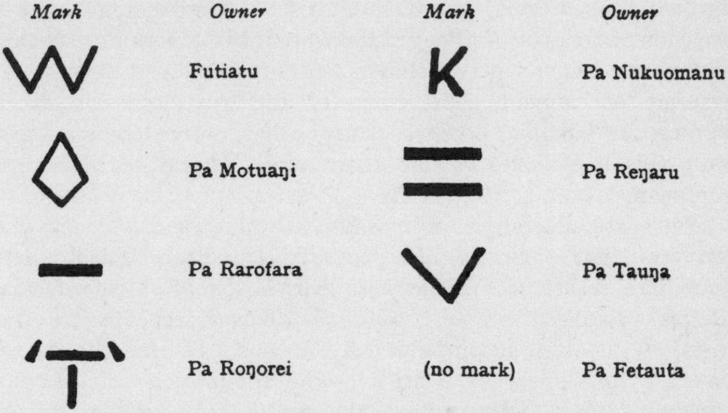

| Mark | Owner | Mark | Owner |
|------|-------|------|-------|
| W | Futiatu | K | Pa Nukuomanu |
| ◇ | Pa Motuaŋi | = | Pa Reŋaru |
| ▬ | Pa Rarofara | V | Pa Tauŋa |
| T | Pa Roŋorei | (no mark) | Pa Fetauta |

Fig. 8

The trunk of each sago palm was split into slabs several feet long, and the slabs of each house were marked by a special set of cuts so that they could be claimed again without difficulty. A list of the marks used is given in the accompanying Figure.

Such marks are not selected *ad hoc*, but are used periodically by the same people for this purpose. Some of them in this case are letters of the alphabet, seen by the Tikopia in the Mission spelling books of the Motlav teacher ; others are old symbols. That used by Pa Motuaŋi is known as *fakafoiika*, a fish design ; those of Pa Rarofara and Pa Reŋaru respectively as *toŋi potutasi* and *toŋi poturua*, "cut at one end" and "cut at both ends". Baskets of *ti* (*Cordyline terminalis*) root were baked at the same time, and were distinguished by differences of leaf wrapping, or by their lashings.

## THEFT AND THE CONSERVATION OF PROPERTY

From what has been said about the freedom enjoyed by other members of the community than the owner to use land for planting, instruments of production such as canoes, and consumer's goods such as coco-nuts, it might be imagined that there is in Tikopia a very vague delimitation of individual rights. This is not the case. Socialization of property does not mean anarchy. Attempts to alienate land permanently or to abstract productive equipment or other goods secretly are fiercely resented, and are characterized as theft (*te kaia*). In practice the line between borrowing and theft is given by the advertisement of the intentions and acts of the person who takes the thing, so that even if the owner's permission is not first obtained there is at least no concealment. The curiosity and free discussion which characterize Tikopia, like so many other native communities, make this line a clearer one than might appear feasible to a European.

There are several possible ways of acting by an owner who discovers that some of his property has been stolen. The immediate reaction is usually to shriek loudly in the formal Tikopia prolonged cry of " *Iefu !* " This is repeated several times, and is often accompanied by furiously beating the house-thatch with a spear or a stick. The commotion brings up a crowd of people, who inquire the reason, and on hearing it, proffer sympathy and suggestions as to who may have been the culprit ; who has been seen carrying a similar article ; who refused to say what he was doing at a particular spot, etc. This acts as a public proclamation of the theft, and may assist in the discovery of the person responsible.

The situation is, however, sometimes more complicated. Thus after a dance festival a man I knew well returned home and shortly afterwards appeared outside, whooped and beat his house in a rage. When we all ran up it was elicited that some tobacco had been stolen from his house during his absence. Everyone sympathized with him. But afterwards people told me that they did not know ; perhaps it had been only a pretence to keep his store of tobacco for himself, since supplies of it were now generally running low. When I expressed surprise at such an artifice, they said that it was sometimes done.  Again, the Ariki Kafika went several times to his orchard of Takarito in Faea, and was heard to give vent to *fuatau*—furious yelling and cursing.  He said that his coco-nuts had been stolen by people of Faea.  When they heard the story these folk denied it ; their account to me was that the chief's sons, who frequently went and worked in Rakisu near by, used to pluck the coco-nuts for drinking purposes and not tell their father.

Assuming, however, that the theft is genuine, the aggrieved owner has several courses open to him.  If he can discover the thief he may go to him and tax him with it, and either receive compensation immediately, or go himself and take something else as indemnity (see p. 320).  But it is often difficult to make certain, especially since the thief will lie vigorously.  One way of relieving the owner's feelings, and perhaps bringing disrepute and shame upon the thief, is to compose a song about the incident and have it chanted as a dance chorus in the ordinary way.  Natives say that the thief, listening to this, is made to feel shame.  The song thus becomes a kind of legal mechanism by which the ridicule of the community is mobilized and launched against the offender.  Here is a typical song of this kind, composed by Pa Rarovi :—

" When a man plucks wantonly from above
Why is he not struck with shame at another's tree ?

My breadfruit have been carried off ;
Have been pronged off in the evening shades.
My coco-nuts have been carried off ;
Have been twirled off in the evening shades."

The reference to " another's tree " (literally, " a tree different ") is to the act of theft.  Breadfruit is taken by means of a long pronged stick ; coco-nuts are twisted off by hand.  In another song the Ariki Taumako, whose areca palms had been raided time after time, despite all his precautions, likened the thieves to paroquets who came and settled in the fronds of the palms and nipped off the nuts.  In irony he asked them to come and dance with abandon after the completion of their nefarious task—a common form of Tikopia appeal to feelings of shame.

A final method of procedure is regarded as the most effective of all.  This is the practice of *tautuku*, the bewitching of the offender.  The aggrieved owner aims at inflicting illness, and even death, on the thief, through the power of his gods. Since the chiefs, their ritual elders, and the spirit mediums are the principal intermediaries with the gods, resort to the *tautuku* is mainly by them. The Ariki Kafika told me a formula he uses when he finds his coco-nuts taken from Takarito. He appeals to a noted ancestor :—

> " Lie you down, Ancestor,
>     In the belly of the person there
>     Who came to eat coco-nut there."

He said that at once the belly of the thief would swell in a sickness known as *te fura*, for which there is no remedy. Other people also stressed to me the virulence of the action of the god or ancestor invoked. A more elaborate technique of the *tautuku* is to employ the *faiŋatā*, the ritual adze with which the chiefs and some elders are traditionally equipped. This metaphorically strikes down the thief. I happened to be sitting with the Ariki Kafika in his house in Uta once when a boy came in with a bunch of areca nut and a message from the Ariki Taumako that areca nut had been stolen from the side of his temple close by. When the Ariki Kafika heard he burst out, " Thy friend, Pa Taumako ! May he be cut with your *faiŋatā* to strike in his belly." He repeated this several times in a bloodthirsty manner.

Resort to the *tautuku* is usually kept secret, partly lest it come to the knowledge of the thief, and allow him to seek means of supernatural protection from it, and partly because its action is generally condemned. It is bad because of its ill effects. Here we meet the frequent Tikopia habit of separate moral judgment upon antecedent and consequent action. Theft is bad, but so also is the punishment of theft. And a man who will use it for his own ends without scruple at one moment will at the next declare that it is evil. The *tautuku*, then, is a traditional institution, regarded as producing real effects, utilized as a means of private retaliation, but categorized as morally bad in general circumstances, even by those who are ready to employ it.

The *tautuku* can be regarded as one of the means whereby the chiefs and other men of rank attempt to maintain their property interests—though as mentioned already they do not form as a whole a solid propertied class. But it is not a very efficient mechanism. Fear of its effects is not sufficient to prevent frequent theft, even from the Ariki Kafika, the premier chief of the land, and the Ariki Taumako, who is acknowledged to possess a very potent and evil deity whom he can invoke.

A more real field of exploitation is given to men of rank, in particular those of chiefly families, by the social power that they possess. On the whole such men have a sense of responsibility, and rarely sequestrate the property of others. But as the Tikopia say, " One man comes, and his thought is good.    Another, no ! Great is his thieving." And occasionally something is taken by a member of a chiefly house. A suspected case of this occurred during my stay. Pa Nukutuŋasau, himself of the chiefly house of Faŋarere, had a new net stolen. The thief was alleged to belong to the village of Potu i Fara, where some men of rank of Taumako lived. He did not go to search for it ; he was frightened to do so, I was told, lest he be beaten. The explanation was given, " It is good if it be taken by a commoner. Thereupon one goes and says to him, ' Now, my net that you here have taken away . . .' But if it has been taken by ' a man of the land ', (that is, a man of rank), one does not go and speak to him ; because if one accuses him one will be struck." People seeing the net and recognizing it say simply, " Oh ! there's the net," but make no complaint to the thief.

I have mentioned in the last Chapter that individuals set up *tapu* in their orchards to conserve their supplies of coco-nut and other fruit. On the whole these operate effectively, and would-be thieves steal mainly from unguarded orchards, or where the owner has set up the barring-sign of the *pipi*, which has no supernatural sanction attached to it. But sometimes a *tapu* is disregarded. The Tikopia say that there are two types of attitude among thieves in such case. One is that of the man " who considers the *tapu* a lie ", that is, who doubts its efficacy, and who goes and steals, paying no heed to the spiritual beings who have been invoked to guard it. In such case he may find himself stricken with illness for his error. The other attitude is that of the thief who is not afraid of the *tapu* because he has previously dealt with its spirit guardians. He knows who they are, and so plucks a coco-nut and pours out the liquid as an offering to them. " He cuts the liquid of the *tapu* " it is said, " he honours the deities." Having thus stolen the owner's thunder, he steals also his coco-nuts, and goes his way, saying that the *tapu* will not harm him. This ingenious, if unsporting, action is regarded as a safeguard by the Tikopia, but I do not know how often it is practised.   On the whole I have the impression that in most cases the first attitude is the more common, and that theft without finesse is the rule.

The purpose of this lengthy account has been to show that theft in Tikopia is a reality, the object of moral judgment, with several methods of coping with it, however ineffectively ;   and that therefore the concept of private property, liberally defined as it is, is regarded as needing social and individual sanctions to uphold it.   Moreover, it is clear that to some extent men of rank are helped more effectively by these sanctions to protect their own wealth, but that the protection afforded them is by no means absolute.

## ENTRY OF GOODS INTO PRODUCTION

The question now arises as to the use of capital in the Tikopia economy.   One difficulty in this lies in the difference of formulation and opinion between economists as to the nature and theory of capital.[1]   L. M. Fraser has summarized these views in giving three main senses in which the term capital is liable to be used : productive equipment ;   use of purchasing power and control over resources ;   and claims to or expectation of interest.   In essence his classification is not one of goods as such, but of their functions in the productive process.

In the Tikopia economy certain classes of goods obviously fall into the category of productive equipment.   In the building of a canoe for instance, adzes, borers, strips of bark-cloth packing, sinnet lashings, and rubbers fulfil this capital function.   It is clear also that many types of consumers' goods definitely must be considered as capital.   Food, bark-cloth, pandanus mats, and sinnet cord are accumulated and employed to further the act of production by being used to maintain and reward the workers. It is important to realize here that ceremonies such as initiation, marriage, and funerals provide for the maintenance and increase of this capital and give a stimulus to future production (see pp. 321 and 330).

To some extent such goods may be regarded as giving control of purchasing power (if this term is reinterpreted for such a non-price economy).   The food, for example, represents resources not specially earmarked in advance for the consumption of the

---

[1] See A. Marshall, *op. cit.*, 787 ; J. M. Keynes, *A Treatise on Money*, 1930, i, 128 ; F. Benham, *op. cit.*, 140 ; L. M. Fraser, *Economic Thought and Language*, 1937, 233–312.

entrepreneur himself or of any other producers, but which can be used by him to meet any variation in his choice or changes in the productive situation. With it he can induce more workers to attend or command the services of more tools. Should a death occur in his family he can convert the food to meet the funeral commitments. In Tikopia there is no extensive borrowing of such capital in the strict sense of the word. A quantity of it is obtained from outside sources but this is interpreted as a conventional contribution to the act of production partly by the workers and partly by the entrepreneur's kinsfolk and neighbours.

The actual process by which the goods accumulated assist production is by meeting the maintenance claims of workers from day to day and by being dispersed to them in a larger quantity at the end of production. As far as claims to future income are concerned Tikopia capital fulfils this function only in a very broad sense. The material assistance given to the entrepreneur by his kinsfolk and workers themselves does give them a future claim upon him. But this claim is not clearly defined in quantitative terms and is a claim to raw materials and to services which yield real income rather than to income as such. This seems to be a reflex of the absence of money as an intermediary between services and income in terms of goods. But the general ideology of the productive system must also be allowed for, since the individual motivation and behaviour of the participants in the productive process are closely regulated by traditional conventions.

In view then partly of the fact that the categories to be found in the economic literature of to-day do not always command general agreement, but more because of the lack of precise correspondence with them of the Tikopia material, I have preferred to pursue the analysis of this aspect of Tikopia economics in more empirical terms.

A complete census of general production in Tikopia is not possible from my data, but it is clear that from the total amount of goods produced at any given time some proportion is reserved for future consumption and to implement further production. There is no preservation of fish in Tikopia, as there is among the Maori, but some kinds of vegetable food are preserved. Taro, banana, and breadfruit are grated into a paste and stored in pits, whence they are withdrawn as occasion demands, perhaps months afterwards. Coco-nuts which may be consumed green are left to mature and drawn upon in a different way for the preparation of puddings. Not only is a small supply of mature nuts often kept in a household, but round enclosures of stakes are made in the orchards and may contain several hundreds of nuts. It is then not an accident that there is a surplus over ordinary household requirements. The setting aside of a surplus is a part of the normal productive scheme. Such accumulated supplies available through the work of single individuals are open to be drawn upon for family wants if the situation requires. When the family of Tafua commemorated the death of the son of Pa Raŋifuri the dry coco-nuts from the enclosure of Pa Nukunefu were utilized ; those of a similar enclosure accumulated by Pa Raŋifuri himself were left to be used for the feast of his father the chief which was to follow shortly afterwards. There may be in addition specific acts of production such as the planting of additional taro gardens directed to objectives envisaged several months ahead.

The Tikopia may be regarded as having a concept of saving, but this is not expressed as a concept of economic investment. The people say " we must prepare for the gifts we shall have to make to the chief "—or whatever be the objective. They do not say " in order to obtain future returns we must save and make these gifts ". De facto of course the latter is what happens but the economic motive does not emerge specifically from the complex scheme of other social dictates.

On the whole it may be said that capital in Tikopia is accumulated by surplus production over immediate requirements rather than by abstinence per se. It might be argued that there is abstinence from leisure but this implies that leisure is an object of satisfaction in such circumstances, and this is not necessarily the case. Work and leisure are not sharply opposed activities ; Tikopia is a society where much production is initiated and carried through with the minimal use of capital of an entrepreneur. A considerable part of the goods necessary for production is contributed by the workers themselves ; hence there is no need for great initial accumulation by individuals taking the initiative. Some stock of goods is necessary ; but this serves as a first stimulus to production rather than as the initial recoupment of workers. One reason for this lies in the dictates of kinship and other social obligations discussed in Chapter III. Another reason lies in the ready lending of tools and other equipment (such as troughs for turmeric and sago making) and in the ease with which raw material such as timber can be obtained without the definite obligation of making an equivalent return.

Some producers, however, operate to more advantage than others. The traditional differences in the ownership of land and other goods gives some families greater possibilities of production. Again titular control of the limited water supplies of the island is vested with ritual sanction in a limited number of individuals. The Ariki Faŋarere, for instance, has no " water " under his control and therefore joins forces with the Ariki Kafika for the manufacture of his turmeric. But the ramifications of the kinship system and the conventions of easy borrowing allow other producers to operate at less disadvantage than the differential ownership of wealth might seem to allow. Their disabilities are potential rather than actual. There is an absence of an exact calculation between contribution to production and reward from the fruits of it, which gives considerable freedom to individuals to take a motive part in the productive scheme.

A further aspect of the situation is the absence of a concept that the goods applied to further production should necessarily yield interest. When the possibility of such a return is mentioned the phrase " at his wish " is the usual reply. As seen in practice this is not simply a verbal concealment of an actual system of interest-taking. Linked with this is the absence of an idea of overheads, that irrespective of its use there should be a constant charge upon productive equipment. There is no onus upon the possessor, for the time being, of such equipment to keep it in use to the limits of its capacity. This again is linked with the absence of any exact measurement of time as of economic worth. Yet there is a tendency to conserve capital, for old sea-going canoes are " retired " to be transport canoes on the lake and finally, when dismantled, they are used as troughs, or their sides are converted into house planks or sounding-slabs for beating time at dances.

An example may now be given of the manner in which productive equipment is contributed in a co-operative activity in which several family groups are involved. In August, 1928 (see Ch. IV, Case H), the Ariki Tafua and some other men engaged in the manufacture of turmeric. The water supply came from a spring controlled by the chief himself—it was adjacent to his residence—and the aqueduct which led from it was repaired some time before by his family. The raw material of turmeric roots was contributed by the respective parties from each of their cultivations, and the final product was not pooled but each portion was manufactured separately and retained by the individual owners. The productive equipment consisted principally of graters, troughs, and bowls and cylinders for baking the pigment. These articles were contributed from the different co-operating families and were pooled for the work. The major quantity was provided by the Ariki Tafua and his sons. Even although two of these sons did not participate in the work because of a marriage tie in one case and a funeral taboo in the other, they helped in the provision of materials. The eldest son, for instance, relashed with sinnet cord his turmeric grater and sent it along. Of the three troughs used, two were the property of the Ariki Tafua and the third of Pa Fetauta, a ritual elder. The other participants had none to contribute. Of the bowls most came from the household of the Ariki Tafua. Those of the smallest size, about 2 feet long and 9 inches deep, were needed in quantity, and 27 of them were taken down from the shelves in the chief's house. One, known by the personal name Faŋarasi, was an ancient highly valued specimen said to have been carved by a man of Rotuma who lived in Tikopia several generations before. Eight wooden cylinders known as " ovens " were used for baking the pigment ; five were contributed from the family of the chief, and included one named Foŋaraŋa. This was fetched from the other side of the island by one of the chief's sons, from a site of previous turmeric manufacture. Its fellow Foŋareŋa had been broken and thrown away some time previously. Two others were brought by Pa Nukuofo and one by another member. The property so used is thus definitely held in individual ownership but is pooled for the process of manufacture without an itemized return being obtained. The chief, though he is the principal contributor of such " working capital ", receives no special economic return therefor. On the other hand, because of his titular ownership of the water supply, his somewhat larger supplies of raw turmeric, and his general expert control of the work, the occasion of manufacture is commonly spoken of as " his ", and upon him rests the primary responsibility for success or failure. His major provision of productive equipment is to some extent a reflection of this premier position.

Where the product was finally obtained the result was six cylinders of turmeric pigment belonging to the chief, four to Pa Nukuofo, five to Pa Fetauta (including two that had first turned out badly and had to be reworked) and three to Pa Nukutauriri (who was represented in the work by his son). That the impulse to manufacture by the chief himself was not the desire for pigment for current use was shown by the fact that he had 16 cylinders of turmeric already hanging in a row in his house—an ordinary commoner such as the other participants having only a couple. Food was provided abundantly for the workers throughout the period of 9 days, each day the onus of supplying the raw provisions being upon one of the participant families.

For the manufacture of a net or of a canoe a similar principle is followed, the attendant workers supplying some of the productive instruments and part of the food provision but here, since the final product rests with the individual and family which initiates the work, the major provision of these items falls on them.

The conventions of Tikopia ownership, allowing of fairly free lending of the instruments of production, sometimes hold back the performance of a task. I saw one instance of this in the sago-making of the house of Fetauta, which had to be deferred for a couple of days till they could get back their trough, which had been lent to a fellow-villager and kinsman. There was some grumbling at this, but no action was taken to get it back immediately, and no charge is ever made for loss so felt or incurred.

### SUMMARY

A brief summary may now be given of the results of our inquiry in this Chapter. It is clear that there is an institution of property in Tikopia, supported by definite social conventions. It is expressed largely in terms of ownership of goods by kinship groups, but allows for some individual holding of smaller items, as well as for the rights of chiefs over certain types of goods such as land and canoes, and rights also over them by other members of the community as a whole. Decisions about the use of these goods in further production are taken in practice by the heads of the kinship groups—chiefs, elders, heads of families, senior members of a " house "—in consultation with other members of the group, so that in the case of the more important goods such as land and canoes " individual ownership " can only be expressed in degrees of responsibility for and enjoyment of the group property.    Moreover, such decisions may be influenced considerably by the opinions and actions of other persons with no direct title to the goods, but who are allowed a partial use of them by the conventions of ownership.    But there is care of property by individuals who have the primary responsibility for it, and the rights of individuals outside the kinship group are limited, the concept of theft being recognized, and there being definite sanctions against it.

The system of property-holding allows of inequality in the possession of goods by the kinship groups, and with this is associated inequality of incomes.

## Chapter VIII

# PRINCIPLES OF DISTRIBUTION AND PAYMENT

SINCE no high degree of specialization has been attained in Tikopia and most people are competent to perform the necessary tasks in food getting, there is no elaborate system of exchange which has as its object the provision of the necessaries of life. The acts of exchange which do take place meet on the one hand the need for some piece of productive equipment, or on the other the need to demonstrate in ceremonial form some social tie. Exchanges of food, though the most common, hardly ever take place to meet a demand for variety of food. In a wide sense acts of distribution of a joint product and of payment for work represent the exchange of goods for labour. But since factually in the Tikopia economy they are of a different order from the specific exchange of goods for goods, it has seemed better to consider them separately. They are therefore examined in turn in this and the following Chapters.

The system of distribution in the native industry comprises two types of operation. One is the apportionment of a joint product among the members of a co-operative group ; the other is the compensating of the factors of production, mainly labour, from a source other than their immediate product. The essential problem raised by the first type of operation is to ascertain the principles upon which the product is apportioned ; the second type of operation brings up additional problems—the source from which the compensation comes, and the basis for equation of the services of labour and other factors of production with goods of a kind other than those immediately produced.

## APPORTIONMENT OF THE PRODUCT OF CO-OPERATIVE WORK

### (i) Fishing

The principles of apportioning a joint product may be first examined. They are not, as might be thought, of the simplest arithmetical order, but are governed by social conventions such as ideas of kinship, a general code of etiquette and ritual obligations. These can be seen even in the commonest and most elementary forms of such distribution, among the members of a household, where the apportionment of the product of their labour is made at the common meal.[1] When the working party is composed of more distant kinsfolk, neighbours, or fellow-villagers, who because they come from different households do not share a common oven and cannot be satisfied at a single joint meal, then division of the raw product is essential. The distributive process in the spheres of industry where this operates particularly, fishing and the extraction of sago and turmeric, may be examined in detail.

First let us consider the distribution of the catch from a fishing expedition in a canoe. Ordinarily the fish are divided out equally, the owner of the craft receiving his portion with the rest in virtue of the participation of the canoe, whether he himself has gone out or not. The equal shares to the crew are justified by reference to the fact that they have laboured in common at the task. There is no attempt to assess the precise amount of each person's contribution. " The distribution of the fish of the canoe is made equally because the crew toiled at the paddling of the canoe at sea." If the owner does not go out with the canoe he may come when the vessel returns and distribute the fish himself. But more often he delegates the job to one of the crew, saying, as I heard one man say, " You, friend, go and distribute the fish ; I am tired."

A couple of examples will illustrate the complications which arise in the system. A canoe named Te Uruakau, property of Pa ŋatotiu, was taken out by a group of young bachelors among whom were two of the sister's sons of the owner. The fish caught numbered about 100. When the vessel returned the catch was first " announced " to the gods of the canoe, and then distributed by the eldest nephew of the owner. On this occasion ten fish and then a few over were counted out to each of the three other members of the canoe crew. With the decimal system in use in Tikopia any less number is often not specified. Each bore off his string of fish to his home. In this case the catch was not fully distributed, rather more than half being kept back. The reason was that they might be cooked in a ceremonial oven for the rededication of the vessel to its gods. This was accepted without demur by the crew, the claims of ritual being regarded as paramount. I have no record or statement of any canoe owner using

[1] A description has been given in *We, The Tikopia*, 112–16.

the ritual sanction in this way as a shelter for his own material advantage. In another case five of a crew went out in Te Aroimata, the vessel of Pa Nukurena. The catch was 40 fish, distributed by a younger brother of the owner and one of his kinsmen. A few only were given to each of the crew and the bulk of the catch went to the household of the owner. The reason was that a kava ceremony for the vessel was to be performed the following day and the food therefrom would be carried to the chief of the clan. When, as in this case, the canoe is a sacred vessel the " canoe food portion " is carried periodically to the chief in acknowledgment of his tutelary position. If the catch reaches the hundred mark, the standard successful yield, " the canoe has attained fish " it is said, or again, " it has got the century." Then the portion carried to the chief may be twenty or thirty fish. If not, he gets ten or so.

The customary freedom of use of other people's productive equipment and the readiness to give labour elsewhere leads to curious situations. In this instance the owner of the vessel did not go out in his own craft but in that of his next-door neighbour. From this he received a share which happened to be ten fish or so. This example illustrates the fluidity of the use of productive equipment and is consistent with a definite system of private ownership. The basic principles are not challenged, individual ownership is not negated, but there is not that unique relation between possessor and user, between ownership and management, which one might expect to find in a primitive community.

The principle of equal distribution is simple to follow when the catch is of flying-fish which are all roughly equivalent in size. A difficulty of estimation arises when a single large fish is caught as well. The Tikopia deal with this not by treating it merely as so many pounds of food with an equivalent in a number of flying-fish, but by making it an object of special presentation. For instance, Seremata went out in a canoe of the Ariki Kafika as a visitor. Besides twenty flying-fish a large *paravao* was hauled up by one of the chief's sons. When the canoe came into shore the chief " announced " the catch ritually and then insisted on giving the large fish to Seremata. The latter protested—he said he could not eat it all himself. But the chief would not be denied, so Seremata took the fish along to his brother's house where many people were living, and it was eaten there. But the next day he and his brother's family prepared a basket of food containing pudding, taro, and breadfruit (without fish) and carried it to the chief's house. Such a gift is termed *fakaara* or *fakaara ŋa ika* [1] and is the normal reciprocation whenever a man is presented by another with a large fish. Should the visiting member of a crew haul up such a fish himself he usually does not keep it. He leaves it either to the owner or the other members of the crew. A native comment on this situation was " the idea is that it is because he himself pulled it up ; it is not good for it to go with him ; and for the others to go away bare ". Another formulation was " a man who has pulled up a fish does not eat it, he gives it to another man because he himself pulled it up ". The owner of a canoe or his deputy sees that this is done. There is, however, a certain elasticity in this procedure and some people hold that it is permissible for the man who caught the fish to take it home —with the consent of his fellows. " Some do, some don't ; it rests with a man's own idea."

The same principle applies when only a few fish are caught. If a man catches one or two only while no one else has any success then he will give them to other members of the crew and not keep any. If he did retain his fish, allowing the others to go away empty-handed, then he runs the risk of slanderous talk. " One man may go and not say anything ; another man may go and criticize, ' that fish which he brought in, he did not give it to me but kept it for himself.' " There is no ritual reason why a man should not eat of his own catch—a reason which sometimes obtains in other communities. The custom is explained on a rational social basis. If a man catches fish with his net in the lake, for instance, it is quite legitimate for him to keep them for himself " because he is alone ". It is when he is a member of a crew that the former custom operates. It is described directly as " the blocking of jealousy " (*te pi o te kaimeo*). The economic principle of equal reward for equal labour, or alternatively of securing reward to the person whose luck or skill gained it, is overridden in favour of a code of etiquette which in its turn is justified by reference to the social value of liberality and the avoidance of personal friction.

When a shark is caught alternative procedure is possible. It may be presented whole to the clan-chief of the owner of the canoe,

---

[1] *Fakaara* means literally " making a path " (*ŋa ika*) " of the fish " but is an example of a vague general term used with a specific significance, not overtly symbolical. Cf. *te aso* (" the day ") for areca nut presentation in *Work of the Gods*. Whether this is a homonym or a forgotten symbol it is impossible to say.

or cut up by the owner at his discretion, and divided between him and the crew. Some men, it is said, give the larger share to the crew, others keep it for themselves. To this no objection is raised. But a qualifying element may come in here. If the shark has been hauled up on a new sinnet cord then the man who hooked it may wish to carry it to the man who has plaited the cord. Such a gift is termed *sunusunu o a kafa* ; it is a kind of celebration of the efficacy of the tackle in doing its work. It is made also for nets and other fishing gear. In such case the fisherman says to the owner, " Son, let the fish be carried for the *sunusunu* of my sinnet." The owner may say " it is well ". But if he wishes to present the shark to his chief, then the claim of the *sunusunu* will be deferred.

There is still another factor affecting the distribution. In fulfilling ceremonial obligations it is usual for the gift of food to contain some fish. Lack of fish at a given moment leads to a considerable amount of borrowing. A man who has to take a basket of food to a funeral or other ceremony next day asks a man who is going fishing that night to give him a string from the catch. " You are going to sea, bring me fish back to give a relish to my shoulder burden." This is done and the loan is reciprocated another time. Sometimes the borrowing is more in the nature of commandeering. The phrase " the relish of my load ", or " . . . of my shoulder burden " exercises a kind of compulsive force since it implies the necessity of conforming to those social obligations which are part of the fabric of the Tikopia community structure. Refusal to hand over the fish desired, even though they were all that a man had, is said not to occur—the sanction being that such refusal might place the churlish one in a difficult position when he himself next wanted fish for a similar purpose. It is taken for granted that the requests will be met. For instance a man caught a couple of fish in the channel. He mentioned it to his cousin who said " where are they ? ". He was told that they had been cooked and eaten. He replied, " If I had only known ! I was wanting a relish for my load." The consent of the other was assumed.

This analysis of direct apportionment of the results of canoe-fishing has shown how social norms may override the obvious principle of getting a reward proportionate to one's exertion. Sometimes one gets more than is proportionate to the amount of labour one has contributed, sometimes less. And frequently this leads to subsidiary transfers of goods (as the *fakaara*) in order to rectify the disequilibrium.

Reference to the distribution of the catch from a fish-drive will show other factors still. When such a drive is conducted along the reef a net belonging to one of the party or borrowed from someone else is taken out, and a score or so of people, mostly men, form a wide circle and drive in towards it. The catch is apportioned by one of the more important men of the group. A share is allotted to the owner of the net, and one also in all probability is sent to the chief, though this is optional. The various households represented in the group then get their share. The more important people are usually given the better fish, or if these are all of one type, such as mackerel, which come in shoals, then such men get one or two more fish than others of the crowd. A ritual elder, for instance, is given a good share. If the fish are few then they are allotted to the owner of the net and a few of the most important people present.

When a new net belonging to the family of the Ariki Tafua was taken out the catch was estimated at 50 fish. The distribution made by Pa Raŋifuri, the eldest son, was as follows : three to the household of the chief, being one for him, one for his wife, and one for his youngest son with whom he lived ; one each to the four other sons who had separate households ; three to Pa Raŋifuri himself, the eldest son ; four each to Pa Tarafaŋa and Pa Korokoro, elderly men of position and experts who had assisted in repairing the net ; three each to Pa Fetauta, Pa Motuaŋi, Pa Nukuomanu, and Pa Nukutauriri, all kinsfolk and neighbours ; three also to Pa Nukuariki, head of another branch of Tafua farther down the coast, two each to Pa Reŋaru and Pa Roŋotaono, fellow villagers.[1] It was said that the fish were distributed to people who helped in the rolling of the thread for the net, but differentiation was clearly made on the basis of rank and kinship as well as economic service.

In the ordinary way it is as beaters and not as prior workers on the net that the men receive their portion of the catch. In this case the drive was partly in order to test the new net, but partly also to give a chance to repay contributors of labour for their services. Pa Korokoro and Pa Tarafaŋa, as experts in charge of the net-making and as having done most of the

---

[1] The residential and kinship ties of these people are given in *We, The Tikopia*, 61–3, 65, 67–8.

construction, got the largest individual shares of the fish. They
had previously each been given a piece of bark-cloth and a basket
of food (reciprocated or not, according to their wish). A sound
portion of the old net had been joined on to the new portion,
otherwise their reward would have been greater.

This scheme of distribution after a fish-drive may be disturbed.
Normally it goes off well, but sometimes, especially when there is
a scarcity of food, individuals of the party pick out fish from the
net, ostensibly to assist in killing them, and then secrete them.
The folds of the waistbelt make a convenient pocket into which in
the confusion a fish can easily be slipped. This is done as quickly
and as unobtrusively as possible, and frequently goes unobserved.
Such conduct is stigmatized but it is common. The owner of the
net has thus often cause to be annoyed at the smallness of his
share, and other members of the party complain when they come
back to shore. If the act is discovered the culprit gets a tongue-
lashing. It is usually the bachelors and the married people of
lesser importance who steal the fish, since they are the ones most
likely to suffer in the distribution. An important man, an elder
or the son of a chief, is not likely to do so, firstly for the sake of
his own dignity which would suffer if he were detected, and
secondly since he will in any case receive a good share of the
catch. Hence such people are most frequent complainants about
the actions of others of the party. This is one aspect, incidentally,
of the way in which underlying inequalities between different
sets of persons in the Tikopia economy come to the surface,
social position giving a title to more than an equal portion of
economic reward. This example shows too that the norms of
behaviour mentioned earlier are not a natural outcome of the
Tikopia mode of life but have to be maintained vigilantly and
may be disregarded if the situation allows. Among the crew of a
canoe nothing can be concealed. The confusion of a fish-drive
allows individual self-interest to seize its opportunity.

Another factor affecting the distribution of the catch of a
fish-drive is the presence of children.

It will be noted that in the fish-drive just mentioned there is
a discrepancy between the number of fish caught (fifty) and
those distributed (thirty-seven). Pa Raṇifuri explained it to me
thus : he said that while the fish were being taken out of the net
children grabbed one each, bit its head to kill it, and hid it away
in his belt. " Each pockets his fish, bolts off laughing as he goes ;

not a person can be angry with him, because he goes off laughing."
Pa Raŋifuri was a kindly man, but it is true that children have
more latitude than grown-ups. The net result in such cases is
that the portion of some households is increased by a fish or two
which does not " show on the books " as it were.

There are circumstances, however, in which convention allows
individuals co-operating in a large-scale task such as a fish-drive
to keep what they themselves take. A set of people who had
prepared a large oven for baking sago assembled the next day to
catch fish. They had two large nets, one a *parae* and the other
a *sikisiki*. Sixty or seventy people participated, the men with
long-handled nets, the women with their scoop nets. They started
from Matautu, worked up the reef to Sapei, then down to Rofaea.
There they waited for the tide to rise and then worked down
farther to Potimua. They worked as an immense circle which
gradually closed in with much splashing leaving only the space
near the nets quiet. The men holding the end of each net had
to be very quick to lift it since some of the fish attempted to
jump over as they were driven near. Folk kept out of the way
of the rear of the net partly because they would have been useless
there but partly also from fear of the garfish, which bound along
the surface of the water and can inflict a dangerous wound. The
main body of the people consisted of the group who had sago in
the oven, but outsiders joined in. They helped in the fish-drive
but did not go to the communal meal which took place afterwards
—the *pureŋa*, or *tafauŋaumu*, " the strolling of the ovens," that
is the meal in celebration of the oven making. All the fish from
the large nets went into the common stock, for the meal. Members
of the " oven " group who caught fish individually were expected
also to put them into this stock. But such obligation did not lie
upon the outsiders ; if they wished they could keep their fish.
" Who then will be expert in the fishing may keep his catch for
himself " was the explanation given me. This was done for
instance by my neighbour, Pa Taitai, who tucked a fish into his
belt as soon as he had caught it.

But on another occasion the same man who had taken out a
seine net of his brother-in-law for mackerel was very annoyed
because members of the party secreted fish from the net and he
got only one out of a total catch of about twenty. He said that
it was no better than stealing. This illustrates the difference
between the conventions of distribution of a catch which has been

taken individually and another which has been taken collectively. That communal distribution of the collective catch is the ideal procedure was shown in the case mentioned by the remark of a young man who listened to Pa Taitai's anger.    With a sly look at the people present, he said, " With folk of Raveŋa that would not happen."    The people, who were of Faea, laughed and chaffed him about his own district.

A further complication in distribution is introduced when the primary object of the fishing is to fulfil the needs of religious ceremony.  Annually, as part of the ritual of Somosomo, which is a section of the Work of the Gods, a fish-drive is made at night by the light of torches.  When I was at Somosomo there was a discussion the morning after the drive.  The man in charge had distributed the fish on the beach, one to each of the party who had assisted from the beach villages.  The Ariki Kafika and the men with him at Somosomo were annoyed.  They said that this was a breach of custom, that all the fish should be brought in to Somosomo unless there happened to be more than thirty or forty. In this case seven only were brought back in the sacred basket which was part of the ritual apparatus.  The man in charge of this, a senior person, who had been present, said that he had not liked to protest, being ashamed lest people should think he was greedy for the fish (either for himself or for the Somosomo group whom he represented).

The apportionment of the catch from co-operative fishing is primarily a matter of satisfying the claims of labour.  Incidentally it has been seen that the major item of capital equipment, canoe or seine-net, is given a share of the product roughly the same as that given to an individual worker.  The minor items of capital equipment borne by the various individuals of the party receive no recognition.  There is of course no payment for raw material, since there is no ownership in fishing banks or the reef waters.

This factor emerges in the extraction of sago flour, as also another factor akin to the profit of the entrepreneur.

## (ii) Sago and Turmeric

The proportion of sago flour allotted to different members of the co-operative labour group varies according to who owns the tree, and who has taken the initiative in proposing the work.

A man wishing to have some sago flour may see a palm of suitable age standing in another man's orchard. He says to him (so I was told) " Hey ! I want the sago palm there that I may come and fell it for myself ". The owner replies, " It is well. You are energetic, go along and fell it." The owner then probably helps in the work, which demands a large party, and other people may be invited to assist, or may volunteer. Each, including the owner of the tree, contributes to the food supply for the workers. " Of the crowd who come and grate, each brings his *fiuri* (contribution of raw food) ; not a person comes empty-handed." But the greater part of the food provided comes from the man who took the initiative. Each day all the workers are fed, and at the conclusion they are rewarded by some portion of the flour. It is divided up while still wet, and each man goes and dries his own.

The major shares are handed over in wooden bowls, the minor on leaf platters. " When it is divided by the man whose tree it was, he gives the greater portion to me who came and spoke my wish to him," said an informant, putting himself in the position of the initiator of the enterprise. If the result be five bowls of sago flour then the man who owned the tree gives three to the man who made the initial request, keeps one for himself and divides the last among the assistants, giving each one two or three leaf platters according to his standing and the amount of work he did. Casual workers will get none. There is no set principle to determine how much a senior man who worked for a short time should receive as against a junior who worked for much longer. It rests at the discretion of the sago producer. But if the owner of the palm has approached another man to share the task as a principal with him then they each bring equal contributions of food, much greater than those of any other men who may assist. " The crowd make *fiuri* only, but the oven has its base in the pair of them, and they provide food in plenty." When the sago is ready the pair share equally in it, while a bowl is divided among the assistants as in the former case.

Sometimes, if another man has taken the initiative in approaching the tree owner, when the product is ready the latter insists on giving all to him, with the exception of one bowl only, which he divides among the assistants. He keeps none at all for himself. He says, " Carry off your own sago. It was felled by your own energy. Sago palms which stand there will be grated or not. You will go there, come back with a crowd to grate my sago." By this he intimates that he will expect help if and when he himself wishes to utilize one of his palms which are still standing. If the other still suggests that he should take a bowl for himself he may reply, "Oh! I don't want to. If I want some sago flour with which to make a pudding I will ask you for it. I won't feed you (i.e. give you any of the pudding) but you will give it to me. Our sago will stay with you." The one suggestion does not preclude the other. The initiator of the enterprise later prepares a basket of food and presents it to the owner—"the payment for the tree". But if the owner has taken the initiative himself then no basket is presented to him.

The principle here is that the man who puts forward the proposition of sago-making is expected to give most in the way of labour, and of food to keep the other labourers going, but he gets the larger share of the product. If he takes a partner they share equally. The owner of the tree gets a basket of food as payment for the raw material—so long as he has not been the prime user of it. He receives also a share in the product, which he may forgo in favour of a claim to future labour services or a future smaller portion of the product, or both. The assistants are paid for their daily labour in food and a small share of the product, while at the same time they contribute a small portion of their own joint sustenance.

This last point may seem strange, that workers should help to pay for their own labour. But this is one of the leading principles of the Tikopia economy. If a person attends any communal gathering where food is to be prepared he obeys the customary rule that he should assist the persons primarily responsible with food, even though he is later to be among those who will benefit.

An interesting case of distribution is given by the manufacture of turmeric. For this several owners of the raw material club together, pooling their capital equipment of troughs, bowls, and baking ovens and working as a group under the direction of one of them who acts as the premier specialist (see p. 276). He takes control in virtue partly of his technical knowledge, but largely also because of his command of the necessary ritual, and his control of a water supply. Chiefs fulfil this function *par excellence* and when one of them decides to manufacture his turmeric several other men are glad to combine with him. The work is marked by a separation of the group from the ordinary social life of the village ; they are physically isolated and also by a rigid set of taboos.  A unique feature of this industry is that unlike all other Tikopia joint enterprises each man's raw material is run through the series of processes separately and the product is isolated as his alone.  This isolation of products may perhaps be correlated first with the value of turmeric, reckoned among the most important types of Tikopia property, and second with the liability to loss in process, or failure to secure the pigment in its proper state.  The large degree of unpredictability of the result is met by the Tikopia with a set of magical reasons.  No member of the working party may leave the group until the whole of the work is over and a desacralizing rite performed.  The motivation to work in any individual case is of a complex kind— desire to assist the chief, respect for the magical aura of the industry, interest in the product which will accrue to him or to the head of his family.  But from the economic angle a turmeric owner who is not a chief contributes cheerfully a much greater amount of labour in proportion to the product he receives.  The chief, since he controls much more of the raw material, may obtain finally half a dozen cylinders of the pigment ; the commoner may obtain four or less.  The situation rests *inter alia* upon the comparatively low estimation of the value of labour *per se*, and a high value of even a small quantity of turmeric. But there are compensations.  The commoner obtains the advantage of the expert technical knowledge of the chief and, more particularly in native eyes, his ritual backing.  Then again the labour is sustained each day by food contributed by all the participants in turn, and a larger share of this is probably borne by the chief.  The major item in the productive equipment is a set of troughs each of which is very valuable.  No payment is made at the time by the other participants who use them.  But when such a trough has been made to the order of a chief or a man of rank, a man who has the intention of participating in future turmeric-making with this person may bring along a piece of bark-cloth as contribution to the payment of the trough. This represents a kind of borrowing-fee in advance, in aid of the production of the capital goods.  But an intending participant in turmeric manufacture is not always so punctilious in paying his contribution towards the use of the productive equipment.

In this industry, then, fixed capital, labour and the capital devoted to accomplishing the act of production, namely the food for the subsistence of the workers, are all pooled. The joint entrepreneurs receive their reward in their respective turmeric cylinders, which represent an aggregate return for the factors of production they employ ; the other workers, who are usually their junior kin, receive their reward essentially in their daily food, though they may be said to have some slight reversionary interest in the turmeric of their particular kinsman.

## FOOD AS PAYMENT FOR LABOUR

We have now to consider that aspect of the distributive economy where it is not a question of the division of a joint product among the workers, but of rewarding them by another medium when the product of their work is not immediately realizable or divisible. This involves a process known to the Tikopia as *tauvi*, which corresponds broadly to our concept of *payment*. (A more detailed analysis is given in Appendix II.) It will have been seen from previous Chapters that both food and other goods are important in this connection. Of the two, food is the more fundamental—not that by itself it can provide the payment for all types of service, but it enters into every transaction, whereas other goods do not. There are several conventional categories of food appropriate for different types of payment. Green coco-nuts (*niu mata*) are presented for drink and refreshment at stages of work, and may, as in collective agriculture, constitute the immediate recompense. Portions (*taumafa*) from a communal meal constitute a further payment, each man's share often being large enough for him to wrap up the remains to take home. Both of these types of payment apply only to non-specialized labour, and moreover to that which does not last more than a day or so. Work of longer duration, and that of a specialist, is rewarded by a large quantity of cooked food, set before the worker or carried to his home, in an openwork basket known as a *popora*. This food should comprise not only baked breadfruit, taro or bananas (*kai tao*) but also a creamed pudding (*susua*). If possible, too, it should include some fish. The *popora*, so equipped, is the unit of major payment in food. Additional types of food presented are green food (*kai mata*) bundles of taro or bunches of bananas, and sprouting coco-nuts (*niu raurau*), but these are rarely given as payment for labour.

These food payments, for economic and social services, bulk

quite largely in the budget of the head of a household, and obviously require the existence of a stock of available supplies over and above daily household needs. How much is this surplus? It is not easy to calculate, since the organization of production in Tikopia shows three striking characteristics. These have been mentioned incidentally earlier, but may be recapitulated here.

(i)   When a payment of food has to be made it is not provided solely by the entrepreneur, but he receives contributions from his kinsfolk.

(ii)  The workers themselves often contribute to their own " wages fund " in virtue of their general assistance to the entrepreneur —and in part also because of kinship ties with him.

(iii) The workers frequently—though by no means always— reciprocate to some extent the payment that has been made to them.

The first two types of contribution are classed by the Tikopia as *fiuri*, the third as *fakapenu*, and both these are categories of social action which operate far beyond the sphere of payment for labour.

Their net effect is obviously to reduce considerably the initial outlay demanded of the entrepreneur and, by reimbursing him subsequently to some extent, to allow him to draw for the moment on the stocks ordinarily demanded for household consumption. He can operate thus on a much smaller margin of " capital " than otherwise. At the same time the relief which he obtains on his own immediate enterprise is not absolute, since in turn he must make his contributions to enterprises which his kinsfolk undertake.

It will be noted from the examples given that the *fiuri* and *fakapenu* are not universally operative : in some cases custom demands them ; in others it is left to the wish of the participant ; in others he is not expected to furnish them. This difference to some extent indicates differences in the quality of the service involved. The absence of *fakapenu*, for example, is apt to be a feature of specialist labour. But the distinction is not absolute.

We may first consider the transference of food as payment for non-specialist labour. When land is being prepared for cultivation, when a sago trunk is being grated up, a house or a canoe built, it is customary for the owner to press into service more or less willing kinsfolk and neighbours as labourers. The reward for such service is food alone. Usually this consists only of maintenance on a fairly lavish scale during the work—including the provision of green coco-nuts for drinking during a morning pause and a meal of cooked food at the close. For some work, however, an additional food item is presented after the conclusion of the task.

In planting shoots of taro for instance a man will " carry off ", as the native term is, a brother or a brother-in-law or a classificatory kinsman. The man he chooses for such work is one who is known to be an energetic labourer. He says, " Brother, let the two of us go and plant seedlings." " Go and plant where ? " " In Rakisu . . . " or wherever it may be. " It is well." The two of them work the whole day, return when it is dark, and eat in the house of the man who has issued the invitation, the oven having been prepared by his wife. If the work is not done then the pair sleep in his house and go back the next day. When the work is finished the helper goes home. A day or so later the owner of the taro prepares an oven and carries a basket of food (*popora*), which should include a pudding, to the house of his helper. This gift is termed the *aso saŋa*, " the day of planting." When the donor comes with it he is scolded conventionally by the other man, " Oh ! What is this ? I only helped you in planting your seedlings." No return gift is made for this basket. If the work is that of felling or grating a sago trunk then such a food gift is not made but the helper receives a portion of the product. The sanctions for such labour have already been discussed.

In a society where everyone is a taro planter such labour assistance as that mentioned above is best described as non-specialist because although the helper selected tends to be one known to be energetic he is not kept in constant employment at such work and any man is liable to be called upon. There is, however, a degree of what might be called semi-specialization in that certain phases of taro agriculture are primarily the work of women. Such are weeding, mulching, and heaping up the earth around the growing plants. In some households, as that of a bachelor or a widower, where a woman is lacking, the men may go and do these tasks. Their acquaintances are apt to twit them when they are at it. " You, spinster aunt, are you weeding your seed plants ? " The other looks up and answers merely " Yes " or may call out " What is to be done ? You, sitting there, why don't you crawl to a woman ? " This is friendly banter and means, " Why don't you get married that there may be a woman available for my work." This reply, apart from allowing a man to defend himself, embodies a reference to a frequent solution. A man without women in his household may invite the services of a woman from another household near by. He may suggest that they go together and work, or he may ask the woman to go alone. In either event she normally does not refuse. Then when the time comes for the taro to be dug he tells her to come along and they will dig out a quantity. Of this the man gives her a backload to carry to her own house as return for her earlier services.

In other cases, so I was told, a woman takes pity on such a man whom she sees carrying his shoots alone and calls out to him, " Come and drop here the seedlings that I may carry them." The man comes and gives them to her, and together they go to the cultivation. She clears the ground while he plants. Only a single woman will work with him in this way. A married woman may take pity on him and carry his "seedlings" to the cultivation but then she will go on to join her husband wherever he is working. If her husband is at home she will not give this assistance since it would make her liable to slander. When the taro is mature if the man remembers this service he will make some return. He will either ask the woman to come and help him dig the taro, a portion of which he will give to her, or will himself make up a bundle and carry it to her house. If, however, he does not reward this service it is quite in order, since it was voluntarily offered from sympathy with him.

## GOODS AS PAYMENT FOR SPECIALIZED LABOUR

Payment for specialist services is usually made in goods in addition to food. As with food, there are definite social categories of goods appropriate to the situation. The basic types are the pandanus mat (meŋa) ; the blanket of bark-cloth (mami) ; and the long strip of bark-cloth (fakamaru) used as a man's waistcloth. When presented in ceremonial form such goods are known as a maro. This term is applied to gifts of bark-cloth alone, as well as to bark-cloth accompanied by a mat, and the number and quality of the various pieces depends upon the type of service for which it is a recompense. As in the case of fiuri and fakapenu, the maro is a category of objects with a much wider range of use than the purely economic.

A specific aspect of the maro category is the fakaepa, the

" honouring " of the bundle either by the inclusion of the pandanus mat or bark-cloth blanket, or more rarely, by the addition of a second *maro* to it (see p. 299, Canoe B). This lends a social distinction to the bundle apart from increasing its value. In accordance with the general principle of closed circuits of exchange the same end could not be achieved simply by increasing the number of pieces of ordinary bark-cloth.

We may now consider how such payments are effected, firstly where work is performed by individual specialists, and then where it demands more elaborate co-operative organization.

If a man wishes to build a large trough for turmeric-making he invites a known wood-worker to his home. The timber is brought there, and the specialist arrives every day with his adze and works. The job may take a month or two, depending upon what other calls of ceremonial or domestic character the specialist may have upon his time. The owner prepares an oven every day and feeds the expert. But he is not left alone to supply the food. Men who wish to join him in turmeric-making in future seasons will come with contributions of green food for his oven, or will cook food at their own home and bring it along. They do not do this every day but at intervals during the work. At last when the trough is finished the specialist is rewarded by a large bundle comprising a pandanus mat, a bark-cloth blanket, and a number of pieces of smaller cloth, from ten to twenty in number, depending on the size of the trough. This is accompanied by a basket of cooked food. Here again, another man who wishes to join in future turmeric-making brings along his contribution of bark-cloth. Neither the food nor the bundle is reciprocated by the specialist.

A set of wooden bowls is made on the same lines. A man digs up a suitable tree root or fells a *fetau* trunk and invites the expert. This man comes each day early in the morning—" as soon as it is light " the Tikopia say, and sets to work with his adze. There is no slacking. The owner says to him, " We two will have a breathing space together when the task is finished ". While the expert works the owner and his wife go and prepare food. The oven is uncovered in the afternoon, the meal taken, and in the evening the expert returns to his house to sleep. Each day care is taken to see that food is properly prepared. If the owner notices that his wife is slackening her energies he scolds her, saying that the bowls are for themselves and their children, and that she must look after the expert properly lest he feels neglected. If the expert sees that the quality of his food is falling off he will probably cease work after he has finished one bowl. He will explain to others outside as his justification " his is the bad reputation who abandoned me ", meaning, " it is the owner's fault, not mine." After the required number of bowls is complete the owner shoulders a bundle of bark-cloth, his wife carries a basket of food, green food termed " the giving drink of the *maro* " (liquid refreshment to go with it), and someone else from the household takes a basket of pudding. Then they go to the house of the expert. As in the case of the trough, no reciprocal gift is made since it is said " the reciprocity is the work of the expert's hands ".

Another object of considerable importance in the economic life of the Tikopia is sinnet cord. Men frequently make their own ordinary cord, especially during the long intervals of waiting for the ovens to be ready at funeral ceremonies. But I was told that in olden times people did not make their own sinnet in quantities but commissioned an expert to do it for them. This was particularly the case for the *kafa tuku kau*, the sinnet for letting down a shark hook, which must naturally be of a thick, heavy character. Such experts used to be few and even nowadays many people do not trust themselves to plait their own shark lines. A man and his family provide the raw coco-nut fibre and the expert and his family roll it into strands and plait it. Every few days food, including a pudding, is made by the owner and brought along to the expert. The work may continue for a month or more, depending on the amount of assistance in the supplementary processes which the expert receives from his family. When the sinnet is finished a *maro* is made—comprising a pandanus mat, a bark-cloth blanket, and ten to twenty pieces of other bark-cloth. If the sinnet cord has been commissioned by a chief or a wealthy man the *maro* is larger. If the cord is not of great thickness the expert " sticks on " another cord to it to equalize the value of the *maro*.

Sometimes owner and expert quarrel during the course of the work—particularly if the former interferes on the technical side. I recorded a song that one sinnet maker, Pa Tuŋatai, had composed. Pae Sao had engaged him to make some cord. When he went to look he told the expert to plait it longer. Pa Tuŋatai was annoyed and told him to complete it himself. Then he composed a song about the incident, in native style.  There was probably some ground for his complaint for no counter effusion was ever produced.  The song is :

> " That one said to take and plait
> The invitation to the fish
> On the sea bottom below.
> As I made it, it had fallen there below.
>
> My back is breaking there,
> Breaking badly."

In the first stanza he defends his judgment that the line— " the invitation to the fish "—was already long enough to reach the bottom, and in the second he draws attention to the very hard work involved.   The implication is that in these circumstances interference was unjustified.

The role of the expert in net-making has already been discussed.  The recompense given to him for his work comprises a *maro* of a pandanus mat topped with several pieces of barkcloth, and a large basket of food.  The food is repaid in kind to the net-owner—in contrast to the payment for canoe-making, where no such return is made.  When the expert gets the payment home he takes out a piece of bark-cloth from the pile and " announces " it to his gods in acknowledgment for their help in his task.

A number of other articles such as hand nets, wooden cylinders for cooking turmeric pigment, betel mortars, bows, may be made by people more skilled than others and handed over by them in return for food, with perhaps a piece of bark-cloth as well.  Nowadays some tobacco may form part of the payment.   An example is given by a bow commissioned by Fuarua from Pa Niukapu.[1] The latter is expert in the minor arts of wood-working, though he is not a noted canoe builder.

Fuarua brought a basket of food and a length of *miro* wood to Pa Niukapu, who reciprocated the food-gift the next day. When the bow was finished he prepared food and took the implement along with it to Fuarua.   The latter then made a

---

[1] According to Pa Niukapu the bow was in use in Tikopia at the time that ŋa Raveŋa were still in the island (that is before the latter half of the eighteenth century).   But quite recently, he said, he had seen a bow from Vanikoro, of a different style, examined it and carved one for himself like it, so that there are now two styles in the island.

return gift of food and a couple of pieces of bark-cloth. Again, Nau Niukapu wanted a bark-cloth beater. She knew that Pa Morotai was an expert in carving these implements, so she prepared a basket of food and setting three pieces of bark-cloth on top carried the bundle to him, presented it and made known her wish. In due time the beater was given to her. It is clear from these instances how gifts of food act as a medium for the conveyance of economic desires ; they smooth the way. The operation of this principle can be seen further in cases where it is desired to acquire an object which is already in use by its possessor (see p. 316).

The most striking example of payment for specialized labour of a co-operative character is on the completion of a canoe. Shortly before the craft is finished the workers, consisting of a group of comparatively unskilled men led by two specialist craftsmen, appoint their " day " and prepare food. This is handed to the canoe owner. It forms a stock for action, of two kinds. In the first place it assists the owner in securing part of the wherewithal to pay the workers. He distributes portions of the food gift to various members of his kin group who then bring in contributions of bark-cloth and food to him. Secondly it gives the signal to the owner that his vessel is ready, and serves as a notice that payment is due. The gift of food to the various kinsfolk is not a simple quantitative payment for their subsequent contributions. It is not exactly equivalent in value to the bark-cloth and food which they bring to him. The food may be regarded as an advance " douceur " for what is known to be coming. To help their kinsman is a duty : moral values dictate economic assistance.

The mass of valuables received is divided up into a number of sections ; one for each of the specialist craftsmen, one which is further subdivided among the group of less skilled assistants, possibly one to pay for the tree trunk used, and one to reciprocate the borrowing of tools. Two examples will illustrate the proportion of goods assigned in each case.

A. A transport canoe was made by Pa Raŋifuri and Pa Siamano for Pa Nukufuti. The distribution shares were as follows :

*Specialists*

| | | | |
|---|---|---|---|
| Pa Raŋifuri | . | . | Pandanus mat and 4 bark-cloths |
| Pa Siamano | . | . | (no mat)       4 bark-cloths |

*Assistants*

| | | |
|---|---|---|
| Pa Roŋotaono | . . | 4 bark-cloths |
| Pa Taraoro | . . . | 4 bark-cloths· |
| Pa Manono | . . | 4 bark-cloths |
| Fopeni | . . | 3 bark-cloths |

*Adzes*

| | | |
|---|---|---|
| Pae Sao | . . | 3 bark-cloths |
| Pa Roŋotau | . . | 1 bark-cloth |

*Tree Trunk*

| | | |
|---|---|---|
| Pa Nukuomanu | . . | 1 hank sinnet, 1 bark-cloth, and 1 small blanket |
| Pa Nukutauriri | . . | 3 bark-cloths |

The collection and assignment of this mass of goods requires much arrangement. In the house of Nukufuti when the bark-cloth was lifted down and unwrapped from its parcels the wife of the canoe-owner held each separate piece on her knees, inspected it, and engaged in low-toned consultation with her husband. Members of their kin group present gave advice as to the apportionment, and occasionally a woman was hastily sent to bring an extra item to help out the family. Thus when Nau Sao, the sister of Pa Nukufuti, arrived, she realized that the amount accumulated was still not enough, and sent one of her children to bring a couple of pieces of bark-cloth from her house. The child returned with the wrong kind of cloth—poor pieces— and was laughingly scolded.

B. A sea-going canoe was built by Pa Vaŋatau and Pa Mea for Pa Roŋotau. Being a larger vessel the payment was greater than in case (A).

*Specialists*

Each received 2 *maro* of the same value. These consisted of :—
(i) Pandanus mat and 10 pieces of bark-cloth.
(ii) Bark-cloth blanket and 8 pieces of bark-cloth (the *fakaepa*).

*Assistants*

Each received a single *maro* consisting of :—
Pandanus mat (or bark-cloth blanket) and half a dozen pieces of bark-cloth.

As far as I know there was no payment for tools, which were provided by owner or specialist. I did not record if there was any payment for the tree trunk.

In the case of both canoes there was a gift of food in addition to every share of goods.

Custom does not require a reciprocation by any of the workers who receive shares in this distribution, since they have already given food to the entrepreneur on their " day ", as well as their labour.[1] The food and valuables are described vividly as " the payment for their shoulders, weary with hewing the canoe ". It is said, however, that a small return gift *may* be made after the payment has been received. Thus in case A, I asked if Pa Raŋifuri would make any return. I was told " We do not speak about it. We don't know about our brother Pa Raŋifuri. He will look upon his *maro*, and then will reciprocate it or not, according to his wish " ; The speaker added expectantly, " He's a knowledgeable man ! " When such a return is made it usually consists of a basket of cooked food, with perhaps a bundle of fresh taro plants, or of mature yams. If the *maro* is a large one, then the recipient might send over a coil of sinnet cord. On the other hand, if he did not there would be no resentment.

This return gift could be regarded by us as an equivalent for an unseen item, namely the excess of satisfaction in payment over the expenditure of energy on the work. This interpretation, however, would not crystallize an element latent in the Tikopia behaviour but would be an intellectualized distortion of the native view—which is that adequate recognition of service by one party tends to promote polite acknowledgment by the other. If a given amount of work $x$ is paid for by an amount of goods $y$ which is regarded as at least adequate compensation, then the small return gift by the worker is not intended to equalize the transaction by representing $y-x$, but represents a third factor $z$, a non-quantitive recognition that he has been properly treated, relative to the status and resources of the entrepreneur. This point is further illustrated by the practice of a chief repaying the specialists not with one or two *maro* apiece but three or four, though their labour is no greater than for a commoner's canoe. In this case $y-x$ may be half a dozen times greater than in the former, but $z$ remains the same.

Introduction of this last illustration leads to the consideration of to what the greater payment by a chief is due. It may be said definitely that it is not due to any difference in the demand for

[1] Personal inclination and recognition of kinship ties may influence the situation. Thus the bark-cloth for Pa Taraoro in Case A was brought by Pa Porima who said that he expected no return " since they were brothers-in-law ". On the other hand, Pae Sao, who lent his adze, received bark-cloth in payment, though he was the brother-in-law of Pa Nukufuti. This was probably because he assisted in the work of preparing the food-gift to the builders, and was a man of rank.

specialized skill or to any greater skill of the experts whom the chiefs employ (the same experts work for commoners). The basis for such conduct is the obligation which lies upon a chief to maintain his rank and prestige by generous use of his wealth. Without knowledge of the local conditions several hypotheses as to the behaviour of a chief in the employment of experts are plausible :

(a) That the chief in the exercise of his power might command their services at less than the customary rate, or even for nothing (cf. the *Corvée* of some African societies, though this was usually of unskilled labour and for public works).

(b) He might pay the ordinary rate of remuneration.

(c) He might pay more than the rate ordinarily given by commoners.

What actually happens is the last of these. The terms *customary rate* or *ordinary rate* do not imply that there is anything of the nature of competitive bargaining for the services of these craftsmen, or by them in offering their services.[1] There is no differential rate of payment for special skill as between experts, nor is there any bidding for the services of experts in terms of increased rates by men desiring canoes. Where there is the tendency for a greater demand for the services of men who are acknowledged as masters of their craft the special inducement (if any) to them to work for some people rather than for others is given by their specific ties of kinship or bond-friendship with the potential entrepreneur. The payment of canoe experts then can hardly be termed *a market rate*. Can it be said that there is a minimum rate ? In a sense, yes. By custom a certain quantity and quality of goods is expected from the owner. He cannot, for instance, hand over an immense quantity of food as a substitute for bark-cloth, and the payment to the specialists is expected to include a pandanus mat or bark-cloth blanket, as the "honouring" (*fakaepa*) of the bundle. Several factors tend to vary the rate of payment :

(i) The size of the canoe.

(ii) The respective number of specialists and non-specialist craftsmen engaged.
    Normally a canoe has an expert in charge at the bow and

---

[1] This principle of non-competitive rates is not true of all primitive societies, e.g. the Trobriands, where there is competitive soliciting by advance gifts. Malinowski, *Argonauts*, 99.

at the stern. A very small canoe may, however, have one
expert only and a very large one a third expert who is in
charge of the middle section. The tendency is for three
specialists to receive slightly less per man than two, this
being to some extent governed by the next factor.

(iii)   Wealth and rank of the canoe owner.
        As already noted a chief is expected to give more than a
        commoner for equal work.

(iv)    A particular desire on the part of one of the workmen may
        cause some variation in the type of payment. I have not
        recorded an instance of this among the working party. But
        the payment for the timber of the canoe of Pa Nukufuti
        included a small bark-cloth blanket, which was unusual,
        but which was given because the wife of the timber owner
        had expressed a wish for such an article.

It will be obvious from this that what is frequently called a
customary or conventional rate of payment for labour in a
primitive society may not be a fixed rate, though at the same
time there is a general level of payment around which fluctuations
occur.

The degree of adjustment possible is seen in an anomalous
case which occurred some generations ago. A man named Pu
Raŋiripo, of the house of Siku, had a canoe made for him. Either
he had speculated on insufficient resources or gone bankrupt in
the meantime but when the vessel was completed he had no means
of paying for it. There were no *maro* for the workers. So he
called them together and told them that he had no valuables
for them, but that each of them could take a wife from among
his daughters. They did so—whether in protest or not is not
recorded—and one girl went to the house of Raropuka, another
to Faraŋanoa, another to Resiake, another to Totiare, and
another to Te Ukatere, later chief of Tafua. It is to be presumed
that the ordinary compensatory payment for marrying a girl
was not given in this case.

The distinction in the rate of payment between specialist and
non-specialist labour is not simply on the grounds of technical
skill, but includes an element of compensation for the direction
and control of the work, which the specialist supplies. In the
main body of workers there may be men whose skill with the
adze approximates to that of the specialist, but since they have
not been on this occasion put in charge of any portion of the
work they are rewarded at a lower rate. On another occasion of
canoe-building, however, they may be in charge and be rewarded

at the higher rate accordingly. If one attempts to disentangle a general principle from the range of Tikopia practice it may be said that labour alone (that is, not of a definitely specialized or expert kind) tends to be repaid by food, while skill (of a specialized kind) receives payment in food *plus* other goods. Tikopia linguistic usage, however, does not make such an explicit generalization. Recompense to assistants in canoe-building is a border-line case.

In describing the amassing of goods to provide the payment it was stated that the canoe owner received contributions from his kinsfolk. Some of these people may have close kinship ties with men of the working party too, and these tend to be taken into account. Thus, one of the kinsfolk of the owner may bring along a pile of bark-cloth and specify that he wishes it to go to his brother-in-law who is in the working party. In such case the net effect is to augment considerably the owner's supplies. Such a close kinship tie induces a man to contribute more than he otherwise would, and this helps to release some of the owner's resources for payment to others. Such is often the case at initiation and funeral ceremonies.

## PAYMENT TO OTHER FACTORS OF PRODUCTION

We have dealt so far primarily with the payment for labour, which is the major item in the Tikopia distributive system. It is very evident that we are not here concerned with a wage economy, with competitive rates theoretically or practically adjustable to changes in the supply and demand for labour. On the contrary the reward for labour has been seen to have a special character according to whether it is the sharing of the results of a co-operative enterprise, the hospitality of a meal, or a gift made with some show of honorific gesture. This is the result of the concept that to put one's labour at the command of another is a social service, not merely an economic service. What the external observer must envisage is the *total contribution* —not merely the handing over of so much physical energy to be converted into material results, but the fact of presence, of assistance and moral support in the activity. It is for these reasons that the reward takes on the forms of politeness, is of a type used in ritual and other social fields, and even seems in part to ignore differences in the skill and application of the

workers. It is for the same reasons also that the workers themselves may contribute to the fund from which their payment is
to be made.

It is even less easy to superimpose upon the Tikopia
phenomena the other elements of the classical analysis. The
payment for raw materials occupies a very small place in the
distributive scheme. Most materials such as hibiscus and coco-nut
fibre, palm fronds, pandanus leaf strips, paper mulberry trees,
shell of various kinds, small timber, and food are obtained from
a person's own cultivations or from those of such near kinsfolk
that no specific economic recognition is necessary. Materials
acquired from other individuals and needing recompense are
mainly large timber for houses and canoes, and sago palms.
Even here ownership is not concentrated in a few hands, and
there is no competitive bargaining for them.

The recompense of a basket of food for a sago palm has been
mentioned earlier. For a house timber, cut on the land of someone
else, a basket of food or a coil of sinnet cord is the customary
return, though this rests at the discretion of the timber-user.
The fact that such timber is often obtained from the orchard of
a kinsman is an element in this. An instance of complications
in payment is given by a case of gift of fish-hooks. Pa Paŋisi
took some fish hooks from Pae Sao, who had just received an
extra supply from me. In return he sent over some fish caught
with them. These in turn were reciprocated by a basket of
vegetable food.

When a tree is felled to make a canoe the usual payment is
sinnet cord ; perhaps some bark-cloth may be given as well.
But sometimes the payment is neglected. When the Ariki Kafika
felled the tree for the wash-strake of his sacred canoe he did so
without asking permission of the owners, the house of Samoa,
and gave them no payment, either from negligence, or relying
on his superior position. They were angry, but could do nothing,
since it was the chief. If it had been a commoner who had acted
in this high-handed way they would have gone and demanded
a coil of sinnet in recompense. " Another chief would have sent
a coil of sinnet " was the opinion of people in Faea when they
heard the news.

I have already mentioned the two bunches of taro presented
to the owner of the soil when the crop has been planted in the
land of another man. These are not reciprocated. The present

is termed *poroporo*, and the same custom obtains when yams are so planted. Never more than two bunches are given, no matter what the size of the area utilized, and what ordinary variation there may be in the yield. Only when the crop is very poor is there a diminution, one bunch alone being given. I was at first inclined to regard this as an economic rent for the use of the land. But it is in part at least as acknowledgment of ownership, of title to the land, that the gift is made, rather than for withdrawing it for a season from the owner's use. This is indicated by the term for the gift, *poroporo*, not *tauvi*. The latter word is used in other contexts for ordinary exchange, the former for a ritual firstfruits offering.

Payment for the use of " capital goods " depends upon the particular category in which these fall. What may be termed " fixed capital " such as canoes, seine nets, adzes, and other European tools, taro graters, bowls are borrowed. When they are returned a payment is made for the use of the more important objects. For taro graters or bowls no payment is given ; the possibility of reciprocal borrowing later is sufficient recompense. In the case of a canoe or a net, it is a portion of the catch, roughly equivalent to the share of an individual worker (subject to certain limitations described earlier in this chapter). But this payment is not calculated according to our conception of interest. If the owner of the canoe or net goes out with it then he does not necessarily receive a larger share, and there is no portion of the product specifically regarded as being due to the apparatus *per se*. In fact it might almost bé said that the reward is given for the participation of the man in the act of production, whether in person or represented by his property. Moreover, there is no calculation of the rate of return on a time basis. The payment is a conventionally dictated quantity or item of goods—for tools a hank of sinnet cord, and a piece of bark-cloth—and is given when the service is finished.

But the case is quite different with the goods used to initiate production and repay participants in the process. The amount of goods of this type which must be at the command of a man for whom a canoe is made may be termed his " liquid capital ", if too close a definition of the term be not insisted upon. These goods must comprise firstly coils of sinnet as payment for the tree trunk and perhaps for the tools used, and, secondly, food resources for the subsistence of the workers during the whole period, and for the provision of the baskets of food which are part of the final payment. This quantity is lessened by the amount of food which the workers themselves present to him a few days before the completion of the vessel, or rather that portion of it which he himself retains. But in addition he must assure the subsistence of himself and his family during the period of the work and keep in hand potential supplies for their further subsistence till the new crops are ready. By fishing he and his family can make up a part of the food by current effort, but the majority must come by drawing upon his resources. Then there are the mats and bark-cloth which constitute the bulk of the final payment. As mentioned, some of this capital is drawn from his kinsfolk. It is a gift rather than a loan. Its repayment depends on the system of reciprocity which operates partly by future gifts in the reverse direction, partly by the future borrowing of the canoe itself or by participating in fishing from it, in either event a portion of the catch going to the user.

The point to note here is that there is nothing which can be regarded as interest accruing from such a loan of liquid capital. In Tikopia there is no developed accounting system and no reckoning of the time during which an object is possessed as meriting recompense. The situation tends in fact to be reversed so that when repayment is made the recipient, that is, the original lender, may even make a small further return gift himself in acknowledgment. The code of etiquette lays stress not on the importance of an increment for use (calculated on the basis of time) but on that of the restoration of equilibrium in act rather than in quantity.

This non-interest-exacting situation is in strong contrast with the practice which obtains in a number of Melanesian societies of making a return higher than the original amount of goods borrowed.

In Rossel Island, as the research of W. E. Armstrong has shown,[1] there are two series of shell objects (which he terms money) which operate in more or less independent but parallel fashion. These two series are not directly expressible in terms of each other. Within each series there are items in a scale of value. These again are not regarded by the natives—to judge from the linguistic data and their behaviour—as multiples of each other.

[1] W. E. Armstrong, " Rossel Island Money," *Economic Journal*, 1924, 423–9, and *Rossel Island*, 1928, 59–84.

$X$, $Y$, and $Z$ are not equivalent to $X$, $2X$ and $3X$. Their difference in value is rather to be expressed in the length of time which elapses before the loan of one is repaid by another. $Y$ equals $X$ repaid after one month, say, $Z$ equals $X$ after six months, or $Y$ after two months (according to Armstrong). This seems like interest, and a more abstract type of calculation than these natives employ would express it as such. But there is no concept to the native of an actual rate of interest, and Armstrong himself does not categorize the system as such. Exact comparison with modern economics is not possible, unless a more liberal definition of interest were adopted. The functioning of the system of borrowing and repayment of these items of " money " is, more-over, highly complex and takes place within a scheme of values depending upon considerations of rank and ritual as well as ordinary advantage in exchange.

Here is an example of the difference between native and European economic categories. It shows also how native categories may differ from one society to another even within the Oceanic area. Evaluation of time as an element in the borrowing situation represents quite a different concept from that of the Tikopia who make no allowance for any time interval. It is worth noting that in Tikopia as in other primitive societies there is no basic antagonism between religious ideals and economic practice, as was presented by the attitude of the medieval church to usury, and is still to be seen in such Christian doctrine as " The love of money is the root of all evil " or the parable of the rich man and the Kingdom of Heaven. In a primitive society production is envisaged in terms of technique, organization, and ritual, and while religion may dictate the times and the conventional forms of exchange it has few moral implications and applies no sanctions against the accumulation of wealth.

In other communities, while interest is as important as in Rossel Island, the relevance of the time element differs. The " tusked pig situation " in Malekula uses the time factor in the calculations of interest, whereas the " shell string situation " in the Banks Islands follows another pattern.[1]

Theoretically, the element of profit can be distinguished in Tikopia enterprise. It might even be calculated, for instance

---

[1] A. B. Deacon, *Malekula*, 1934, 196–7 ; cf. Tom Harrisson, *Savage Civilization*, 1937, 26–8 ; Codrington, *The Melanesians*, 1891, 325–7. (In the Banks Islands interest is paid " cent per cent without regard to time ".)

in the case of a canoe, in terms of the surplus of fish yielded to the owner through a period of, say, a dozen years, over his total expenditure in food and other goods in having the craft built. However, this would involve making several assumptions as to the relative values of different types of food and goods, which, as will be seen later, would be of a very arbitrary nature. In the case of extraction of sago flour the calculation would be easier. But even here there is no clearly recognized standard of evaluation which allows the cost of production in terms of labour and food to be related to the yield of, say, three bowls of sago flour—if only for the fact that the role of sago flour in the food æsthetic of the Tikopia is not the same as an equivalent nutritional quantity of the foods supplied to the workers.

But it must be borne in mind that the Tikopia in practice do not engage in this type of calculation. Their system of mobilization of working capital from kinsfolk, without payment of interest, and the small part which the payment for raw materials plays in their economy, means that they are not in the position of having continually to offset their borrowing charges against the possibility of getting an adequate yield. Nor, in their lack of concern with extensive accumulation are they driven in a continual search for alternative and more profitable avenues of employment of their capital.

Again, the " profit " of the enterprise goes in effect to many more persons than the entrepreneur himself. The extensive system of borrowing and participation in use means that the balance of advantage is finally shared in a communal fashion. Profit gained, like labour given, is a social service.

The lack of any clear comparison between interest and profits and the difficulty of expressing in any numerical terms the profit of an enterprise is one of the implications of a price-free economy. Associated with it also, perhaps, is the slowness of the tendency to increase production beyond the level of providing goods for ordinary use.

## Payment for Non-labour Services

There is in Tikopia a considerable transfer of goods for services other than ordinary labour. For instance, a young man who used to go out frequently at night and set his net in the lake, hung it up always at the side of a house of a neighbour of mine, since he himself lived about a mile away. One evening he gave two fresh fish to my neighbour in compensation for this service. The next day a reciprocal gift was made of a basket of cooked food as acknowledgment. This is of the type known technically as *fakaaraŋaika* (cf. p. 282). In the custom known as *sunusunu* referred to earlier, if a man has made for another or helped him to make a hand net, or ordinary fishing line or sinnet cord, then it is usual when the first fish is caught by such means to present it to him. This is not only a payment for his labour but also an acknowledgment of the efficacy of his help.

In another category are the gifts handed over by men to women with whom they have had intercourse. Adultery with a married woman is not common, but if a man meets a former mistress by chance alone in a cultivation he may persuade her to have relations with him. After this he may give her some taro from his garden which she will represent to her husband as being from their plot. Such a gift, though a payment for sexual services, may be also a recognition of past sentiment. A bachelor may give to a young woman betel nut or tobacco as an expression of his desire for her. This she accepts, but that does not mean that she consents to have intercourse with him. If she later refuses he will naturally be angry, but the woman is in no way bound by his gift. The gift is meant as a stimulant to her emotional interest in him, not as an economic payment.

In the sphere of social services there are a number of payments of a highly conventionalized kind. Such are those at initiation and burial [1]; after conducting a boy on his first torch-light fishing expedition; and after taking charge of a boy or girl on their first sight-seeing trip round the crests of the hills. In all these cases a basket of food is a basic item in the payment, with sinnet cord, bark-cloth, or wooden bowls as the other item, according to circumstances. Each of these types of transaction has its specific name.

A service of an interesting kind classed by the Tikopia as demanding payment is the composition of a song in one's honour, or the acceptance of the leading part in the first production of a song that one has composed oneself. This principle is extended to cover payment for a song sung on formal occasions to one's deities. The conventional payment is a length of bark-cloth,

---

[1] For initiation payments see *We, The Tikopia*, ch. xiii; for mortuary payments v. Chapter IX of the present book.

trailed out in public by the donor and deposited before the composer or expert performer as the case may be. It is known as *te ufi*—the " covering ". The economic gain in this case is negligible, since every cloth must be reciprocated on the spot, in the same manner.

Here we have a specific and clear example of a basic Tikopia convention—that a service demands some acknowledgment, which may be termed payment (*tauvi*), but that this in its turn requires a reciprocal payment (*fakapenu*). In economic terms neither party gains or loses, since such bark-cloths are all of the same value. In social terms both parties have gained, the one by the compliment of the song composed or performed, the other by the public acknowledgment of the compliment.

From this and other examples in this section it will be seen how difficult it is in many cases to separate " payment " from " gift " in Tikopia. " Payment " in our sense is often made by the Tikopia in the guise of a gift ; and a " gift " is frequently an item in a chain of reciprocities. Linguistically there is a phrase *sori mori fuere* for something handed over ostensibly without *arrière pensée*, but the range of this in Tikopia speech is extremely limited. To describe even many of the transfers of goods enumerated above as " payments " gives them an undue harshness and rigidity of interpretation. (In our own society it is only by using the term in a very elastic sense that we should describe a return of hospitality as a " payment ".)

## COVERT EXCHANGE

A reference may now be made to certain types of transfer of goods which, whatever be the guise they assume, take the form of, or result in, covert exchange, as distinct from the overt exchange of a non-ceremonial and ceremonial order examined in the following Chapter. These are broadly classified by the Tikopia as " gifts ", though in fact they often ultimately are followed by " counter-gifts ".

In the first place there are gifts of food, tobacco, or betel materials, given on the basis of hospitality to any person who is present on an occasion when these are being distributed. The Tikopia are always careful to see that any person who attends at such a time is not left out, whatever may have been his contribution to the preceding activity. To give two instances

—At the repair of the temple of Kafika the young son of Pa Fenumera of Faŋarere clan, a boy of six or seven years old, was present. He was of no particular rank, and did no work, but he was treated as a representative of his father and referred to as " our friend ". The Ariki Kafika said to the crowd of people, " You look after this boy who has come, though his father has not. We have looked at one another," meaning that the lad had attended the ceremony. He got a good share of the food. Again, at another Kafika ceremony a huge basket of food known as the *tua popora* was allotted by the chief to his principal elder, Pa Rarovi, a virtual return gift to a similar basket received from him earlier. Pa Rarovi was entitled to keep it and take it home, but he insisted on dividing it up there and then, and giving a share to the other elder present, Pa Tavi, despite the protests of this man and others.

How far in such cases it is thought by the donor that he will reap an advantage from his gift it is impossible for me to say. Certainly in most cases some ultimate return is received. But it is at least theoretically possible for something to be given without the idea of reciprocity being necessary. As an explanation of the term *sori mori* (or *sori more*) a Tikopia said " one does not think that it will be returned by something or other ".

An example of Tikopia care to observe at least the forms of disinterestedness is given by an experience of my own. A man brought me a gift of green coco-nuts. As it was a hot day he opened one for me to drink. I invited him to have one himself, but he refused. On being pressed he explained that it was not etiquette for a person to consume part of a gift that he had brought, and that if he did so he would become the object of slander. The native expression for a person who breaks this rule is " He who carries and eats thereof " (*Nea e mori nea e kai*). My visitor, however, had no objection to drinking from another coco-nut brought by someone else. Akin to this attitude is that of ceremonial exchange, which prescribes that as far as possible goods should not be exchanged within the immediate patrilineal kinship group, and should go to other groups, in other localities. Breach of this is termed *sori taŋa*, " giving into one's own basket."

There are, however, circumstances when it is quite permissible to partake of one's own food contribution. When one brings a *fiuri* to assist someone else's food preparations, then it is quite in order should one by accident receive in the subsequent distribution part of what one contributed.

A Tikopia convention is that one is allowed and even expected to ask for the small change of social intercourse, such as tobacco and betel materials, from people one meets on the path, or from anyone whom one happens to visit, or to turn the tables, from a visitor himself. Such requests are made irrespective of rank, though chiefs are expected to be more free with such articles than other people. There are individual differences in generosity, some people resorting to small artifices to keep their supplies for themselves. The custom is included under the term *kaisi*,[1] " asking " (as distinct from *fesiri*, asking for information). This freedom of request is undoubtedly to be correlated with the reciprocity that it entails, so that in the long run " gifts " of this type are really items in a series of covert exchanges. When, as sometimes happens, a request is refused, or evasion is practised, the thwarted person is ashamed, and may even give vent to his feelings in song. Here is a sample, composed by Pa Rarovi. In a time of shortage of tobacco he had gone to the house of Pa Faioa to ask for some ; he had found him unwrapping a package of it, which on his arrival had been hastily concealed. Mortified, he returned home and issued this complaint.

" The Heavens smoke towards me, O !
The silver money is tinned hither
The pound buried in the earth.

The Heavens will be veiled over ;
Look at the cloud,
In the Heavens.
I row back my boat."

The original contains some curious jargon of English terms in a Tikopia rendering, given for their prestige value, and not properly understood (as in the verbal use of the slang noun " tin "). The idea of the song is that the smoke of the owner's tobacco rises to heaven ; yet he refuses it ; is it money that it should be covered up and hidden ? All that the composer could do was metaphorically to " row his boat back ", to return home in chagrin.

[1] It is similar to the Fijian *kerekere*, which, however, operates on a much more elaborate scale, and has been inaccurately described by Europeans as " begging ". See W. A. Deane, *Fijian Society*, 1921, 119–124, who holds that " the whole tendency of *kerekere* is to create an idle class ".

## THE CONCEPT OF RECIPROCITY

For convenience I have used the term reciprocity for any transfer of goods made in response to an initial transfer. But the notion of reciprocity covers several categories of transaction differing in their quantitative effect upon the parties and in their intent from the native point of view. The Tikopia have a number of different terms for them, the connotation of which is explained in Appendix II.

It will be seen from the analysis there given that it is necessary in using the term reciprocity to distinguish in the concrete material these different elements : transactions where the net effect is to restore the former economic equilibrium of the parties ; those where the second transfer abates but does not neutralize the disequilibrium ; and those where whatever be the quantitative effect, the emphasis is laid upon the act of return rather than upon the quantity or quality of the goods returned.

The importance of such distinctions in Tikopia leads one to think that they might also be made for other societies. The term reciprocity has been freely used in anthropology but so far there has been little attempt to clarify the quantitative aspect of the phenomenon in economic terms as distinct from the qualitative aspect in social terms. When the expression " gift exchange " has been used it probably implies that the emphasis is laid by the native peoples themselves largely upon the wider social implications of the transaction.

To summarize the results of this Chapter it may be said that the Tikopia economy embodies a definite concept that all participants in a productive activity should receive a share of the product, but that social considerations do not make it necessary for this share to be exactly proportionate to the contribution in time, labour, or skill that each individual has made. Moreover, the position is complicated by the convention that in any kind of activity persons who give their labour should also contribute food for the sustenance of the working group. This is linked with the absence of a very clear distinction between entrepreneur and workers. There is also a definite convention that services require material recognition though here again the form and amount of the reimbursement are governed by social considerations which are wider than the purely economic.

## CHAPTER IX

# EXCHANGE AND VALUE

A T the back of all the transactions described so far is obviously some idea of the " value " of goods in a broad sense, some comparative rating of their worth. In ordinary economic analysis the term value means value in exchange, and is connected with the existence of a market. In the descriptive sense there are no markets in Tikopia, that is, a visitor sees no assemblies of people for the barter or buying and selling of things, such as he would see in some Melanesian islands or in many areas of East or West Africa.[1] But from the economic point of view we may perhaps speak of a market for goods and services in that the differential possession of them throughout the community as a whole leads to their transference from one person to another, in ways which affect one another. Thus there can be said in this sense to be a market for the services of canoe-builders and other specialist craftsmen, or a market for fish or cooked food. But it must be understood from the accounts already given that such a market has no unitary spatial character, is non-pecuniary, and has no middlemen whose function it is to serve as a link between producers and consumers. Moreover, the market is an imperfect one, not because of the ignorance of some producers or consumers of the rates of exchange existing in other spheres, or quantities of goods available or desired, but through the absence of any constant flow of *all* kinds of goods and services through it, and the lack of an impartial choice in the selection of producers and consumers. The traditional character of the Tikopia economy involves definite limitations on the type of transactions which can occur. Thus there is little direct barter of one object for another, but much transfer in accordance with set procedure ; and while some types of goods circulate freely, others rarely, if ever, come into the market.

The characterization of the Tikopia " market " as imperfect raises the question of whether the distinction drawn by R. F. Kahn between rational and irrational consumer preference is

[1] See R. Thurnwald, " Markt," in M. Ebert's *Reallexikon der Vorgeschichte*, 1924 ; and *op. cit.*, Ch. VII.

applicable to this situation. Irrational consumer preference exists, Kahn holds, if a consumer is attached to the product of a certain seller when the product of another seller would satisfy him just as well, so that if removed from his original attachment he would suffer no loss of satisfaction.[1] The conditions of the imperfect market examined by Kahn are different from those in Tikopia, in that it is the price economy of an industrial civilization that is discussed. But it seems as if the kinship and other attachments of the Tikopia, which limit their field of economic relationships, might be classed as irrational preferences. The argument at the end of this Chapter shows that this is not the case. Reliance on kinship ties in securing labour services, for instance, or in acquiring goods, does give the consumer certain satisfactions, of a social and economic kind, that he could not get if he transferred his demands elsewhere. They are rational preferences from this point of view. And even if the economic satisfaction in quality of goods or services be not evident, if the linkage is of a traditional or customary kind, the preference is still hardly to be called irrational, since the simple following of customary procedure is in itself regarded as satisfactory—as " good " by the people themselves. It might be possible, in fact, to argue that any preference for one seller over another, even in a modern civilized community, has always certain satisfactions of an undefined order associated with it—perhaps those derived from credulity in an advertisement slogan. And certainly in a primitive society such as Tikopia there appear to be always more positive elements than mere inertia or lack óf knowledge of other sources of supply which determine the specific attachment.

## EXCHANGE OF GOODS

To complete the empirical background necessary for a discussion of the problem of value in Tikopia a description may now be given of some types of exchange of goods not so far examined. These fall into two broad categories, non-systematic, those which are not part of any wider scheme of transactions, and systematic, those which take place in virtue of some more general structural arrangement. Those of the first category can be termed again non-ceremonial, since though they follow a

---

[1] R. F. Kahn, " Some Notes on Ideal Output," *Economic Journal*, xlv, 1935, 25–6. See also J. K. Galbraith, " Rational and Irrational Consumer Preference," ibid., xlviii, 1938, 336–342.

traditional procedure of etiquette the primary emphasis is upon the objects wanted by the party initiating the exchange, and not upon the act of exchange itself. Here are examples in the first category.

A couple of shell arm-rings recently ground were given to a young man who wanted them for a dance. Later a basket of food was sent in return. This is an example of the simplest type of exchange. A man wanted a betel mortar to help make up a funeral payment. A son of the Ariki Tafua gave him two. Later on the first man, who himself was a craftsman in wood, made two others, giving one to the chief and another to the son. With these he brought a basket of food, which the family of Tafua reciprocated by another basket the following day. Here is the equivalent of goods for goods, with a basket of food as an acknowledgment of the service of the loan and demanding in its turn an acknowledgment in food. It is a good example of the operation of exchange on two levels of economic and of social interest.

## Forced Exchange

The importance of the social category comes out more clearly in cases such as when a man wants a coco-nut-grating stool. If he knows of a close kinsman who has an extra one, he goes and asks for it and should get it without ceremony. " You give me a stool for myself ; your stools are two." It is said that the kinsman " rejoices " to give it because of the tie between them. Sooner or later he in turn comes and asks for something that he fancies and this too will be handed over freely. Such freedom of approach obtains only between members of a small kinship group, and depends upon the recognition of a principle of reciprocity.

If a man is going to apply to someone not of his own kin, a " different man " as the Tikopia say, then he cooks food, fills a large basket and tops it off with an ordinary piece of bark-cloth or even a blanket. Armed with this he goes to the owner and asks for the article. He is usually not refused. " The owner does not object because the doing of things has been brought, and the *maro*." The " doing of things " (*faiŋa nea*) is the gift of food, and the *maro* is the cloth. It is recognized that the owner may inwardly be unwilling but that he will say " O, certainly ".

The reason is that if the other is refused and has to return home with his bark-cloth he will be ashamed. " His face is not good." Someone may refer pityingly to him : " What is that one there ? He is a bat, that person." A " bat " is the conventional metaphor for a poor person who, like that mammal, has no property. Moreover people in general, when they hear, laugh at the man who has refused and may criticize him severely. They say " Why not give the thing to him ? Why does he let him go ? The other desired the thing. That person, isn't he ashamed because his *maro* has been made ? Are there no valuables still there in his possession ? " So much may a person be involved in social disapproval by a churlish refusal that he invites the other man again—" Bring me my *maro* "—and will hand over the article required.

The description of the basket of food as " the doing of things " is noteworthy here. It shows the explicit recognition of the activating role of food in the native system of exchange. A present of food is the initial stimulus applied in many kinds of transaction. The above is a standard native description, in this case from Pa Raŋifuri, of what occurs. But in fact a man may accept the refusal calmly and not pursue the matter unless he wants the object badly.

Heirlooms, however, are in a special category from ordinary objects. Spear-staves, bonito hooks, coco-nut-grating stools, head-rests, often have a sentimental value. If other people ask for them the owner may reply " that is the speech of grandparent and grandchild, the one thing only left to me, to abide with me. His own token of affection that he left to me."[1] If the other person insists then the object will probably be handed over after all. The recipient in such cases goes to his house, observes which of his own more important property is equal to it, and presents this to the donor as a further acknowledgment. Sometimes the donor himself specifies a particular equivalent at the moment he hands the object over. The generalization is a summary of native statements, not of direct observations. But it is in keeping with native attitudes that the context of social situation should allow of what is in effect a forced exchange.

Even in a simple scheme of distribution such as this, there is an intrusion into the more purely economic situation of social

---

[1] The term " speech " is a figurative usage, analogous to the citation of a coco nut palm as " my hearing " (*roŋo*), v. p. 263.

factors which control the operation of the principle of economic advantage. Put another way, in the very act of distribution far wider ends than the purely economic are secured. This is symptomatic of the distributive economy as a whole.

The technique of forced exchange in Tikopia may be compared with that in two other communities—Australia and the Maori of New Zealand. In North-West Australia, according to W. E. H. Stanner, there are complex series of exchanges by which goods pass through a great number of hands. A man can secure an object which he desires, which is as yet several stages off in the exchange process, by " bespeaking ahead " the object. Each man may have several exchange partners, and in order that the object may not be diverted from himself, the person wishing it " calls it before " in the pidgin English phrase. This verbal claim is usually honoured.[1] Among the Maori of olden times the object desired might be named after a portion of the body of the person wishing it, or might have a thread from his garment tied to it. This association with his personality obliged it to be handed over to him, in return for some material equivalent. In these three societies the economic result is the same, though the sanctions differ somewhat. In Tikopia the fear of scandal and of uncomplimentary references impels the transfer. In Australia these factors also operate but in addition the distaste for derogatory remarks about meanness, with perhaps the fear of private sorcery, and the ultimate risk of having to fight. Among the Maori the idea of insult, of breaking a bodily taboo (even by verbal association) which might have to be wiped out in blood, was of fundamental importance.

It will be seen that it is impossible by formal economic analysis to understand either the exchange system of these people or how the uneven distribution of goods tends to be levelled out. Social norms at every turn condition the economic situation. The situation of forced exchange in Tikopia has, however, a practical as well as a sentimental limitation. The difference between primary and secondary objects of need is recognized, and it is the latter which are more open to requisition by others. If a man has only a single knife, then his claims for it for his work are recognized as valid and there is no social obligation upon him to surrender it.

[1] W. E. H. Stanner, " Ceremonial Economics," *Oceania*, iv, 1933–4, 156–175, 458–471.

## BORROWING, THEFT, AND COMPENSATION

To a considerable extent the need for exchange through scarcity and the uneven distribution of goods is minimized by extensive borrowing, for which kinship ties and neighbourliness serve as bases. Frequently no compensation is given for the use of the article borrowed when it is returned afterwards. For instance at a marriage ceremony four taro graters were borrowed for the preparation of a feast by the people living at one end of the Namo beach from those at the other. As a rule each household has only one of these graters and so must obtain others for any big event. When they were finished with they were given to a child to take back. Nothing was sent in addition " because when one person is doing something he takes it and when another person is doing something he takes it. It is not paid for." This balanced form of expression, uttered to me in explanation on the spot, embodies the idea of the reciprocity in borrowing and lending of many small objects which is a feature of the Tikopia economy. But, as has been mentioned earlier, for more important things some form of payment is made, particularly when there is a direct yield from their use. If a canoe is borrowed for even a short journey something is usually given to the owner when it is returned. If the borrower has been catching fish, then a couple are handed over.

Linked with borrowing and exchange is the concept of indemnity. Damage to borrowed property is expected to involve compensation, the rate of which varies according to the extent of the damage, the nature of the object, and the rank of the owner. For example, my friend Pae Sao borrowed the new axe of his kinsman Pa Porima to cut a tree for bark-cloth. He chipped the edge on a stone, and soon after returning the implement sent along a coil of sinnet cord as compensation. This was approved by people, who told me of it as being the proper thing. Unauthorized borrowing occurs when a man takes someone else's canoe to go off to sea either to commit suicide or to voyage to other lands. Not infrequently the man is caught by a searching fleet and the vessel brought back, or sometimes he returns of his own accord.[1] In such case he is expected to send along a present to the owner of the canoe, in addition to making a food gift to the crew of the vessel which caught him, as some compensation

[1] *We, The Tikopia*, 245-6.

for their labour. Even when he does not return his family are expected to make up a *maro* of a bundle of bark-cloth and take it with food to the owner. When the owner is a chief, as happened in a case which occurred when I was in Tikopia, the family are very careful to make this atoning gift to appease the chief's anger.

With this type of situation can be linked the attitude in cases of theft. A fuller discussion of the reaction to theft has been given in Chapter VII. But it may be said here that the element which seems to be foremost is not so much the return of the stolen property as the exaction of compensation for the loss of it. I found for instance when three knives were stolen from me that the opinion of people who heard of the theft was that the act was bad ; that the man, obviously wanting the knives, should have come to me and asked me for them in the usual native manner of initiating exchange ; and that having taken them, the proper course for him to pursue would be to come and give me a pandanus leaf mat as an equivalent for them. My protestations that I wanted, not a mat, but the knives returned, went practically unheeded. Again, if a man takes seed taro without permission from the garden of another, when the theft is discovered the owner goes and rates the thief, telling him, " You have taken seedlings from my garden ; now I am going to yours to pull out the payment (*tauvi*) for them." He goes and removes an equivalent quantity to that which he has lost.

## CEREMONIAL EXCHANGE

The need for individual exchange, either of the commissioned or forced type, is minimized not only by borrowing but also by systematic ceremonial exchanges. These are an important channel of distribution of goods, since these goods are used also in ordinary production and consumption. Their effect, however, is not so much to provide the necessaries of life as to give a stimulus to production above the subsistence level.

Such transactions are frequent, and to some extent are predictable, so that provision is made for them, and to some extent the income from them can be reckoned upon. A family, for example, may be cautioned by a relative to begin to accumulate stores of pandanus mats and bark-cloth in view of the elaborate exchanges consequent upon the approaching death of an ageing parent. A father wishing to initiate his son, or the kinsfolk of a chief's son who has taken a mistress will begin to plant taro, plait sinnet, and accumulate wooden bowls against the probability of having to provide the things for exchange in six months time.[1] If a man marries a woman of Kafika clan he makes in the first year of his marriage a large gift of food to the Ariki Kafika and certain other men of rank at the annual ceremonies of Somosomo. This is reciprocated. The amount of food required is huge— from twenty to forty baskets—and preparations have to be begun months in advance. On the day appointed the man receives help from his kinsfolk and neighbours, and two or three ovens are needed to cook the food. In olden days a similar transaction took place with the Ariki Tafua at Fiora.

Ceremonial exchange occurs on a great variety of occasions— at birth, initiation, marriage, sickness, death, and other social events, as well as at much religious ritual. At a communal dance festival, for instance, it is a convention that the groups from the two districts shall not consume the food that each has brought, but that their supplies shall be exchanged, and that each shall eat the food of the other. Again, when a chief is ill, or on a visit, and people take gifts of food to him, custom provides that these people must be fed, but not from the gifts that they have brought. When some folk of Kafika paid a visit to the Ariki Tafua the food they brought was received by the Tafua clan, who handed over in return food from their own ovens. The Kafika folk then retired outside the house and ate this. A couple of baskets of the Kafika food were then presented by the son of the Tafua chief to some other visitors from Namo, and he and the other local people ate the rest.

In ceremonial exchange there is not always an exact equivalence between gift and counter-gift. Thus in the marriage gifts at Somosomo just mentioned, the Ariki Kafika and three other men of rank each get a very large basket of food. This is reciprocated by a single basket, in which they combine. The opinion expressed to me was that this is " an evil custom "— a bad bargain, though in conformity with traditional procedure. On the other hand a large gift of food presented by the family

---

[1] If a person should marry without such preparation having been made people may say " he marries there, but where does the food stand ? " More distant kinsfolk have to give the major supplies, and are annoyed.

of a bridegroom to that of the bride is reciprocated by one of equal size. The opinion given about this was that the second gift—the *tauvi* of the first—should be of good amount to compensate for the heavy labour of the women who carry the first.

In many cases where the incidence of ceremonial exchange is not apparently equal the balance is redressed later by further exchanges, and the total situation over a number of years may have to be taken into account. For example, in the case of the Somosomo marriage gift again, for the second year of the marriage a much smaller present of food, comprising only two baskets, is made, and reciprocated by a single basket as before. But this is not necessarily the end of the series. If the man has a son born to him, then at all funerals of the chiefly house of Kafika this son will probably be given handsome presents of goods. In such case the man continues to give an annual present of food to the elders at Somosomo. Moreover, in virtue of his relationship, the man goes as cook to such funerals, and as such is the recipient of a pandanus mat or bark-cloth. The result is a set of lifelong obligations wherein food, services, and goods are exchanged, tending on balance to cancel one another out, though at any moment there may be some disequilibrium in the position of the parties concerned. On the whole, too, the Tikopia attitude of reciprocity is such that a liberal interpretation of an obligation on one occasion is likely to promote a more elastic reply on another.

The alignment of persons within the exchange and the basis of their contributions rest primarily on kinship ties. An instance has been given of a man carrying some food and a paddle to a marriage ceremony because he had married into the group of the bridegroom. Standing in this affinal relationship he had also to give his services as cook. In this capacity he might receive a pandanus mat as equivalent, but more likely he would get only bark-cloth, since his kinship ties were not close, though his services would be of approximately the same character. Here again economic action can only be understood against the social background.

Again, the alignment in such ceremonies often involves a splitting of functions : people contribute through one set of kinship ties and are recipients through another. At times, as with the pandanus mats of *tama tapu* at initiation, care is taken

## MARRIAGE EXCHANGES

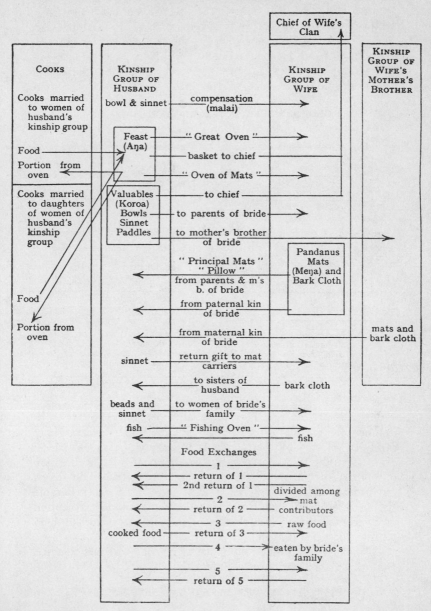

Fig. 9

to mark their contributions so that they do not receive the same items back again. But bark-cloth is not so marked, every piece being like every other, and is redistributed indiscriminately. Such ceremonial exchange may be illustrated by a diagram of what happens at marriage (Figure 9).[1] Here there are no less than nine major transfers of goods between the kinship group of the bridegroom and that of the bride, with more than that

GROUPINGS AT A TIKOPIA FUNERAL

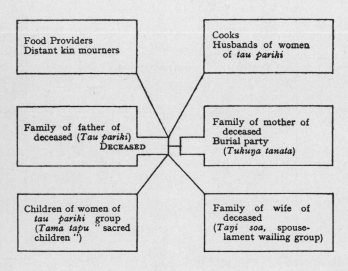

FIG. 10

number of subsidiary transfers. The objects exchanged can rarely be selected by the recipients in advance. The net effects are : a stimulus to increased production ; a change in the direction of normal consumption (the food received satisfies the day's nutritional needs though coco-nuts, sago, and other durable supplies are drawn upon to an unusual extent) ; and the reception of some immediately useful objects (paddles and bowls) which go into the general stock.

The exchanges which take place at marriage are less complex than those at initiation or a funeral.

[1] A detailed analysis of Tikopia marriage economics has been given in *We, The Tikopia*, 544–563.

### EXCHANGE IN MORTUARY CEREMONIES

A full description of the transfers of goods which take place at a Tikopia funeral is not possible here, because of their complexity. But I give two diagrams to show the major groups of people involved in the ceremonial, and the major types of

MAJOR EXCHANGES AT A TIKOPIA FUNERAL

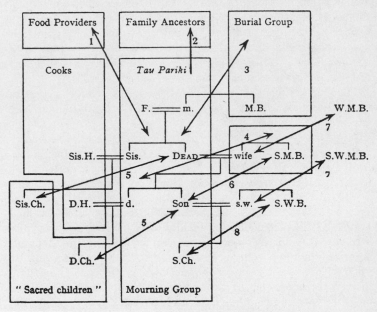

FIG. 11

Abbreviation : F., Father ; m., mother ; B., Brother ; w., wife ; S., Son ; d., daughter ; H., Husband ; Ch., Child.

The relationships are expressed in terms of the transactions that take place because of the death. Thus the dead man's wife's brother makes a gift to the dead man's son because he is the son's mother's brother from the point of view of funeral exchanges.

transaction which occur. The segregation of these groups takes place on the basis of closeness of kinship with the deceased ; patrilineal as against matrilineal affiliation : and affinal as against consanguineous kinship.

From the native point of view the transactions are directed to feeding the immediate mourners (that is, the family of the deceased), paying others who attend in various capacities for their services, and making acknowledgment through food and other goods of the ties of persons with their maternal kin. As will be seen from the description of Figure 11, many of the " gifts " are reciprocated, but the net effect is a heavy drain, both of food and of other goods, upon the resources of the family of the deceased. For clarity, I have excluded from Figure 11 any mention of the gifts to the clan chief of the deceased, of the complex principles of accumulation of green food (*putu*) in honour of the deceased, and of the presentation of pandanus mats and other grave cloths for the burial. With exception of the *ara manoŋi*, I have also not mentioned the apportionment of food on occasions other than the transfer of goods.

The following list briefly describes the major types of transaction that occur at a funeral, with reference to the numbers cited in the Figure.

1. *Vai*—" water ". Food brought on three successive evenings by " outsiders " to feed the members of the mourning group. Each bringer of *vai* selects a mourner to whom he presents the food, and this is reciprocated on the third evening by a gift of a wooden bowl, a coil of sinnet cord and supplementary articles such as a few fish-hooks, a piece of tobacco, a couple of shell arm-rings, a betel mortar, a paddle, or a coil of hibiscus fibre fish line. A mourner frequently receives several *vai* from different men, and hands on one or more of them to be reciprocated by other members of the mourning group. Again, a recipient may invite other members of the mourning group to share his *vai*, and they then contribute to the reciprocation (*penu* or specifically, *kauŋaroŋa*). This contribution is known as *soaki*, " assisting." The service of the *vai*, and the consequent reciprocation, is later returned at a subsequent funeral.

2. *Koromata*—the " novitiate ". A concluding item in the funeral rites is the preparation of a large mass of food, and of a *maro* of bark-cloth, for offering to the ancestors, who are believed to descend in spirit form and bear off the spirit of the dead person to the Heavens. The rite is known as the *ara manoŋi*, " the scented path," from the sprig of fragrant leafage stuck in the bundle of bark-cloth. From the Tikopia point of view this is a transaction with the ancestors, who in return for their service take away the essence of the cloth and the food. The food is later distributed among the members of the mourning group.

3a. *Punefu*—the payment to the mother's group of the deceased, whose responsibility it is to bury him. The *punefu* consists on the one hand of coils of sinnet cord laid in wooden bowls, and on the other of piles of bark-cloth with a pandanus mat at the bottom of each. An ordinary *punefu* numbers 20 or so pieces of bark-cloth, and 6 or 8 bowls and sinnet coils ; that for a member of a chief's family 50 or more pieces of bark-cloth and a dozen to 20 bowls and sinnet coils. A large mass of food is also divided among the burial group. The mats, bark-cloth and food are not reciprocated—thus making a heavy drain on the resources of the mourning group—but the bowls and sinnet coils are reciprocated the same day by goods of precisely the same kind and quality. Great stress is laid upon equivalence in this respect. The *punefu* is given to the mother's group as a whole, and is distributed among them all. In addition, however, the few men who actually dig the grave take away with them the tools used—a spear, a wooden bowl, a digging stick—which they have seized from the house of the dead person. No return is given for these things.

*b. Mori ŋa taŋata*—" conveying the man ". This is a further transfer of goods to the burial group, on the fifth day of the funeral. It consists of pandanus mats and bark-cloth—about half a dozen pieces—and a large quantity of food. The food is reciprocated in kind, but the other goods are not.

4. *Penu te taŋi soa*—" reciprocation of the spouse-lament ". If the deceased is a married man, his widow and her brothers and sisters have the duty of chanting a special lament for the dead. For this they receive payment from the sons of the dead man. Several wooden bowls, coils of sinnet cord, paddles, fish-hooks, and pieces of tobacco are distributed by the chief mourner among the " spouse-lament " group. These are not reciprocated ; they are " *te tauvi te soa fuere* ", " the payment for the spouse-lament, simply." The service of the chant suffices.

5. *Koroa ŋa tama tapu*—" valuables of the sacred children ". The children of women of the mourning group, as so often in Tikopia ceremonial, receive special gifts. In an ordinary funeral green food alone is presented to them, but at the funeral of a wealthy family, " a funeral raising valuables," gifts of wooden bowls, sinnet cord, etc., are made to them. Reciprocation is made to a much smaller extent than the gifts, though there are several complications which cannot be described here. In effect

such gifts give some recompense to the cooks, who are the fathers of the " sacred children ".

6. *Kupukupu.*—This is a gift made to the chief mourner by his mother's brother. It consists of a large basket of cooked food, brought on the second evening of the *vai*, but topped off by a piece of bark-cloth. If the chief mourner has several mother's brothers he may receive a corresponding number of baskets. The *kupukupu* is reciprocated by a coil of sinnet cord and a piece of bark-cloth, the latter having been specifically set aside on the day of burial.

7. *Kava.*—This is the counterpart of the *kupukupu*, but is a gift to the female chief mourners from their mother's brothers, and is distinguished by the absence of any piece of bark-cloth on top. *Kava* are usually given to the wife of the deceased, his son's wife, and to the daughter of the deceased (often as an alternative to the *kupukupu*). The reciprocation is the same as in the case of the *kupukupu*, a coil of sinnet cord and a piece of bark-cloth.

8. *Kura.*—On the day on which the corpse is buried goods consisting of a pandanus mat, a sheet of bark-cloth, and some other pieces of bark-cloth are brought into the house and presented to the children of the son of the dead man by their mother's family. Though this is a gift to the paternal grand-children of the dead man, it is in effect another instance of the mother's brother sister's child relationship which is so important in Tikopia society. It is reciprocated by the father of the children in goods of the same type as presented. If owing to the other mortuary obligations he has not the bark-cloth on hand at the moment, he announces at the time of the presentation of the *kura* " Its repayment stands in the middle of the woods ", meaning that the trees to provide the bark-cloth are still uncut in his orchard, but that he has noted the obligation.

In quantitative terms the effect upon the economy of the individuals and households involved in these transfers of goods is considerable. As an example, I give a summary of the transactions concerned with the *vai*, *kupukupu*, and *kava* at a funeral at the house of Pa Fetauta, a commoner, but the head of an important kinship group, a ritual elder, and therefore a man of rank.

| *Vai* (three baskets of food each) | *Reciprocation* (a) by principal recipient of *vai* ; (b) etc., by others who *soaki*, i.e. helped him. |
|---|---|

1.
 (a) sinnet, tobacco.
 (b) bowl, sinnet, 2 yams, fish-hooks.

2.
 (a) bowl, sinnet, bark-cloth sheet, 2 fish-hooks.
 (b) bark-cloth beater, fish-line.
 (c) paddle.

3.
 (a) bowl, sinnet, 2 fish-hooks.
 (b) sinnet, 4 fish-hooks.
 (c) paddle, fish-line, fish-hooks.
 (d) sinnet, shell arm-rings.

4.
 (a) bowl, sinnet.
 (b) sinnet.
 (c) fish-line.
 (d) 2 yams.

5.
 (a) bowl, 2 sinnet coils, fathom of cloth, fish-hooks.
 (b) tobacco, 2 dry coco-nuts.

6.
 (a) sinnet, betel mortar.
 (b) sinnet, paddle, 2 shell arm-rings.
 (c) bowl, tobacco.
 (d) 1 fish-hook (small boy).

7.
 (a) bowl, sinnet, fish-hooks.
 (b) sinnet, tobacco.
 (c) (no reciprocation ; *soaki* to another *vai*, No. 9 *c* ; an unmarried woman.)

8.
 (a) sinnet.
 (b) sinnet.
 (c) bowl.

9.
 (a) bowl, bark-cloth.
 (b) sinnet, dry coco-nuts.
 (c) fish-hooks, 2 shell arm-rings (see No. 7).

10.
 (a) sinnet, bark-cloth, 2 *taumako* (vegetables of yam type).
 (b) sinnet.

11.
 (a) bowl, sinnet ? further goods.

12.
 (a) bowl, sinnet ? further goods.

13. (presented by Mission teacher)
 (a) paddle, bark-cloth sheet, sinnet.
 (b) paddle, bark-cloth, sinnet.
 (c) bowl, sinnet (an exceptionally good reciprocation ; " great is its size ").

14.
 (a) paddle.
 (b) sinnet.
 (c) fish-line, fish-hooks.

15. (presented by half-brother of Pa Fetauta)
 No reciprocation in goods ; it had been accounted for by gift of similar food the day before.

*Kupukupu* (one basket each, with one bark-cloth)
 *Reciprocation*

1.
 (a) sinnet, bark-cloth.

2.
 (a) sinnet, bark-cloth.

*Kava* (one basket of food each)    *Reciprocation*
1.                                   (*a*) sinnet, bark-cloth.
2.                                   (*a*) sinnet, fish-hooks.
                                     (*b*) bark-cloth sheet.

In these three types of transaction, then, 49 baskets of food
were handed in to the group of mourners, and in return 29 coils
of sinnet, 12 wooden bowls, 6 paddles, 4 fish-lines, 6 yams and
*taumako*, over a score of fish-hooks, more than half a dozen
arm-rings, 3 bark-cloth sheets, 6 strips of bark-cloth, a fathom
of calico and a small amount of other goods were given by this
group. The original details of the transactions which I recorded
(too complex to reproduce here) show that the food was provided
by 16 households (a few giving more than one *vai*), and distributed
ultimately to members of 20 households, by whom the
reciprocation was shared. In this the chief burden was borne
by the household of Pa Fetauta, the " basis " of the funeral.
He received nominally 6 *vai*, Nos. 1–6 (i.e. 18 baskets of food),
which he allotted to his wife, his son, his unmarried brother,
a nephew, and a classificatory kinsman, keeping one for himself.
He thus had to provide from his household resources the
reciprocation for 4 *vai*. In addition he received one *kupukupu*,
which he handed over to a kinsman, and his wife received a
basket of food from a *kava*, which she kept and reciprocated.
*In toto* goods from his household were handed over to the amount
of : 5 sinnet coils, 4 wooden bowls, 2 dry coco-nuts, 4 fish-hooks,
3 pieces of tobacco, 1 bark-cloth sheet, and 1 strip of bark-cloth ;
in addition to the food given prior to the reception of *vai* No. 15.

If in addition to this it is remembered that his household
handed over without return four or five pandanus mats and
about 30 pieces of bark-cloth as part of their obligations of the
*punefu*, etc., then it will be realized what a heavy drain is imposed
upon the property of a household by a funeral. Over a period
of years, they tend to recoup these losses by participating in
other funerals in a different capacity. But it is evident that the
need to assemble from their own resources such a quantity of
goods for immediate out-go exerts a considerable effect upon the
production of any household, and upon that of the community
as a whole over a period of time.

The death of a person in a chiefly family involves a much
greater transfer of goods. Firstly, the quantities of each type of
transaction must by convention and wider kinship ties be greatly

increased. Thus I was told that at one mortuary ceremony of the house of Tafua, 128 baskets of food were received in *vai*, etc., meaning that over 40 transactions took place, or nearly three times as many as in the case cited above. Secondly, additional transactions such as the " valuables of the sacred children " are often initiated, involving a still further heavy expenditure of goods.

Arising out of this brief review of ceremonial exchange in Tikopia a comment may be made on some propositions on primitive exchange made by M. Marcel Mauss in his admirable *Essai sur le Don*, a stimulating theoretical treatment of the subject. Mauss stresses the binding nature of the obligations underlying much primitive exchange, the social constraint—to return a present made, and the motives of rivalry often involved. He points out too that ceremonial exchange is primarily between groups rather than individuals, and that not merely goods, but a whole system of rites, feasts, and courtesies is transferred, in a manner which he describes as *prestations totales*.[1]

Each of these propositions could aptly cover some aspects of the Tikopia situation. But they must not be stressed too strongly. As we have seen, the motives underlying Tikopia marriage and funeral exchanges, as well as those in exchange of other kinds, involve a strong response to complex social obligations. But these may be considered as part of a rational economic choice, if a preference for other types of advantage or satisfaction than the mere increase of wealth be regarded as legitimate, in view of the value of securing and maintaining social co-operation. Moreover, one must not ignore the more purely material aspects of the transactions. Again, while from a general standpoint funeral exchanges, for instance, may be viewed as group-exchanges, the fact is clear that these take place through the acts of separate individuals, who concentrate a great deal of attention on the accumulation of their personal contributions, the drain that these make on their personal as well as household resources, and on the personal relationship to them of the individual with whom the exchange takes place. Group-exchange conceived as a set of individual transactions is a more adequate formulation. Finally, in Tikopia, material goods are frequently the sole commodity in the exchange, the rites and courtesies being part of the whole cultural matrix in which the transactions take

---

[1] M. Mauss, " Essai sur le Don," *L'Année Sociologique*, n.s., I, 1925, 36–7.

place, and not forming an element in the total complex handed over. This does not, however, appear to be the case in some institutions such as the potlatch of the American Indians of the north-west coast, where the term *prestation totale* is more properly applicable.

A further hypothesis is put forward by Mauss in terms of an evolutionary sequence. He suggests that the principle of the gift-exchange may be characteristic of societies at a stage intermediary in the development from total group exchange to the later purely individual contract, using the idea of money price.[1] If this be so, it is almost certainly not the result of a development of the exchange institution *sui generis*, but a correlate of a much wider scheme of changing institutions, depending upon technical advancement, alteration in moral and religious codes, and the emergence of a different type of legal system linked with a more complex social and political structure.

## THE ECONOMIC VALUE OF GOODS

This descriptive account of various types of distribution, exchange, and compensatory payment has been given in detail, with quotation of actual transactions observed, in order that the reality of the Tikopia system may be appreciated, and the empirical basis of my generalizations be made clear. Two facts are obvious : the Tikopia attach different utilities to different classes of goods (including labour also) ; and the loss of goods, by whatever means, requires compensation. How far does this represent the existence of a scheme of values, comparable with that operating in our own society ? And in so far as there can be said to be economic values, how are they determined ?

In answering these questions it is first essential to decide what is meant by value in an economic analysis. The modern economist is quite clear on the point. To him, value is a relation between goods in exchange, at a particular place and time. And in practice, since this relation in civilized communities is normally expressed through the medium of money, value is expressed in price.[2]

Strictly speaking, then, in a primitive community with no

[1] Ibid., 125–6.
[2] See, e.g., A. Marshall, *Principles* (8th ed., 1922, 61–2) ; F. Benham, *Economics*, 1938, 15–16. Cf. G. Cassel, *Fundamental Thoughts in Economics*, 1925, 41, " Value always means a price paid under certain circumstances."

money, no prices in the ordinary sense of the term, and not even a thorough-going system of exchange of goods, there are no economic values. We seem to be left with simply a set of relative utilities of goods—their " values in use ", according to an older economic terminology.

Anthropologists discussing primitive economics have usually ignored this issue, and have spoken of " values " without giving any definition of the term or attempting to relate their usage to that of economists.

For instance, Lloyd Warner holds for the Murngin of north Australia that the governing principle in the evaluation of objects intended to be kept permanently by their owner is the ease with which they can be transported by human carriage or by dug-out canoe. Allowance is made for their relative scarcity, and for the amount of labour expended upon them, but the final desideratum is held to be the relative ease of transportation of the article. This hypothesis, interesting as a criterion of " value " in a nomadic tribe, might be compared with Viljoen's time and elaboration criteria of " value " for more settled communities.[1] But this acceptance of ease of transportation as the final determinant in the demand situation obviously leaves out of account the importance of other facts such as the comparative utility of these things, as ornaments, and in food production. Warner again does not bring into the generalization the value of non-transportable things, e.g. land and waterholes, which are owned by clan groups and which are so linked with them by myth that a clan is never dispossessed by an act of war. Furthermore, although the economic structure is explicitly stated to be secondary to the other aspects of the social structure it is not made clear what are precisely the primary forces in the social structure which determine relative " values ". And finally, in the absence of any statement as to the meaning of the terms used, it is not clear whether indeed economic values are discussed, or a more general relation between persons and things.

Again, the analysis of exchange and distribution by Viljoen contains no reference to the problem of primitive economic values—though there is a descriptive chapter on Money—and the term value is used elsewhere in a vague way. For instance, in the course of an examination of Arts and Crafts Viljoen gives a series of generalizations, which, though not consecutive, are

[1] Warner, *op. cit.*, 148 ; Viljoen, *op. cit.*, 151.

related to one another, and merit scrutiny.[1]    These generalizations are :

A.  The tools of the primitive remain undeveloped, inadequate,
unspecialized ; the result is that the process of manufacture requires
a very long time.  On account of the amount of work expended on
the construction of some Samoan mats these are symbolical of the
wealth and the rank of their possessors.

B.  Primitive objects are often overladen with ornament.  The
amount of work embodied on [sic] an object seems in fact to be the
criterion of its value.

C.  As wealth in primitive societies has a concrete form and can
be embodied in relatively few objects, the elaboration of articles is a
means of acquiring distinction.

First in statements A and B there is no clear definition of
what is meant by " amount of work ".  Is it simply the amount
of physical energy expended, or that physical energy which is
regarded as labour and is treated as of economic value ?  The
distinction is important since in some primitive societies the
division between working time and leisure time is not made so
sharply as in an industrialized society—partly because of the
absence of wage labour and partly perhaps because of less diversity
of the forms of recreation.  Hence once the prime technological
requirements of the object are satisfied occupation with it may
go on, bringing it to a high degree of elaboration.  But the result
may make little or no difference to the demand for it or its
value in exchange.  Where work as a drive and work as a
pleasurable interest may be so closely joined upon the same
object it is difficult to measure values in terms of the amount
of work unless we know more precisely of what type it is.

Moreover statement B appears to be a loosely formulated
expression of a labour-cost theory of value.  It ignores the part
played by scarcity of the materials required, and by the type
of demand for the object (nor is any subsequent reference made
to them by Viljoen as determinants of value in this context).
In the case of Samoan mats the situation is much more
complicated than Viljoen's account suggests.  Plaiting of these
fine mats was done only by women and involved months of

[1] S. Viljoen, op. cit., 150–1.  In the chapter on Trade there is mention
of " subjective value " and " intrinsic value " ;  of " value " that must be given
in return for a gift ;  of the lower Congo people haggling half a day over a trifle
and then giving away " more than half its value " ;  of the " value " of Kula
bracelets and necklaces being derived from symbolic and historical associations
rather than from their beauty or intrinsic value.  (Ibid., 213, 214, 216, 224.)
One is entitled to expect from a professed economist some clearer statement of
the use of these terms.

concentrated labour. They have often been called " Samoan currency ", and according to Margaret Mead are an excellent illustration of a currency *originally* founded upon labour value. But Mead points out that their economic value is ceremonially enhanced by their age, by the high lineage of the ladies who have plaited them, and by the exchanges in which they have played a part. Some mats which have personal names have a history attached to them and are normally the property of high chiefs. All this shows that Viljoen's generalization is superficial. Moreover, Margaret Mead says that it is plausible to suppose that the value of the mats has not increased proportionately as the technique of manufacture has become more difficult and laborious. Thus it is still more difficult to accept Viljoen's casual sequence between the amount of work alone expended on them and their function as a symbol of rank. In fact Te Rangi Hiroa suggests that the converse is to some extent the case, that the importance and value of the fine mat directed the attention of the craftswomen to still further laborious attempts at refinement and made them keep to check plaiting with a restriction on the development of other forms of decoration.[1] This last statement further bears against Viljoen's attempt to link ornamentation, labour, and value together.

In statement C we have apparently an incomplete sequence of argument due to the loose coalescence of four separate elements, the possible alternatives to which are not examined. In the first place, on a question of fact, it can be shown that there are forms of immaterial wealth in some primitive societies, to mention only songs, dances, and ceremonies, which in Melanesia and Australia are exchanged between tribes or " bought ".[2] In the second place, the final part of the proposition may hold where wealth is embodied in very many objects. For instance, in modern conditions of industrial mass-production the elaboration of articles by individual craftsmen is a very definite means of acquiring social distinction. In furniture, glass, and metal-work, the hand-made thing, personally designed and ornamented, gives reputation to its maker. In those primitive societies where everything is hand-made it is possible that no special kudos

[1] Margaret Mead, " Social Organization of Manua," *B.P.B.M. Bulletin*, 76, 1930, 73–4. Te Rangi Hiroa, " Samoan Material Culture," *B.P.B.M. Bulletin*, 75, 1930, 228, 231.

[2] W. E. H. Stanner, *Oceania*, iv, 1933, 172 ; Margaret Mead, *Sex and Temperament*, 1935, 9.

accrues to any individual for this alone. Again, it may not be only the elaboration of articles that gives distinction. Why not the multiplication of them, or the destruction of them ? In theory, if the objects are relatively few, either of the attitudes would attract attention to the person concerned. In fact, this can be so, as the potlatch of north-west America shows. This consists essentially in the destruction of wealth as a means of obtaining rank and prestige (see also the section on ceremonial destruction later in this Chapter). Moreover, the statement implies that there is a demand in primitive society for elaboration *per se*. This may be by no means always the case. The demand for a type of article may be such that any item of it which conforms to the ordinary conditions has the same value, and an elaboration of it is treated as an individual idiosyncrasy on the part of the maker, satisfying his æsthetic interests but giving to the object itself no higher exchange value nor to its maker any special distinction.

This series of statements by Viljoen is not necessarily inaccurate for any given case, but distorts the situation when applied as a general principle.

In attempting to clarify his own position on the problem of the existence and nature of economic values in a primitive society the anthropologist is compelled to decide how far he wishes to adhere to current economic terminology. In most primitive communities values as expressions of exchange ratios in prices cannot be found—assuming that by price is meant the sum of money paid for a thing. If, however, the economic value of a thing is taken in the more general sense as the amount of that thing that can be got in exchange for another, having regard to circumstances of time and place, then there are many primitive economic phenomena to which the term can be applied, even though there be no single general medium of exchange. The difficulty arises when we come to consider things which are not exchanged against one another, but which nevertheless are ranked by a general consensus of opinion in a hierarchy, so that the possession of one is regarded for all ordinary situations as more desirable than that of another. To the economist this can be simply treated as a scale of comparative utilities—the things have different " values in use " ; the preferences shown for some as against others express their differential capacity to satisfy desires, or as Pigou argues, more strictly, the differential

intensity of the desire for them.[1] But the anthropologist may
not be content to have the problem thus flung back into the
vaguely speculative realm of comparative desires. He feels
that a more objective element is involved, and that the agreement
of people upon a set of common standards about the relationship
of their different types of goods to one another deserves to be
considered more closely as part of a scheme of economic values.
To any Tikopia a canoe ranks higher than a wooden bowl, a
pandanus mat than a strip of bark-cloth. Yet they are never
exchanged against each other, and there is no expression of the
" value " of a canoe in terms of so many bowls, or of that of a
pandanus mat in terms of so many strips of bark-cloth. A concept
which may help us here is that of equivalence. Without being
able to find the expression of one item in terms of multiples of
another, or of a common denominator, we can yet discover that
a wooden bowl is not " equivalent " to a canoe, nor a strip of
bark-cloth " equivalent " to a pandanus mat in the various
customary transactions in which these things are used, or in
discussions about them. In a community where actual exchange
of the items against one another may never take place the idea
of an imagined substitution or theoretical exchange can still
allow us to construct a scale of what might be termed " economic
values ". This means a substantial rather than a formal use of
the term. Goods are related to one another by a process of
tacit comparison in which measurement is given by the possibility
of substitution and not by actual transfer against one another.

The position of different types of goods on this scale of relative
values is determined partly by the institutional setting in which
they are used, and partly by the relative ease with which their
raw material can be procured and converted into the object
desired. The lower " economic value " of bark-cloth to the
Tikopia as compared with that of a pandanus mat thus depends
upon the greater quantities of paper-mulberry trees than pandanus
palms available, the much less amount of labour necessary for
the manufacture of bark-cloth, its shorter durability, and the
different place which it occupies in the native system of household
requirements and ceremonial transfers.

The terminological argument as to whether we are to
speak of " values " or of " comparative utilities " in a primitive
non-price economy is, however, of less moment than an elucidation

[1] A. C. Pigou, *The Economics of Welfare* (2nd ed.), 1924, 23–4.

of the relationships that exist between the different types of goods, and the native ideas about them. In the following section I give some data of this kind for Tikopia. If I seem to stress unduly the factors involved on the demand side it is because the treatment of " values " by anthropologists has often tended to throw too much weight on the side of cost of production, particularly on the scarcity of materials and the labour of manufacture.

## THE RELATIVE WORTH OF GOODS IN TIKOPIA

A Tikopia, Pa Raŋifuri, whom I induced to formulate statements on the comparative utilities or " values " of goods, began by putting them into two major categories : those which are " weighty " (*mafa*) and those which are " light " (*mama*). There terms are ordinarily used to describe the degree of heaviness of objects, but can denote also the degree of ritual sanctity attaching to names of the gods, formulae, and ceremonial institutions. Here it is the degree of importance in the economic scheme that is meant, though this is related in some cases to the ritual background. As " weighty " goods he included bonito-hooks, sinnet cord (that for catching sharks only), bowls, and spears ; as " light " goods he mentioned bundles of arrows, bows, and pandanus mats. Having done so he drew comparisons between them. " The mat and the bonito-hook are not equivalent ; they are not exchangeable. The mat is somewhat heavy (*mamafa*), but the bonito-hook, it is alone, in the forefront. And the sinnet for the shark-hook is next to the bonito-hook, while next to it is the mat. The mat and the sinnet (of ordinary type) are reciprocally equivalent." (This is the most exact translation of the expression *fakafetau faŋatasi*). Another man explained the kind of transaction in which a bonito-hook is used and its peculiar position. If a commoner has a good tree for a canoe growing on his land, he said, and a chief desires it, the man may be unwilling to part with it. But if the chief presents him with a bonito-hook his objection vanishes. I was told that he will hold the hook among his treasures, but he will not term it his ; it is held as " the property of the chief ". When the time comes that he goes to " the hearings of the chiefs ", an important ceremony such as the death of a chief and the succession of his heir, he takes the bonito-hook and presents it to the new ruler. It is not handed over to another commoner. If in exceptional circumstances a man should wish to acquire a canoe already built, and the owner refuses to part with it for the goods offered, the man takes a coil of shark line, lays it on the goods, opens his basket of bonito-hooks, chooses one, lays it on the sinnet coil, and carries the pile to the owner of the canoe. No more words are spoken ; the owner says " Go and take your canoe ". He rejoices to see the bonito-hook, and the heavy sinnet cord. In all these cases the hook must be what is termed a *pa tu maya*, that is, with the turtle-shell barb attached to the shell shank. (The shank is frequently worn separately, as an ornament, and is also termed *pa*.)

Between commoners the same retention of proprietary interest in the bonito-hook which is transferred does not apply. The unique social position of the chief conditions the former situation. Moreover, a commoner's stock of bonito-hooks is normally small—many people do not even possess any.

The categories here are shown to be broadly significant but not strictly defined nor mutually exclusive. Though there is a general rating of objects on the basis of their respective utilities this is not finely adjusted, and there cannot be said to be a comprehensive scale on which every type of good is placed and bears a measurable relation to the type of good above and below it.[1] As far as material goods are concerned there is no class of object which serves as a unit of measurement for all the others, and there is no conversion of the worth of different classes of object into one another in a systematic way. It might be thought that labour might provide such a measuring unit, but this is not the case, if only from the fact that labour is a social service as well as a contribution to production.

It may be asked what is the function of the notions of comparative utility that the Tikopia do possess, if they cannot be related to a general system of exchange and a market. To this the answer may be given that such notions are related to the perception of differences in the relative potentialities of objects or classes of objects to serve any particular want, and the

[1] To some extent, by my barter of European goods for specimens of native work I instituted such a scale. But the measurement of goods in terms of each other was primarily my intellectual construction, and even here there was no common denominator, fish-hooks, beads, cloth, and steel tools tending to operate in separate series. Natives did not argue that the price of a pandanus mat, for instance, should bear any particular relation to that of a wooden head-rest, but stressed the quality of their specific offering, and the need they had for the article they asked for (see Appendix III).

acceptance of a certain ranking of them assists in the taking of decisions.

These general statements may now be exemplified in a further consideration of spheres of exchange.

## SPHERES OF EXCHANGE

From the transactions in labour and goods described it emerges that there are at least three separate series of exchanges, or spheres of exchange, the goods in which are not completely convertible into those of the other series. At the lowest level there is the food series. Small objects such as arm-rings, small services such as the loan of a canoe, non-specialist labour of taro planting, paddling, or ordinary timber working, are paid for by food. Gifts of food, whether raw or cooked, are returned in kind, though not necessarily in the same state. On the next level is the bark-cloth sinnet series. Payment for timber, for bowls, coco-nut grating stools, or specialist skill in canoe or house-building, damage to valuable tools, the unauthorized use of a canoe, and in some circumstances payment for a ritual presentation, is made in one or other of these items (the sinnet here is of the ordinary light kind). Attached to this series is the pandanus mat which is its highest expression. The third and most important series from the point of view of utility of the goods, though not from the frequency of the transactions, is that including bonito-hooks, turmeric cylinders, and canoes. The objects and services in these three series cannot be completely expressed in terms of one another, since normally they are never brought to the bar of exchange together. It is impossible for example to express the value of a bonito-hook in terms of a quantity of food, since no such exchange is ever made and would be regarded by the Tikopia as fantastic.

One could present a set of equations representing transactions having a canoe as their basis, but the items on the other side of the equation in each case cannot be fully measured against each other. The physical equivalent for the production of a canoe is the labour on a tree trunk of two specialists and perhaps a dozen non-specialist workers, with several adzes, for a number of months. Expressed as cost of production of the canoe this means a coil of sinnet cord, with perhaps bark-cloth, as payment for the raw material ; bark-cloth as payment for the use of borrowed tools ;

a few pandanus mats and many bark-cloths plus a number of food baskets, plus subsistence for the period of the work as payment for the labour, skill, and management—from which must be subtracted a quantity of food handed over by the workers themselves. The exchange value of a canoe is a bonito-hook, a coil of heavy shark cord, a bundle of bark-cloth, and food. A second value in exchange is given when, as I observed at one funeral in a chief's family, a canoe is handed over to the principal man of a burial party as one item in return for their services. It replaced the gift of a wooden bowl which is usual on such occasions. It might seem from this as if a bowl would be a correct economic equivalent for a canoe. But it must be noted that the vessel handed over was a small one, and that it was a kind of honorific substitute for the ordinary gift, conferring prestige upon the donors. Moreover, a canoe and a bowl are essentially of the same shape ; the largest Tikopia bowl—the trough—is very similar to a canoe hull. No amount of bark-cloth could have acted as substitute in this way. Put generally, it can be said that the social context is different in each case. The services of a burial party at the death of a chief or the son of a chief are of a complicated kind charged with a high emotional significance, and though compensated for by economic goods could not be paid for only in bark-cloth and food, the types of goods by which specialist and non-specialist skill are rewarded. In other contexts again, obligations which are satisfied by bark-cloth or sinnet cannot be met simply by an increase in the amount of food handed over. Each kind of object is appropriate to a particular kind of social situation. It is as if, allowing for the obvious differences, in our society gold, silver, and copper were used as media of exchange in three series of transactions but there was no accurate means of rendering them in terms of each other.

Because the goods or services in these different spheres of exchange cannot be expressed fluidly in terms of each other, the cost of production cannot be measured exactly against exchange value. Theoretically it would seem that one should be able ultimately, by considering the various exchange transactions into which a canoe enters, to relate the value of a canoe to its cost of production in terms of that of the other items, e.g., a bonito-hook, and to find some common measure in the labour involved. In practice this is never done by the Tikopia. Moreover, while the bonito-hook has a high value correlated, *inter alia*, with its ritual use for funerals, for atonement, etc., it is primarily, after all, an instrument for catching bonito. The hooks are not kept only by the few acknowledged experts in the fishing but also by other men as valued property to be used when the social occasion offers. But there are no Tikopia who accumulate them principally for purposes of commercial exchange. The reason for this seems to lie in the general character of the institutions by which exchange is conditioned.

It must be noted that there is no effective monopoly of bonito-hooks. Of the materials, clam shell for the shank, turtle-shell for the barb, and hibiscus fibre for lashing and tassels, only turtle-shell is at all scarce. But of this sufficient comes to hand to allow of making more hooks than are in existence. Some at least is utilized for ear-rings, which rank comparatively low in the scale of utilities. Alternative conversion of the shell into hook-barbs would have a much greater exchange value. The labour of making a bonito-hook, though perhaps dull and lacking the stimulus of collective work, is not very onerous ; it could be done largely in spare time. It demands no high degree of skill, being mainly grinding. Competence in lashing on the barb is recognized as necessary and the precise method is not common knowledge. But one can always get the hook relashed by an expert at small cost, and in exchange attention is not directed to the adequacy of the lashing—though for fishing purposes it is very critically appraised.

I have always thought it remarkable that the Tikopia do not make more bonito-hooks. The question why some sharp individuals do not accumulate a stock for trading purposes and why all men do not put in more labour in the production of them is difficult to answer. It seems that the attitude of the Tikopia in this is governed by other factors than those mentioned. Supply does not necessarily respond to demand because of indifference which is the result of attitudes towards time, labour, and material objects which themselves are part of a wider scheme of social values—indeed, almost of a philosophy of life. There is in Tikopia a lack of stimulus to ultimate acquisition ; they have other channels for the expression of their interests. For this reason they divorce the values of their end-products from the values of the labour and material involved in the production itself.

This is a hypothesis rather than an empirical generalization, since I have made no intensive observations on bonito-hook making. But I am sure that an attempt at constructing theoretical equations in terms of comparative costs of these items would distort the native economic ideas.

We may return for a moment to examine the three spheres of exchange from the point of view of the mobility of the articles appearing in them. Food produced by every household is a common medium for initiating or liquidating a great variety of economic and social obligations. Even here there is an element of non-conversion since many forms of obligation must be met by cooked food and not by an equivalent or greater amount of raw food. But since such food is usually consumed immediately at the end of such a transaction or at the most is handed on only one stage further, it cannot form anything like a true medium of exchange. The only exception to this are dry and sprouting coco-nuts which need not be consumed at once but can be stored and used in another transaction.

Sinnet and bark-cloth, the common articles in the second sphere, are the most mobile in the Tikopia economy. Like food they are home-produced, by personal labour from the raw materials of the family. Sinnet is plaited by the men, bark-cloth is beaten out by the women of the household, with assistance from the men in preliminary stages. But such articles, being in frequent circulation, are received also from outside. Ultimately both are consumed, the sinnet in fishing or lashing, the bark-cloth in wearing. But so frequent are the needs of payment for economic, ritual, and social services that these articles may pass through many households before being finally consumed. Because of their durability, which food does not possess, they can serve as embryonic media of exchange. As measures of exchange value, however, they operate only to a very limited degree because of the limitations of sphere which social convention puts upon them. To some extent they are alternative or even convertible in terms of each other, there being a number of transactions in which either a coil of sinnet or a piece of bark-cloth can be offered. But in many others an appropriate item must be rendered. Bark-cloth (of the *fakamaru* type) is much better adapted for serving as an embryonic medium of exchange than sinnet ; there is so little difference in quality between individual pieces that any piece is accepted. With sinnet, however, it is frequently a matter of finding or matching a coil of appropriate quality.

In the third sphere bonito-hooks, shark cord, turmeric cylinders,[1] and canoes are of much greater durability, but are not of great mobility in exchange. When the transfer of them from one individual to another takes place the situation is usually charged with emotional significance. Turmeric cylinders are broken over the body of a dead chief, bonito-hooks are hung round his neck, or in the lobes of his ears, a canoe is handed over to his mother's kin, as part of the payment for his burial.

Apart from the three spheres of exchange mentioned a fourth may be recognized in cases where goods of unique quality are handed over. Such for instance was the transfer of women by the man who could not otherwise pay for his canoe. Transfers of land might be put into the same category. Women and land are given in satisfaction of unique obligations ; they are alike in that their productive capacity is vast but incalculable !

## CEREMONIAL DESTRUCTION

Mention of the emotional situation surrounding the transfer of goods of the third category raises some interesting points with regard to exchange and value. Sometimes the heir to a dead chief, on his succession, as a token of sentiment, determines to allow one of his canoes to rot in its shed. When word of this goes round, if the canoe is in good order another chief may attempt to secure it for himself. It might be thought that since the vessel was now of no further use to the new chief he would part with it for a smaller quantity of goods than otherwise. But the emotional rejection of the vessel does not tend to lower its exchange value but to cause it to rise. Since it has been doomed to decay, some special form of compensation must be offered to appease the owner's determination. This is given in the form of the bonito-hook, backed up by shark cord and a quantity of bark-cloth. The special function of the bonito-hook here is to meet the emotional element in the situation. With this may be correlated its use as an ornament of chiefs, an indemnity for offence, and a tribute to dead chiefs. I do not of course mean to imply that the emotional factor is of a simple kind.

This situation was explained to me by Pa Fenuatara. Before his death a chief indicates which canoes he desires to be left as

[1] Turmeric properly prepared will last a lifetime. Pa Nukutai told me that when he was a little boy he made some turmeric. He grew up, grew old and grey-bearded, and it was still there, quite good.

" an orchard " for his son, that is, in active service, and those which he wishes to be neglected. When he dies the bark-cloth ritual vestments of the canoes indicated are buried with him. Hence they can no longer be sacralized in any ceremonies. They are left in their sheds untouched. If they are already beyond repair they will be abandoned, but if not then on the day that the chief is buried one of the visiting chiefs who may desire such a canoe says, " That is the hull of the canoe which will be resting with me." If the new chief approves the canoe is taken away that day by members of the other's clan. But he may object. He may say, " O, you have come to speak for my canoe but it will not go with you ; my canoe has been laid up in its shed to fall to pieces, that it may rest and decay." Pa Fenuatara said, " He is mindful of his canoe not to give it ; he has affection for his father and for his canoe, he does not wish that another clan shall take it and go and paddle at sea while he sits and looks on it. He objects, he does not wish to see it (used thus)." But if the chief who wants it has a suitable tree in his orchard he replies, " You, friend, object on account of your canoe, but your canoe will go with me ; there stands by me its equivalent, its replacement." If, however, he has no tree available in his orchard he says, " O, friend, your canoe will go with me. I am possessed of its equivalent." When he has spoken thus he goes to his house. He makes no mention of property but the other chief knows that a bonito-hook is ready for the exchange. When the chief returns home his relatives assemble, each with a piece of bark-cloth. These are heaped up in two piles each containing about twenty pieces and topped with an orange piece. Then the chief takes down his roll of sinnet cord, extracts a hank of the best quality (that for shark fishing) and lays it by the bark-cloth. He says, " The equivalent for my canoe is there." He then takes a bonito-hook with its barb and sticks it into the sinnet cord. He adds, " The equivalent for my canoe is there also." He stays in his house while the pile of property is carried to the other chief. When this man sees the bonito-hook in the sinnet then he consents to let the vessel go. It is said, " He gives thanks to the chief whose equivalent has been good." The gift is termed *motuŋa vaka*, " severing of the canoe," an indication of the weight of the transaction. No return present of food or valuables is given for this ; just the canoe is taken. The equivalent is reckoned a good one. " The exchange has been good, the bonito-hook and the sinnet cord are just the same as the canoe. Because the bonito-hook with standing barb, and the sinnet, great are their weight, they are the property of chiefs alone."

The canoe thus acquired may even be consecrated by its possessor and made into one of his sacred canoes. The natives speak as if these canoes are actually meant to rot, but it is probably rare for a seaworthy one to be allowed to do so. At the same time the statement of intention is not a simple polite fiction ; there are strong emotional elements there which might easily lead to the abandonment of the craft.

Actual destruction of economic goods is to some degree institutionalized in Tikopia. Thus if on the death of a *maru*, a man of rank of a chiefly house, he has no son to succeed him, but only daughters, his kin group may cut down coco-nut palms, areca palms, and chestnut trees in their grief. At the death of Pa Resiake the Ariki Taumako ordered his younger relatives to go and cut down such trees in the three orchards of Osiri, Korofau, and Resiake, and this was done. Pa Paŋisi, who was married to a daughter of Pa Resiake, had to do a great deal of fresh planting to restore these orchards to their former condition. It was said, " They were destroyed, to vanish away, because the man was dead." Such goods destroyed are described as " property making pungent in affection " (*a koroa fakamasi*). Again, if a man's only son dies he will destroy wooden bowls or similar valued goods. But an eye is kept on expediency. Thus when during my stay Pa Maevetau, a brother of the Ariki Tafua, died, no such destruction was practised, since he had sons to succeed him.

A great deal depends on the discretion of the individual owner of the goods. When Noakena, son of Pa Raŋifuri, was lost at sea, the people of Raveŋa, when they came over for the wailing ceremonies, broke up a large number of small canoes, and took others back with them to their homes. The reason was that Noakena had gone off alone in a little one-man canoe, and his grandfather the Ariki Tafua, in grief and anger at the loss of the lad, ordered all such craft to be broken or confiscated. The funeral rites which were performed for the boy (in the absence of the body) took place when I was on the island, about a year after his loss. On this occasion his mother's brothers considered that their " affection " was not complete (so they phrased it). One of them went out during the ceremonies and broke up one of the family canoes—one in quite good repair. Again, the reason for this special concentration of destruction on the canoe was because Noakena had gone off in one. The rest of the family of mother's brothers wailed ceremonially while this was being done.

As in the case of the chief's canoes mentioned earlier, intercession by another person can often save property from such destruction. For instance, Noakena, when a young boy, had planted two Canarium almond trees. After he had gone on his suicide voyage the father in passing one day with a younger son noticed one and proposed to cut it down. The lad objected. The father said, " O, the two of us have been deserted by him, he went off to sea ; cut it out." But the boy persisted in preserving it so he let it stand. Afterwards, when he told the incident to people in his house, they said, " Yes, let it grow." He told me of this at the funeral. Again, he had marked down a tree to build his son a canoe. After the lad's death the tree was cut down and half of it was made into the small transport canoe of Pa Nukufuti, mentioned earlier. Pa Raŋifuri acted as chief builder. He announced his intention of having the other half burnt as firewood because of his son's decease. But when Pa Nukufuti took over the bundle of bark-cloth and the pandanus mat to him in payment for his work he asked that the other half of the trunk might be preserved and later hewn into another canoe. The amount of goods that he took was rather larger than normal, partly because Pa Raŋifuri was a chief's heir, but partly also to provide a basis for his request. Here we see factors of family sentiment entering into an economic situation and conditioning rates of exchange.

The economist might regard this as a response to partial monopoly ; the Tikopia look upon it as a concession to standard cultural attitudes, proper and necessary in order to save useful material.

## EXCHANGE IN A PERSONALIZED ECONOMY

We may now summarize the general features of the Tikopia exchange system, and try to suggest the kind of social factors on which this system depends.

In the first place Tikopia acts of exchange are not characterized by an appeal to a general market ; they are essentially a series of individual transactions. But this does not mean an entire absence of valuations. Linguistically, and in material comparisons, ideas of equivalence and greater or less worth are in operation. Things have comparative utility, though in the absence of a price mechanism or common denominator, and of a widespread exchange system, there is no close measure of comparison. The absence of a price system means that personal knowledge of conditions replaces the more automatic money regulator of relations between producers and consumers, and acts as a rough indicator of potential demand.

Again, in the demand situation of the Tikopia " buyer " and the reception of the counter-article by the " seller " an element of interest in social advantage rather than in material gain plays a large part. This may even run counter to the ordinary propositions of economic analysis. There is an absence of an " interest " convention for loans of capital ; exchange can be forced ; labour is estimated as a social obligation and service ; and the convention is that the labourer brings to the " entrepreneur " what is in effect a contribution towards his own reward.

To understand the workings of the Tikopia economy one needs then at some points a radically different series of assumptions about conduct in exchange than those which serve to explain the operation of our commercial markets.

In all these transactions the Tikopia work on what are in effect conventional exchange rates. The sanctions which stand behind these rates do not allow of much elasticity of response to changes in supply or demand. But they do not mean simply an automatic conformity to an arbitrary rule of custom, once established, and followed insensately ; they fluctuate according to specific conditions, and their efficacy is linked essentially with the concept of reciprocity. This principle, which has been shown by Thurnwald, Malinowski, Mauss, and Maunier to be extremely important in primitive societies, is one of the foundations of Tikopia social relationships. In the economic sphere, it supplies the long-period view which is necessary to the working of the conventional exchange rate. This rate is by implication not for the immediate individual transaction alone, but for an infinite series of transactions in which the idea of reciprocity is embedded.[1]

---

[1] Incidently, the general sphere of exchange, and the mechanisms of reciprocity and delayed payments give no support to such statements as those of Marshall that " modern methods of trade imply habits of trustfulness and a

Fluctuations in demand and supply which on a short-period view threaten the conventional rate are met by the promise of future transactions in which any balance of advantage will be reversed. This may be interpreted as a fixed present return plus a fluctuating future return. And in this situation super-economic advantages have their place : maintenance of one's kinship position, of one's social position as a *taŋata laui* (a good man), and relative freedom from slander, are all factors to be considered. It may be asked if these conventional rates do not sometimes change. They may do. The explanation is presumably that in this case the perception of immediate economic advantage by some individuals is too strong to be withstood by the long-period advantages. (The influence of personality on social and political institutions may be compared with this.)

It is useless to inquire into the historical reasons which have provided the Tikopia with this type of economic system, lacking a price mechanism to facilitate it. But some of the major predisposing features may be indicated, at least as a hypothesis. One of these seems to be the absence of any significant external market (that of Vanikoro and Anuta is negligible). Concerned for some centuries only with an internal market, the personal relations of producer and consumer enter into their economic position and condition the evaluation of goods and estimate of requirements. The essence of a modern price economy is its impersonality. An essential feature of the primitive system is the control of the good faith of the giver by manifold relations with him, and his endeavour to keep faith in view of these relationships. Our commercial system is characterized on the whole by the want of concern for the satisfactions of the other party to the contract, once it is concluded. The principle of *caveat emptor* would not function well in a primitive society.

This absence of an external market is only one factor. Another is the small size of the community ; if it were very large then the conditions of an external market would tend to be created *ipso facto* for small units in it. But the smallness of a community alone is not a determining factor in its economic arrangements,

power of resisting temptation to dishonesty which do not exist among a backward people ". (*Principles of Economics,* 7.) Trust and honesty do exist among primitive peoples, without any written or even verbal contract, not necessarily because of moral virtue, but because the social norms demand them, and continued attempts at evasion would lead to a severance of vital social and economic relations.

as witness the trading groups of New Guinea coast (Trobriands, Manus, Tami, Wogeo, etc.) who range far afield with products for exchange.[1]

Allied with the small size of the community is the personal character of the economic relations of its people. Linked with this is the estimation of ultimate social advantage as more important than immediate material gain. This means that all members of the community must share the same idea of where their advantage lies ; they must have a set of unified social conventions by which to regulate their own behaviour and give to that of others the requisite degree of predictability. These conventions have been discussed fairly fully in the course of this book—rules of kinship and hospitality ; bond-friendship ; obligations of initiation and mourning ; concepts of labour as a service to be rendered ; freedom in the use of planting land ; moral views as to goodness and badness in these matters. Christians in Tikopia at the present day respond in common with the pagans to the authority of these conventions, even when they are backed by the old native religion. (Religious differences have made a breach in the community, but kinship and chieftainship still bridge it to some extent.)

These factors seem to provide the major clue to the nature of the Tikopia economy ; they are the basic conditions which are correlated with it. That they are substantially accurate as an explanation is seen by the fact that similar conditions of sinking economic advantage in favour of wider social advantage tend to occur in other small communities which are tolerably self-sufficient, even in the villages of Europe, and that in the smallest economic unit, the family, they are predominant. Here, above all, economic principles of exchange of services and distribution of goods are held in subordination to wider social ends in which, however disguised as sacrifice or other moral idea, the concept of reciprocity plays a large part.

A comment on the thesis of Karl Bücher is of interest at this point. Bücher's system of stages of economic evolution regarded primitive societies as either engaged in a " pre-economic " individual search for food, or practising an " independent household economy ".[2] On the question of fact Bücher was certainly

---

[1] Note that the small size of a community does not mean that everyone has access to all types of goods ; there is strong ownership, complex exchange, and the specific making of some objects for exchange.

[2] K. Bücher, *Industrial Evolution* (transl. of 3rd German ed.), 1901, 1–89.

wrong. But he would have been right if he had laid stress in his second stage not on the factual identification but on the similitude. As investigation has shewn, a primitive economy of the Polynesian or Melanesian type is not simply a household economy, but the wider economic relations of the people *resemble* in many respects those of a household. Such characteristics of the household as the forgoing of present economic advantage for future social advantage ; and the treatment of labour as an obligation, and a service not requiring exact indemnification, are found in the wider primitive community. This is feasible since the relations of the people concerned are manifold and are intended to endure, not to lapse after the immediate economic relationship has ended. They constitute a kinship economy. In a sense then, primitive economy and household economy are species of a single genus— the " small unit economy " not oriented to an external market.

That a primitive economic system is correlated with these factors mentioned above, and is not the outgrowth of an intrinsic type of primitive mind *per se*, is seen by the behaviour of the people when they come under the influence of a European economic system. Given an external market to regulate the conditions of supply and demand, with an enlargement of the scale of economic relationships, these tend to become more impersonal ; there is more insistence of immediate and exact indemnification of services ; the transfer of goods by gift is replaced by barter and sale ; exchange can no longer be enforced by appeal to weakened social sanctions ; a price mechanism is introduced, and operated by the people among themselves. The initial period may be one of some strain to the people, in the conflict of the two sets of norms, and some of the economic transactions may seem incomprehensible to Europeans, but the adjustment is finally made.

## CHAPTER X

# CHARACTERISTICS OF A PRIMITIVE ECONOMY

OUR survey of the economic life of the Tikopia has revealed the complex fabric of social institutions which serve to regulate the satisfaction of material wants among a primitive island community. We find here no trace of the artificial concepts by which the economic behaviour of primitive man has been sometimes interpreted : the opposed figments of " primitive communism " and the " individual search for food " now appear as equally barren principles of interpretation, " Man Friday " and the " nuts for arrows " savage alike disappear, while the popular idyllic picture of the Golden Age primitive man sitting beneath his tree and waiting for the fruit to fall before him is seen to find no place in a community where the struggle to wrest a livelihood from the environment is a very definite reality.

The means by which this problem is met by the Tikopia have been the theme of this work. We have sketched the forms of productive organization and of the principles of exchange, distribution, and consumption, observing the way in which these are affected by kinship obligations, the institutions of chieftainship, by magico-religious beliefs and practices, and by the system of values embedded in the cultural tradition. We have noted the chronological sequence of economic activities, observing how these are fitted in with other pursuits which profoundly affect their incidence and intensity, sometimes stimulating the forces of production when the demands of ceremonial call for unusual productive effort, and at other times causing a complete cessation of work through the obligations of funeral etiquette or the imposition of taboos.

Realizing the manner in which these social elements interpenetrate and overlay the economic organization, and finding none of the complex industrial and commercial institutions which form the subject matter of modern economics, we might even be tempted to deny the existence of Tikopia *economics* in the sense in which the term is ordinarily employed. Yet the facts remain that problems involving the provision of material goods and questions of human material welfare do exist in

Tikopia, and they are solved by an organized and intelligible system of activity.

This type of problem is not new to the anthropologist. In the sphere of law he has been faced with the anomaly that whereas the elaborate legal institutions of modern civilization are mainly lacking among primitive peoples, these communities have none the less organized methods of dealing with murderers, thieves, and adulterers. The resolution of such anomalies is not to be found in a simple denial of the existence of " law " or " economics " among primitive peoples, but in the wider re-formulation of the existing theories, concepts, definitions, and methodology which have been employed in dealing with our own highly specialized society.

We may now attempt to answer in summary form some of the questions raised at the end of the first Chapter. It is evident that the basic aspects of the Tikopia economy do correspond to the data of ordinary economic analysis, and can be covered by the same general propositions. There is a scarcity of the means available for satisfying wants, these wants are arranged on a broad scale of preferences, and on the whole choice is exercised in a rational manner in deciding how the means to hand shall be disposed of. The employment of the factors of production is governed by some recognition of the advantages of the division of labour and specialization in employments according to differential skill, and economies of scale are also secured in an elementary way in agriculture, fishing, and other co-operative work. Productive equipment and other goods are accumulated specifically to engage in further production, so that one may speak of the employment of capital, though it does not fulfil all the functions of this factor in a modern industrial system. Moreover, there is an implicit concept of a margin in the use of the various factors of production, as in the transference of labour from one area of land to another according to variation in its productive capacity, or from one type of fishing to another according to the conditions operating at the time, or in the tendency for the size of the working group to vary directly with type of employment. In certain fields of the Tikopia economy there is therefore some realization of the operation of the law of diminishing returns. Again, there is a system of property rights which regulate the relations of producers and consumers to resources and to the things produced. Finally, notions of value can be said to exist with the forces of supply and demand as a regulating influence, though these are not expressed through a general system of exchange of commodities, or a price system such as we know it.

Certain other aspects do not conform to the type of situation envisaged by current economic analysis. It is not only that the level of material achievement is elementary compared with our own, and that the whole fabric of the economic setting lacks the complexity of an industrial concentration, a banking and monetary system, and a position in the scheme of international trade. Nor is it that the Tikopia economy is a skeleton system, with the bare bones of the articulation of resources and wants showing because of poverty, and a population too tiny to indulge in complication. It is an economy complex along its own lines, rich in personal relationships, and in concepts of exchange of goods and services, but arranging these to fit a scheme of wants dictated by a variety of cultural values. It is a primitive economy on the material side ; and in its absence of any marked progressive development of technique it may be termed a stationary economy. But its positive character is given not by its poverty of resources or by its simple technique for using them, or by the limitations of its knowledge of the further potentialities in the resources. It is rather in what may be loosely termed the modalities of its economic system that its essential difference lies.

In the first place the Tikopia economy is non-competitive in the sense that there is no constant and admitted struggle between producers to offer their goods to sets of consumers also in competition among themselves. And there is no attempt by producers to thrust themselves forward by generating new wants in consumers, and little or no attempt by consumers to have new wants met in ways in which will lead to revolutionized methods of production. Where there is competition it is in social emulation rather than in economic emulation *per se*. Again, there is in production a high degree of mobility of labour and capital, due not only to the elementary character of specialization in employments, but also to the limitations placed upon the use of private property by social requirements, and by the traditionalized concepts of conversion whereby the same object is acceptable without change of form in a variety of different functions. Bark-cloth accumulated as a consumer's good for clothing, a ritual offering, or an indemnity payment, can be used instead as a means to pay for the production of a canoe, or as a medium of exchange in a complex series of ceremonial transfers. Yet though there is this great horizontal mobility there is not the same vertical mobility. There are to some extent closed circuits of exchange of objects and services of different kind, defined by a traditionally dictated scheme of values in which certain types of commodity are regarded as appropriate to specific social situations. Again, labour is a social service, not merely an economic service, and the reward for it takes this into consideration. Exchange, too, is conditioned by the kinship and other bonds between " buyer " and " seller ", is circumscribed by widely operative conventions about loans bearing no interest, and when it does take place is often designed to meet other wants than that for the goods in themselves.

In brief, economic relationships are also explicitly social relationships.

This may be put in another way in the form of three pro-positions. First, that an important feature of the Tikopia system is the personalization of its economic relations, as contrasted with the impersonal relations of participants in the economic field which are at least theoretically true of our own society. Secondly, the operation of the profit-motive is conditioned by other psychological factors concerning the social role of the accumulation and use of wealth. Thirdly, there is a code of reciprocity in economic transactions, but this is but part of a wider code which obtains for all types of social relationship, which linguistically as well as practically are brought into line with it, and receive much more overt and institutionalized expression than in our type of society.

It will probably be agreed, however, that the differences between a primitive economy and a civilized economy, as far as the " spirit " of the relationships is concerned, are quantita-tive rather than qualitative. To some degree the elements characteristic of Tikopia can be paralleled in modern industrial life.

A review of the somewhat limited material available for other primitive communities would show that the characteristic features of the Tikopia economy are widely found. But considering the variety of institutionalized economic arrangements that have been recorded it is evident that Tikopia is but one of a series of types. An important problem for the comparative economist is then, granted that the basic economic principles are valid for a primitive as for a civilized economy, to define the types of particular system in which these principles operate, so as to use them for the interpretation of actual economic behaviour. What indices of classification of these types of economic system can be adopted ?

It is not my province to examine these here. But it may be suggested that such indices can be found in the spheres from which the economist ordinarily takes the " given factors " in his analysis. These might include :

   (i)   The dominant technique of production, with reference to the relative frequency of the various techniques employed.

  (ii)   The system of exchange, considering the amount of dependence upon external markets, and the existence of internal markets.

 (iii)   The existence of a price system. Here it may be necessary to distinguish a non-price type from others with an embryonic, a partial, or a fully operative price mechanism.

 (iv)   The system of control of the means of production, by reference to the forms of ownership, and inequalities in the possession of resources.

  (v)   The system of regulation of consumers' choices.

 (vi)   The nature of the ties between the participants in the economic process—the degree of personalization involved, control by factors of tradition, ritual, etc.

The separation of types of primitive economy hitherto has relied primarily upon the first of these indices ; more adequate classification would seem to require a consideration of them all in conjunction.

A general problem of interpretation emerges from the method of analysis of the Tikopia economy, and propositions about its character, which have been given in this book. How relevant is the role of the non-economic factors which have so frequently appeared in the treatment ? To answer this question we may remind ourselves of the position of some modern economists as described in Chapter I.

Three associated postulates are taken by such an economist as necessary to his formal analysis : that economic activity consists in the application of scarce means to alternative ends ; that this application is governed by principles of rational choice ; and that the aim of all individuals engaged in economic activity is to maximize their satisfactions. And there is often an express rejection of the validity of any inquiry into the nature of the ends themselves, of why one is preferred to another, and of the kind of satisfaction that is derived when they are secured.

But as an anthropologist I have had occasion to examine the importance of a wide range of " non-economic " factors to the processes of production, distribution, and exchange in Tikopia. Is there any defence for this procedure from an economist's point of view ? My reasons are in the first place that unless the nature of the ends desired by the people be understood, and their relative strength be compared, it is not possible to explain why at any given moment there is a change in the volume of production, a diversion from one factor of production to another, an increase or diminution in any single factor. Without understanding the weight attached to kinship obligations in Tikopia, and the ritual conventions of mourning for dead kin, one cannot explain a sudden failure to employ productive equipment such as canoes and nets, and a diversion from fishing to agriculture at a period when fishing would give a yield apparently greater than that on the agricultural margin. It might be argued that from the economic point of view all that it is necessary to know is that such a diversion takes place, and to estimate its effects on the economic system by logical processes of analysis. But the result would be an analysis which would lack reality, and which would rule out the possibility of prediction for the future, save on the basis of averages, which would need data for longer periods of time than the anthropologist can afford.

Couching the argument in terms of maximization of satisfactions would not be of much value here. If all conduct in the economic sphere is directed to maximizing the individual's satisfactions, then this becomes meaningless as an aid to the interpretation of changes in demand, or differential application of the factors of production, unless an attempt is made to examine the various types of satisfaction aimed at, and consider how they influence one another. If a Tikopia drops his digging stick and lets his taro plants wither where they lie in order to go and wail at his aunt's funeral, or breaks up a canoe because his nephew has committed suicide by going off to sea, or refrains from canoe-building because loud noise is taboo while the yam seed is still unplanted, it can be postulated that this change in his activity or destruction of his property is a choice made with consideration of the alternatives, that the satisfaction he gets from his choice is greater than he would have got from adopting the other alternative course of action, and that for the economic analysis the important thing is the effect produced. But it is doubtful if it is permissible to compare the different types of satisfaction involved in this simple way if any generalization is required to explain fluctuations in economic activity. It is true that the concept of maximization of satisfactions is employed to describe only a long run tendency ; but it has been somewhat crudely asserted that a long run is only a combination of a number of short runs, to each of which analysis should be applied if possible. Again, as far as Tikopia is concerned, I have shown that the processes of exchange which result in extensive transfers of goods, with considerable effect upon the system of production, may embody satisfactions not directly arising from the nature of the goods themselves, but from the fact of exchange in itself. This has far-reaching repercussions upon the system of production and the economic process as a whole—as it would in our society if people bought clothing, groceries, and tools in large amounts, and sold them again or gave them away not simply for their utility as consumer's goods, but for the satisfaction of maintaining social relations with the persons from whom they got them and to whom they handed them on. But where such cases occur in our society they form but a small proportion of the total volume of transactions.

The postulate of rational choice can also be examined from this point of view. This is intelligible for a primitive community if it be admitted that it is rational for such choice to be largely dictated by the traditional pattern of the institutions and values of the culture. In theory, the ends presented to the individual are alternatives, and he is at liberty to decide between them on the basis of the relative satisfactions they yield him ; in practice he may follow one, with or without conscious deliberation, because his social circumstances prescribe it for him.[1] The interest of the modern economist in notions of an imperfect market, in " irrational " consumer's preferences, and in the " frictions " of the economic mechanism, as well as in the concrete phenomena of exchange control or the planning of dictators, is all part of an admission that the formal theory of free and rational choice between ends needs to be supplemented

---

[1] To use the term "irrational" to describe much primitive economic behaviour seems to me inadvisable, in the absence of an exact definition of its meaning. See R. Thurnwald, *op. cit.*, 177 (cf. also 285 ibid.), and R. H. Lowie, *op. cit.*, 216.

by subsidiary postulates about human behaviour in defined cultural situations in order that actual economic organization may be adequately treated.

In stressing therefore that a native economic situation cannot be understood without a study of the effects produced by cultural factors of a wider kind, some of the conclusions from the Tikopia material may be mentioned again. For example the economic initiative of a chief may act as an incentive towards large scale labour on the part of others ; or at other times his action may cause abstention from labour, as when people would dig up their lands for cultivation to provide food for the future if the chief did not forbid them, or draw upon their supplies of coco-nut. Here the strictly economic motive is conditioned and inhibited by respect for authority, and a choice is made not on the basis of each individual's own estimate of his food requirements and the most advantageous utilization of his resources, but by the chief's example in the one case and fiat in the other, supported by the values attached to his personality and his position. For the time being he is in the situation of a dictator, or final consumer, upon whose choice all other choices by his clan depend. And this being so, the reasons for his choice are relevant, if only one wishes to understand the periodicity of such phenomena. Again, let us consider the fishing which takes place after the annual ritual consecration of a canoe. The greatest desire of the natives at this time is that a shark may be caught, and to this end a considerable amount of time is spent in fishing with large tackle. If this is successful on the first expedition and a shark is caught, the fishing with large tackle is continued the next night, but not to the same extent ; less time is spent on this, and more attention is devoted to the netting of flying-fish, an occupation which gives a more certain yield. But if a shark is not caught on the first occasion, energy is not diverted to the netting of flying-fish to the same extent, or to work on shore—the fishing with large tackle is assiduously pursued, perhaps to the detriment of the total food supply, and much time is spent on long ritual appeals. The choice between a continuation of intensive shark fishing as against the diversion of energy towards the netting of flying-fish is here determined by whether a single shark has been caught, the stress placed upon this depending upon the need to have shark, additional to flying-fish, to offer as an appeasement to the gods.

If no shark is caught, custom requires a repetition of the offering of flying-fish in lieu of the shark.

In this case ritual needs dictate productive effort in a field of less profit for the time being. And a further modification has taken place as a result of the introduction of Christianity among the people of Faea. With this change in the ritual system the need for concentration upon shark fishing to the partial exclusion of other kinds of fishing has disappeared, while the time and energy expended upon ritual appeals for shark has been diverted towards other ends.

The emphasis upon the influence of such non-economic motives in the economic behaviour of the Tikopia is necessary as a *caveat* to the popular tendency, in our own society, to regard the profit-seeking motive as "natural". In our own civilization the occurrence of elaborate institutions, such as the money market and the stock exchange, offer striking examples of the operation of strictly economic transactions and behaviour in response to the profit motive acting to all intents and purposes in isolation. The result of this is the partial realization of the traditional economist's picture of economic motives operating under "ideal" conditions. If the supply decreases, demand remaining the same, prices "tend" to rise, the adaptability of sellers to this situation being limited by peripheral factors such as ignorance or inertia only. But in a primitive economy the equilibrium may be re-established in a different manner. There is in Tikopia a system of friendly borrowing, by those in need from those with stocks in hand, of goods of which the supply has temporarily decreased; and this borrowing is not at a premium. On the contrary, the goods borrowed at such times are subsequently repaid at a time of increased supply by the same amount as that borrowed; that is, in terms of modern exchange economy, by a repayment of less than the equivalent of the original value borrowed. In other words, a temporary shortage in supply is met by what we might call "dis-hoarding" at a discount.

Such contrasts between the generally accepted norms of our own society and the economic behaviour of the Tikopia might lead us to describe the latter as "bound by custom" or "not alive to their economic advantage". Such is not the purpose of the present argument. The Tikopia native, like all primitive people, is a realist, and is keenly alive to economic considerations ;

he recognizes the necessary relation between labour and production, and embodies this in the ethical values attached to work ; he is keenly critical of the quantity and quality of the goods which he receives in exchange ; and, most important of all, he is quite ready, at times by evasion, to secure his own economic advancement in spite of the dictates of tradition which impose irksome self-denial. It is not a case of a simple contrast between economic advantage and the inertia of traditional ways of behaving—rather do the traditionally dictated patterns of behaviour limit and define the lines of action along which economic advantage is pursued. And one of these limitations lies in the fact that advantage is *not* habitually taken of a fall in supply in order to increase the exchange value of commodities. To state the case in general terms, primitive man is definitely alive to his economic advantage, but his traditional background does not allow him to treat this as the universal, unique, and dominant imperative in the determination of his behaviour.

So far we have been comparing generalizations from the Tikopia economy with those from some aspects of formal economics.

But a special type of approach to the problem with which we are dealing is adopted by one Marxist school of " historical materialism ". This theoretical point of view is of particular interest to the anthropologist in that it stresses two general assumptions which are of great importance. Firstly, that the specific principles formulated in relation to the data of modern capitalistic systems are not necessarily applicable to all human communities, and secondly, that there is a basic interrelationship between economic facts on the one hand and non-economic institutions, values, and motives on the other. With this the anthropologist is in agreement. But the essential principle of historical materialism is the ætiological primacy of one set of factors within this complex, namely the level of development reached by the productive factors and the methods of production, and linked with it is a methodological stress upon the chronological aspect of this set of causal factors throughout human evolution.

Against such a view the anthropologist has two objections. In the first place as a theory of change it is based upon certain assumptions concerning the evolution of society from postulated communistic forms which are nowhere open to observation, through the various forms of primitive and feudal society to modern capitalism, and so on or back to communism again. This is not the place to enter into a discussion of the evolutionary theory originally formulated by Morgan, used polemically by Engels, and more recently adopted as the official *credo* of the leading ethnologists of the U.S.S.R.[1] But it is clear that such a theory can be of little use to the anthropologist who is interested in the dynamic, present-day significance of the facts of native life.  When a Tikopia fisherman gives a share of his catch to another man without any immediate return, to describe this as a " survival " of " primitive communism " merely distorts the native reality, for the giver very definitely expects a corresponding return at some future date.  Or when a chief uses his authority for his own economic advancement against the interests and public opinion of his community, it helps us little to describe this act as an embryonic emergence of individual acquisitiveness from communism.  Admittedly chronological interpretations, both for the past and future, may follow from a detailed empirical investigation of the observable phenomena of the present, but this investigation is merely stultified when it proceeds from initial *a priori* assumptions as to what human society was like in the past and what it is likely to develop into in the future.

This objection to the historical or evolutionary approach is more concerned with the methodology actually employed in anthropological science than with abstract epistemology.  The suggestion is not that such evolutionary speculations are from their very nature scientifically impossible or undesirable.  But in the actual history of anthropology reconstructions have been founded upon inadequate evidence, tenuous hypotheses have been regarded as established laws, and above all the stress upon the past has largely prevented the study of present-day reality.[2] Those ethnographic facts which, vital as they may be in the

[1] *Vide* the articles by representative anthropologists in *Ethnography, Folklore and Archæology in the U.S.S.R.*, Voks, iv, 1933.

[2] This position is of course by no means confined to Marxist anthropology. The later work of Morgan and of W. H. R. Rivers, each of whom in his earlier writings produced a most valuable study of the ethnographic reality of a primitive culture (*League of the Iroquois*, 1851 ; *The Todas*, 1906), is open to grave objection on this score.  But nowhere is this distortion of observation by evolutionary hypotheses so marked as in the work of Soviet ethnographers in the sphere of kinship, where the hunt for " survivals " has concentrated attention on the bare formalities of kinship terminology and unusual, sporadic deviations of custom cited in records which any modern anthropologist regards as superficial and out of date.  Against these striking and supposedly archaic variations in kinship usage the more universal and significant, though less spectacular, aspects of

dynamics of culture, do not fit neatly into the evolutionary scheme have been ignored or distorted. But in considering how societies actually work and the totality of forces operative in social organization, the field-worker is forced not only to admit, but to record, study and analyse a vast range of present-day facts which the limited view of the evolutionist usually leads him to ignore.

Apart from this general methodological objection there is a more fundamental difference between the outlook of the social anthropologist and that of the Marxist, namely the postulate of the latter as to the primacy of productive· organization as a social determinant.

It is here that the social anthropologist would insist upon a multiple as opposed to a unitary determinism. On a sociological level he would not for one moment deny that every phase of social life—religion, kinship and political organization—must be related to the material implements of production and the organization which regulates their use in economic life. But the study and analysis of such relationships is only one of the many sets of functional inter-connections which must be traced out in the investigation of cultural facts. Thus, in considering the family, the anthropologist insists upon the basic sentiments (empirically ascertained) of sexual attraction, parental affection, and social prestige as essential determinants, though these cannot be considered apart from the motives arising through economic co-operation within the family and in wider social groups. Systems of law, again, are directly correlated with economic institutions through the principles of land tenure and the rules of property. But they are seen to depend primarily upon the fact that in all communities investigated the disruptive elements existing in the greed, envy, malice or lust of exceptional individuals are inhibited by some mechanism of social control. In considering such institutions as chieftainship, the systems of rank are demonstrably correlated with inequalities in the distribution of wealth and with the privileged direction of productive enterprise. But they also depend upon the tendency towards the social emergence of standards of personal value, which are perpetuated through the individual family (as in hereditary systems) or by the recognized

human kinship (revealed by the work of Malinowski, Radcliffe-Brown, Margaret Mead, Warner, Schapera, Audrey Richards, Fortune and many others) have been brushed aside as subsequent and therefore irrelevant developments, or as biased interpretations of the data.

admission of individuals into the privileged class not only on the basis of wealth, but also through prowess in war, technical and ritual knowledge or merely age. These processes are seen by the anthropologist to be universal. They depend upon a variety of determinants, upon individual differences in temperament and intelligence, upon the social regulation of human vanity, and upon the need for efficiency in economic and social control.

This point of view has led the anthropologist to a reformulation of the old contrast between " individualism " and " communism ".[1] For him, this antithesis is a false one, for he would hold that the two sets of motives, and the two forms of organization, co-exist. Certainly this is the case in Tikopia where individual evasion and " exploitation " exist side by side with, and manifest themselves in spite of, strong mechanisms of social control and regulations in the interests of community welfare. The limitations placed upon individual greed and acquisitiveness are of three kinds : firstly, there is the force of tradition, the binding obligations of kinship, respect for rank, and magico-religious taboo. Secondly, there is the lack of the means for individual economic assertion, the low level of material culture and the limited range of possible satisfactions. And, finally, there is the difficulty of evasion, the fact that in a small island community public opinion is hard to deceive, easily mobilized and effective by reason of the close and intimate nature of the personal bonds uniting the members of the community. But subject to these limitations, and sometimes in spite of them, individual greed operates. A chief may use his position for economic advancement in spite of public criticism and the traditions of his rank ; the introduction of European material goods has provided new expressions for the desire for individual wealth. And finally the force of public opinion in inhibiting greed is only effective because of the publicity of most economic activities—in canoe fishing, the amount of the catch is known by everybody, and pilfering is very difficult ; but in a communal fish drive it is possible for men to secrete fish in their loin-cloths and in fact they do so.

These facts have a bearing upon modern economic problems considered in their more normative aspect, that is when the value of change in the existing forms of production, exchange, and distribution is under consideration. Consideration of the

[1] See B. Malinowski, *Crime and Custom*, 18–21, 28–32.

Tikopia material might seem to point a moral for our own society. There is in Tikopia a community in which (barring droughts and shortage) everybody is fed, where there is little difference in individual wealth, as compared with the enormous inequalities of modern capitalist society, and where social tradition and community welfare, as opposed to the motive of individual profit, play a very much greater part.    But application of these generalizations to our civilized conditions would be meaningless. Consider, for example, the factors limiting individual greed, to which reference has been made above : in the first place in modern European society the tradition of religion, morals, and even recreation is different. Secondly, the vast range of material culture, and the almost infinite variety of material satisfactions provide powerful incentives towards the acquisition of wealth, which simply do not exist in Tikopia.    The absence of unity of cultural ideals, norms of group conduct and individual training lead to an opposition of interests and a differential statement of social obligations.    Finally, the size of our social groupings and the essentially private character of individual life facilitate evasion and make difficult the mobilization of public opinion and public repression in order to enforce communal obligations. The inference is, therefore, that social change must take into account the whole body of existing institutions and values which go to make up a culture.

Comparative studies of economic systems, whether dictated by scientific interest or reformatory zeal, must employ concepts which will fit the facts of primitive life as well as the specialized developments of modern communities.    Assumptions which can be made with some assurance for our own highly depersonalized society are not necessarily valid for others. For primitive communities the anthropologist is in a position to offer suggestions as to what form these assumptions should take, and to what extent they should supplement those of existing economic theory. At the same time it will be obvious that he himself must refine his analysis a great deal more, and define his categories much more carefully before really valuable comparison can be made.

| | JULY | AUGUST | SEPTEMBER | OCTOBER | NOVEMBER | DECEMB |
|---|---|---|---|---|---|---|
| | ←————————— Toŋa —————————→ | | | ←————— Raki ————— | | |
| **PRODUCTION OF VEGETABLE FOOD** | Ground cleared for taro, yams, manioc.<br><br>Breadfruit harvest.<br><br>Pastes eaten (time of scarcity). | Taro planting.<br><br>Yam planting.<br><br>Manioc planting.<br><br>Taboo on coconuts in Rofaea lifted. | Taro planting (sporadic).<br><br>Sago prepared. | Taro planting (increasing).<br><br>Taboo on coconuts in Faea imposed.<br><br>Forest foods gathered during period of mourning.<br><br>Store pastes utilized. | Ground cleared for taro.<br><br>Taro planting.<br><br>Yam planting.<br><br>Breadfruit harvest. | Breadfruit harvest.<br><br>Bananas ga▾<br><br>Breadfruit ▾ made. |
| **FISHING** | Reef fishing.<br><br>Canoe fishing in Tafua taboo owing to mourning. | Seine-net fishing for mackerel.<br><br>Mourning taboo in Tafua lifted.<br><br>Reef fishing. | Canoe and reef fishing.<br><br>Opening of channel to lake (te ava).<br><br>Lake fishing. | Canoe and reef fishing taboo in Faea.<br><br>Lake fishing. | Canoe fishing everywhere.<br><br>Seine-net fishing.<br><br>Taboo in Faea lifted.<br><br>Lake fishing.<br><br>Crabs ; bird netting. | Canoe fishi▾ |
| **ARTS AND CRAFTS** | Bark-cloth prepared for initiation ceremony. | Bark-cloth prepared.<br><br>Ritual manufacture of turmeric (9 days). | Bark-cloth prepared.<br><br>Canoe built.<br><br>Woodwork. | Much plaiting of mats and beating of bark-cloth. | Tafua net made.<br><br>Canoe repairing. | Canoe build▾ |
| **SOCIAL ACTIVITIES** | Tafua in mourning ; games played in Faea ; no dancing. | Work of the Gods.<br><br>Initiation ritual (5 days).<br><br>1 Funeral.<br><br>Games ; no dancing in Faea. | Repair of sacred oven house of Taumako.<br><br>3 Funerals.<br><br>Games ; no dancing in Faea ; mourning almost lifted in Tafua. | Initiates return to Faea ; funeral of brother of Ariki Tafua ; funeral of child ; dancing in Raveŋa, none in Faea ; dispute over orchards.<br><br>Young men in Faea limed heads in preparation for dance. | Kafika taro harvest rite.<br><br>Funeral.<br><br>Work of the Gods.<br><br>No dancing. | Ritual danc▾ Raveŋa.<br><br>Secular dan▾ Faea.<br><br>Dance festi▾ |

FIG. 12.—CHART OF ECONOMIC AN▾

| January | February | March | April | May | June |
|---|---|---|---|---|---|
| ————RAKI————→ | | | ←————TOŊA———— | | |
| ɔoo on coco-nuts Faea lifted. / nanas gathered. / estnuts thered. | Taro planting. / Breadfruit harvest. / Sago prepared. / Coco-nuts gathered. / Bananas gathered. | Taro crop more plentiful. / Taro planting. / Yam planting. / Breadfruit harvest. / Coco-nuts gathered. | Taro fields mulched. / Communal sago ovens (food shortage). / Coco-nuts gathered. / Forest foods gathered during scarcity. | Taro planting (sporadic). / Breadfruit appearing. / Pastes eaten. | Taro planting. / Manioc harvest. / (Sago dominates diet.) / Thefts of coco-nuts and yams. / Forest foods. / Pastes eaten. |
| ɔoe fishing minished. / h channel ened (te ava). / ving for green ail. | Sporadic lake and sea fishing. | Sporadic sea fishing. / Bonito fishing. / Lake fishing. / Crabs. / Diving for green snail. | Sporadic sea fishing. / Reef fishing. | Sporadic sea fishing (few fish caught). / Birds netted. | Turtle caught. / Seine net fishing. / Fish channel opened. |
| t making. / ɔoe building. / e felled for noe. | Net making. / Houses rebuilt. | Sacred Canoe of Ariki Kafika repaired. | Bark-cloth prepared. | Bark-cloth prepared. | Bark-cloth prepared. / Sinnet cord plaiting. |
| ness of son of riki Tafua. / e ; houses rengthened. / ki Taumako sited Ariki afua. / nce festivals. / ts between iefs. Sighteing tour. | Illness of Ariki Tafua. Funeral of children. Attempts at voyages. / Dancing in Raveŋa only. / Anger of Ariki Taumako. | 1 Funeral. / Attempted suicide voyage. / Exchange of gifts between bond-friends. | Rite for rain by Ariki Tafua. / Marriage ceremony. / Dance festivals. / Dart matches. | Ariki Kafika living in Faea. Illness of Ariki Taumako. Ariki Faŋarare performed rite to avert disease. Dancing ; funeral of child ; initiation ritual. | Work of Gods begun. / Funeral rite of Tafua. |

SOCIAL ACTIVITIES, 1928–1929.

## SYNOPTIC RECORD OF A TIKOPIA YEAR (1928–1929)

The aim of this Diagram is to give a synoptic picture of the institutional activity of the Tikopia over their two seasons which together approximate to our calendar year, and in particular to indicate how their economic activities are fitted in with their social and ceremonial events. The Diagram is divided into sections corresponding to our months, not because these have any significance for the Tikopia, but because they provide a most convenient frame of reference.

The material is taken from the daily records of my diary, written up every evening. While it was not possible to observe all the doings of people in other parts of the island than that in which I was living, the inter-relationships between the various groups made it possible to obtain news of events of major importance, to attend some phases of them, and to keep in touch with what was happening in my absence.

It will be understood that at any given moment the life of the Tikopia community showed to external observation a mosaic of events. Some people were engaged in ceremonies, others in craft work, others in ordinary food-procuring tasks. A day later there was usually a re-grouping in terms of new social events. And at times a single event was so significant for the community as a whole—a dance festival or the illness of a chief—that the energies of all the groups in the island were oriented to some degree towards it.

The following summary shows the type and number of major social events which occurred during my stay ; they all had direct economic repercussions of one kind or another.

*Events in the Individual Life Cycle*

| | | |
|---|---|---|
| Births . . . . . 60 | (approx. 5 still births, no ceremony) |
| Initiations . . . . 2 | (1 of 2 and the other of 3 boys) |
| Marriages . . . . . 3 | |
| Illnesses and Injuries Ceremonialized . . . 6 | |
| Funerals . . . . . 15 | (21 deaths, but 5 still births and 1 death of a child a fortnight old had no ritual). In addition 1 burial of grave clothes of boy lost at sea earlier. |

*Major Productive Events*

| | | |
|---|---|---|
| Building of canoes . . . | 4 | (and 1 repaired) |
| Nets made by chiefs . . . | 3 | |
| Sago ovens . . . . | 15 | approx. |

*Recreation*

| | | |
|---|---|---|
| Secular dance festivals . | 13 | |
| Sight-seeing Tour . . . | 1 | |
| Dart Matches . . . . | 5 | approx. |

*Fortuitous Events*

| | | |
|---|---|---|
| Demonstrations by chiefs and group quarrels . . . | 6 | |
| Visits between chiefs . . . | 5 | |
| Attempted voyages . . . | 5 | (also 1 threatened group voyage) |
| Hurricane . . . . | 1 | |
| House burnt . . . . | 1 | |

*Religious Events*

| | | |
|---|---|---|
| Specific Rites, not part of series . | 5 | |
| Rites of Work of Gods . . | 3 | periods of approx. 6 weeks each. |

Without taking these figures too seriously the occurrence of an event of wide social interest on the average every two and a half days (even apart from the concentrated Work of the Gods) shows that the economic life of the Tikopia is by no means a monotonous round of food getting for simple nutrition.

## VARIATIONS IN DAILY PRODUCTION

In the Diagram it has not been possible to show more than the general sequence of productive activity. The daily variations were much more marked than this. The extent of these fluctuations are illustrated by a transcription from my diary, giving a day-to-day record of fishing for two months, August and December, 1928. Since the first was in the trade-wind season and the second in the monsoon this incidentally shows the seasonal variation in this type of production. In each case the record refers primarily to the activities of one village, where I was living at the time, in the first case to Matautu in Faea, and in the second to Potu sa Taumako in Ravena. The fact that these are on opposite sides of the island does not affect the major fluctuations.

### DAILY AND SEASONAL VARIATIONS IN FISHING

| Day of Month | *Faea* August, 1928 (Trade wind season) | *Ravena* December, 1928 (Monsoon) |
|---|---|---|
| 1 | 20 women, 3 children, 6 men with rod and line. | Canoes went out, first time for some nights; catch: 50, 40, 30. (In Faea: 80, 70.) Nets in lake, 2, 6 fish. |
| 2 | Seine net dragged at night. | Large number of canoes in two fleets; 80, 70, 60 fish (*mau ika*). |

| Day of Month | *Faea* August, 1928 (Trade wind season) | *Raveŋa* December, 1928 (Monsoon) |
|---|---|---|
| 3 | Seine net dragged at night, 25 women and children; with hand nets; 12 men with rod and line by day. | Fleet caught 60, 50 fish. |
| 4 | Wet, little fishing. | Canoes got 80, 60, 50 fish. |
| 5 | (Sunday; no fishing.) | 6 men with rod and line; 1 canoe diving for green snail; women on reef, canoes at night 80 (3 vessels), 60, 40, 20 fish; nets in lake. |
| 6 | No observation; most people engaged with ceremony of removing taboo on coco-nuts. | Men with rods; canoes out at night. |
| 7 | Men and women on reef, 4 men on outrigger floats off reef. | 12 canoes out at night, 70, 60, 40, 30 fish (Faea 10 only); nets set in lake. |
| 8 | Women on reef. | 2 canoes at night, 10, 7 fish. |
| 9 | 15 men and lads dragged seine net. | 6 canoes out at night. |
| 10 | No observation; initiation ceremony begins. | No observation. |
| 11 | Initiation. | Nets set in lake; swell running, canoes observed. |
| 12 | (Sunday; no fishing by day; a score of women out with torches on reef at night.) | Nets set in lake; no observation of canoes. |
| 13 | 16 women on reef, 5 men. Taboo on flying-fish lifted and canoes went out. | Men with rod and line; 1 man caught 10 fish. |
| 14 | 1 family poisoned fish in reef pool. 4 canoes out at night, 15, 7 fish (8 p.m.—midnight). | Women out with torches fleet of canoes out. |
| 15 | Large number of people on reef (8 a.m.—1 p.m.); 1 canoe off shore. Canoes out at night, 1 caught 10 fish. | Nets in lake; most men assembled for ritual in Uta; 1 canoe out, 20 flying fish, 2 small shark. |
| 16 | Many people on reef. | Some reef fishing; nets set in lake; 12 canoes out at night; 60, 40, 30 fish. |
| 17 | No fishing; bad weather. | Nets in lake, 2–6 fish per net; 5 canoes at night; 80, 70, 50, 30, 20 fish. |
| 18 | Turmeric making; no observation on fishing (? none owing to bad weather). | Collective drive (ritual basis) on reef by day, catch about 20 fish per person; no canoes out owing to ritual dancing. |
| 19 | (Sunday) (turmeric making; ? no fishing). | Ritual dancing. A couple of canoes out at night, crew leaving dance on purpose. Little food prepared. |
| 20 | A little fishing on reef; weather too rough to catch much. | Ritual dancing; little food prepared; doubtful if any fishing except nets in lake. |
| 21 | Fine weather. 11 women on reef; several men with rods and others on floats. | Ritual dancing; nets set in lake; sea fishing in canoes, 100, 80 fish. Large preparation of food for the morrow. |
| 22 | Weather very wet; practically no fishing. 8 men with seine net at night caught 2 fish. | No observation. |

| Day of Month | *Faea* August, 1928 (Trade wind season) | *Raveŋa* December, 1928 (Monsoon) |
|---|---|---|
| 23 | Men and women on reef ; seine net dragged. | No observation ; little food prepared. |
| 24 | Strong easterly wind ; a little reef fishing ; sea too rough for canoes ; complaints about lack of fish. | No canoes out owing to moon. |
| 25 | Some reef fishing ; 2 men on floats outside reef. | No canoes out owing to moon. |
| 26 | (Sunday) No work ; 1 man made torches for canoe fishing, but too much moon. | No canoes out owing to moon. |
| 27 | Little fishing ; abortive attempt to catch shoal of mackerel. | Fishing on reef at night ; no canoes out owing to moon. |
| 28 | Wet, only a few women on reef. | Nets set in lake ; fishing on reef ; flying-fish nets repaired ; a few canoes went out, 10–30 fish. |
| 29 | Some women on reef ; 40 men and lads netted a shoal of mackerel (many men planting taro). | 2 fleets of 20 canoes went out ; first large expedition for some nights ; some canoes remained on shore from lack of crew. Total catch 800 fish ; 2 canoes 100, others 90, 80, etc. |
| 30 | Many women on reef ; a woman and some children building a fish corrall ; a number of men fishing at edge of reef. | A small fleet out at night. |
| 31 | 20 people on reef. | 6 canoes out at night. |

Several points arise from this synopsis.

It will be noted that there is a very great variation in the nightly catch of flying-fish. This is due very largely to weather conditions. A light wind facilitates the rising of the flying-fish above the surface and increases the catch, but if the wind is very heavy the surf on the reef may prevent the canoes on one side of the island from going out to the channel or may stop all but the hardiest seaman. The method of fishing with torches again means that it is not worth while for the canoes to go out when there is a long period of moonlight.

The people of Faea are nominally Christian and therefore do not normally engage in fishing on Sundays. The Sabbath, however, is treated by them as the period of daylight only and therefore torchlight fishing on Sunday night is possible. Moreover, other economic activities such as turmeric making, which follow a traditional sequence of daily operations, are not blocked by the coming of the Sabbath.

It may be thought that the great variation in the number of persons and canoes engaged may be partly due to an idea that the resources of the sea—especially those of the reef—should be conserved from time to time. This is not the case. There is no native theory that the number of fish may be exhausted, and in practice it seems that the daily resort to the reef from ancient times has not diminished the supplies. There have been occasions periodically, recorded in tradition and in recent memory, when fish have been extremely scarce.   This is attributed not to natural exhaustion or to any seasonal migration, but to magical action by some offended person of rank ; it is believed that the quantity of fish available is under the control of specific gods and ancestors who can be swayed by human influence. The periodicity of collective fish drives is not due to any idea of waiting for supplies to be replenished, but to the specific need for a large quantity of fish for some collective purpose, such as a sago oven or a funeral.   Linked with this is also the traditional concept that certain kinds of ceremony demand collective economic action. The ordinary daily work of households frequently draws just as many people out on to the reef as does a collective drive.   The main difference is that the catch in the former case is individual.

Unfortunately there are gaps in this record :  there are few observations on the catch of fish in August, and on the number of people engaged in reef-fishing in December.   I did not realize when the notes were made the possibility of obtaining from them empirical generalizations of a quantitative order, relating production to what may be called a normal standard of consumption.   But it may be noted that reef-fishing assumes a less important role in the monsoon season, when the catch of flying-fish from the canoes is the major source of supply.   Again, it is more difficult to get quantitative data for reef fishing than for canoe fishing.   This is due to the more individual technique of the one, and to the greater social interest in the other. The yields of canoes and fleets are compared by gossip the morning after they go out, as a matter of rivalry as well as of pure curiosity. But the individual catch by men or women on the reef is not treated in the same way, although in bulk it may provide an important addition to the general food supply.

# SOME LINGUISTIC CATEGORIES IN TIKOPIA
## DISTRIBUTION AND EXCHANGE

In Chapters VIII and IX an analysis has been made of various aspects of the Tikopia system of distribution and exchange, the part they play in the economic process as a whole and their economic effects. The classification there adopted was primarily in our own terms. By the Tikopia these transactions are classified in a somewhat different way, in categories represented by certain linguistic expressions. Since language can be regarded as a nexus between thought and bodily action, a means of controlling and moulding other behaviour, it is relevant to re-examine the material briefly from this angle. I shall not try to discuss the deeper psychological aspects of these linguistic categories, to explain them in terms of native modes of thought, but simply to give them in empirical terms, with a short explanation of their overt meaning. This will serve also as a glossary to the earlier descriptive material. I abjure etymological analysis here, though it is very suggestive from the psychological point of view.

The native terms here given show that the Tikopia possess a wide range of concepts for this aspect of their economic life. And though many of them are descriptive of specific types of action, it is clear that there is no lack of terms to express general ideas.

These various terms might be grouped in a number of ways: terms for things and terms for actions; referring to distribution and to exchange; of specific and of general application; relating to food and to goods other than food; for initiating action and for reciprocating it. It is difficult, however, to draw any clear line between them on such principles. The distinction between terms for things and those for actions, for example, is complicated by the Tikopia habit of using many words either verbally or substantively, so that *ufi*, for instance, may mean either the bark-cloth given in acknowledgement of the composition of a dance-song in one's honour, or the act of giving it, by trailing it out in front of the advancing band of dancers. It will be simpler here, then, to consider first a number of terms most commonly met with, as referring to many types of situation, and then others which are quantitatively less current.

Two features of the Tikopia language may be noted at the outset. One is the frequent use of homophones, the meaning of which may differ very greatly (as in the case of *ufi* mentioned above, which in other contexts means the yam). The other is the existence of what might be regarded from the historical point of view as primary and

371

derived meanings, but which here will be considered rather as general and specific meanings, in different contexts. Examples will be seen below. In an analysis of the psychological processes involved in these categories the existence of these general and specific meanings would make it very difficult to decide just how far the user of the particular word is thinking in terms of the immediate situation and how far in terms of its wider associations.

The first broad categories of things to be distinguished are *kai* and *koroa*.

*Kai* means " food ". In economic and social relationships the expression *fai te kai*, " prepare food " is very frequently heard, and signifies the preliminary act of initiating the relationship, since a basket of food is the common medium of prefacing a request, atoning for an injury, or fulfilling an obligation. In native descriptions of how to act in a variety of situations the words " go to your house, prepare food . . . " often begin the instruction. The more specific types of food concerned are discussed under *monotaŋa*, *fonokava*, etc.

*Koroa* means wealth other than food, and may be translated in different contexts as " goods ", " property ", " valuables ". Sometimes the significance is fairly abstract. I have heard the Motlav mission teacher, in discussing the Tikopia fondness for recreation say " In this land their *koroa* is the dance "—an immaterial possession by which the people set great store. The term has a wide range, from bark-cloth to canoes and, as mentioned earlier, can be roughly divided into " heavy " and " light " according to importance. The expression " *koroa* of chiefs " has been discussed on page 218.

In actions a broad contrast can be drawn between *sori mori* and *tauvi*.

*Sori* is a term of very general application, meaning " to transfer from one person to another ", " to hand over ", " to give " in the most undifferentiated sense. *Mori* means " to carry " or " convey " (apart from the homophone *mori*, the name of a particular type of dance). The compound term *sori mori* (or *more* as Seremata insisted) means " to give " in the sense of not demanding a return. Hence the expression " *E sori mori fuere, sise e tauvi* ", " It is a gift simply ; it is not presented for exchange ".

*Tauvi* embodies the concept of an equivalent, of reciprocity, of exchange, or of payment. It comes nearest to the European conception of buying and selling when applied to transactions such as the barter of native specimens for my European goods (see Appendix III), or the exchanges of native mats and other goods on the deck of the *Southern Cross* and other vessels which call. The absence of free competitive market conditions in Tikopia, however, makes translation in these terms generally inapplicable. The term *tauvi* is applied much more widely again than to purely economic transactions. The goods handed over to the father of a bride, for example, are described as " *te tauvi o te fafine* ", " the indemnity for the woman ", and cannot be properly described as " buying " the woman. Again, the *tauvi* is not always in material goods. When a canoe-owner gives his formal thanks to the builders in phrases stating that he is eating their excrement their reply of " *Tapuraia* " is termed " *te tauvi o te kai tae e fai* " " the reciprocity of the eating of excrement which is stated ". In opposition to this return of politeness is the returning of one insulting song by another. Here the term *tauvi*, which is applied to the song in reply, is analogous to the English expression " paying someone out " for an injury.

Two more terms, which come under the general head of *tauvi*, reciprocity, are *toŋoi* and *fakapenu*. These are distinguished by the first being related to food and the second to non-food goods.

*Toŋoi* means food given in return for food. It normally applies to a basket of cooked food, and may be given in response to raw food such as fish or cooked food of various types. According to convention it may be of approximately the same size as the initial gift, or less.

*Fakapenu* is the return of *koroa* for *koroa*. It is often by convention much less than the initial quantity received, and then takes on the character of an acknowledgement of the service rather than an equivalent of the goods. A standard object used for *fakapenu* is sinnet cord ; though it can be the reciprocatory gift for wooden bowls, pandanus mats or paddles, they are not used for this function.

Three types of food presentation may now be mentioned, *fiuri*, *taumafa*, and *fakaariki*.

*Fiuri* does not properly form a part of the distributive scheme, but enters into the exchange situation as giving a prior stimulus to apportionment and reciprocity. It is the contribution of green food which a person brings with him to an act of production or to a ceremony.

*Taumafa*, in the most general sense, is the portion of cooked food distributed at a meal. It is often *de facto* a reciprocation for the *fiuri*, which does not demand any other equivalent. In a ritual sense, again, it is the portion of food set out as an offering to one or more ancestors or gods, in which case it is withdrawn after the ceremony and handed over to the person who is the human representative of the spirit being concerned.

*Fakaariki* is a special type of food apportionment, consisting in separating off from the general mass of food from an oven four large baskets, often supplemented by sprouting coco-nuts and other goods, one for each of the clan chiefs. Hence the name—" making the chiefs." Each of the individual gifts is known as a *rau*, a term meaning in this connection a " share ". These are *toŋoi* by baskets of food later in the usual way.

Each of the above three terms implies a sharing ; in the *fiuri*, a sharing of responsibility, and in *taumafa* and *fakaariki* a sharing of food produced. Other terms of food presentation are concerned more with the individuality of the act. Such are *vai* and *fonokava*.

*Vai* in the ordinary context of everyday life means " water " or
" liquid ". But in a deprecatory sense it is applied to a food present
—the Tikopia say because to speak of one's food gift as *kai* implies
a boasting about it. Periodic gifts of food to men of rank or to chiefs
by commoners are so described ; they are reciprocated in due course
by the *toŋoi*. But in a still more specific sense *vai* is applied to the
gifts of food brought at funerals to the close kinsfolk of the dead
person. These are reciprocated first by a *fakapenu* of sinnet cord
(one of the few occasions on which food is so met) and later by a
return of the complete service, the former mourner taking the *vai*
to his former " feeder " when the latter is one of a mourning group.
A reinforcement of the literal meaning of " water " is given by the
fact that the " feeder " brings with him a water-bottle from which
the mourner must drink before partaking of the food. *Fonokava* is
a kind of analogy to *fiuri*, in that it is the contribution brought by
a person who attends a ceremony. But it is in the form of a basket
of cooked food. If a chief is holding a kava rite, for instance, then
convention demands that a man of another clan who attends it should
go along with his *fonokava*. He is not expected to eat of it himself ;
he presents it to the chief, who hands over to him in return a similar
basket from the food prepared in connection with the ceremony.
At dance festivals of large size it is the custom for each household
to " make *fonokava* ", and these are then exchanged on a clan or
district basis. Reciprocation for *fonokava* is thus received on the
spot, in kind.

A number of other more specific food presentations may now be
mentioned.

*Monotaŋa* is a gift to the clan chief from one of his constituent
kinship groups holding an important ceremony, such as a marriage,
a funeral, or a reconsecration of their sacred canoe. From the
canoe, in particular, it is supplemented by a parcel of cooked fish.
It is *toŋoi* by a basket of cooked food. *Fonakava* (not to be confused
with *fonokava*) is a basket of cooked food presented to the clan chief
by a major kinship group, even his own—when one of their ancestral
temples is being reconsecrated. This also is *toŋoi* in kind. *Fakaara*
(or *fakaaraŋaika*) is a basket of cooked food given to a person from
whom one has received a gift of fresh fish, either spontaneously or
by request.

*Sunusunuŋa kafa* is a gift of cooked food, but embodying fish
in particular, which is made in acknowledgement of the efficiency
of a piece of fishing equipment that an expert has made for one, as
a shark line or a bag-net. This is in addition to the *tauvi* of property
handed over at completion of the article.

*Poroporo* is in general a harvest acknowledgement. When performed
by a chief it consists in a rite celebrating the yield of the crop over
which he is in especial religious control—as the *poroporo* of the taro
by the Ariki Taumako or of the breadfruit by the Ariki Faŋarere.

(The elder of Fusi also performs the *poroporo* for the sago.) It has, however, no particular ritual significance when it consists of a bundle or two of taro shoots given to the owner of land by the man who has had the use of it for a season's cultivating (see p. 261). A special rite of the *poroporo* type carried out with the taro of a particular sacred cultivation by the Ariki Taumako is known as the *Pora*, and has as its chief item the preparation of an enormous taro pudding several feet across.

We may now consider several transfers of *koroa*.

*Maro*. This has been described already in connection with the payment for specialist skill in Chapter VIII. Here is a noticeable case of the use of a word in a general and a specific context, as mentioned above. In the most general context *maro* is a man's waist-cloth, and is equivalent to the equally common term *ɳatitara*. Either word can be correctly applied in ordinary speech. But *maro* is also a technical term with several connotations. It refers in kava ritual to the offering of such bark-cloths to ancestors and deities, and is one of the trio of elements—*maro, taumafa*, and *kava*, vestment offering, food portion, and libation—which constitute the basis of the rite. Again, it is the *koroa*, in which bark-cloth forms an indispensable element, which constitutes the reciprocation or payment to a specialist in tattooing, canoe-building, etc. As such it is often followed by a *fakapenu*, as already described. What may be regarded as a different word, though often difficult to distinguish in practice is *maro*, in which the *r* is slightly trilled, and which connotes the prize of victory, or victory itself without material reward, in a competition or ceremonial struggle.

*Malai* is essentially a gift in indemnity, compensation. It is made to the head of a kinship group from which a woman has been taken away in marriage, or to a chief whose canoe has been taken for a " suicide voyage ", or who has been insulted. Its form depends on the nature of the offence, but it always consists of *koroa*, and not of food. It is not *fakapenu*.

Finally, there are two categories of activity which though applicable to general contexts, have a specific economic connotation.

*Fakaepa*, meaning generally " to honour ", " to treat with distinction ", applies in economic transactions to the raising of the value of a gift—usually a *maro*—by the addition of an item to the normal amount. This is done not by simply putting one more piece of bark-cloth into the pile, which would be taken as a normal variation, but by adding an extra pandanus mat, or by making up an additional pile of bark-cloth. It is either a recognition of special service or, more often, of the rank of the recipient. A food gift can be also *fakaepa* by topping it off with a piece of bark-cloth, which again singles it out from the normal run of such gifts. The *rau* of chiefs in the *fakaariki*, the *fonakava*, and the *monotaɳa* are frequently treated in this manner.

*Fakafeuviake* is the process of " pairing " or " matching " in exchanges, whereby two parties to the exchange, one on each side, agree to hand over their gifts to each other. Their contributions thus cancel out by prior agreement, and relieve the organizers from the obligation of having to account for them in the mass of transactions to be arranged. This usually happens in a few cases at initiation, marriage, and funeral exchanges. In such case the *fakapenu* is made in the ordinary way ; it is merely the line of the transaction that is predetermined.

There are a number of other terms of a specific connotation, for transfers of goods at marriage and other ceremonial occasions, but they can be disregarded here, since they follow the general scheme of *tauvi*, a presentation of food being followed by a *toŋoi*, or one of goods by a *fakapenu*, of the type described.

From this analysis it will be clear how the Tikopia use the distinction between food and non-food goods as a basis for their categories of distribution and exchange, and how deeply the concept of *tauvi*, of equivalence, or reciprocity enters into their economic and social life. It may be pointed out here again that in speaking of " present " or " gift " I have used these terms simply for convenience, leaving out of account the element of reciprocity with which nearly all of them are associated.

# EXCHANGE RATES IN A CULTURE CONTACT SITUATION

In Chapter IX I have shown that in ordinary Tikopia life there is no means of expressing the comparative values of all objects in terms of any common denominator, though there is a kind of rough scale of comparative utilities of things. This is borne out to some extent by the exchanges which I conducted of European articles for specimens of the native crafts. I knew before I went to the island that money was not in use there, and so took a variety of trade goods which I hoped would be appropriate. Practically all turned out to be in demand by the Tikopia for one purpose or another. Some types I did not use in ordinary exchange, but gave as presents to selected persons. The seven adzes I took—the most valued objects of all to the Tikopia—went as gifts to the chiefs and other men of rank in acknowledgement of their divulgence of religious and traditional information ; and my small stock of printed cloths went as ritual offerings to canoe and temple deities. Apart from these and similar gifts, I bartered for specimens, mostly at times appointed beforehand, when anyone could bring objects which he wished to exchange. A summary of the resulting rates is given in the Table.

The native types of object are roughly arranged in order of importance, judged by Tikopia preferences for the things I had to offer. A vertical line indicates the different " prices " given for different objects of the same kind.

## TABLE X
### EXCHANGE RATES IN A CULTURE CONTACT SITUATION

| Tikopia Article | European Article |
| --- | --- |
| Clam-shell adze blades (no longer used). | 1 fish-hook. |
| Net gauge. | 2 fish-hooks. |
| Sinnet beater (wood). | 3–4 fish-hooks. |
| Wrist ornaments (shell). | 1–3 fish-hooks. |
| Darts. | 3 fish-hooks. |
| Wooden hooks (furniture). | 4 fish-hooks. |
| Arrows. | 4 fish-hooks. |
| Wooden top (toy). | 4 fish-hooks. |
| Coco-nut leaf fans. | 4 fish-hooks. |
| Stone adze-blades (no longer used). | 4–6–7 fish-hooks/1 clay pipe. |
| Bow. | 6 fish-hooks. |
| Bag-net (*kuani*). | 6 fish-hooks. |
| Net-shuttle (*sika*). | 6 fish-hooks. |
| Plaiting board. | 7 fish-hooks. |
| Betel mortars (*soka*). | 7 fish-hooks (average)/1 pipe (for two). |
| Neck ornaments of shell (*pa*). | 3–4/8/12 fish-hooks. |

| Tikopia Article | European Article |
|---|---|
| Neck ornaments of shell  (*tifa*). | 5/8 fish-hooks/1 fathom blue calico (ancestral specimen). |
| ,,    ,,    ,,    (*tavi*). | 6–10/20 fish-hooks/1 fathom white calico. |
| Bark-cloth beater. | 7–9 fish-hooks. |
| Dance-bat. | 7–8 fish-hooks/1 pipe/1 fathom red calico. |
| Wooden head-rest. | 8–9/10 fish-hooks/1 pipe/1 cotton belt/1 plane-iron. |
| Short club (*tuki*). | 10 fish-hooks. |
| Taro grater. | 10–12 fish-hooks. |
| Wooden shark-hook. | 11/20 fish-hooks. |
| Man's sinnet belt (*maia*). | 15 fish-hooks. |
| Wooden slab (for grating hibiscus fibre). | 1 pipe. |
| Coco-nut waterbottle. | 1 pipe and 1 stick tobacco. |
| Tattooer's equipment. | 1 pipe and 6 fish-hooks. |
| Bark-cloth sheet (*mami*). | 2 pipes and 5 fish-hooks. |
| Bag of coco-nut fibre. | 1 razor. |
| Whalebone betel pestle. | 5 fish-hooks/3 strings beads. |
| Coco-nut shell beads. | 3 strings beads/6 strings small beads. |
| Turmeric grater. | 16 fish-hooks/3 strings small beads. |
| Spear. | 9 strings small beads/1 fathom white calico. |
| Club. | 3–4 strings beads/1 fathom white or red calico/1 plane iron and 1 string beads (ancestral specimen). |
| Kava bowls. | 15 fish-hooks/40 fish-hooks, 1 pipe and 1 fathom calico. |
| Food bowls, small. | 11/12/15 fish-hooks/2 pipes and 5 fish-hooks. |
| ,,   bowls, large | 1 plane iron/1 fathom white calico, 1 fathom red calico, and 3–6 fish-hooks. |
| ,,   bowl and spear. | 1 axe. |
| ,,   bowl and kilt. | 1 tomahawk. |
| Bonito-hooks (medium quality). | 2 pipes and small beads/1 fathom white calico/1 fathom red calico. |
| Hibiscus fish line (*matai*). | 1 sheath knife/1 12 in. knife. |
| Pandanus kilts (*kie*). | 4 strings beads/1 12 in. knife. |
| Pandanus mats (*meŋa*). | 3 strings beads/1 pipe and 1 string beads/1 fathom calico/1 12 in. knife. |
| Wooden turmeric baking cylinder. | 1 12 in. knife/1 14 in. knife. |
| Ritual shell adze blade (*toki tapu*) ; owner now Christian. | 1 14 in. knife. |

For services which I received I also paid in similar goods, either directly, or in later reciprocation. For the building of my house, for instance, I expended the following :—

| To thatch-makers and casual helpers  . | 28 lb. bag of rice, 2 tins meat, and 12 sticks tobacco. |
|---|---|
| To principal builders (two men) .     . | 1 ¾ axe, 2 plane irons, 2 pipes, and 10 fish-hooks to Fakasiŋetevasa. 1 14 in. knife, 2 sticks tobacco, and 10 fish-hooks to Seremata. |
| To secondary builders (three men)   . | 1 14 in. knife, 1 pipe, 1 stick tobacco, and 10 fish-hooks each. |
| To assistants (four men) .   .    . | 1 12 in. knife and 1 pipe to one ; 1 pipe and 5 fish-hooks to the others. |

This was done soon after my arrival in Tikopia. In the light of my later experience this was a princely reciprocation, but it served as a major gift to the chiefly family of Taumako, the relatives by marriage of Pa Paŋisi, the Motlav mission teacher, who organized the job and suggested the payment.

Something may now be said about the rates of exchange. My purchase of specimens was by no means the first acquaintance of the Tikopia with an external market, but it was by far the most intensive, and lasted for practically a year. The exchanges concluded by the Tikopia with Europeans on the *Southern Cross* and other vessels are spasmodic, and hardly merit the name of barter, since in their almost total ignorance of English and small knowledge of Mota by only a few individuals, the Tikopia have to rely on the generosity of the recipients of their goods. Often, too, things are given them not so much in exchange for their articles as gifts out of pity for their poverty. My residence among them gave them a considerable increase of wealth, an opportunity of rejecting the exchange and returning later if they were not satisfied, and the facility of discussing their wants and the qualities of the articles they offered, in their own vernacular. As a result, we tended to establish something like standard rates of exchange for most of the ordinary goods brought forward. My position as a monopolist controlling a limited supply of goods to them of great utility enabled me to dictate to some extent the initial rates of exchange. But my practice of asking the intending seller to name his want, and discussing it with him, coupled with the etiquette of gift and counter-gift which obtained, meant that in practice the Tikopia themselves had a considerable say in determining the comparative rates. I soon found out the rough order in which they tended to evaluate the objects they offered, and the " prices " below which they were not.prepared to let their things of different kinds go. From my side I tended at first to base my offers on what I had paid myself for the various kinds of goods in the first place. But I soon found that though there was some correspondence between the original money prices I had paid and the rating of the things in Tikopia eyes, there were some types of object where this did not apply at all. A clay pipe costing rather less than one penny was about equivalent to half a dozen fish-hooks costing the same. But a sheath knife, sheath, and belt for which I had paid 6s. 3d., for instance, being smaller, was much less valuable to the Tikopia than a 12 in. knife for which I had paid 3s. 6d. ; and a cotton belt costing 1s. 6d. was worth very little more than a clay pipe of about one-twentieth its money value. Hence I abandoned altogether any consideration of the original cost of the articles to me, and regulated my offers of goods by the supply I had on hand (with no possibility of increasing it) and their relative utility to the Tikopia.

To begin with, both my estimate and that of the Tikopia was often arbitrary ; I tried to judge the worth of an article to me by the quality of its workmanship, and the Tikopia hazarded a request which he hoped I might be gullible or polite enough to fulfill. Soon, however, our respective demand schedules became more comparable, and for the commoner objects, such as head-rests, betel mortars, bark-cloth and pandanus mats, rates of exchange crystallized out to some extent. These became practically standard rates, and I found that as time went on and surplus stocks grew less the tendency was not for a higher rate to be sought for them by the Tikopia, but merely for them to be offered to me less frequently. At no time, however, did we establish any overt rates between the different things I had to give ; there was no common agreement, for instance, that a pipe was equivalent to six fish-hooks of a certain size, or ten of a smaller size ; nor was any definite relation of a fathom of a calico to a trade knife set up. The rates always remained fairly fluid.

The differences in the objects given for the same type of Tikopia article were due to several factors : the variation in the quality of the article itself (often considerable, and depending to some extent upon its age) ; the individual preference of the owner of the article ; my calculation of my decreasing stocks ; and my desire to please or reciprocate a particular person.

There was a tendency to insist on receiving certain types of European goods in exchange for certain Tikopia types. Clubs, pandanus mats, and bonito-hooks, for instance, were never offered for fish-hooks, but for calico, beads, and knives ; and though I tried on various occasions to substitute fish-hooks these were refused.

Again, it will be noted that certain types of Tikopia article, such as the wooden cylinders for baking turmeric, received more in exchange than others, such as the bonito-hook, which I have mentioned earlier as being of greater " value " to the Tikopia. Here it is a matter of the exchange situation itself. The bonito-hook is one of the items of supreme importance in the native exchange system, as in the acquisition of a canoe, or indemnity for wrong, and cannot be replaced. No one would dream of attaching a turmeric cylinder to a gift of bark-cloth and pandanus mats on such an occasion, though more European goods were demanded for it. This bears out the statements on spheres of exchange made earlier.

When my goods were received they were fitted into the productive and consumptive economy of the Tikopia, often in unexpected ways. But on the whole they did not feature in the elaborate native exchanges, but were retained by the families who obtained them. Only a few were so utilized, and fitted into the closed circuits of exchange mentioned earlier. My fish-hooks formed part of the payment of mortuary obligations, being linked with paddles in a series of secondary importance ; and a fathom of calico, regarded as an equivalent of a *mami*, a square of bark-cloth, entered into initiation and other ceremonial exchanges.

This brief description may be of interest in showing the operation of the forces of supply and demand in a situation of barter presented in the setting up of a novel market, with elements of monopoly present.

# INDEX

## A

Abasement, ritual, 224
Accumulation of goods, 243, 253–4 (*see also* Food)
Æsthetics, of food, 38, 51, 161; form, 84; of sex, 155
Age differentiation, 33–4, 112
Agriculture, 15, 17; possible changes in Tikopia, 48–53; nature of Tikopia system, 66; native theories of, 90, 93–4 (*see also* Breadfruit, Coconut, Food plants, Land, Taro, Yam)
Ancestors, 210
Anthropology, research methods, 2–5 (*see also* Economics)
Anuta, 21, 84, 349
Arensberg, C., 25 n., 28 n.
Armstrong, W. E., 306
Australian aborigines, 108, 318

## B

Banana, new varieties, 47
Banks Islands, 307
Bargaining, absence of, 142
Barkcloth, 20, 22, 24, 32–3, 35; manufacture of, 134, 228, 252–3; used as payment, 294–304; in exchange, 322–331
Barter, see Exchange
Benham, F., 25 n., 272 n., 332 n.
Birds used as food, 60, 75
Blackstone, W., 19
Boas, F., 4
Borrowing, 24, 319 (*see also* Exchange, Reciprocity)
Bow, use in Tikopia, 297 n.
Breadfruit cultivation, 65, 72
Bücher, K., 350
Buck, P. H. (Te Rangi Hiroa), 166 n., 335 n.
Burling, R., 9 n.

## C

Canarium almond, 47, 75, 347; origin, 84
Canoes, 12, 27, 31; use of hard wood for, 47, 79; design, 82; effect of size, 61–2; borrowing of, 62; types, 117; repair of, 117–131, 134; ritual association with chiefs, 218–19, 249; life of, 249; ownership of, 244–250; reward for builder of, 298–303

Capital, 17, 24; classification for Tikopia, 237–8; accumulation of, 243–257; economic concept, 272; uses in Tikopia, 272–7; payment for use of, 305, 308
Cassel, G., 332 n.
Celibacy, 36–7, 42–5
Chiefs, 27, 28, 31; wants of, 34; and infanticide, 43–4; ownership of land by, 53; control of water supply by, 64; control of production by, 88–9, 276; technical knowledge of, 102; ritual function of, 102, 180; incomplete control by, 142, 196; work done by, 112, 173, 194–8; obligations to, 146; nets of, 175; political position of, 188; economic position of heir, 189–190; ritual duties of, 191; restrictions on, 193; wealth of, 200; economic obligations of, 219; income of, 221; feast given by, 222–231; as consumer, 212–222; ritual link with canoes, 218–19; role in production, 190–200; general economic role, 231–6; accumulation by, 243; exploitation by, 271; payment by, 300–1
Childe, V.G., 79 n.
Choice, 28–9
Choice, 28–9
Christianity, 45, 49, 53, 80, 177, 182–3, 234, 265, 307, 369
Clan, see Kinship
Climate, 72; effect on work, 157
Clothing, 32
Coconut, mats, 32; as wealth, 53–4; as source of protein, 51; planted by chiefs, 54–8; cultivation of, 64, 71; as preserved food, 75; *tapu* on, 206–8; planted on other's land, 263; use of, 274; as gifts, 311
Codrington, H., 307 n.
Communism, primitive, 59, 364
Comparative study of economics, 11, 13–14, 365
Conn, H. W., 51 n.
Contraception, 42–5
Cooking methods, fish, 81
Co-operation, see Labour
Counting, method of, 99–100, 227, 280
Crawfurd, B. E., 42
Culture contact, 19, 21, 31, 80, 84, 87, 182–3, 234, 377, 339 n., 380 (*see also* Christianity)
Currency, 6, 22, 23, 166, 307

## D

Dalton, G., 25 n.
Dancing, 36, 161, 235, 275
Deacon, A. B., 307 n.
Deane, W. A., 312 n.
Decision-making, 29–30
Demand, for European goods, 19, 87; economic principle, 35–6; situation of, 348; effect of ritual on, 184; for canoes, 248
Destruction of property, 344–7
Dillon, P., 84 n.
Distribution, role of chief's son, 190; principles of, Chapter VIII; of fish, 280–7; of sago, 288; of turmeric, 290

## E

Ebert, M., 314 n.
Economic growth, 2, 13
Economics, definition, 7, 26–7, 352; modern theory in relation to anthropology, 7–14, 272, 314–15, 332, 352; notion of economy, 2, 17, 24–8; problems in primitive society, 6–7, 15–16, 313, 353–5
Eddystone Island, 183 n.
Eels, ritual associations, 61
Einzig, P., 22
Ellice Islands, 84
Entrepreneur, use of concept, 134; status of, 138–9; chief as, 199; position in Tikopia, 273; outlay of, 292; profit of, 308
Equipment, see Resources
Exchange, 5, 6, 10, 16, 17, 18, 19–20, 21, 23; with Europeans, 19, 47, 377–380; a characteristic of Tikopia production, 149; with chiefs, 221–2, 226; classification of, 315; forced, 316–18; ceremonial, 320–32; circuits, 238, 338–344; group, 331 (see also Gifts, Payment)
Experts, canoe, 117–131, 142; turmeric, 289; payment of, 291, 294–303 (see also Specialization)
Exploitation, absence in Tikopia, 166, 231; by chiefs, 271; according to Radin, 171

## F

Famine, 12 n., 18, 73
Faulkner, 50 n.
Feasts, given by chiefs, 222–230; reciprocal aspects of, 222; social effects of, 230; planning of, 240
Fiji, 103 n., 249, 312
Firth, J. R., 147 n.
Fishing, 12, 15, 17, 28, 29, 30; resources, 61–3, 179; fluctuations, 76; for shark, 61, 162, 214, 359; for bonito, 113–14, 163; for flying-fish, 61; for green-snail, 76, 81; experts, 103, 113–14; by chiefs, 193; distribution of catch, 214, 279–287
Food, 32; social context of, 37–9; consumption of, 49; fluctuations in supply, 48, 73–7; nutritive value, 50–3; conservation of, 75, 239, 273; taboos, 206–8; gifts to chiefs, 213–17; exchanges, 322–331; accumulation, 223, 227, 243, 253; used as payment, 291–4
Food Plants, introduced from abroad, 47; cultivation of, 64–73; economic and ritual value, 65
Foresight, 228, 239–241, 266, 274
Fortes, M., 27
Fortune, R., 362 n.
Fox, C. E., 183 n.
Fraser, L. M., 272
Frazer, J. G., 91
Freeman, J. D., 21 n.
Fusfeld, D. B., 28 n.

## G

Galbraith, J. K., 314
Geddes, W. R., 21 n.
Gifts, 6, 19, 21, 22; of food, 53, 215, 239, 298; to chiefs, 191, 213–17, 282; as payment, 148, 310–11; expressing kinship, 215
Gilbert Islands, 249
Goodfellow, D. M., 5 n., 24

## H

Haddon, A. C., 4
Harrisson, T., 307 n.
Hawaii, 152
Herskovits, M. J., xiv, 5 n.
Hocart, A. M., 169
Housebuilding, 134; in Samoa, 166 n.
Houses, 32, 35

## I

Inefficiency, 107
Inequality, 34
Indemnity for theft, 269, 320
Infanticide, 42–4
Interest, 17, 275, 306
Invention, 86–8
Investment, 274

## K

Kagarov, E., 234, 262 n.
Kahn, R. F., 314–15
Kapauku, 17 n.
Keesing, F. M., xi n.
Kenya, 108
Keynes, J. M., 272 n.
Kinship, 2, 10, 11, 12, 15, 27, 28, 31, 92, 362 n.; of chiefly houses, 54–5; ownership, 58, 62, 275; plant affiliations, 65; transmission of

knowledge, 106; of working groups, 118, 134–7, 140–1; effect on production, 130; obligations, 147, 292–3; exchange, 215, 322–331; chiefs, 235; effect in distribution, 284

Knowledge, transmission of, 106–8; technical, 78–87; agricultural, 93–4 (*see also* Specialization)

L

Labour, supply, 11, 29, 31, 41–2, 109, 138–142; recruiting by Europeans, 48, 142; division of, 111–12; co-operation of, 115–16, 134–9, 173, 275–6, 298; efficiency of, 165–7; kinship services, 293–4 (*see also* Specialization)

Land, ownership of, 6, 28, 53–7, 259–264; taro cultivation, 49; utilization of, 58–9, 262

Language, as property, 103 n., 312; role in work, 131–3, 146, 151–160; transmission of culture, 146; ownership concepts, 257–8; categories, 63, 371–6; in technical procedure, 101

Leadership, 6, 143–5 (*see also* Chiefs, Experts)

Le Clair, E. E., 25 n.

Lipsey, R. G., 25 n.

Lowie, R. H., 5 n.

M

Mackie, 50 n.

Magic, *see* Ritual

Maine, H. S., 19

Malaya, 11

Malekula, 307

Malinowski, B., 4, 18 n., 21 n., 42 n.; on magic, 91, 169, 184; on language, 102, 146 n.; on reciprocity, 348; on competition, 301; on kinship, 363 n.; on primitive communism, 364 n.

Mana, 89–90

Management, 27, 30–1

Manu'a, 335 n.

Maori, xi, 75, 218 n.; art, 84; House of Learning, 106; proverbs, 152; culture contact among, 183 n.; slavery, 259; exchange, 318; ritual, 170; preservation of fish, 273

*Mara*, 66–70

Market, 9, 11, 15–16, 17, 24, 25, 31, 349; absence of in Tikopia, 88, 301, 314; effect of, 351

Marquesas, 84

Marriage, exchange, 321–3; social status of, 34

Marshall, A., 17, 33, 35–6, 272 n., 332 n., 348 n.

Marx, K., 19, 20

Marxism, 234, 361–3

Maunier, R., 348

Mauss, M., 331, 348

Maximisation principle, 10, 13, 16

Mead, M., 112 n., 335, 363 n.

Mediumship, 177–8

Meillassoux, C., 25 n.

Models, economic, 9, 25

Money, 1, 9, 10, 11, 16, 19, 21, 22, *see also* Currency

Morgan, L. H., 362

Mortuary rites, 12, 20, 22, 27, 29; effect on food supply, 76; effect on consumption, 216; *tapu* as part of, 206, 216; destruction of property, 100; 346–7, exchange, 325–330

Mukerjee, R., 13, 14 n.

Mulch for taro, 67

Murngin, 7 n., 333

Myths of origin, 86–9, 112

N

Neighbour's obligation, 147

Net making, 95–100, 135–6; ritual, 174–181; reward for, 297

New Guinea, 1, 17 n., 19

Ngata, Sir A., xi n.

Ngoni, 172 n.

Nutrition, 50–2

O

Ogden, C. K., 147 n.

Ownership, concepts, 89, 257–8; by chiefly houses, 53–7; by kinship groups, 58, 62, 275; by chiefs, 218; of water, 64; effect on labour, 148–9; of land, 259–263; of canoes, 244–7; of goods, 263–8; marks, 267

P

Pandanus mats, 35; as property, 250–2; as payment, 295–304; as exchange, 322–331

Pawpaw, 47

Payment for knowledge, 103, 106–7; for labour, 119, 140, 148, 291–303; for use of property, 281; for capital goods, 290; for non-labour services, 308–310; categories, 292–4; principle, 303 (*see* also Gifts, Exchange, Reciprocity)

Pearson, H. W., 25 n., 28 n.

Piddington, R. O'R., xi

Pigou, A. C., 336

Polanyi, K., 25 n., 28 n.

Political structure, 187; power of chiefs, 235

·Population, pressure, 17, 26, 46; general problem, 39–48; map, 40; of chiefly houses, 54–57

Pospisil, L., 17 n.

Potlatch, 241
Price system, 16, 23, 24, 25, 30–1, 35, 60, 166
Primitive, 1, 17, 19, 20, 21, 23, 24
Proclamation, 44
Production, possible changes in Tikopia, 48–53; role of chief in, 88, 191–200; theory, 130; ideology, 146–151; effect of ownership, 148–9; effect of ritual, 179–186; factors governing quantity, 238–243; annual quantities, 255–6; characteristics for Tikopia, 293; types, 237, 244, 264, 272; role of expert, 296–7 (see also Resources)
Profit, 308
Protein content of food, 51–2

Q

Quality, appreciation of, 251
Quantitative data, 4–5; difficulties of obtaining, 139; on population, 41–2; on food consumption, 49; on kinship groups, 55; on labour, 109; on various activities, 134–8; on canoes, 245–7; on production, 253–7; on land utilization, 262; on turmeric production, 277; on fish distribution, 284; on payments, 299; on funeral exchanges, 329; on fishing, 367–9; on culture contact exchange, 377–8
Quarrels, 143–4
Queensland, 103 n.

R

Radcliffe Brown, A. R., 363 n.
Radin, P., 171
Rank, see Chiefs
Rationality, 16, 25
Raw materials, cost of, 304
Read, M., 172 n.
Reciprocity, 140, 289; by chiefs, 199; by workers, 292, 306; general concept, 313; kinship, 348 (see also Exchange, Payment, Gifts)
Reddaway, W. B., 8 n.
Redfield, R., 18
Religion, see Ritual
Rent, 59
Resources, of Tikopia, 37; land, 53–6; fish, 61; equipment, 33, 62, 78–84, 244–7, 272 (see also Production)
Richards, Audrey, 363 n.
Richards, I. A., 147 n.
Ritual, 10, 15, 21, 23, 27; a factor in productive system, 6, 31; effect on demand, 35, 184; for attracting fish, 63; effect on cultivation, 64; associations of plants, 65, cultivation of mara, 66–70; forms still preserved in Tikopia, 79; relation to technical knowledge, 85–92;

functions of chiefs, 102; knowledge of, 104–5; sex differentiation, 111, 265; during canoe repairs, 119–120, 125, 129; formulae, 120, 122, 160, 176–8, 217, 224, 270; in production, 131, 150–1; definition, 168; classification, 170; in net-making, 174–181; effect on demand, 184; beliefs about, 185; of chiefs, 191; waste, 242; canoes, 250; distribution, 281, 287; in exchange, 320–332
Rivalry, 162–4
Rivers, W. H. R., 3, 4, 183 n., 362 n.
Robbins, L., 9
Rossel Island, 306
Rotation of crops, 66, 93
Rotuma, 84, 86

S

Sago, cultivation, 64; extraction, 115, 135, 267; loan of equipment, 277; distribution, 287–9
Samoa, 64 n., 84, 86, 152, 166 n., 335 n., 249
Samuelson, P.A., 9 n., 25 n.
San Cristoval, 183 n.
Saving, 239, 274 (see also Foresight)
Scarcity, 18, 19, 25, 26
Schapera, I., 363 n.
Sex, differentiation, 34, 105, 111, 251, 264–5; economic aspects of, 309; ratio, 41 (see also Celibacy, Contraception)
Shark, 61, 162, 214, 359
Sheddick, V. G., 11
Sinnet, 22, 24, 35; as property, 252, 296; as payment, 304–5
Sleep, 32, 156–7
Solomon Islands, 15
Songs, 153–4, 163, 214, 229, 269, 297, 312
Sorcery, 164, 269–270
Specialization, in technique, 63, 113; in fishing, 103; by women, 105 (see also Experts)
Spillius, J., xiii, xiv
Stanner, W. E. H., xi, 318, 335 n.

T

Taboo, 2, 28 (see also Tapu)
Tami, 350
Tapu, 58; of mara, 69–70; pipi, 119, 203; of chiefs, 104, 189–192; imposition of, 201–212, 240; classification, 202; breach, 266; against theft, 271
Taro, land under cultivation, 49; cultivation of, 66–70, 93, 134, 228, 293; effect of moisture on, 73
Tattooing, 113, 115
Technique, in agriculture, 93; in net-making, 95–8; in canoe repairing,

121–6; in a fish drive, 285–6

Technology, 17, 21, 26, 78, 334 (*see also* Resources)

Te Rangi Hiroa, *see* Buck, P. H.

Thatch-making, 195

Theft, 260, 268–272, 320

Thurnwald, R., 5 n., 112 n., 213 n., 314 n., 348 n., 358 n.

Tlinkit, 241

Tonga, 86

Tools, 21, 47, 66, 79, 87, 334, 299, 378

Trade (external), 19, 37, 47–8, 351

Trikojus, V. M., 51 n.

Trobriands, 36, 42, 60, 102, 169 n., 301 n., 350

Turmeric, 21, 64; properties of, 81; methods of extraction, 83–5, 90, 276; women's work on, 111–12; extraction by Ariki Tafua, 137–8; ritual importance, 157; accumulation, 254; distribution, 289–291; in exchange, 340

Tylor, E. B., 91


U

Uvea, 85–6


V

Value, 6, 16, 20, 23–4, 27, 37, 314, 332–8

Vanikorô, 21, 42, 84, 349

Viljoen, S., 5 n., 172, 186 n., 333–4, 336


W

Wants, in Tikopia, 32–7; for European goods, 48, 87; effect of ritual on, 184 (*see also* Demand)

Warner, W. L., 7 n., 333, 363 n.

Waste, 41, 241

Water, 63, 275

Wealth, differentiation, 53; control by chiefs, 222; types of, 244–257; effects on-payments, 302

Wenner-Gren Foundation, xv

Witchcraft, *see* Sorcery

Wogeo, 350

Work of the Gods, 36, 66 n., 110, 117 n., 141, 150, 181, 184, 199, 217, 287


Y

Yam, 51; cultivation of, 70–1; preserved food, 75

Yamey, B. S., xv